The Travels of Olearius in Seventeenth-Century Russia

SUÆ LV. ✶ ADAM OLEARIUS ASCANIUS SAXO. IN AULA CIMBRICA BIBLIOTHECARIUS & MATHEM. ÆTATIS

Simbl. ex Psalm 73.
In Consilio tuo duces me, et
postea in gloriam me.
suscipies.

Quisquis es, huc adhibe visus, OLEARIUS eccum.
ILLE MEUS præbet vulta tuenda tibi.
Quæ Ruthenrum dignatus noscere Cæsar,
Et quæ Sofij tuus Persia dives, Herus.
Ingeny nequiit quia cœlo fingier instar,
Noscendum ingenio se dedit ipse suo.

M. V. Sommer Fec.
Norib A. 1656.

Polyc. Wirth Lips.
I. V. D.

To my Mother

Preface

Adam Olearius's account of the journeys of an embassy from the Duke of Holstein to Muscovy and Persia was first published in Schleswig in 1647. Appearing with little fanfare, the work enjoyed a sensational success. By the close of the seventeenth century, it had gone through numerous German editions, and it also had been brought out several times each in French, English, and Dutch, and once in Italian. Moreover, for decades after its initial publication, foreign works on Russia were deeply colored by what Olearius had written. As in the sixteenth century Baron von Herberstein's treatise largely shaped Europe's image of Russia, so Olearius's work influenced European opinion in the seventeenth.

In the nineteenth century, scholars confirmed the justice of the acclaim and the tribute of imitation accorded Olearius's work in his own day. In his important bibliographical study in 1846, Friedrich Adelung described Olearius's book as "one of the most excellent and valuable works on Russia, down to the present." The prominent historian N. I. Kostomarov wrote a laudatory introduction to the first Russian edition, published in 1861. And in V. O. Kliuchevskii's dissertation, *Reports of Foreigners on the Moscow State*, no seventeenth-century work is cited more frequently. Interestingly enough, Soviet specialists on the seventeenth century yield nothing to their prerevolutionary predecessors in their regard for Olearius. For example, the respected Academician M. N. Tikhomirov has written: "Of all the works [by foreigners] on the history of Russia in the first half of the seventeenth century, Olearius's is the most significant. For accuracy of detail and clarity of exposition, Olearius has no equal." Olearius's account appealed sufficiently to the imagination, it may be added, to inspire the writing of two historical novels: F. T. Wagenheim's *Paul Fleming, oder die*

Gesandschaftliche Reise nach Persien (Leipzig, 1842) and V. L. Sne-girev's *Pokhozhdenie Berngarda Shvartsa* (Moscow, 1928).

Notwithstanding the accolades bestowed upon him by the reading public in the seventeenth century and by Russian historians more recently, Olearius and his book are scarcely known in the English-speaking world, and least of all in the United States. This is hardly surprising, and not just because copies of the English editions are rare. For if Americans deplorably neglected all of Russian history prior to the Second World War, since 1945, while doing much to make amends, they have slighted the earlier centuries. Too few scholars venture back into the pre-Petrine era; and, in textbooks and courses as well, the greater part of Russian history usually is given short shrift. The price of disproportionate attention to recent periods of Russian history is high. The student is apt to get no more than a glimpse of the seventeenth century, a colorful and intrinsically interesting era; his impression of it, if indeed he has any, is accordingly schematic and bloodless. More important, he may be deprived of valuable insights. A knowledge of the century is indispensable, for example, to an adequate conception of the much-discussed problem of Russia's relation to the West. To mention another point, familiarity with seventeenth-century customs and usages helps one to judge the degree to which Soviet behavior is rooted in old Russian rather than Marxist-Leninist sources. On these and a host of other subjects, Olearius furnishes invaluable evidence.

The 1647 edition of Olearius's work was followed by a second, also published at Schleswig, in 1656. Bibliographies and catalogs disagree on subsequent editions. The consolidated list I have compiled contains German editions published at Schleswig in 1661, 1663, 1666,* 1669,* 1671,* 1673,* and 1694,* and others at Hamburg in 1694* and 1696. French editions were issued at Paris in 1656, 1659, 1666, and 1679, at Amsterdam in 1656* and 1727, at Leyden in 1718 and 1719, and at The Hague in 1727.* Dutch editions were published at Amsterdam, Utrecht, and Groningen in 1651, and at Amsterdam in 1652 and 1658.*

---

* Editions marked by an asterisk I have found listed in only one source, as follows. Loviagin's Introduction to the 1906 Russian edition: the Schleswig editions of 1666 and 1671. Recke-Napiersky, *Schriftsteller Lexicon*, III: the Schleswig edition of 1669. Adelung, *Kritisch-literärische Übersicht der Reisenden in Russland deren Berichte bekannt sind*: the Schleswig editions of 1673 and 1694, the Hamburg edition of 1694, the Amsterdam edition of 1656, and the Hague edition of 1727. Koninklijke Bibliotheek: the Amsterdam edition of 1658.

English editions were issued at London in 1662, 1666, and 1669, and an Italian edition at Viterbo in 1658. In addition, many extracts and abridged editions have been published, the most recent at Munich in 1960.

No Russian edition of Olearius appeared until the nineteenth century. Although some Russian political authorities were sufficiently interested before then to order the work's translation—a late-seventeenth-century manuscript survives to the present day—they were understandably reluctant to give currency to its candid and uncomplimentary views of the Russian government and people. The first Russian edition, an abridgement comprising three of the original six books, was published in St. Petersburg in 1861. The complete work, translated by P. Barsov, was published for the first time in the periodical *Chteniia v imperatorskom obshchestve istorii i drevnostei rossiiskikh pri Moskovskom Universitete*, 1868, Nos. I–IV; 1869, Nos. I–IV; 1870, No. I. This translation was brought out as a separate book in Moscow in 1870. In 1906, A. M. Loviagin made a new translation for a deluxe edition, published in St. Petersburg by Suvorin. This edition included Olearius's illustrations and maps, which Barsov had omitted, but most of the material on Persia and other sections considered uninteresting to the Russian reader were eliminated.

Most of the translated versions, as well as the German editions, were based upon Olearius's second Schleswig edition (1656): *A New Enlarged Description of Travels to Muscovy and Persia*. In contrast to the first, the second edition included an index and a bibliography; moreover, it was enlarged from the 546 pages of the 1647 edition to 778 pages, in the same format. Olearius so enriched the second edition with historical information and descriptions of a wide range of cultural phenomena that it is not just an excellent travel account but a study of a civilization as well. The impressive scholarship that went into the second edition is reflected in its bibliography of over 160 titles.

This edition is a new translation of Olearius's second edition. I initially intended to use the old English translation, modernizing the language and making other changes as a check against the German edition of 1656 made necessary. It soon became apparent, however, that the seventeenth-century English edition would not do, for the translator evidently was more concerned with felicity than with accuracy. Many passages were excised, and many others transposed, with no indication to the reader that this had been done. Although the translator did preserve the sense of most of the passages he included, he made a great many errors and on occasion even improvised.

To be sure, Olearius offers serious difficulties to the translator. Although his material is presented in an interesting manner, many of his sentences are extremely long and involved, and of course much of his language is archaic. To further complicate matters, many of his renderings of Russian names bear little resemblance to the originals. In grappling with these and other problems, I was greatly aided by Loviagin, whose conscientious and able Russian translation I relied upon heavily. Unfortunately, Loviagin chose to translate each and every word of Olearius's wordiest sentences, and as often as not to retain the incredibly involuted constructions of the originals. In my own translation, I have tried to avoid excessive literalness, and the awkwardness inseparable from it, while rendering the author's thought as accurately as possible. I have followed Loviagin, however, not only in the spelling of Russian names but also in translating *schloss* as *kremlin,* and the King of Persia as the Shah. Obvious errors in dating made by the author or typesetter have been corrected, usually without comment. Quotations that Olearius gives in Latin are here rendered in English.

The present edition contains slightly more than half of Olearius's 1656 edition. Essentially, I have translated only the portion of the account that deals with Russia, omitting the part of Book IV that treats the embassy's journey from Astrakhan to Persia, and all of Books V and VI. Book V deals only with Persia, and Book VI, which treats the return trip from Persia to Germany, adds little to what is said of Russia in the first three and a half books. Thus, although the embassy did not arrive back in Holstein until 1639, the present edition leaves the Holsteiners in late 1636, as they are about to move on from Astrakhan to Persia.

Of the first half of Olearius's account, approximately four-fifths is presented here, the remainder having been deleted chiefly on grounds of irrelevance. Olearius could not refrain now and then from dilating on matters connected only in the most tenuous way with the embassy's travels and experiences. In the most flagrant case, he devoted a long chapter to Greenland, using as a transition a briefer chapter on the Samoeds, a small, eccentric tribe that dwelt in Russia's far north. Both of these chapters in Book III have been excised, as have parts of Books I and II that were integral to Olearius's travel account but are marginal to his work considered as a treatise on Russia. These sections deal with the embassy's return from the Russian frontier after its first visit to Moscow, its voyage to the Russian border on the first leg of its second journey, a shipwreck suffered by the embassy, the people and towns of Livonia (Estonia and Latvia)—which the embassy passed through on its way to Russia—and rules of conduct laid down by the ambassadors for those in their company. These and other omissions of some magnitude are indicated in the text by bracketed notes. Smaller omissions— from one to several paragraphs—are indicated by ellipsis dots and are treated briefly in footnotes. In the latter category are scholarly digressions—often based on classical and ecclesiastical texts—antiquarian material, repetitious matter, and descriptions of trivia.

A few deletions are not indicated by bracketed notes or ellipses. These include all but two of the poems by his friend Paul Fleming that Olearius added to the second edition. Fleming, a well-known German poet, accompanied the embassy on both of its journeys and memorialized many of its experiences in verse. Also deleted without ellipses are references to illustrations that have not been used, cross-references that do not particularly assist the reader (including references to the Persian material), and German equivalents of Russian weights and measures or monetary sums.

I have retained Olearius's division of the work into books. His numerous, short chapters, however, produced a rather choppy, disconnected narrative; so, without altering the sequence, I have consolidated his chapters into longer ones (the 17 chapters of Book I have been reduced to two, the 32 of Book III to eight) with new titles. Paragraphing within the chapters has also been revised in many places. At the top of each page of the translation, in brackets, the corresponding pages of the 1656 edition are cited for the benefit of anyone who may wish to compare my version with the original.

The reader should also be apprised of two difficulties Olearius inadvertently introduced into the text. The Russians called all West Europeans, whatever their nationality, Germans (*nemtsi*). Olearius's practice is even more troublesome: he sometimes follows suit and calls all the Westerners in Russia Germans, and he sometimes reserves the term for people actually from Germany. A difficulty involving the dating of certain events derives from the revisions made in preparing the 1656 edition. Interlarded with the earlier material is a good deal of information on events subsequent to the embassy's visits to Russia, and subsequent even to the publication of the first edition. This produces a curious effect, especially when, as is frequently the case, an episode is said to have occurred "a year ago" or at some other indeterminate time. Although Olearius was aware of this problem and tried to avoid it, there remain instances in which the context does not indicate whether the point of reference is 1647 or 1656. Where the date seems important, I have attempted to fix it in the notes.

The value of Olearius's work was decidedly enhanced by the numerous illustrations it contained. As he pointed out with pride, they were not copied from other books but were drawn from life—most of them by Olearius himself, a few by Dr. Gramann, another member of the embassy. After the embassy returned from Persia, the drawings were made into engravings under Olearius's personal supervision. The artistic value of these plates is more limited than their historical worth. Striving to represent their subjects truthfully, the illustrators vividly portrayed the people and places they had observed. Olearius's engravings have been widely borrowed for both books and museums to illustrate the life of seventeenth-century Russia. A small proportion of the more than 80 engravings in the first three and a half books of the 1656 edition are reproduced here.

Despite their virtues, the modern—that is, the Russian—editions have suffered from sparse annotation. The 1861 edition had no notes at all, and Barsov's few notes to his edition, though they did set right several errors, were generally concerned with trivial matters. Loviagin provided more substantial annotation, though much of it was concerned with minor geographical points and other relatively unimportant items. However, a few of his notes, and also part of his Introduction, were based on archival research and clarified some important questions. The present edition offers by far the fullest annotation of Olearius to date, although I do not pretend to have produced such a thoroughgoing examination and evaluation as that made by S. M. Seredonin of Giles Fletcher's *Of the Russe Common Wealth.*

I am indebted to earlier scholars whose investigations furnished much helpful information. This work would have been much the poorer but for the researches of Kliuchevskii on foreign accounts of the Muscovite state; Rushchinskii, Pascal, and Tsvetaev, on the religion of the time; Basilevich on economic affairs; Kurts on the contemporary reports of Rodes and Kilburger; Bakhrushin on the Moscow rebellion of 1648; and Muliukin on the conditions of foreigners in Russia. References to their works, as well as to the contributions of earlier editors, are given in the notes.

It is a pleasure to acknowledge other debts as well: to the Inter-University Committee on Travel Grants, the American Council of Learned Societies, and the American Philosophical Society for grants that made this work possible; to Marc Raeff and Walther Kirchner, who read the Introduction and offered helpful suggestions for improving it; to Frank Silbajoris and Andrew Brown for help in the translation of some passages from the German; to John Crossett for similar assistance with Latin passages; to Dirk Baay for the translations of the Fleming poems; to Father Georges Florovsky and Serge Zenkovsky for help on a number of points in the notes; to Professor G. A. Novitskii of the University of Moscow, Dr. Kurt Hector of the Schleswig-Holstein Archives, David Miller, and Richard Hellie for bibliographical assistance and suggestions for the notes; and to my wife for her willingness to look after a host of tedious details connected with the editorial work.

S.B.

Contents

Weights and Measures

Ahm   A wine measure equal to 130 to 160 liters.

Chetverik   A dry weight measure equal to 22½ pounds.

Ell   A linear measure of variable length. The Flemish ell equaled 27 inches, the English 45. It is not certain that Olearius used the term consistently.

Last   4,320 pounds.

League   A German mile, equal to 4.6 English miles.

Loth   A weight of half an ounce.

Pud   36 pounds.

Sazhen   Slightly less than 84 inches.

Span   Slightly less than eight inches.

Verst   3,500 feet, or about two-thirds of a mile.

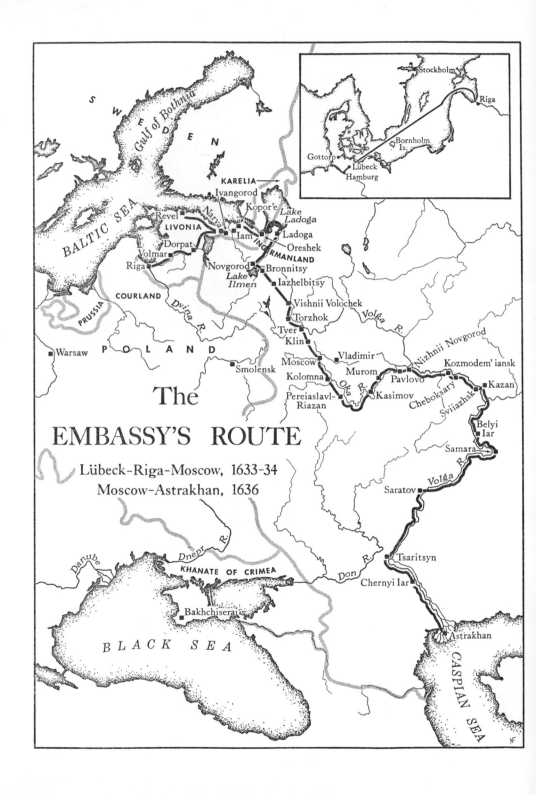

The

EMBASSY'S ROUTE

Lübeck–Riga–Moscow, 1633-34
Moscow–Astrakhan, 1636

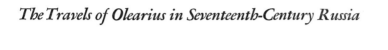
The Travels of Olearius in Seventeenth-Century Russia

Introduction

MANY DECADES after Henry the Navigator first dispatched Portuguese seamen to reconnoiter the obscure coasts of Africa, fleets of vessels were still leaving European ports on voyages of exploration. The charting of a new route to the East, the discovery of the New World, and the circumnavigation of the globe, far from exhausting the urge for exploration and expansion, gave it added impetus. Thanks to their feats of navigation in the fifteenth century, the Portuguese replaced the Arabs, the Turks, and the Italians as principal middlemen in the commerce between Europe and the East, and reaped enormous profits. The emergent competitive state system and the rise of dynamic commercial classes spurred other powers to encroach upon or displace those whose pioneering efforts had won them a lucrative advantage. The Dutch largely superseded the Portuguese around the end of the sixteenth century, and in the course of the seventeenth, the French and English in turn challenged the commercial supremacy of the Dutch.

In the same period, Russia enlarged its territorial holdings by expanding into contiguous areas, but it did not extend itself overseas. Not only did it lack the necessary ports and fleet but, perhaps most important, it lacked an enterprising merchant class.[1] Insofar as Russia was involved in the overseas movement, it was in the manner of China, Japan, and India in the sixteenth century—as an object of the exploratory-expansionist activity of others. The European powers hoped to tap the great wealth they imagined was to be found in Russia, but they

---

[1] Russian merchants apparently were more enterprising in an earlier age. From the tenth through the twelfth centuries, they were reported at Cracow, Prague, and Regensburg, and Russian merchant ships plied the Baltic to Denmark and Lübeck. The decline of Russia's active foreign trading dates from the beginning of the thirteenth century. Although the trade at Novgorod remained at a high level into the fifteenth century, the Germans took over the carrying business. See Cross, "Medieval Russian Contacts with the West," pp. 141–42. See also Kirchner's "Über den russischen Aussenhandel" for a perceptive examination of Russia's failure to develop an aggressive, ongoing foreign trade. (Complete authors' names, titles, and publication data for all works cited in the notes are given in the Bibliography.)

also thought of Russia as a land through which trade routes might be opened to the fabulous East.[2] Remarkably enough, in the same year (1553) that the Englishman Chancellor found a way around the North Cape to a Russian harbor on the White Sea, a Venetian merchant attempted to negotiate with Russia the establishment of a trade route linking Venice with the East by way of Moscow and Astrakhan.[3]

The English expedition was ostensibly seeking an all-water route to China and India, but Sebastian Cabot, its inspirer, may actually have expected it to reach Russia's shores.[4] Having been cordially received by Ivan IV, the English established the Muscovy Company to develop their trade with Russia. From the first, however, the company sought also the right of transit for trade with lands farther east; and the tsars, though they exacted a price, were amenable. As further efforts to reach China by way of the northern seas or Central Asia proved fruitless, the English increasingly concentrated their attention on the more accessible Persia. The potential of this trade was described with some awe by Michael Lock, one of the company's agents:

> The traffic of Persia through Russia would be of exceedingly great importance to England for jewels, spices, silks, drugs, galls [an insect product, used in tanning and dyeing], alum, and other merchandises there to be had at their fount; all of which might pass safely, without danger of the Turk, and without knowledge of Italy and Spain, and with no license from the King of Portugal. And all those commodities of Russia and Persia would pass abundantly by this North Sea into England, and through England out again into Flanders, Germany, France, Spain, and Italy, through the hands of Englishmen.[5]

---

[2] This attitude was by no means new. As B. D. Grekov observes: "The Normans ... were drawn to [Rus] not only by the wealth to be found there, but also by the possibilities of establishing relations—through her—with Byzantium, Iran, and the Arabian lands." *The Culture of Kiev Rus*, p. 25.

[3] Friedrich Adelung (I, 194–95) calls attention to the Venetian merchant's bid. It was characteristic of Muscovy's sociocultural situation that although her own seamen had already sailed westward around the North Cape and a Russian merchant had pioneered a route to India, these feats went unappreciated and the opportunities they created unexploited. On the Russian doubling of the North Cape, see Hamel, pp. 36, 50–54. The account of Afanasii Nikitin, the merchant who traveled to India, is printed in English in *India in the Fifteenth Century*, R. H. Major, ed.; a deluxe edition, with the text in modern Russian, English, and Hindi, was published in Moscow in 1960 under the title *Khozhenie za tri moria Afanasiia Nikitina, 1466–1472 gg.* For a discussion of Nikitin's account, see Kirchner, "The Voyage of Athanasius Nikitin," pp. 46–54.

[4] Lubimenko, *Les Relations commerciales*, p. 25.

[5] Bond, p. xi. Attempts by Englishmen to develop trade with Persia by way of Russia are treated in Morgan and Coote. This Hakluyt Society publication contains many interesting documents.

Between 1557 and 1581, six English expeditions were sent down the Volga to Persia. Hazardous conditions on the lower reaches of the river, however, combined with wars between the Persians and Turks and the stiff competition of Near Eastern cloth to frustrate the Muscovy Company's designs. Then, in the 1590's, the company was deprived of the right of free transit.[6]

Although the English initiatives had failed, a lively sense of the great potential of the Persian trade persisted. The English themselves returned to the charge and in 1616 opened trade relations in the Persian Gulf. In 1620, having concluded an alliance with the Shah, they used their naval power to oust the Portuguese from their favored positions on the Persian coast, and became important purveyors of Persian silk to Europe.[7] The Dutch established themselves in Persia around the same time, and their volume of trade soon surpassed that of the English. However, a good deal of Persian silk continued to be exported by way of the old caravan route across the Turkish Empire to Aleppo, where it was sold to Italian merchants. For all that, interest in developing the Persian trade by way of Russia waxed in the first decades of the seventeenth century. Between 1615 and 1631, the English, the Dutch, the French, the Danes, and the Swedes all tried to secure transit privileges from Tsar Mikhail Feodorovich.[8] It is particularly striking that in the 1620's and 1630's, in spite of the special position they already enjoyed in Persia, the Dutch endeavored to win the Tsar's assent to free transit across his domains.[9] What was denied to all these was granted in 1634 to an embassy sent to Moscow by Frederick III, Duke of Holstein.

A shrewd diplomat and a ruler devoted to the arts of peace, Frederick successfully avoided entanglement in the Thirty Years War, then

[6] Lubimenko (*Les Relations commerciales,* pp. 56, 88–89), who considered the Muscovy Company's trade with Persia highly profitable, believed that its termination was the result of action by the Russian government. T. S. Willan, however, suggests that the company abandoned the Persian trade because it had proved unprofitable, so that the action of the Russian government had no practical effect. See Willan, pp. 151–54.

[7] Sykes, II, 273–81; Kieksee, pp. 46–47. A study that includes many interesting documents is Bayani's.

[8] See Zevakin, pp. 135–38, for the Dutch, French, and Danish bids. The Swedes tried unsuccessfully to gain free transit to Persia under the Treaty of Stolbovo, concluded with Russia in 1617. The English tried repeatedly to regain what they had lost. See Lubimenko, *Les Relations commerciales,* pp. 153, 163, 167; Konovalov, "Anglo-Russian Relations, 1617–1618," pp. 69–70, 86, 100; and "Anglo-Russian Relations, 1620–4," p. 73.

[9] A Dutch bid was made as late as 1631. For data on its rejection, see "Otchet niderlandskikh poslov," pp. 167–68.

devastating most of northern Germany. In the early 1630's a Hamburg merchant named Otto Brüggemann submitted to the Duke a proposal that promised to lift little Holstein into the ranks of the commercial powers.[10] In the course of travels on business in the Netherlands and Spain, Brüggemann had become interested in the Persian trade and had learned something of the economic and political conditions controlling it. Thereafter he devised a grandiose plan to make Holstein an entrepôt for trade with Asia, to win for it a monopoly of the European commerce in silk, and, possibly, to make it a center for the manufacture of silk cloth. Enticed by the prospect of not merely equaling but surpassing the handsome profits the Dutch reportedly were earning in the silk trade, Duke Frederick readily fell in with Brüggemann's plan.

The project was designed to take full advantage of Holstein's geographical position. With its shores washed by the Baltic Sea, Holstein could receive Persian goods shipped by way of Russia, Swedish Livonia, and the Baltic. Its easy access to rivers connecting the North and Baltic Seas with inner Europe would facilitate the distribution of both raw and finished products.[11] After calculating the comparative costs of bringing silk to Europe by way of Russia and by way of other routes, Brüggemann contended that the market must inevitably fall under Holstein's control. The Dutch would be driven from the field, since the distance from Persia to the Netherlands via the Cape of Good Hope was almost four times the distance from Persia to Holstein via Russia.[12] As for the Italians trading at Aleppo, although they were much closer

---

[10] Several Russian writers have viewed Brüggemann as a representative of Hamburg financial and commercial interests, and these interests as the dominant element in the Holstein venture. This judgment is based on Jean Chardin, a French agent who traveled to Persia later in the seventeenth century and left an account of what he had seen and heard. According to Chardin, as rendered by G. F. Müller (I have been unable to locate the passage in Chardin's work), Hamburg used Holstein as a cover for its scheme, assuming that Moscow was more likely to grant the transit privilege to Holstein than to the old Hanseatic city. See Lappo-Danilevskii, "Rossiia i Gol'shtiniia," p. 258; Zevakin and Polievktov, p. 4; Müller, VII, 492–93.

Chardin's statement is implausible. Kieksee, a careful modern student of the subject who used the Holstein archives in Copenhagen, presents full information on Brüggemann and his scheme (pp. 42–52), but none of it confirms Chardin's thesis. Besides, Hamburg's alleged desire to conceal its involvement in the project can hardly be reconciled with Holstein's willingness to have Sweden openly join her in negotiations with Moscow (see note 15). The Tsar would have been even more likely to oppose Sweden's participation in the enterprise than Hamburg's.

[11] Viskovatov, p. 55.

[12] For the same reasons Holstein could expect to displace the English traders. The eagerness of the Dutch, the English, and others to obtain the right of transit through Russia shows that Brüggemann's reasoning was not unsound. Undoubtedly all the contenders viewed the Russian route as the least costly.

to Persia, their ability to compete effectively was impaired by the heavy tolls imposed on Persian silk that passed through the Turkish Empire. Economically, the scheme appeared sound enough.

Since the project's fulfillment required the cooperation of Sweden, Russia, and Persia, however, Holstein was compelled to launch a diplomatic offensive. Stockholm's acquiescence proved not very difficult to secure, for the Holstein scheme accorded well with Sweden's own policy of diverting Europe's trade with Russia from the White Sea port of Archangel to her own eastern Baltic ports. Nevertheless, Holstein had to pay dearly for the Livonia transit privilege: she agreed to turn over to Sweden four to six hundred thousand reichsthalers annually, and to accept Swedish participation in the projected enterprise.[13] For her part, the Queen of Sweden contracted to give diplomatic support at Moscow to Holstein's bid for the right of transit through Russia.

Brüggemann was confident of Persia's cooperation: not only did his scheme provide for a substantial annual gift to the Shah, but it appeared likely to serve Persia's political interests as well. The Shah could not refuse his blessing to a proposal to shift the trade route, inasmuch as trade through Aleppo worked to the advantage of his neighbor and foe, the Turkish Sultan, who levied a 100 per cent duty on Persian silk passing through his domains.[14] Incidentally, just as the economics of the silk trade was counted on to eliminate Dutch competition with Holstein, so a Persian decision to re-route the trade across the Turkish Empire promised to deprive the Italians of their share of the trade. Neither Sweden nor Persia, therefore, but Russia, appeared to present the thorniest problem. As no tsar since the 1590's had agreed to grant foreign merchants free transit to Persia through his territory, Holstein's diplomacy was put to the greatest test in its dealings with Moscow.

We may be sure that Holstein benefited from a cardinal distinction between itself and the other petitioners for the privilege of establishing a trade route through Russia. Although they differed considerably in stature, England, Holland, France, Sweden, and Denmark were all powers of some consequence. Muscovy's rulers were loath to risk encroachment upon their territory and independence by giving special

---

[13] Kieksee, pp. 57–61. The treaty, concluded in June 1633, is reproduced in *Sverges traktater*, V, 263–70.

[14] Kieksee, p. 51; Zevakin and Polievktov, pp. 2–3. Documentary evidence of the Shah's desire to re-route the silk trade is given in Bayani, p. 98.

rights in their lands to states that in recent times had demonstrated acquisitive propensities. Holstein enjoyed a decided advantage in being a small, inoffensive state, unlikely to impair Russia's independence or seriously to damage its interests.[15]

But this circumstance alone would hardly carry the day. Holstein had to convince the Tsar of the positive benefits he would realize from an accord. Long before fully revealing its own wishes, Holstein began to woo the Russian court, employing tactics similar to those that had won favor for England 80 years earlier. In June 1632, just as Russia was preparing a campaign against Poland, Brüggemann was sent on a mission to Moscow. He brought a gift of 12 cannons, a supply of ammunition, and permission for Russia to purchase military equipment in Holstein. And, just when Russia was endeavoring to enlist thousands of foreign soldiers in its forces, he invited the Tsar to send his recruiting agents to Holstein. In return, Brüggemann asked only that Holstein be allowed to purchase Russian grain and that its merchants be permitted to trade in Russia—rights that other states already had. The next year, having already sent a group of cannoneers, the Duke ingratiated himself further by promising to provide one of his physicians to attend the Tsar.[16]

When, in 1634, negotiations finally began on Holstein's request for free transit through Russia to Persia, it was no doubt understood that Mikhail could continue to count upon Holstein for munitions, soldiers, and skilled technicians. In gratitude for similar assistance, Ivan IV had once granted to the English a privilege like that the Holsteiners were now seeking. Holstein, however, could hardly expect a like *quid pro quo,* for in the 1550's England had risked the displeasure, and more, of Russia's neighbors, who were striving to keep Russia weak by denying her access to the technical aid that such a country as England could impart.[17] By the 1630's these efforts had been frustrated, and several states were contending for Russia's commercial and political favors. Therefore, in order to secure so signal a privilege, Holstein had to

[15] Holstein nearly destroyed this advantage when it brought Sweden into the negotiations. This step so aroused the Tsar's suspicions that he would not consider meeting Holstein's request unless Swedish participation in the enterprise were dropped. See Kieksee, pp. 67–69.

[16] See Loviagin's Introduction to the 1906 Russian edition, *Opisanie puteshestviia v Moskoviiu,* pp. vii, xv.

[17] Bond, pp. xvi–xvii. See also I. I. Polosin.

offer a special inducement in the form of substantial financial compensation. This gambit awakened the interest of the Tsar, who was perennially short of funds, especially precious metals. Nevertheless, he drove a hard bargain. The Holstein ambassadors were granted the coveted right, but not until they had pledged an amount substantially larger than their original offer: six to eight hundred thousand reichsthalers annually for the first ten years, and a million annually thereafter, should the privilege be renewed.[18]

The Holstein embassy, having left home in the fall of 1633, returned triumphantly in April 1635. Later that year a second embassy was dispatched, this time to Persia by way of Moscow, to negotiate an agreement with the Shah and initiate trade with his subjects. Not until early in 1639 did the ambassadors reappear at the Duke's court. Their experiences in the interim cast serious doubt on the feasibility of the entire scheme. Contrary to expectations the Shah was not eager to cooperate, and a series of other, unanticipated difficulties made the earlier perspectives now appear illusory. Accordingly, in 1640 and 1641, the Duke strove as zealously to disengage himself from the contract with Russia as he had earlier to obtain it.[19]

Following the route that trade between Persia and Holstein was expected to take, the second embassy had traveled down the Volga and onto the Caspian Sea. The navigation of the Volga proved far more difficult than anticipated; and, as if the natural hazards were not enough, on the lower reaches of the river the vessels were constantly threatened by lawless bands of Cossacks and Tatars. (The account of this part of the voyage shows how precarious was Moscow's control of these areas some eighty years after they had been formally incorporated.) On the Caspian, the splendid ship especially built for the voyage was wrecked in a storm. This was the second such disaster for the embassy—the ship in which it had left Germany had also gone down. In parts of Persia, too, savage peoples had endangered the lives and property of the Holsteiners. Besides, by his behavior during the journey, one of the ambassadors, Brüggemann, sowed discord in the embassy and seriously jeopardized its mission.

An enigmatic figure, Brüggemann gave no hint early in the journey

---

[18] Kieksee, pp. 69–70.
[19] *Ibid.*, pp. 87–89; and Amburger, *Die Familie Marselis*, p. 85.

of the irascible, imprudent, and violent nature he revealed later on. In the course of the waterborne voyage southward through Russia and on the Caspian, where vigilance was certainly called for, the ambassador proved flagrantly trigger-happy. His abusive behavior not only alienated many members of the embassy, Olearius perhaps most of all, but also deeply offended their Russian and Persian escorts. In Persia, he engaged in shameless debauchery, insulted a high official by refusing to accept a gift, and wantonly had a Persian soldier thrashed and killed.[20] A few decades ago it was discovered that he also had hatched a plan, in which he tried to interest Russia, for the seizure of Persia's silk-producing region.[21] All in all, his conduct was as far removed from the discretion expected of an ambassador as can be imagined. Complaints pressed against Brüggemann by other members of the embassy after their return to Holstein resulted in his being tried and executed.

Though these circumstances surely contributed to the collapse of the enterprise, undoubtedly the economic factor was decisive. The Holstein project could be sustained only if profitable, but experience demonstrated that serious miscalculations had been made. Contenting themselves with the prospect of controlling the sale of Persian silk, the Holsteiners had not contested the exclusive right the Tsar claimed for Russia's merchants to trade in most other Persian wares.[22] Thus the volume of trade left to the Holsteiners was too small to cover expenses and still earn a profit. For in addition to the normal costs of a commercial venture, they were obliged to spend large sums for what were essentially political purposes: luxuriously equipped embassies to foreign courts, costly gifts for the rulers whose favor was sought, and security forces to convoy vessels between Moscow and Persia. To make matters worse, little or no margin had been left for losses incurred at the hands of marauders or in shipwrecks and other accidents. It was no wonder that the Duke wished to cancel the contract. The Holsteiners had bid too high.[23]

[20] Olearius's report on these matters is omitted in the present edition.

[21] Zevakin and Polievktov, pp. 9–16.

[22] The articles in which Holstein could trade are listed in the treaty of 1634, which is reprinted in *Akty istoricheskie*, Vol. III, No. 181.

[23] Loviagin's Introduction, pp. xii–xiii, gives a glimpse of the Duke's maneuverings. Incidentally, Brüggemann's irresponsible conduct in Persia perhaps stemmed from his growing realization that the scheme on which he had staked his reputation, and possibly his fortune, was in fact uneconomical; his plan for the seizure of Persia's silk-producing region was probably a desperate effort to keep alive the goals of the initial project while radically changing its form.

Nevertheless, the Holstein venture's failure did not extinguish interest in trade between Europe and Persia by way of Russia. The tsars continued to receive requests for the transit privilege. Around 1650 Sweden once again demonstrated its desire to participate in the silk trade, and in 1675 the Dutch formally applied once more for the right of access to Persian wares and markets, but in vain.[24] In 1667, in an interesting reversal of the traditional pattern, Tsar Aleksei Mikhailovich granted an Armenian trading company based in Persia the right to travel north from Astrakhan across Russia, to sell Persian merchandise to European buyers.[25] This enterprise soon foundered too. By then, still another obstacle to the realization of the imagined potential of the Persian trade had arisen: the heightened opposition of Russia's merchants to special privileges for foreign trading interests.

Although the primary aim of the Holstein enterprise was thwarted, a secondary objective was admirably realized. Duke Frederick, a patron of the arts, letters, and learning, had directed his embassy to Muscovy and Persia not only to negotiate with the rulers of these states, but also to gather information on their lands and peoples, their institutions and customs. This duty devolved upon Olearius, who served in the embassy principally as a scholar.[26] The laurels subsequently bestowed upon his work were a tribute to the energy and talent with which he fulfilled his charge, as well as a consolation to the Duke for the failure of his commercial ambitions.

Adam Olearius was born in 1603 in Aschersleben, a town in the German principality of Anhalt.[27] His father, Adam Oelschläger, was a tailor. Intelligent and eager to learn, young Adam proved himself worthy of the support of his family, who made it possible for him to study. Upon completing secondary school, he entered the University

---

[24] See the dispatches of Rodes, the Swedish agent in Russia, in Kurts, *Sostoianie Rossii*, pp. 12, 38–39, and *passim*. On the Dutch petition, see Zevakin, p. 136.

[25] The terms of this very involved agreement are given in *Polnoe sobranie zakonov*, Vol. I, No. 409.

[26] Olearius speaks of the Duke's charge to him in his Preface to the 1647 edition.

[27] Little is known of Olearius's personal life. The brief sketch given here is based upon several biographical articles, notably those in *Allgemeine Deutsche Biographie*, Vol. XXIV; *Russkii biograficheskii slovar'*, Vol. XII; *Dansk biografisk leksikon*, Vol. XVII. Of these, the last is the most recent, and according to Dr. Kurt Hector, curator of the Schleswig-Holstein archives, the best (letter to the author, July 18, 1964). This Danish account, which is apparently based on fresh research, disagrees with previous articles on such particulars as Olearius's date of birth, usually given as 1599, and his father's name.

of Leipzig, where he devoted himself to philosophy, literature, mathematics, astronomy, and geography. In 1627 he was awarded the degree of Master of Philosophy. During the next few years, he engaged in physical-astronomical investigations, the results of which were published. His ability and achievements impressed the scholarly community so favorably that he was made an assistant in the university's Faculty of Philosophy and a member of a distinguished learned society. He went on, as was then the custom among scholars, to adopt a Latin name—Olearius.

The young Olearius had not been established at Leipzig very long when the Thirty Years War engulfed Saxony, forcing him to abandon his scholarly pursuits. In 1633, he was rescued from a difficult situation by an invitation to enter the service of Duke Frederick of Holstein.[28] We do not know whether Olearius was an avid reader of Marco Polo and an enthusiast for travel in foreign parts, as the author of a Russian historical novel portrays him, but he had been recommended as a person well qualified to carry out a scientific mission like the one the Duke envisioned for the embassy he was just then organizing.[29] Olearius joined the embassy as secretary for its initial journey; in recognition of the distinguished service he had rendered, for the second he was made a counselor as well.

Olearius spent more than five years in the company of the Holstein embassy, and his whole subsequent life was deeply affected by the experience. Returning to the Duke's court in 1639, he was occupied during the next eight years in preparing for publication the voluminous material he had gathered. Between 1647 and his death in 1671, much of his time was spent arranging for other editions. But before his book was first published, Olearius made one more trip to Moscow; having visited the Russian court in 1634, 1636, and 1639, and having become knowledgeable in its ways, he was chosen by the Duke to carry a message to Tsar Mikhail Feodorovich in 1643. In 1639 the Tsar, knowing of Olearius's accomplishments, had attempted to enlist him in his service, and in 1643 he renewed the offer. On neither occasion did Olearius reject the proposition out of hand, perhaps because of un-

---

[28] According to the Danish account cited above, friends at the Holstein court interceded on his behalf.

[29] V. L. Snegirev, *Pokhozhdenie Berngarda Shvartsa,* pp. 59–60.

certainty about his position at the Duke's court, perhaps out of a feeling that he was valued there at less than his true worth. Each time, however, after due deliberation he decided against entering Muscovy's service, probably after receiving assurances of a distinguished and satisfying career in Holstein.[30] On his return from Moscow in 1643, he was appointed court mathematician, librarian, and counselor to the Duke.

If any uncertainty about his position persisted, it was dispelled by the praise showered upon him once his book appeared. The many-faceted character of his work, and the impressive erudition that underlay it, earned him the sobriquet "the Holstein Pliny."[31] But his fame did not depend upon this one book alone. His published writings, which reflect the breadth of his interests, include numerous scientific, historical, and literary treatises. He was placed in charge of the Duke's collections of curiosities, which he organized into a museum and which he described in detail in one of his publications. He oversaw the construction of a globe, remarkable for its time, which later was presented to Peter the Great. As an aftermath of his travels in the Shah's domains, Olearius devoted particular attention to Persian studies. He translated the poet Saadi's *Gulistan*, and left behind an unpublished Persian-Turkish-Arabic dictionary. The contemporary Dutch orientalist Jacobus Golius called him the best Persian linguist in Europe. With all these achievements, Olearius became a treasured ornament to the Holstein court, which he served until his death.

Such are the external facts of Olearius's life. From his book we may discern something of his character and cast of mind. He might have said with Terence: "Nothing human is alien to me." For, far from restricting himself to a description of institutions like the state and the church, he also treats personal relations and moral conduct—and a wide range of such mundane but fascinating matters as the Russians' dress, food (he includes a number of recipes), bathing habits, marriage ceremonies, sex life, holidays and amusements, crime and punishment, drinking habits (including an antidote for hangover), and lexicon of abuse. Two centuries later Olearius's skill as an ethnologist received

[30] He owed a good deal to the patronage and protection of an important official at the court, J. A. Kielmann, as he himself acknowledges in the Preface to the 1647 edition.

[31] Olearius recalled the ancient Roman scholar both in his zeal for study and in his special interest in astronomy, geography, and ethnology.

high praise from Friedrich Ratzel, one of the founders of modern cultural anthropology.[32] To his description of Russian civilization Olearius added abundant geographical and astronomical data.

Olearius was a man of avid curiosity, and he spared no effort to satisfy his craving for knowledge. It was gratified in part by the studies that made him a man of notable erudition and his book an exemplar of conscientious scholarship. Olearius's extensive bibliography, to be sure, includes relatively few works devoted specifically to Russia, but there was little published material on the subject in his day. He attempted to compensate for this scarcity by gleaning bits of information, and background and comparative material, from a wide variety of ancient and contemporary works. He made full use of the writings of Baron von Herberstein, Matthiae a Michovia, Antonio Possevino, Paolo Giovio, Alessandro Guagnino, and Jakob Ulfeldt, and he borrowed more heavily than he admits from Peter Petrejus.[33] Of the more important foreign accounts, one misses only those in Richard Hakluyt's collection of travel narratives (especially Giles Fletcher's) and Jacques Margeret's *L'Estat de l'Empire Russe.*[34]

A review of his bibliography suggests that Olearius knew neither English nor French; all but one of the titles listed are in Latin or German.[35] On Russia, the one English source he cites (though not in the bibliography) is Clement Adams's expanded version of Chancellor's account, which was included in Hakluyt's collection but was also published in Latin. It is unlikely that Olearius's account would have been significantly altered had he consulted English sources; nevertheless, had he known of the travels of Jenkinson and other Englishmen, he might have added another dimension to his narrative of the Holsteiners' voyage to Persia, which took much the same route. Olearius's bibliography lists no Russian titles. This will not seem surprising, however, if we recall that few books had been published in Russia prior to his time, and virtually none on Russian history and institutions.

Not just a cabinet scholar, Olearius took advantage of every oppor-

---

[32] *Allgemeine Deutsche Biographie,* XXIV, 274.

[33] References to these works are given in the notes to the text.

[34] Queen Elizabeth suppressed the first edition of Fletcher's work at the insistence of the Muscovy Company, which feared that the book's hostile tone might bring the Tsar's wrath upon itself. Nevertheless, abridged editions of Fletcher appeared in Hakluyt (1598–1600) and Purchas (1625). The company's petition is printed in Bond, pp. 352ff.

[35] See Herbert. This work has some importance for Persia, but none for Russia.

tunity for firsthand observation. At Narva (in Livonia), even before reaching Muscovy's frontier, he goes to see a Russian community pay its respects to the dead before Pentecost. From Moscow he rides out to watch the Tsar's officials receive a Turkish ambassador. At Astrakhan he goes incognito to a public bath to see how the Russians perform their ablutions. In Moscow as the Duke's messenger in 1643, he makes an experiment to discover whether the information purveyed by the Tsar's corruptible officials is accurate: he contrives to transcribe a purported copy of a letter from the Tsar to the Duke (made by a bribed official for another foreign representative) in order to see if it is in fact a true copy. Many passages in the book demonstrate Olearius's resourcefulness in gathering information. Even as late as 1653, when a Russian delegation came to Holstein to negotiate some business for their sovereign, he met with and interrogated its members daily.

No one has ever doubted the devotion to truth that Olearius declares in the preface to his book. As a student of astronomy and mathematics, he was imbued with the ideal of scientific objectivity. The reader encounters this spirit in the very first pages of the book, where apropos of stormy weather at sea Olearius neatly refutes a prevailing notion about the causes of seasickness. In the course of the account, he repeatedly tells of having taken readings with an astrolabe to determine the exact longitude and latitude of a town; and now and then he corrects the data reported by a predecessor. Olearius attempted to describe the people, institutions, and mores of Russia with similar objectivity. He made careful observations, meticulously recorded his data in a diary, and strove to present his findings with a maximum of clarity and accuracy.[36] His drawings and engravings, too, were painstakingly made. Moreover, Olearius used the works of earlier writers critically. To cite one example, despite his obvious regard for Herberstein's authority, he refutes the latter's widely quoted allegation that a Russian woman gauges her husband's love by the beatings he gives her.

The public success of Olearius's work may be explained in part by the attractive and interesting way in which it is written. To the modern reader, Olearius's zeal for completeness, especially in descriptions of

---

[36] Olearius carried an album in which he asked people he encountered to set down some lines, possibly not only as a remembrance but also as a source of information. If so, he must have been disappointed in the results. For, perplexed by the request and suspicious of his motives, most Russians wrote verses from the Bible. See *Moskvitianin,* pp. 452–53.

ceremonies, may occasionally seem tedious; but for a work of such large dimensions, these occasions are few indeed. The book is full of human interest because it does not concern itself just with the great impersonal institutions, the people at the summit of society, and the public aspects of life—although it neglects none of these. Olearius embellishes his work with a wealth of anecdote that brings the people to life as perhaps no other piece on seventeenth-century Russia does. Besides, the narrative is spiced by Olearius's wit and his sense of the humorous and the ironic in the folkways and episodes he describes.

For all its merits, Olearius's account is of course not flawless; it contains errors of fact and interpretation, internal contradictions, and lapses from objectivity. Many of these errors may be traced to Olearius's unfamiliarity with the Russian language; for, the contrary opinion of earlier editors notwithstanding, Olearius probably did not know Russian when he first traveled to Moscow. It seems likely, given his inquisitive nature, that he studied it while in Muscovy and in the interval between the two journeys. Still, he must have known the language imperfectly at best, for he used an interpreter in interrogating some Russian-speaking Samoeds he met in Moscow.[37] Besides, his misinterpretation of the meanings or nuances of certain words leaves little doubt that he had not mastered the language, a handicap that must have made the task of understanding the phenomena he observed extraordinarily difficult.

In comprehensiveness, systematization, and integration, Olearius is less than completely satisfying. Like the modern cultural anthropologist, he is comparatively indifferent to political and military events, although he presents a vivid description of the Moscow rebellion of 1648. More important, his data on the social structure and the economic basis of Russian culture are rather scanty. Significant facts are given in passing, but these subjects are not investigated or described as thoroughly as some less consequential matters. For example, he scarcely explores the all-important relationship between the nobles and the peasants; indeed, he devotes relatively little space to conditions in the countryside, the center of Russian socioeconomic life. In spite of the patently commercial nature of the Holstein embassy's journey to Russia

---

[37] Loviagin, p. 166. The seventeenth-century English translator gives the opposite impression, since he fails to mention that Olearius used an interpreter (p. 50, 1669 edition).

and Olearius's good contacts among the foreign merchants in Moscow, he imparts less information on trade and industry than one might wish. He also pays little attention to the arts, although his work is no more deficient in this respect than other foreign accounts of seventeenth-century Russia.

The form Olearius gave to his work operated against a fully systematic presentation of his data. Whereas the first two books and the fourth are preeminently a log of the embassy's travels and experiences, Book III constitutes a treatise on Muscovy and the life of its people. At times these two principles of organization clash. For example, in Book III Olearius discusses Muscovy's cities, including an absorbing description of the capital; but he treats Novgorod, Kazan, and other towns in Books I, II, and IV. Occasionally material included in the travel account is repeated in Book III, and sometimes information appears in one of the two main divisions that would be more appropriate in the other. Although the chapters of Book III are supposedly systematic, sometimes one finds within them material that is irrelevant to the subject announced by the chapter heads, and points relating to a single topic are sometimes dispersed throughout several chapters.

On the matters of generalization and integration, Olearius's work produces contradictory impressions. On certain questions involving a low order of generalization, he makes judgments on the basis of insufficient data. For example, having traveled through a good deal less than all of Russia, he draws conclusions about the fertility of the soil throughout the country. Similarly, in discussing the moral conduct of the Russians, he now and then generalizes from what appear to be sensational and exceptional cases. But if he is occasionally too hasty in generalizing about matters of this order, Olearius seems reluctant to make generalizations of a higher order. He gives the reader a plethora of interesting details on a multitude of topics but little on their interrelation and even less in the way of overall interpretive comment. Still, able ethnologist though he was, he should hardly be reproached for failing to produce the sort of unified analysis one expects of a modern social scientist.

On another vital point, sensitivity to cultural relativism, Olearius is more vulnerable. More than fifty years earlier Montaigne had observed: "Each man calls barbarism whatever is not his own practice;

for indeed it seems we have no other test of truth and reason than the example and pattern of the opinions and customs of the country we live in."[38] By contrast, Olearius failed to appreciate that his attitudes were culturally conditioned and that his objectivity might be limited. To view Russia through the eyes of a Westerner, as he did, of course had certain advantages. The outsider may report features of the culture before him that its members, who take them for granted, would not; and what is taken for granted are often precisely the most characteristic features of that culture. However, the outsider is barred from discovering its internal logic and values so long as he persists, as Olearius did, in making judgments exclusively from the frame of reference provided by his own culture. Thus—to cite one conspicuous example— he dismissed Russian painting, whose style and principles were unfamiliar to him, with a few disdainful words.

The reader must keep in mind that Olearius was a German by nationality, a Protestant by faith, a scholar by training, and a high functionary by social rank. Like other foreigners, the Germans in Moscow, among whom Olearius collected much of his material, were distrustful of the Russians and contemptuous of their culture. If Olearius strove to be fair (for example, he credits the Russians with technical aptitudes and their government with religious tolerance toward foreigners within Muscovy's frontiers) he still shared the sentiments of his compatriots to some extent.[39] We may be disposed to agree with his assertion that German, or at least foreign, example had caused some tempering of Russian manners. But Olearius is unduly haughty about Russian behavior, while leaving out of the balance such matters as the legendary drunkenness of the foreign soldiers formerly garrisoned in the Naleika district of Moscow (to which he refers elsewhere) and the misdeeds of the German mercenaries in Russia's employ, of which the Holsteiners caught a glimpse during their first journey to Moscow. And on one occasion, in the course of comparing German and Russian baths, he delivers an ill-tempered, chauvinistic diatribe against the Russians.

In matters of religion, Olearius had much in common with other seventeenth-century intellectuals. His scientific studies disposed him

---

[38] Montaigne, pp. 77–78.

[39] It is significant that modern Russian writers consider Olearius fairer than most other foreign observers. See, for example, Kostomarov's *O sostoianii,* p. vii; Rushchinskii, p. 21; and Zagoskin, p. 291.

to naturalistic explanations of what he observed, and he was accordingly skeptical of the miracle-working power of religious rituals. His ironical remarks on the ceremonies of Russian religion convey plainly his conviction that it was heavily freighted with superstition. His critical attitude does not extend to religion in general, however: his judgments on Russian religious practices and ideas betray a mind steeped in the Protestant thought of the time. Characteristically, in contrasting the Russian Orthodox with the Protestant system of reckoning years, he praises the latter for being "in accord with the true Bible story of the creation of the world 3,949 years before the birth of Christ."

In view of his humble background, one might expect Olearius to have been sensitive to the plight of Russia's downtrodden common people. In fact, he had thoroughly assimilated the aristocratic point of view of the Holstein court. Like other high-ranking visitors to Muscovy, he was appalled by the abased condition of the nobility there. As against this, he speaks resentfully of being obliged to spend some time with "the rabble." And elsewhere he remarks that in a massacre perpetrated by Ivan IV at Novgorod almost three thousand were slaughtered, "not counting women, children, and the common people." In an estimate of the sort one expects from the masters of a society based on inequality, Olearius pronounces the Russian people fit only for slavery.

If Olearius fails to provide us with a coherent image of Russian culture, he does furnish us with a great deal of material for one. Although Olearius regards the Russians, with some reservations, as a Christian people, he considers most Russian institutions so different from their Western counterparts as to constitute a distinct civilization.[40] Among other things, he notes its treatment of women, its painting, its alphabet, its calendar, its preoccupation with ceremony, and its distrust of foreigners. His experiences in Russia are set in the frame of two characteristic occurrences: when he first reaches Russia's western frontier, he witnesses a curious performance acted out by the Tsar's officials to demonstrate their sovereign's superiority to any foreign ruler who might send him an ambassador; and when the embassy was leaving Russia for Persia, they were forbidden by the governor of Astrakhan to fraternize

---

[40] This attitude was shared by practically all English observers of Russia in the sixteenth and seventeenth centuries. Anderson, pp. 28, 39–40.

with the Tatars in the vicinity. But overshadowing, and encompassing, such particulars in Olearius's account are three aspects of Russian culture that he repeatedly emphasizes: political tyranny, moral debasement, and indifference or hostility toward intellectual pursuits.

Olearius's opinion of Russia's political system was similar to Herberstein's and Fletcher's. Although crediting Tsar Aleksei Mikhailovich with mildness and compassion for his people, he attributes this not to a diminution of the ruler's extravagant power but rather to a disinclination to exercise that power to the full. The despotism of the political order was evident in the dependence of the lives and property of the people—the notables no less than the commoners—on the Tsar's goodwill, and in the regime's apparent ambition to exercise an all-embracing control over the activities of its subjects.[41] When we learn from Olearius that before a corpse was lowered into the grave a passport calculated to secure his admission to Heaven was placed in his hands, we are tempted to view the practice as symbolical of a society which assumed that nothing could be done without official papers. And so that this state of affairs might be perpetuated, Olearius observes, "They are forbidden, on pain of corporal punishment, to travel out of the country on their own initiative, [for they might then] tell [their countrymen] of the free institutions that exist in foreign lands."

Olearius supplements his description of the political system with sketches of its barbaric punishments and the people's servility. But on this and other points one must use his testimony with some reserve. It is not that his facts are wrong, but his evaluations sometimes are. On the matter of punishments, for example, some perspective is needed. The Russians' methods were indeed frightful, but those of the West were hardly beyond reproach—Giovanni Beccaria's famous condemnation of the cruel methods of punishment employed in Western Europe was not yet written, let alone the practices corrected. On the matter of the people's subservience, Olearius does not reconcile their alleged love of slavery with the turbulent and ferocious Moscow uprising of 1648 that he describes so vividly. Whereas he writes, "this despotic government seems best suited to their humor, which is insensible to the advantages of liberty," he later cites the insurrection to prove "that the

---

[41] On the type of system this phenomenon suggests, see Wittfogel.

Muscovites, no matter how submissive and slavish they may be, will endeavor to recover their liberty when the government becomes insupportable to them."

Olearius gives a most unflattering description of the Russians' moral character. With an abundance of evidence, he depicts them as a people given to drunkenness and sexual license, coarse and repulsive speech, lying, deception, cruelty, and criminal behavior. The masses' servility has its counterpart in the nobility's arrogance. Olearius was no more shocked by the sordidness of what he saw than by the prevalence of such behavior in a society pervaded by religious ritualism; for he makes plain how large religious events and activities loomed in the affairs of the average Muscovite. Coming from an Evangelical society in which a man's behavior was viewed as an expression of his spiritual condition, he reproaches the Orthodox church for failing to exercise its authority on behalf of Christian conduct. Unfortunately the important movement for moral reform then afoot in Russia escaped his attention; and in his indictment he overlooked certain of the patriarchs' acts on behalf of moral improvement that he himself reported.[42]

The strictures that the historian V. O. Kliuchevskii laid down against the use of foreign sources for the study of Russian moral life of course have some point.[43] One must be wary of taking isolated incidents as typical, and of measuring Russian manners and morals against Western ideals rather than Western practice. Still, if Olearius sometimes seems insufficiently cautious, it does not follow, as some offended Russian writers later intimated, that everything written by foreign observers of Muscovy was slanderous and without foundation. After all, Iurii Krizhanich, a Croat whose sympathies lay with the Russians, also was dismayed by the national vices, and reproached his fellow Slavs for their ignorance, laziness, stupidity, filthiness, rudeness, and drunkenness.[44] Still it must be conceded that most foreign writers, Olearius among them, either never inquired into, or failed effectively to deal with, the sources of the moral situation they confronted.

---

[42] Abundant information on the reform movement is presented in Pierre Pascal's fine book, *Avvakum et les débuts du raskol.*

[43] Kliuchevskii, *Skazaniia inostrantsev,* pp. 8–10. Kliuchevskii omitted such material from this work, his doctoral dissertation. Although this study is still valuable today, it was omitted from the recent Soviet edition of Kliuchevskii's works.

[44] Petrovich, p. 86.

Nothing about Russian civilization astonishes Olearius so much as the low esteem in which intellectual affairs are held. The Russians neither know nor study foreign languages, and they do not occupy themselves with the arts and sciences. If he perceives some slight change for the better, he nevertheless feels that this deplorable situation will not soon be remedied. Schools, the agencies for propagating and extending knowledge, are few in number and rudimentary in character. The ignorant populace is intensely suspicious of natural science, which they are unable to distinguish from witchcraft.[45] Furthermore, the church authorities, who ought to favor the spread of enlightenment, are intensely hostile to the free discussion of religious questions, fearing it would only lead to discord and heresy. Similarly they seek to prevent free communication between the Russians and more intellectually advanced foreigners, lest established doctrines and practices be brought into question. As befits a scholar, Olearius identifies wrongly understood religion and the attendant opposition to intellectual endeavors as the root cause of Russia's cultural predicament.

He does not, however, push this point very far. Not surprisingly, given the time of his writing, he does not systematically use the historical approach as a device for integrating his material. Although his narrative is supplemented by a wealth of historical data, and although he is aware that "a great deal has been written about the Russians which no longer applies, . . . because of general changes in time, regime, and people," he simply does not ask how this peculiar combination of institutions and ideas came into being. His few incidental observations on the subject are rather more contradictory than complementary. For instance, the people's servility, in his view, is partly a consequence of the terror to which they had been subjected by Ivan the Terrible. Yet, he sometimes explains national traits not historically but in terms of innate qualities—remarking at one point that the Russians "are cruelhearted by nature." At another point, he relates the high incidence of robbery and murder in Moscow to the inadequate wages paid by the

[45] Of course Russia was not unique in this respect; and Olearius's Germany was hardly blameless. As Edgar Johnson writes: "Because of the witchcraft mania a 'century of [scientific] genius' (the seventeenth) has also been called 'the darkest age of superstition' . . . [and] in Germany the witch mania reached its height." Johnson, II, 143.

grandees to their serfs. But like nearly all other foreign reporters on Muscovy, he does not generally relate the moral situation of the people to social conditions.[46] Instead he charges it to lack of enlightenment or to the Church's neglect of its duties.

Considerable attention has been given here to the limitations of Olearius's work because it has not previously been subjected to an overall, critical scrutiny. We should remember, however, that the faults in his work are faults peculiar to the better minds of his time. Even though he has the advantage of hindsight, the reader cannot fail to be fascinated and charmed by Olearius's immensely informative, lively, and perceptive account of seventeenth-century Russia.

Of the many themes Olearius illuminates, perhaps none is of greater interest than Russia's relation to the West. The reference is not to diplomatic relations, a subject our author discreetly declines to discuss, except for the externals, despite his considerable firsthand knowledge of it. Diplomatic contacts are but a small part of what we have in view, namely, the meeting of two cultures and their interaction, and above all the West's impact upon Russia.[47] Although Russia had had limited contacts with Western Europe prior to 1553, the establishment of a trade route to Archangel via the North Cape opened a new era. Relations with the West, particularly with England to the end of the sixteenth century, became more regular and stable.[48] Its immediate neighbors sought to isolate Muscovy, envisaging her as the heir to the Tatars, a savage and barbarous state threatening to overrun and destroy Western civilization. The English were adept at securing commercial advantages from the tsars without either satisfying or flatly rejecting their pleas for diplomatic support. However, the tsars themselves successfully exploited the English merchants' desire for profit to split what might have been a united front of the Western powers, and to obtain

[46] The English diplomat Giles Fletcher was a notable exception to the rule. See his remarks in Bond, pp. 64, 151.

[47] General studies of this subject are Brückner's *Kulturhistorische Studien;* the same author's *Die Europäisierung Russlands;* and Platonov's *Moskva i zapad.*

[48] It is of course true that until the end of the fifteenth century Novgorod had enjoyed uninterrupted trade relations with the Hanseatic League for several centuries. In contrast to the process set in motion by the establishment of Anglo-Russian relations, however, ties with the Hansa appear to have had a very limited impact upon Russia.

military supplies and technical aid that strengthened their country vis-à-vis its immediate neighbors. During this period foreign doctors, soldiers, and artisans entered Russia's service, and foreign merchants became a familiar sight along the main arteries of trade. Contacts between the two civilizations were as yet superficial, however, and the changes they wrought relatively insignificant.

The Time of Troubles provoked an anti-foreign reaction in Muscovy. In 1612, in response to an offer by certain foreigners to serve in Russia's army, Prince Pozharskii, a leader of the uprising that defeated the Polish-Catholic attempt to dominate Russia, proclaimed his country's mistrust of outsiders and its intention of relying exclusively upon itself.[49] This bold declaration did not become the basis of policy. In practice Tsar Mikhail, the first Romanov (r. 1613–45), generally avoided relying upon the Catholic nations but increased overall contacts with the West. After the Time of Troubles, English influence waned, as Dutch traders and German military and technical advisers became more prominent.[50]

By the time Olearius first went to Moscow, Russia had many more ties to the West, both diplomatic and commercial, than she had at the death of Ivan the Terrible some fifty years before. Sweden had achieved some success in the 1630's in using Russia's antipathy to Poland to the advantage of the Protestant coalition in the Thirty Years War. As we know, several Western states were competing at the Russian court for the privilege of a trade route to Persia. Some of them also were competing for the right to purchase Russian grain. For its part, the Russian government controlled the flow of grain and other commodities with an eye to the political advantage to be obtained.[51] Many Western states permitted Russia to recruit soldiers and technicians within their borders.[52] Meanwhile, foreign merchants had penetrated Russia's markets so successfully that a mercantilist reaction began to take shape there.[53]

In Russia Olearius meets Westerners everywhere: en route to Moscow, officers and soldiers returning home from service in the Tsar's un-

[49] *Sobranie*, Vol. II, No. 285.

[50] The Dutch triumph over the English is treated in Lubimenko, "The Struggle of the Dutch."

[51] This point and the one concerning Sweden's use of Russia are discussed at length in Vainshtein, Chap. 2.

[52] See Lappo-Danilevskii, "Inozemtsy."

[53] For Basilevich's excellent articles on this theme, see the Bibliography.

successful campaign against Poland at Smolensk; in Moscow, members of the West European community, which numbers no fewer than a thousand people; in Nizhnii Novgorod, a number of Protestants sufficient to support a church; in Astrakhan, an Austrian who became a Russian Orthodox monk and introduced the art of viniculture to the area. He hears of the many foreign merchants who annually come to Archangel and of German ironworks at Tula. He also finds foreigners engaged as doctors and apothecaries, interpreters and translators, bell casters and makers of luxuries for the court. Moreover, there are representatives of foreign governments, pastors of the Protestant churches, and men prospecting for gold and promoting other industrial enterprises.

Although the presence of foreign merchants and government representatives requires no particular explanation, that of the many other Westerners in Muscovy does. The influx of foreigners was in part a consequence of religious intolerance and international conflict in the West. Among those who came to Russia were persons barred from advancement in their homelands by religious restrictions; mercenaries, unemployed between campaigns or attracted by offers of higher pay; and adventurers, a type whose proliferation was favored by the upheavals of the time. Olearius's memorable portrait of the Bohemian adventurer von Slick and his notes on the terror the German mercenaries inspired among the peasants make it clear that the foreigners in Russia were not an unmixed blessing.

Nevertheless, Russia had to take the bad with the good. Although the Muscovite rulers were loath to acknowledge it, their policies eloquently expressed the need of their backward country for the more advanced, Western civilization's assistance in developing its resources and power. Why else did such a populous land employ foreign mercenaries? Why else did a country with rich resources give advantageous concessions to such Western entrepreneurs as Peter Marselis to develop them? Why did the tsars extend valuable privileges to foreign merchants to the detriment of their own? Why were their doctors, apothecaries, interpreters, and so forth, almost invariably foreigners? If there is any doubt of the answer, it may be deduced from the fact that most contracts with foreigners required that they train Russians in their specialties.

To grasp the full extent of Russia's need, one must realize that ever larger numbers of foreigners were recruited despite the country's deep-seated aversion to them.[54] The sources of this sentiment were various. They were partly of recent inspiration, partly ancient; partly political and economic, partly religious and cultural. What the Russians had suffered under the Tatar yoke strongly colored their attitudes toward outsiders, and their recent experience in the Time of Troubles, when the country once again was nearly subjugated to a foreign power, had unquestionably intensified their xenophobia. Russia continued to resent earlier European efforts to isolate her,[55] although the situation was now changed for the better. Still, some foreign technicians continued the embargo by failing to impart the secrets of their crafts to the Russians who worked with them.[56] Whether the Russians were disturbed about this is not clear, but there is abundant evidence of anxiety caused by foreign competition with Russian merchants.

It has also been suggested that Russia was wary of foreigners for fear they might be spies.[57] Even though few cases of spying seem to have come to light, this suggestion should not be dismissed out of hand. The Russians' attitude toward West Europeans derived in considerable measure from a sense of weakness and vulnerability to exploitation.[58] Compounded principally of fear and enmity, it often tended to produce exaggerated and irrational suspiciousness. Krizhanich, one of those who warned against the danger of espionage by foreigners, expressed this feeling in the 1660's, when he wrote:

> Not one people under the sun since ancient times has been so wronged and shamed by foreigners as have we Slavs by the Germans. No other people has had as much reason to guard against dealing with foreigners as have we Slavs. And how is it that we guard ourselves? Nowhere under heaven have foreigners half the honors and profits that they have here among the Russians and the Poles.[59]

---

[54] This matter is brilliantly discussed in Pypin, pp. 255–96.

[55] For a brief account of the Schlitte affair, one of the more notorious such efforts, see Platonov, *Moskva i zapad*, pp. 9–11.

[56] Brückner, *Kulturhistorische Studien*, II, 81; and Tsvetaev, *Protestantstvo i protestanty*, pp. 397–401.

[57] Muliukin, *Priezd inostrantsev*, pp. 33, 49–50, 58.

[58] See Plekhanov, XX, 322–25.

[59] Krizhanich, I, 182.

Even deeper roots of the antipathy to foreigners may be found in Russian religious attitudes. In one of the first Russian places Olearius visited, he saw a painting of the Last Judgment in which the Russians were evidently being directed to Heaven and those in foreign clothes were consigned to Hell. One might be inclined to regard this painting as a graphic expression of the Third Rome Doctrine, which implied the distinctiveness and superiority of the Russians—the true Christians. However, the first manifestations of these attitudes antedate the proclamation of the Third Rome Doctrine by several centuries. As early as the eleventh century, only decades after the separation of the Eastern and Western churches, Metropolitan John II of Kiev had warned against eating with the "Romans" or traveling in their lands. If someone knowingly ate with a foreigner, he had to be cleansed "by prayers of purification." And anyone who had traveled abroad could be admitted to communion only after "making atonement by [offering] certain prayers enjoined as a penance."[60] Obviously, contact with members of other faiths was considered defiling. Consistent with this belief, marriage between the Orthodox and the non-Orthodox was forbidden. Such regulations, which reflected Greek Orthodox antipathy to the Latin West, may not have been rigorously enforced in Kievan times, but there is no doubt that the spirit that underlay them not only persisted but was reinforced in the Moscow era.[61] Thus, as Olearius's account makes clear, the entry of foreigners to the country was carefully controlled and restricted, and Russians were permitted to go abroad only on official business. Moreover, like earlier visitors, Olearius observed during a public audience with the Tsar the ewer, basin, and towel he used to wash his hand after it had been kissed by foreign envoys.

It seems likely that the taboos on intercourse with Western Christians, although framed as if to prevent physical pollution, were really directed against religious and cultural subversion. In spite of the proclamation of the Third Rome Doctrine, it is difficult to escape the impression that Russian church authorities suffered from a sense of weak-

[60] Fedotov, pp. 186–89. Metropolitan John's regulations are set forth by Herberstein, I, 66–68.
[61] According to Muliukin, *Priezd inostrantstev*, there were no restrictions upon foreign entry into Russia before the Moscow era; see his Introduction.

ness. Perhaps a tacit admission of it was the ban they imposed upon religious disputation. The ignorance of the clergy was proverbial, and one may imagine the inability of either clergy or laity to make an adequate defense of its beliefs. Having only the most tenuous connection with classical Greek culture, Russian Orthodoxy lacked a spirit of rationalistic inquiry, and it failed to develop an intellectual tradition geared to rigorous and dialectical thinking. Accordingly, Russia produced no Aquinas or Calvin, and indeed, as G. P. Fedotov has argued, it failed to produce a single scientific work on theology before the seventeenth century.[62] Understandably, church authorities wished to inhibit communication with Western Christians, which might undermine the edifice of their faith.

In the seventeenth century, then, if not earlier, serious discordances were introduced into Russian culture. Inasmuch as its keystone, the Orthodox religion, was proclaimed to be the true faith, in theory the entire culture was superior to others. Yet, in glaring contradiction, Russia was obliged to seek instruction and assistance from the West. Humiliating though this must have been to nationally-conscious Muscovites, they were able to rationalize the necessity in much the same way that the Chinese dealt with a similar conflict in the nineteenth century. The Russians were not as explicit as the Chinese in the era of the "self-strengthening movement," but they too, in effect, conceded the superiority of Western technology,[63] while vaunting the superiority of their own spiritual culture, something far more important in their hierarchy of values.[64]

Nevertheless, the guardians of Russia's traditional culture sensed that the large number of foreigners entering the country for extended periods created an unprecedented danger. If the spiritual base of Russian civilization were to be preserved against erosion, better ways had

[62] Fedotov, p. 38. The relationship between classical Greek culture and Russian Orthodoxy's failure to develop an intellectual tradition is treated in Fedotov, Chap. 2. For other views, see Florovsky, "The Problem of Old Russian Culture" and the discussion articles that follow it. Florovsky's interpretation of Russia's "intellectual silence" is developed in his *Puti russkago bogosloviia.*

[63] See Kliuchevskii, "Zapadnoe vliianie," pp. 380 ff. For a study of the Chinese self-strengthening movement, see Wright.

[64] This position was foreshadowed as early as the time of Ivan the Terrible. Ivan was extremely eager to draw Western technicians to Russia, but he also engaged in polemics against both the Catholic and Protestant faiths.

to be found to demarcate the foreigners sharply from the native population—the existing strictures no longer seemed an adequate barrier to
communication. Since the implementation of a more stringent policy
occurred in Olearius's time, he reports a series of actions that pushed to
new extremes the process initiated in Kievan times by Metropolitan
John. The measures of the seventeenth-century patriarchs converted
the Westerners into a caste and relegated them to a physically segre-
gated community.[65]

As Olearius relates, foreigners were forbidden to wear Russian
clothes and Russians to wear foreign clothes, so that free mingling
might not take place unobserved. The Russians were forbidden to
smoke tobacco on pain of severe punishment, whereas the foreigners
were free to smoke. Other decrees made it illegal for West Europeans
to own estates in Russia or to have Orthodox servants. Western Christians (the Russians actually did not consider them Christians) were
not admitted to Russian churches. If a foreigner somehow entered a
church—and something of the sort sometimes held for private homes
as well—the place was swept out and reconsecrated. In the most dra-
matic measure of all, in 1652 the Westerners in Moscow were ordered
to move from their homes in the city to a separate quarter. Thus came
into being the famous Moscow foreign suburb (nemetskaia sloboda),
widely thought of as an enclave of Western civilization in the heart of
Muscovy.[66]

It should be pointed out that the Church was not alone in fostering
such decrees and practices and in cultivating among the populace the
anti-foreign sentiment that occasionally erupted into a pogrom. Although they did not attract Olearius's attention, the merchants whose
interests were threatened by foreign competition were becoming increasingly vociferous. From the 1620's on, they addressed to the government a series of petitions for protection. It is plain that if the petitioners had had their way, the foreign merchants would have been

[65] It should be noted, however, that a counter-tendency was promoted by Russia's incorpora-
tion, in 1654, of the strongly Polish- and Catholic-influenced Ukraine, and by the reform movement that sought to bring Russian church practices into accord with the Greek. An incidental
result was a slight reduction of the distance between Russian and Catholic religious practice; for
example, Catholic converts to Russian Orthodoxy were no longer obliged to be rebaptized.

[66] The suburb, which has yet to be studied in depth, is the subject of short chapters in Platonov, *Moskva i zapad*; Schuyler; and Brückner, *Die Europäisierung Russlands*. See also Nechaev,
Zviagintsev, and Bogoiavlenskii.

banned from the country and obliged to deal with their Russian counterparts at the frontiers.[67] The Russian merchants eventually received
some satisfaction, but even Tsar Aleksei Mikhailovich (r. 1645–76),
who did the most for them, never fully met their demands. He realized, as they did not, that his backward country could not afford the
policy they urged.

The limited action taken against the foreigners did not cause them
to withdraw from Muscovy. But neither did their segregation achieve
the desired result. In the last half of the seventeenth century, Western influence steadily increased—with the encouragement of the same
Tsar Aleksei who promulgated many of the anti-foreign measures. The
frequent visits of Aleksei's son Peter to the nemetskaia sloboda had a
decisive effect in the policy of accelerated and intensified Westernization that Peter instituted when he became Tsar.[68] Years before he
seized a sector of the Baltic coast, Peter cut a window through to Europe by entering into free communication with the residents of Moscow's foreign community. Later, he definitively subordinated the
Church to the State, by suppressing the office of Patriarch, and thus
neutralized the most serious opposition to the termination of Russia's
cultural isolation. As was later true of the Chinese and other civilizations, defensive measures did no more than delay Westernization.
Paradoxically, Russia had to undergo cultural change in order to preserve its territorial and national integrity.

Olearius could not of course fully comprehend the process in which
Russia was caught up, for both its origins and its outcome were obscure.
Yet no student of seventeenth-century Russia or of Russia's relations
with the West can afford to ignore him, for his work abounds in the
precious material of which the historian reconstructs the past.

---

[67] There were pressures for such a policy vis-à-vis the English even in the late sixteenth century. See Willan, p. 226. In 1649, they were finally forbidden to trade in Russia. A more com-
prehensive decree was published in 1667, but it allowed numerous exceptions and was not rigorously enforced.

[68] See Kliuchevskii, "Zapadnoe vliianie"; and Schuyler.

BOOK I

The First Journey to Moscow

[*The first part of Book I, in which Olearius discusses the benefits of foreign travel, is omitted.*]

M Y MOST ILLUSTRIOUS and noble Prince and Lord, Frederick, Heir to Norway, Duke of Schleswig, Holstein, Stormarn, and Ditmars, Count of Oldenburg and Delmenhorst,[1] having resolved to organize and dispatch a grand embassy, designated as envoys two of his counselors, the noble, honest, highly respected, and most learned gentleman Philip Crusius of Eisleben, Licentiate in civil and canon law (now a nobleman, thanks to the special favor of the King of Sweden, who named him Philip Krusenstierne and made him a royal counselor, Burgrave of Narva, and general director of commerce in Estonia and Ingermanland), and Mr. Otto Brüggemann of Hamburg.[2] On October 22d, 1633, both were sent for the first time from the Duke's residence in Gottorp to Moscow, to the great sovereign Tsar and Grand Prince, Mikhail Feodorovich, Autocrat of all Russia, etc., to request free passage across Russia to Persia. When everything necessary for the voyage had been prepared, they departed from Hamburg on November 6th with a company of 34 persons, arriving in Lübeck on the 7th and in Travemünde on the 8th. There an experienced sea captain named Michael Cordes was taken aboard, having been engaged for the journey on the Caspian Sea.

On the 9th, with the good wishes of many friends who had accompanied us from Hamburg and Lübeck to the coast, we set out to sea. The ship in which we sailed was called the *Fortune,* and its skipper

---

[1] Frederick III ruled Schleswig-Holstein from 1616 to 1659. Because of his sponsorship of the arts and sciences and his interest in promoting economic enterprises, he may be considered a forerunner of the enlightened despots.

[2] Olearius spells the Hamburger's name variously in his work. I have used the spelling given here throughout. Brüggemann had gone to Moscow in 1632 on Frederick's behalf.

was Hans Müller. We also had along with us Mr. Wendelin Sybelist, a physician whom the Grand Prince had invited to become court doctor and whom his Princely Excellence the Duke of Holstein had recommended to His Tsarist Majesty.[3] In the afternoon, we put out from shore in high spirits and lay at anchor in the road. About nine in the evening we invoked God's blessing and set sail. With a favorable southwest wind, that night we made 20 leagues.[4] The next day, with the approval of the ambassadors and the skipper, certain ship's rules and regulations were established so that the men might conduct themselves in an orderly manner. The fines paid by offenders were later to be distributed to the poor. Several of the notables were authorized to see that the rules were followed and to fine offenders. The regime was so rigorously enforced that by the end of our sea voyage, that is in just four days, 22 reichsthalers had been taken in. The money was turned over to the captain, with instructions to distribute half to the poor of Riga and half to the poor of Lübeck.

Toward evening on the 10th of November we passed Bornholm Island, which lay a good league to our right and some forty leagues from Lübeck. It is a high-lying island, rocky in places, three leagues in both length and breadth, with good pastures. It is said to yield several lasts of butter annually.[5] By the shore is an ancient castle named Hammershausen. The island formerly belonged to the city of Lübeck but for certain reasons was transferred to His Royal Majesty the King of Denmark as a christening gift, and it is still subject to him. Near the north side of the island lie the dangerous Erdholm reefs, which seamen greatly fear in the autumn. Since at night these rocks cannot be

---

[3] Russia's failure to produce doctors was one indication of her backwardness. Western doctors were employed at least by the early sixteenth century, for Grand Duke Vasilii III was attended by foreign physicians as he lay dying. In the reign of Ivan IV they became a permanent fixture of the Russian court; England supplied the first practitioners, and in the seventeenth century German doctors predominated. It is thought that the first Russian to receive a medical degree was P. B. Postnikov, who graduated from Padua in 1695. However, in the last decades of the seventeenth century, Russians who had been trained by the Tsar's foreign physicians engaged in a wide range of medical tasks. On medical practice in Russia before the eighteenth century, see Rikhter, Vols. I–II; Lakhtin, Chaps. 1–3; *Chteniia*, 1911, No. 4, Part 3, pp. 41–51; and Platonov, *Moskva i zapad*, pp. 137–38.

Sybelist, formerly employed at the Holstein court, replaced Dr. Artemius Dee, an Englishman, who retired in 1633. Dr. Sybelist served the Tsar from 1633 to 1642 and from 1644 to 1646. See Rikhter, II, 48–62.

[4] Olearius most often uses the so-called German mile, the equivalent of 4.6 English miles, as the measure of distance. To avoid confusion, I have translated the German mile as a league.

[5] A last is a measure of weight equal to 4,320 pounds.

detected even with the aid of a plumb—in their immediate vicinity the water is very deep—many ships are sunk here.

On the 11th, with good weather and wind, we reached the 56th latitude at noon. Toward evening the wind behind us began to increase, continuing through the night and obliging us to take in our sails. Most of us who had not traveled by sea before became seasick, and some became so weak that they expected to die. This ailment is not caused by the stench of the salt water—as [Jovianus] Pontanus (in *Bellaria Attica*) and others write—but exclusively by the motion of the ship. Although in most people it calls forth stomach spasms and dizziness, those who are accustomed to this motion and are therefore not inclined to dizziness do not experience discomfort. In my opinion, that is the main reason why small children, who are accustomed to being rocked in the cradle, are very rarely affected. The cause of this illness is also apparent from the fact that it is not experienced at the very beginning of a sea voyage, while the wind is still weak, but only after several days, when a strong wind rocks the ship. Also, when stormy weather lasts some days, for most people the illness passes of itself. I observed the same phenomenon among some of our party on the Volga River, where salt water is not in question. In fair weather they sailed along for extended periods feeling nothing; but when a gale blew up, with the wind going against the river's current, and when the ship began to roll, they again felt discomfort. Therefore, Pontanus's remark (*Bellaria Attica*, p. 524) that "those who sail on a river do not experience such discomforts because there is no smell of the sea" is baseless, for in fact it all must be attributed to the motion alone.

With the aid of the stiff wind just mentioned, we kept to our course and on that night made 15 leagues. The next day, the 12th, was so still that not the slightest breeze blew, and the ship was becalmed. In this mild weather, we had our musical instruments brought up on deck and thanked and praised God with singing and playing for having mercifully preserved us through the preceding night. Toward noon, we again got a good wind from the south, which carried us easily to Domesnes, a cape that juts out from Courland into the sea. Here we anchored and remained until the evening of the 13th, when a west wind came up, enabling us to sail around the cape into the bay. Thus early on the 14th we reached the fort of Dünamünde, which lies two leagues from the city of Riga at the mouth of the Dvina River (whence its name).[6] As a thick fog descended, making it impossible to see any distance, we announced our approach with a trumpet blast, in order to secure from the fort a pilot, without whose aid someone unacquainted with the place could not proceed. Soon afterward customs officials came aboard to determine whether the ship carried any taxable merchandise. Finding nothing, they sent us a pilot, with whose aid we went forward; and very late in the evening, thanks be to God, we reached the city of Riga.

After the ambassadors had advised the city authorities of our arrival, they and a few others of us went ashore and entered the city. There we were met by some army officers with an empty coach, which the local governor had sent to meet the ambassadors. Since they were not far from the inn, however, the ambassadors declined to mount, and were instead accompanied on foot to Hans Krabbenhoft's inn, where they and the most important members of the suite put up, while the rest were sent to neighboring houses. On November 21st the ambassadors received gifts from His Honor the Magistrate, namely an ox, some sheep, hens, rabbits, and many game birds, as well as several loaves of wheat and rye bread and an *ahm* of Rhine wine.[7] Three days later the ambassadors arranged an entertainment, to which they invited the Governor (Herr Andreas Erichsen), His Honor the Magistrate, the Superintendent (Magister Samsonius), and some high-ranking officers of the city.

We spent five quiet weeks in the city, until the frost and snow had prepared a good sledge road for us across the outlying swamp. Thence lay the way to Dorpat; and on December 14th some of our people were sent ahead with our train and baggage on 31 sleighs, the ambassadors following the next day. As most of us were unaccustomed to riding in sleighs and driving sleigh horses, which we were now obliged to do, the first day several people were thrown from the sleighs, after which they would pick themselves and their things up out of the snow. On the 18th we arrived at the little town of Volmar, where we were received by the commandant. This town, 18 leagues from Riga, had

---

[6] The Dvina is called the Düna in German. Dünamünde means the mouth of the Düna.

[7] An ahm is an old wine measure equal to 130–60 liters.

been devastated by Russian and Polish attacks. Here, on and around the old walls of ruined houses, the inhabitants erected wooden dwellings in the Swedish and Russian styles. We left there on the 20th and went six leagues to the castle of Ermes, belonging to Colonel de la Barre, where we were well received and entertained with two princely meals.

On the 21st we got four leagues farther, to the country estate of Halmet, where a young elk (*elend*), taller than a horse, was brought to our table at the inn. Such animals are abundant in this region, and some years ago were used to attract artisans and workers from Germany to cultivate the soil. The land was so rich and there was such an abundance of food here—they were told—that the elk ran into people's houses. However, since the Germans were unaccustomed to the heavy work involved in tilling the fields, they fared badly, became indigent, and *elend* [poverty] really came into their houses. With the help of good-hearted Germans some of them returned to Germany, as others whom we met complained to us.

On December 22d we advanced four leagues to the castle of Ringen, and the following day reached the town of Dorpat. This town lies in Estonia, or Estland, on the Embach River in the middle of Livonia; it is surrounded by a circular stone wall and bastions, which like the houses are built in the old style. In the course of many wars, especially the Russian action in 1571, the town had been nearly destroyed, as one may read in Henning's *Livonian Chronicle*.[8] Dorpat formerly belonged to the Muscovites, who called it Iur'ev. In 1230 it was taken by the master of the Teutonic Knights and made an episcopal seat. [Later] Magnus, Duke of Holstein and son-in-law of the tyrant [Ivan IV], was bishop there, as Hamelmann recalls in the *Oldenburg Chronicle*.[9] In 1558 the tyrant Ivan Vasil'evich again conquered Dorpat. In 1582

---

[8] Solomon Henning, *Lieffländische Chronica* (Leipzig, 1594). Henning was an envoy sent by the Master of the Livonian Order to the Holy Roman Emperor to request aid against Russia during the Livonian Wars. Dorpat was ravaged during Ivan IV's campaign to seize the Baltic coast. For a recent account in English, see Kirchner, *The Rise of the Baltic Question*.

[9] H. Hamelmann, *Oldenburgische Chronicon* (Oldenburg, 1599). Like many sixteenth- and seventeenth-century writers, Olearius habitually speaks of Ivan IV as "the tyrant." Magnus, who wedded Ivan's niece in 1573, was the only foreigner in the sixteenth and seventeenth centuries who married into the royal family without being obliged to embrace the Russian faith. On the diplomatic considerations that led Ivan to seek the marriage, see Kirchner's *The Rise of the Baltic Question*, pp. 113–18; on the marriage, see Tsvetaev, *Protestantstvo i protestanty*, pp. 212–15, 420–26.

King Stephen Batory [of Poland] subjugated the town; but when Duke Charles of Sudermanland acquired the Swedish throne and again made war on the Poles, he captured Dorpat, among other towns. Even now it is subject to His Royal Swedish Majesty.[10]

In Dorpat there is located a Livonian higher school, or university, and a royal court of justice. The school was founded and supported by Johann Skytte, Baron of Duderoff, formerly the attendant and tutor of King Gustavus Adolphus, and was dedicated October 15th, 1632.[11] Johann Skytte's son, Jakob, was the first rector of the university, and during his administration Andreas Virginius, a Pomeranian nobleman and Doctor of Holy Scripture, was designated vice-rector. Among the learned people and famous professors whom we met there were: Dr. Virginius; Johann Balau of Rostock, a doctor of medicine who later was called to Moscow as physician to the Tsar;[12] Friedrich Menius, whom the Emperor [Ferdinand II] named poet and professor of history; and Magister Petrus Andreas Schomerus, a mathematician from Sweden. When we were there, however, the number of students was still very small, amounting to only ten Swedes and a few Finns.

Having celebrated Christmas in Dorpat, on December 29th we proceeded on our way to Narva. On January 3d, 1634, we arrived in Narva, where we stayed with Jakob von Köllen, a leading merchant and innkeeper. To our great dismay we remained there 22 weeks, awaiting the arrival of the Swedish ambassadors, who for certain reasons were to accompany us to Moscow.[13] However, we were not without amusing diversions for passing the time. Not only did we daily set a princely table, at which we were well entertained by music and the good conversation of notables who often visited the ambassadors; we also attended divers sumptuous banquets and were invited out walking, riding, and hunting. Nevertheless, a passionate desire to be on our way

[10] Dorpat remained Swedish until Peter the Great conquered Livonia in the Great Northern War, concluded in 1721. It has been under Russian rule ever since, except for the interval between the two World Wars, when it was included in independent Estonia.

[11] Skytte was a Swedish senator and the governor of Livonia. The University of Dorpat, or Tartu as it is now called, is the oldest university in Russia.

[12] On Balau, or Belau, see Rikhter, II, 73–83.

[13] Olearius alluded to "certain reasons" when he wished to avoid discussing diplomatic matters he did not feel at liberty to disclose. The facts are as follows. Negotiations between Sweden and Holstein led in the spring of 1633 to an agreement granting Holstein's merchants the right of transit through Swedish Livonia. The two parties also contracted to make a joint representation in Moscow on behalf of free transit through Russia for Holstein's trade. See Kieksee.

made all this amusement unbearable. In addition, our underlings, forced to remain idle for so long, frequently got into quarrels and brawls with the Narva soldiers, and the ambassadors and the Governor were constantly having to mediate and set things right.

When we realized that we should be unable to depart until spring and that it would then be very difficult to travel the road between Narva and Novgorod, Magister Paul Fleming and some others, with packhorses and the heavy baggage, were sent ahead to Novgorod on February 28th, by the good sledge road.[14] At the same time, Dr. Wendelin [Sybelist] and his people also went ahead, and they soon continued on to Moscow.

At last provisions became so short at Narva that our Russian suppliers had to go as far as eight leagues to find chickens and sheep. Although for certain reasons we still could not hope for the early arrival of the Swedish ambassadors—chief among whom was Mr. Philip Scheiding, Governor of Revel—our ambassadors set out for Revel with 12 others, leaving the rest in Narva.[15] In Revel the gracious Magistrate saw that we were well received with gun salutes and presents. Here we stayed another six weeks, in the course of which the Governor, the noble Magistrate, and the notable citizens extended to us every manner of honor and friendship.

When on May 10th the Governor learned by post that the other members of the embassy assigned to him had arrived at Narva, he readied himself for the journey; and on Ascension Day, that is May 15th, he departed with us. On the 18th we were back in Narva. The Swedish ambassadors, Colonel Henrik Fleming and Messrs. Erik Gyllenstierne and Andreas Bureus, came with a considerable company to meet us a league from the city, received us cordially, and conducted us into the city, where once again we were welcomed with artillery salutes.

In a conference of the ambassadors of both sides, it was decided that

---

[14] Fleming, a well-known German poet and a member of the Holstein embassy, wrote many poems inspired by what he saw in Russia, some of which Olearius included in his 1656 edition. I have omitted all but two. Fleming's poems were reprinted at Stuttgart in 1865 under the title *Deutsche Gedichte.*

[15] By this time the Stockholm authorities had had some second thoughts about the agreement with Holstein, and delayed sending their envoys while attempting to devise a scheme that would draw the chief benefits of the Persian trade to Sweden. Evidently such notions were abandoned, however, for the Swedish representatives presently appeared. See Kieksee, pp. 63–64.

the two parties should proceed across Karelia to Novgorod by way of
Lake Ladoga. Word was sent by courier to the voevoda of Novgorod
so that he might know where to meet us and so that we need not wait
too long at the border. For it is the custom in Russia, as in Persia, that
when foreign ambassadors reach the frontiers they must declare their
business and then wait until the ruler of the country is notified by
courier of their arrival and sends the governor (*namestnik*) of the
province instructions for receiving and entertaining them.[16] The Muscovites and the Persians defray the expenses for both provisions and
transport of all ambassadors and messengers sent by great foreign
rulers, and also furnish a security escort for as long as these visitors
remain within their borders. Therefore the ambassadors were provided
a conductor (*pristav*) and some soldiers to escort them through the
country [to the capital]. After the courier had been sent to Novgorod,
on May 22d the Swedish ambassadors left Narva and went on toward
the Russian border, to the fortress of Capurga [Kopor'e in Russian], to
observe Pentecost.

On May 24th, the Saturday before Pentecost, I went to Russian
Narva to see how the Russians honored the memory of their deceased
relatives and friends.[17] The cemetery was full of Russian women, who
had spread upon the graves and gravestones beautifully sewn, vari-
colored handkerchiefs, on which they set dishes containing three or
four long pancakes and pies, two or three pieces of dried fish, and
colored eggs. Some standing and some kneeling, they wailed and cried,
and put different questions to the dead, as they are said to do also at
funerals.[18] If one of their acquaintances passed by, they turned to him
and spoke with a smile, but when he moved on they again began to

---

[16] Although foreign merchants, soldiers, artists, and clerics were freely admitted to Russia in
Kievan times (ca. 850–1240), the Muscovite rulers instituted a much more restrictive policy.
Although there were exceptions, on the whole they did not welcome foreigners. Even foreign
merchants, who were permitted to trade in such border towns as Archangel, Novgorod, Pskov,
and Astrakhan, were supposed to obtain permission if they wished to penetrate farther. In 1696
Peter the Great abolished the impediments to foreign access to the country. See Muliukin, *Priezd
inostrantsev*; Peter's 1696 decree is reprinted in the Appendix. For a fuller study, see the same
author's *Ocherki*.

The official rank of *namestnik* was defunct by Olearius's time. The term survived, however,
and sometimes was used interchangeably with *voevoda*. A voevoda was an appointee of the Tsar
who governed a town and the surrounding area.

[17] Though Narva at the time was in Swedish Livonia, Ivan IV had controlled it between 1558
and 1581. However, the Russian quarter of Narva dates back to the fifteenth century.

[18] Olearius describes Russian funeral ceremonies in Book III.

wail. Among them went a priest, with two servants, who carried a censer, into which from time to time he threw bits of wax, and censed the graves, while repeating a few words. One after another the women told the *popy* (thus they call their priests) the names of their deceased friends, some of whom had been dead for ten years; others read names out of a book and some gave them to the servants to read, and the priest was supposed to repeat them. Meanwhile the women bowed to the priest, sometimes making the sign of the cross, and he waved the censer toward them.

The women pulled and pushed the priest from one place to another, each wanting her departed to be served first. When the priest had completed the censing and praying, which he performed in an inattentive and not particularly reverent manner, the women gave him a large copper coin, like a Holstein sessling or six pennies of Meissen money.[19] The priest's servants took the pies and eggs for themselves, sharing some of them with us Germans who had witnessed the spectacle. We in turn distributed them to some poor children.

On May 26th, we made our peace with God and took communion; and having sent our train and baggage on by water to Nienschans with some of the common people, on the 28th we ourselves followed by land. To the firing of salvos from the city's guns, we entered the fortress of Iam [Gam in German] in the company of the commander, Colonel Port. Iam lies three leagues from Narva (and not 12, as Herberstein writes[20]) in Ingermanland, on a stream called the Iam that abounds in fish, especially salmon. Here one crosses the stream by ferry. Though not very large, the fortress is surrounded by strong stone walls and eight bastions. This town was taken from the Russians at the same time as Narva. Nearby is a Russian farming community, which, like the fortress, is subject to His Royal Swedish Majesty.

Here we obtained fresh horses, which on the 29th carried us six leagues, to the fortress of Capurga, where we were again greeted with

---

[19] Olearius frequently states monetary figures in terms of German currencies, but he usually gives both the Russian denomination and a German equivalent. Meissen money circulated in Saxony.

[20] Baron Sigismund von Herberstein, an envoy of the Holy Roman Emperor to the Russian court in 1517 and 1526, wrote a famous account of Muscovy, *Rerum Moscoviticarum commentarii*. Subsequent references are to the English translation, *Notes on Russia*, by R. H. Major. On Herberstein and his work, see Adelung, I, 160–75.

a fine gun salute. The commander of the fort, Bugislav Rosen, entertained us excellently. That evening he gave a banquet in our honor,
with 48 dishes and various wines, mead, and beer. The feasting on the
next day was even more ample, and was supplemented by music and
other amusements. At 3 o'clock in the afternoon we were sent on our
way with gun salutes and fresh horses. From Capurga the way went
across the estate of a boyar named Nikita Vasil'evich, but since the
estate was seven leagues away and we had departed late, we were
obliged to travel through the night until we reached the house. At 3
o'clock in the morning, the boyar received us kindly and feasted us
with various foods and drinks in silver vessels. He had two trumpeters
who played gaily while we were at table, and especially when we drank
toasts, a practice he probably had learned from the Germans. It was
abundantly evident that he was a gay and brave fellow. He had participated in the battle before Leipzig in 1631 and showed us scars of
wounds he had received.[21]

Before we left he brought his wife and one of her relatives to meet
us; both had young, lovely faces and were richly dressed. They were
accompanied by an ugly attendant, the better to emphasize their beauty.
Each lady had to sip a cup of vodka in honor of each of the ambassadors,
then hand it over and bow to him. The Russians consider it the greatest
honor they can pay a guest to show him in this manner that he has been
agreeable and welcome. Where friendship and intimacy are very great,
the guest is permitted to kiss the wife on the mouth, of which more
will be said below.

On May 31st at 1 o'clock in the afternoon, we took our leave, and by
evening had gone four leagues to Johannesthal. Here the noble Baron
Johann Skytte planned to build a town, and the church was already
nearly completed. A triple echo can be heard here, and our trumpeter
amused us with this a good part of the night, since the many mosquitoes
kept us from falling asleep. Because the area is so swampy, we encountered here our first great discomfort and unpleasantness: during the
day from large flies and wasps, which raised big welts on us and our
horses, and at night from mosquitoes, which we could drive away only
by smoke, which was also hard on our eyes and our sleep.

---

[21] Who this boyar was, why he was living in Swedish territory, and how he had happened to
participate in the Thirty Years War (apparently at the Battle of Breitenfeld, 1631) is unknown.

Learning that the Swedish King's ambassadors awaited us in Nienschans, we set out at once, at 3 o'clock in the morning of June 1st to be
precise, and arrived there at 6 o'clock. Nienschans, or Nie as some call
it, lies two and one-half leagues from Johannesthal on a navigable
watercourse that rises in Lake Ladoga and empties into the Gulf of Finland and the Baltic Sea, dividing Karelia from Ingermanland.[22] Good
food is available in Nienschans. Here we found the King's ambassadors,
who, after discussing certain affairs in secret with ours, went on to
Nöteburg.[23] We followed them on June 2d. The Governor there, a
brave-looking man named Colonel Johann Kunemundt, came out to
meet us in a gondola, or covered boat, received us courteously, and
brought us in to a salvo of guns.

The fortress of Nöteburg, eight leagues from Nienschans, lies at the
mouth of Lake Ladoga, 53° 30′ from the equator.[24] It is situated on a
nut-shaped island, surrounded on all sides by deep water, from which
it gets its name, Nöteburg [the nut fortress]. Here I found a magnetic
declination of 5° 30′ toward the west. The fortress was built by the
Russians and is surrounded by walls two and one-half *sazhens* thick.[25]
Since the embrasures are pointed directly ahead, i.e., their outside
dimension is scarcely wider than the inside (as in all the old Russian
fortresses), they are neither very convenient to shoot from nor very
effective for defense. In one corner of the fortress is a special, strongly
fortified little citadel, from which the fortress may be fired on from
within. This fortress was taken for His Royal Swedish Majesty by
Colonel Jakob de la Gardic.[26] We were told that the besieged Russians
held out until only two men were left; when, under the terms of the
surrender, all survivors were obliged to quit the fortress with their
belongings, only these two emerged. Asked where the rest were, they
answered that all the others had died of a contagious disease. In general, the Russians are believed to fight harder and more bravely in
holding fortresses than in field battles, of which more hereafter.

[22] The navigable water course is the Neva River, and the point at which it empties into the
Gulf of Finland is where St. Petersburg was later built.
[23] The fortress of Nöteburg, or Oreshek as the Russians called it then, was captured in 1702
by Peter the Great and renamed Schlüsselburg, for he considered it the key to the sea. See
Solov'ev, VII, 641–42.
[24] The correct reading is 63° 30′.
[25] A sazhen is a bit less than 84 inches.
[26] During the Time of Troubles.

Although the place is pleasantly situated, the freshwater lake and the many surrounding swamps make it unhealthful. For a whole three weeks in June there was such a multitude of gnats of the genus *Pyraustis,* or firefly, that one could not see air free of them a hand's length away, and it was impossible to go walking, face uncovered, without discomfort. Every year at this time masses of these pests swarm over Karelia, though in smaller numbers than at Nöteburg. The inhabitants call these insects "Russian souls" [Russische Seelen].

Surmising that we should be forced to wait a while in Nöteburg, the ambassadors kept only six men with them and sent the rest on to the Russian frontier, where provisions were easier to obtain. We ourselves stayed seven weeks, during which our ambassadors were daily invited to dine with the King's ambassadors so long as the latter remained there. (The invitations were brought by their marshal, the noble Wolf Sparr, and their *hofjunkers* [courtiers].) We who accompanied our ambassadors were also well received and entertained. On June 17th [Arend] Spiring, sent by His Royal Swedish Majesty with the rank of royal ambassador, arrived in Nöteburg with a small retinue.[27]

Since word came on the 25th that the voevoda of Novgorod had sent a pristav to the frontier to escort the Swedish ambassadors, first of all and separately from the others, they set out on the 26th and went up to Laba [Lava]. At their departure, the Lord spared them from a great misfortune. The salute was fired from a tower just when the boat conveying Ambassador Bureus passed, and the discharge caused a large timber from the roof to fall very close to the ambassador's head. Our ambassadors accompanied the King's a full four leagues. With their permission I rode with them all the way to the Russian border to observe the ceremony and customs with which the Russians received envoys. On the 27th at 4 o'clock in the morning, they arrived at the little river, forty paces wide, that flows past the village of Laba and is the frontier between Russia and Sweden. When the King's ambassadors learned on their arrival that 17 boats awaited them on the Russian side, they immediately sent their interpreter across to the pristav to request that he dispatch several boats to carry their things over without delay,

---

[27] Arend Spiring was the chief of the customs administration in Swedish Livonia. He was Sweden's expert on Russian affairs in the mission. Here and elsewhere, Olearius ought to have written *Her* Royal Majesty, for Queen Christina ruled Sweden from 1632 to 1654.

so that they might be on their way as soon as they had been formally received. However, the pristav, an elderly man, sent a reply that he dared do nothing of the sort before the ambassadors had been received: "Did they think that His Tsarist Majesty had not provisions enough to feed them an extra day, in the event of a possible delay?"

Around midday the pristav sent over his interpreter with four *streltsi*, or musketeers (of whom he had 30), with instructions to say that he would be very pleased to receive the ambassadors; did they not wish to come ahead? At that, one of the ambassadors had word conveyed to the pristav that they already had been obliged to sit and wait five weeks, so the pristav ought not to be offended if he now waited one extra day for them. However, he did not wish to take it entirely upon himself to answer, and his fellow ambassador had lain down for an afternoon nap, for they had traveled all through the night. They had adopted Russian habits at the Russian frontier, and everyone knew that most Russians took a rest every afternoon. When the interpreter was asked when the Holstein ambassadors would be received, he intimated that it would hardly be sooner than three weeks, [that is] after the Swedish ambassadors' arrival in Moscow. He explained that he did not believe there were enough boats and horses to permit both embassies to make the trip at the same time.

At 4 o'clock in the afternoon the ambassadors sent word to the other shore that they now wished to be received and that the pristav should therefore come ahead. Then they and their interpreters sat down in one boat and their hofjunkers, whom I joined, in another. The pristav, with 15 well-dressed Russians, then came to meet us in a boat. To impress upon us the pristav's rank and dignity, the Russians dipped their oars into the water very slowly, moving the boat so little that they scarcely came away from the shore. From time to time they quit completely, waiting for the Swedish ambassadors' boat to draw near them. They extended an oar to the ambassadors' boat so that they might be pulled along beside it. They also prompted the ambassadors' helmsman to the same end. When the ambassadors realized what the Russians were up to, one of them called to the pristav to come more quickly: "What is the use of such pointless ceremony?" The pristav would gain as little for the Grand Prince as they could lose for their sovereign. When the boats came together in the middle of the stream, the pristav spoke up and said that the Great Lord and Tsar, Mikhail Feodorovich, Autocrat of all Russia (rendering the full title), had instructed him to receive the King's ambassadors and had ordered that they and their attendants be furnished with provisions and conveyances sufficient to take them to Moscow. When a reply had been given, the pristav escorted the ambassadors to the shore and into the house of a certain *syn boyar* or *dvorianin*.[28] We all entered a small, overheated room, black as coal from smoke. The streltsi gave a salute with their flintlocks (which, along with swords, are part of their general equipment) without the slightest semblance of order, as if each wanted to be first to finish. By way of welcome, the ambassadors were offered several cups of very strong vodka, two kinds of bad-tasting mead, and some pieces of gingerbread. They gave me some to try, too, saying [in Latin]: "Add a pinch of sulphur, and you'd have a drink fit for Hades."

After an hour of such entertainment, to the accompaniment of drum rolls, the Swedish ambassadors in 12 boats and the Russians in three sailed off to Novgorod. I returned across Lake Ladoga to Nöteburg, where, true to the Russian interpreter's words, we had to wait three whole weeks. We passed the intervening time very cheerfully. The lake affords pleasant views of its surroundings, and there are several small islands in it, with various kinds of game. Two of these islands, four leagues from Nöteburg and not more than a musket shot's distance from one another, are covered with vegetation, including many raspberry bushes. On the smaller of the two stands a small chapel, in which Russians who are out fishing say a prayer. The large number of birds nesting in the chapel caused such a stench that we could not stay there for long. Several of us went hunting on these islands a number of times. Around the islands were countless seals of every hue. When they sunned themselves on the outlying broad rocks, we could shoot them easily from behind the bushes. We also had the good company of the nobleman Peter Krussbiorn, a learned, experienced, and brave man, whom His Royal Swedish Majesty was sending to Moscow as his Resident.[29] He and his suite were also awaiting an invitation from the Russians to come ahead. We enjoyed his friendship.

[28] A low-ranking member of the serving nobility.
[29] At the time Russia maintained no permanent diplomatic representatives in foreign capitals, but it occasionally permitted a foreign power to have a representative in Moscow. England

On July 16th we were advised that a pristav, Semen Andreevich Krekshin by name, had arrived in Laba to receive us, and on the 20th we set out for Laba. Several hours after we had arrived, the pristav sent an interpreter and a musketeer to our side [of the river] to inquire whether the ambassadors were ready to be received. When we asked whether he would receive us on his side or on the water as he had the Swedes, he replied that we should come across; there was no need to meet on the water, since there could be no quarrel with us over borders that we did not share.

When, accordingly, we came across, the pristav, wearing a red damask robe, came forward and halted several paces from the shore. When the ambassadors stepped ashore, he advanced to meet them with his head covered, and did not remove his hat until he began to speak and mentioned the Grand Prince's name. As before, he took out a piece of paper and said: "His Tsarist Majesty Mikhail Feodorovich, Autocrat of all Russia, etc., has sent me here to receive you, Philip Crusius, and you, Otto Brüggemann, ambassadors of the Prince of Holstein, and to furnish you and your party with provisions, boats, horses, and whatever may be necessary to bring you to Moscow." The interpreter, Anthony by name, could not speak decent German, and his translation was so wretched that it was almost unintelligible. Only after the ambassadors had replied did the pristav extend them his hand. Then he conducted us between rows of streltsi (20 Cossacks, with flintlocks at the ready) into his residence. The salute the streltsi then fired was executed so carelessly that the secretary to the Swedish Resident, who was standing by us watching the ceremony, had a large hole torn in his jacket. The refreshment the pristav served us consisted of gingerbread, vodka, and freshly preserved cherries. Having stayed a half hour, we returned across the river, to the accompaniment of a salute from the streltsi, and continued our journey. After a dinner tendered to us at midday by the commander of Nöteburg, who accompanied us a little way and regaled us with all sorts of delicious farewell toasts, we set out in seven boats across Lake Ladoga.

secured the right to maintain an agent in Moscow after Chancellor opened a trade route to northern Russia; Sweden gained the same right in 1631. Krussbiorn was appointed to replace the first Swedish Resident, Johann Miller, who had recently died. Two of the Swedish residents, Pommerening and Rodes (the latter was not accredited), wrote dispatches and accounts which are valuable sources on seventeenth-century Russia. Pommerening's reports are printed in Iakubov; Rodes's in Kurts, *Sostoianie Rossii.*

When early on the 22d we completed our 12-league trip across the lake and reached the shore at the Nikol'skii Monastery in Volkhonskii inlet, a Russian monk welcomed the ambassadors with bread and dried salmon. Our pristav, who was responsible for our feeding and provisioning, asked whether he should procure provisions and have them prepared daily or whether we should prefer to receive the money allotted by His Tsarist Majesty and have our cook prepare the food in our own manner. We elected to follow the custom usual for ambassadors in these parts—to receive the money and do the purchasing ourselves. However, the pristav set the prices everywhere, so we got things very cheaply. In Russia generally, as a result of the fertility of the soil, produce is very inexpensive; for example, for a chicken, two kopeks (which is equal to two schillings or a groschen of our Meissen money); for nine eggs, one kopek. We daily received two rubles and five kopeks (that is four reichsthalers and five schillings). Each person was allotted a share proportionate to his rank.

After dinner we set off on a stream that took us that evening to Ladoga, a little town 17 leagues from Laba. On the way we met a pristav who was conveying three boats to the Swedish Resident, whom we had left at Nöteburg. In our entire journey we never saw a larger throng of four- to seven-year-old children than here in Ladoga. When some of us went walking, the children swarmed after us, shouting and asking if we did not wish to buy the red berries they called *maliny* [raspberries], which grow in such profusion throughout Russia. They gave us a hatful for a kopek, and, when we lay down on a grassy hill to eat them, fifty of them surrounded us. All of them, girls and boys alike, had their hair close cropped with locks hanging on either side, and they all wore long shirts, too, so that one couldn't tell the boys from the girls.

Here we first heard Russian music. At midday of the 23d, while we were at table, two Russians with a lute and a fiddle came to entertain the ambassadors. They played and sang about the Great Lord and Tsar, Mikhail Feodorovich. Observing that we liked their performance, they added some amusing dances and demonstrated various styles of dancing practiced by both women and men. Unlike the Germans, the Russians do not join hands while dancing, but each one dances by himself. Their dances consist chiefly of movements of the hands, feet, shoulders, and hips. The dancers, particularly the women, hold varicolored, embroidered handkerchiefs, which they wave about while dancing although they themselves remain in place almost all the time.

After dinner we again took seats in our boat and sailed off on the Volkhov River. More than a hundred children and old people stood on the walls to see us off. On the shore was a monk, whom the streltsi called over to bless them as is their custom. Afterward, in the course of the journey, we often observed how, when they passed a priest or a monastery, they would approach and ask a blessing, or would bow and cross themselves before the crosses on the roadside chapels, saying, *Gospodi pomilui!* [Lord, have mercy!] When the wind began to favor us, we hoisted a sail. But hardly were we under sail when a rope broke, and the sail fell on one of our streltsi, who lay as if dead. However, after an hour he began to revive, and when he had had a cup of vodka, he recovered completely.

The Volkhov, though almost equal in breadth to the Elbe River, does not flow as swiftly. It rises at Great Novgorod in the lake they call Il'men and empties into Lake Ladoga. Seven versts from Ladoga (five versts equal one German league),[30] there are rapids in the river, and seven versts farther some more, through which it is very dangerous to pass in boats; at these points the river shoots like an arrow over and between large boulders. Therefore, when we reached the first rapids we disembarked, walked along the shore, and waited until the boats were dragged on ropes, by a hundred people, through the most dangerous places. All came through well except for the last, in which we had been obliged to leave Simon Friese—son of a Hamburg merchant—who was seriously ill. When this boat reached the spot where the current was strongest, the rope suddenly snapped and the boat shot backward. It probably would have been smashed in the falls—through which it had been hauled with great difficulty—if, by a stroke of fortune, the part of the rope that was still attached to the boat had not lodged so tenaciously under a big rock protruding from the water that it could only be freed with great effort. We were told that, some time ago, a bishop and his boatload of fish had gone down at this very place.

Toward evening we passed through the other, less treacherous

---

[30] A verst is equal to 3,500 feet, or about two-thirds of a mile. Actually seven versts, not five, equal one German league.

rapids. Having arranged to spend the night at the Nikoly na Posade
Monastery, we stayed until our lagging boats caught up with us the
next day. Here, as throughout the journey, because of the unbroken
forests and bushes we were so bothered by gnats, flies, and wasps that
neither by day nor by night could we travel or sleep in peace. Since
most members of our party did not take the necessary precautions, their
faces were as ravaged as if they had smallpox. Insects are so prevalent
all over Livonia and Russia in the summer that many travelers are
forced to protect themselves with nets or tents made of finely woven
linen with tiny holes. When they wish to rest, they put up these tents
and take refuge inside. The peasants and coachmen, who have no such
tents, build large fires and sit or lie as close to them as possible; but
even so they have scarcely a moment's peace.

An old monk from the monastery (which had only four friars) appeared and welcomed the ambassadors with radishes, cucumbers, green
peas, and two wax candles. He so much liked the gift given him in
return that, to please us, he departed from custom to don his priestly
garb and open the church for us to see. On the walls of the porch was
what he called "The Miracle of St. Nicholas," naïvely and inartistically
portrayed, like most of their paintings. Over the doors was depicted
the Last Judgment. Here, incidentally, the monk showed us a person
in German dress and said: "Germans and others peoples may be saved,
too, if only their souls are Russian and if, fearing no man, they behave
in a way pleasing to God."[31] He also showed us a Bible in Slavonic;
none of the Russians, neither ecclesiastics nor laymen, know any language other than their native tongue and Slavonic.[32] He read us the
first chapter of the Gospel according to St. John, which proved to be
entirely in accord with our text, and used a bit of wax to mark his stopping place. He told us that he had once been in Revel and that the
priests there had wanted to test his knowledge of the Bible. In truth,
he had not understood the German translator well, but as soon as he
saw the Biblical pictures he was able to tell the stories. He undoubtedly

---

[31] Olearius does not make entirely clear what was undoubtedly the case—that in the picture
those in foreign dress were relegated to Hell. This conception was evidently quite common, for
Paul of Aleppo describes a similar picture he saw in Kiev's St. Sophia Cathedral. See Paul of
Aleppo, I, 230.

[32] This is a slight exaggeration, for Olearius himself encountered several Russians who knew
foreign languages. Such people, however, were rare.

would have taken us into the church if our streltsi had not come up and begun to grumble that he already had allowed us to go too far.[33] We rewarded the monk with another thaler, in gratitude for which he bowed to the ground several times. When we sat down in a grassy meadow to dine (the surroundings were so pleasant that we did this daily), the monk came up to us again with a large radish and a full cup of cucumbers. He said the favorable wind, which had arisen in the meantime, was sent by St. Nicholas because of our kindness.

We got under sail at 2 o'clock in the afternoon, and with this wind went four leagues to the village of Gorodishche. As the riverbank seemed more cheerful to us than the village, we set up our kitchen and table there. The pristav sent a young bear to entertain the ambassadors, since they wished to move on after the boatmen had rested rather than spend the night there. After midnight we went four leagues farther, to the village of Sol'tsy. Our pristav, who had remained behind for the night, caught up with us again, bringing with him his host, who had entertained him so well that both were drunk. This host, a Russian prince named Roman Ivanovich, had come to visit the ambassadors. Since he still wanted to drink, we served him vodka and Spanish wine, which we always carried with us, and helped him so effectively to make up what he still lacked for complete intoxication that he fell to the ground unconscious.

In the evening we went six leagues farther, to the village of Gruzino, from which all the peasants fled before us.[34] We set ourselves up on a grassy meadow by a pond outside the village, made three large fires, and sat there as night fell. Since none of us who had slept in the boats during the day were inclined to sleep any more, we passed the night telling diverting stories and amusing ourselves. The streltsi, having

[33] The monk's behavior was exceptionally liberal. As Olearius later recounts, and as most foreign reports on seventeenth-century Russia confirm, Western Christians were forbidden to enter Orthodox churches.

[34] The peasants undoubtedly were frightened off by the foreign appearance of the party. About this time, the countryside was being ravaged by foreign mercenaries who had been hired by the Tsar to recapture Smolensk from the Poles. For documents on the recruitment of foreign regiments, see *Sobranie,* Vol. III, Nos. 81–88. After the campaign failed, many foreign soldiers were discharged. As they made their way home, they evidently caused far greater unpleasantness for the Russians than they had for the Poles. The failure of the foreign regiments led the Russian government to cease engaging whole units of them in favor of hiring foreign officers to develop foreign-style units manned by Russian troops. In 1660 and 1661, however, large numbers of rank-and-file mercenaries were hired once again, several thousand of them in England. Borodin, pp. 193–94. On the Smolensk campaign of 1632–34, see Vainshtein.

drunk several cups of vodka, helped entertain us with two lutes and games with the bear. The place was so plentifully stocked with cranes that we saw more than three hundred of them standing side by side in the pond.

On July 26th, around 3 o'clock in the morning, we set out again; toward midday, having gone four leagues, we arrived at the village of Vysokaia. When the pristav sat down to dinner with us and heard the name of Jesus as we said grace, he crossed himself in the Russian manner and asked to be told our prayer in Russian. When he heard it, he said that he liked it very much and that he had not expected Germans to be such good Christians and God-fearing people.

On the 27th we rode all day and all night, arriving at sunrise in the village of Krechevitsa, where we had to stop and wait until the pristav had notified the voevoda of Novgorod (two leagues away) of our arrival and had received an answer. A good musket shot's distance from this village lies a well-built monastery, which some call Khutyn', others Krechevitskii Khutynskii Spasov Monastery. The monastery, which is in a lovely setting, has an abbot, 60 friars, and 400 peasants who support it. They say that it must maintain one hundred people in the Tsar's service at Novgorod, at its own expense.

The next morning, July 28th, we at last arrived at Great Novgorod. Some of our party, who had been sent ahead by the sledge road and had impatiently awaited our arrival more than four months, came more than a league by boat to greet us. To welcome us the voevoda sent to our inn barrels of beer and mead and a cask of vodka. He was sent a gilded silver cup in return. We remained in Novgorod four full days, and toward evening on the last day of July went on to Bronnitsy by water, since the marshiness of the place made it impossible to go by land.

On August 1st, as we brought our things ashore at Bronnitsy, a procession of Russians came to sanctify the water. First came two men carrying long poles; on the first pole was a cross with apostles depicted on the four ends; on the other was an old ikon covered with a white cloth. After them came a priest in ecclesiastical vestments, carrying in both hands a wooden cross, a span long.[35] He sang in unison with a boy who followed him carrying a book. Then came all the peasants with

---

[35] A span is a linear measure of about 20 centimeters.

their wives and children. Each adult carried a burning wax candle; behind them went the sexton, holding more than ten candles twisted together and burning. When the priest had sung and read for a good half hour on the shore, he took the twisted candles and plunged them into the water. Then all the others extinguished their candles too. The priest then immersed the candles in the water three times and collected the runoff in a vessel; this is considered the holiest water. When he had finished, the women grabbed their children, large and small, in their nightshirts or without, and submerged them three times in the stream. Some of the adults also jumped in. Finally, they brought the horses, too, to drink of the holy, health-giving water. Afterward, they returned to the church to be blessed. Noise and shouts, of young and old people alike, such as one might hear in common bathhouses or taverns, issued from the church.

At 4 o'clock in the afternoon we mounted our horses and sent our baggage ahead on 50 wagons. On the road the baggage train met some German soldiers who had been discharged in Moscow. They raided the provision baskets, broke open a barrel of beer and drank their fill, and took away the saber of our musketeer escort. When they reached us and what they had done became known, our pristav gave two of them a severe beating, and took their swords and guns. That evening we went three leagues to the village of Krasnye Stanki. On the 2d we went eight leagues to the coach station Krestsy. The Russians call the places where horses are changed and fresh ones procured *iamy*. On the 3d we went six leagues to the little village Iazhelbitsy, where again the peasants fled. Because our cook had gone two leagues ahead to set up the kitchen, and the bad road made it impossible for us to catch up with him that evening, we were obliged to bed down in a field without supper.

Around this time we met several officers who were returning home from Moscow after the campaign at Smolensk. For example, on the 4th of the month we met Colonel Fuchs at the Zimogor'e coach station, and Colonel Charles and other officers at Volochek, another coach station. When they came to visit the ambassadors, they were treated to Spanish wine. After drinking for several hours our trumpeter, Kaspar Herzberg, became so intoxicated that in a drunken rage he fatally wounded one of our streltsi with a sword. We left the wounded man there, gave him and those who were to look after him a little money, and went on. After the Persian expedition, this trumpeter entered the service of the Grand Prince in Moscow. Later on, he was stabbed by some scoundrel.

Early on the morning of the 5th, we passed through a village that had been deserted by the peasants, who fled to the forest to avoid the German soldiers coming from Moscow. In the evening we came to the village of Kolomna, situated on the shore of a stagnant lake. Not far from this village we found in the bushes along the roadside a great, broad rock, lying just like a gravestone. The tyrant Ivan Vasil'evich had ordered it transported from Livonia to Moscow, but when the cartmen heard that the tyrant had died, they immediately rid themselves of the stone, dropping it beside the road. Similar stones, which were to have been brought from Revel to Moscow, lay a day's march farther along, by a stream that we had to cross.

On the 7th we arrived in the village of Budovo, where a Russian prince resides. We had hardly entered the village when the horses began to prance, kick, and run about in such a frenzy that some of us were thrown to the ground before we could dismount. At first we were perplexed, but then we discovered that a swarm of bees in the village had caused the trouble. We, too, were defenseless against them, so we threw our cloaks over our heads, left the village, and settled ourselves on a grassy hill. Later we were told that the peasants had stirred up the bees to drive us out of the village. As history relates, others have resorted to similar tricks. In one town, the besieged inhabitants flung beehives over the walls into the enemy's ranks, causing panic among both horses and riders. The kicking horses inflicted so much injury on each other that the enemy was forced to retreat.

On August 8th we reached another coach station and soon afterward arrived in the little town of Torzhok. It lies a short distance to the right of the road and is surrounded by a palisade with blockhouses at intervals. We found excellent bread, mead, and beer here. Since we were not admitted to the town but were assigned some houses outside it, the ambassadors instead ordered a bower of leafy branches set up on a grassy hill. Here they dined and spent the night with some of their entourage.

On the next day we crossed two streams, one just beyond Torzhok,

the other two versts from Mednaia. In the evening we came to Tver,
12 leagues from Torzhok. Tver, which is somewhat larger than Torzhok, lies on a hill beyond a river. It is an episcopal seat, and, like
Torzhok, has a resident voevoda.[36] Near the city the Tver[tsa] River
(from which the city takes its name) and the Volga (which flows 600
leagues across Russia and Tartary to the Caspian Sea) join to form a
rather wide river. At Tver we had to ferry across, and we were put up
outside the town in a country house. Since this was the last coach station,
we obtained fresh horses, which were to take us the rest of the way to
Moscow. On August 13th we reached Nikoly Nakhimskogo, the last
village before Moscow and two leagues from it. From there the pristav
sent a courier to Moscow to announce our arrival.

[36] As Olearius himself later points out, Tver was an archepiscopal seat.

CHAPTER TWO

Our Experiences in Moscow

EARLY ON THE MORNING of the 14th the pristav, with his interpreter and his scribe, came to the ambassadors, thanked them for the kindnesses they had rendered him during the journey, and begged pardon if he and his staff had not served us properly. The pristav was given a large goblet, the interpreter and the scribe some money. When our courier returned from the city, we prepared to enter in the following order.

1. In the lead went the streltsi who had accompanied us.

2. Jakob Scheve (quartermaster), Michael Cordes, and Johann All-geier, in one rank.

3. Three horses, a black and two dapple-grays, led single file by the bridle.

4. The trumpeter.

5. The marshal.

6. The hofjunkers and table servants in three ranks of three men each.

7. The secretary, the court physician, and the major domo (*Hofmeister*).

8. The ambassadors, each preceded by a bodyguard of four streltsi armed with carbines.

9. The pristav, riding some distance to the ambassadors' right.

10. Six pages in two ranks.

11. A carriage drawn by four dapple-grays.

12. The coachman and eight other people in three ranks.

13. Some of our prince's gifts for the Grand Prince, carried on five carpeted, litter-like racks.

14. A wagon bearing the sick Simon Friese.

15. Forty-six ordinary wagons with our baggage.

16. At the very end came three boys.

When we had advanced slowly in this order within half a league of Moscow, mounted couriers began arriving at full gallop. Ten of them, one after another, came up to us, told the pristav the point reached by the Russians who were to receive us, and brought orders to proceed either more rapidly or more slowly, so that one party should not arrive earlier than the other at the appointed place and be compelled to wait. As we drew nearer, various groups of well-dressed Russians rode out to meet us, swung by, and went back again. Along the way were some members of the Swedish ambassadors' retinue, but they were not permitted to extend their hands to us, and had to hail us from a distance. A quarter league from the city, we came upon four thousand mounted Russians, in costly dress, drawn up in very fine ranks [on either side of the road]. We were obliged to pass between them.[1]

When we moved forward at the firing of a pistol, two pristavs dressed in gold brocade and high sable hats rode up on beautifully groomed white horses. In place of bridles, the horses wore silver chains with links over two inches wide, yet no thicker than a knife's edge, and so large in compass that a man could put his hand through them. These chains produced a loud, strange ringing when the horses moved. Behind the pristavs came the Grand Prince's Master of the Stable, with 20 white horses led by their bridles; he was followed by many people, some mounted and some on foot. When they drew near each other, the pristavs and the ambassadors dismounted from their horses, and the senior pristav bared his head and said: "The great Sovereign Tsar and Grand Prince Mikhail Feodorovich, Autocrat of all Russia, Vladimir, Moscow, and Novgorod, Tsar of Kazan, Tsar of Astrakhan, Tsar of Siberia, Lord of Pskov, Grand Prince of Tver, Iugra, Perm, Viatka, Bolgaria, and others, Lord and Prince of Novgorod on the lower lands [Nizhnii Novgorod?], Riazan, Rostov, Iaroslavl, Beloozero, Udora, Obdorsk, and Kondinsk, and ruler of all the northern lands, Lord of the Iversk country, of the Kartalinsk and Georgian Kings, and of the Kabardian lands, of the Cherkass and Gorsk princes, and sovereign and lord of many other states, etc., has ordered us to receive you, the Grand

[1] For such ceremonies, according to Kliuchevskii (*Skazaniia inostrantsev,* p. 48), the people of neighboring communities were ordered to turn out in their finery to impress foreign ambassadors with the numbers and well-being of the population. It is plain that Potemkinism long antedated the well-known efforts of Catherine the Great's favorite to deceive Emperor Joseph II of Austria by similar means.

Ambassadors of the Duke of Schleswig, Holstein, Stormarn and Ditmars, and Count of Oldenburg and Delmenhorst. He grants you and
your hofjunkers the privilege of entering upon his horses, and has
designated us as pristavs to serve you and procure everything you need
during your stay in Moscow." When Ambassador Philip Crusius had
answered, two large white steeds, with embroidered German saddles
embellished with various ornaments, were brought forward for the
ambassadors.

As soon as the ambassadors had mounted, the pristav and the Cossacks who had escorted us from the frontier to Moscow left us. The new
pristavs were Andrei Vasil'evich Usov and Bogdan Feodorovich. Ten
more white horses, with Russian saddles covered with gold brocade,
were brought for the most distinguished members of the embassy. The
ambassadors rode between the two pristavs. Generally the Russians consider that when three or more persons walk or ride side by side, the
place of greatest honor is on the right. Behind the horses came Russian
servants carrying saddlecloths of leopard skin, brocade, and scarlet.
A throng of other Russians on horseback accompanied us into the city
and to the ambassadors' residence. We were put up in the area called
Tsargorod (the emperor's city), which is within the white wall. During our entry we were watched from the streets and houses by countless numbers of people. The streets had been devastated by a great
fire just before our entry, reducing more than five thousand houses
to ashes. People were forced to live in tents wherever they could.
Since the ambassadorial residence had also burned down, we were installed in two wooden houses belonging to townsmen.

Half an hour after our arrival, by way of welcome we received
provisions from the Grand Prince's kitchen and cellar, namely eight
sheep, 30 chickens, many wheat and rye loaves, and 22 kinds of drinks—
wine, beer, mead, and vodka—each one more delicious than the others.
They were brought by 32 Russians who came in single file. We were
daily supplied in the same manner with similar, but only half as many,
provisions. Their custom is to provide a double ration on the day of
an ambassador's arrival and on any day when he has an audience with
the Tsar.

When the provisions had been handed over, the porch of our dwelling was locked and 12 streltsi were placed there as a guard so that none

of us could go out and no stranger could visit us until we had had our first audience. Each day the pristav came to visit the ambassadors and to see whether anything was needed. One of the Russian interpreters stayed in the house with us to dispatch musketeers to buy various things we requested. This interpreter, named Ivan, was Russian by birth. He had been captured by the Poles, and thereafter served His Princely Grace Jan Radziwill. The Prince spent two years studying at the University of Leipzig, and it was there that [Ivan] learned the German language.

On August 15th the Russians celebrated a great holiday, the Assumption of the Blessed Virgin, when the fast begun on August 1st ended and they could again eat meat. Two days later His Tsarist Majesty made a pilgrimage to a certain village. Had it not been for that, the pristavs told us, we would have had an audience that day. We gave thanks to God for our safe arrival, with prayers, a sermon, and music. With the permission of the Grand Prince, Balthazar Moucheron, who serves as Resident Commissioner of our gracious Prince and Sovereign, came to see us on this holiday.[2] He reported that the Russians were very pleased with our procession as we entered the city. They were astonished to learn that there were princes in Germany powerful enough to fit out such an impressive embassy. Their princes, even those most richly endowed with landed property and income, are comparable to our ordinary German noblemen.

On the 18th the pristavs came and informed us that His Tsarist Majesty wished the ambassadors to attend a public audience the next day, and that we should make ourselves ready. In the name of the State Chancellor, they requested a list of the gifts to be presented to the Grand Prince, which we gave them.[3] In the afternoon, the junior pristav came to tell us again that on the next day we should be brought into His Tsarist Majesty's presence. On the preceding day we had heard

[2] Moucheron, the son of a Dutch merchant who had been involved in trade with Russia, accompanied Brüggemann to Moscow in 1632. At that time, in return for gifts and favors to the Tsar, Brüggemann obtained permission for Holstein merchants to trade in Russia. Apparently in conjunction with this, Holstein was allowed to maintain a resident in Moscow. Moucheron filled the post from 1632 to 1640. See Loviagin, pp. vii, xii; Kieksee, pp. 55–56.

[3] The Muscovite government had no position corresponding to prime minister. A few of the departments of state (*prikazi*) had at their head or as second in command a *dumnyi d'iak*, which Olearius generally translates as "State Chancellor." Foreign embassies transacted their business with the dumnyi d'iak and other officials of the *Posol'skii Prikaz*, the Chancellery for Foreign Affairs. See Belokurov, "O Posol'skom Prikaze."

countless salvos from heavy guns and from our apartment had seen many weapons on a field, but we did not know what it was all about. The pristav explained to us, "His Majesty ordered that some new weapons be tried out, and he himself had watched through a window." Others, however, contended that it was intended to impress upon the Swedish ambassadors that not all the guns had been left at Smolensk, as reported, but that many remained [at His Majesty's disposal].

Early on the morning of August 19th, the pristavs came again to ascertain whether we were prepared to proceed, and when they saw that we were fully ready, hurriedly rode off again to the Kremlin. Soon afterward the Grand Prince's white horses were brought for the procession. At 9 o'clock the pristavs returned in their usual garb, having arranged for the new robes and high hats, which were borrowed from the Grand Prince's wardrobe, to be brought after them. They brought these into the ambassadors' antechamber, where, in our presence, they dressed themselves in the finest manner. Then, in our cloaks, but without swords (according to their custom, no one dares to appear before His Tsarist Majesty with a sword), we mounted the horses and rode to the Kremlin in the following order: in the lead, 36 streltsi; our marshal; three lesser hofjunkers; three other hofjunkers; the commissioner, the secretary, and the doctor, in one rank.

Then came the Prince's gifts, one after another, led or carried by Russians, as follows.

1. A black stallion covered with a beautiful cloth.

2. A dapple-gray gelding.

3. Another gray horse.

4. A horse's harness, finely worked in silver and embedded with turquoises, rubies, and other stones, carried by two Russians.

5. A cross, almost a quarter of an ell in length, made of chrysolite and encased in gold, carried on a basin.[4]

6. A costly chemical-apothecary apparatus. The cabinet was made of ebony and stamped in gold; the boxes were also made of gold, and decorated with precious stones. It was carried by two Russians.

7. A crystal receptacle stamped with gold and set with rubies.

8. A large mirror, five quartiers [?] long and an ell wide, framed

[4] The length of an ell varied from place to place. Olearius may have used the Flemish ell, which equals 27 inches, or a smaller one.

in ebony, adorned with pictures and thick layers of silver leaf. It was carried by two Russians.

9. A chiming clock, shaped like a mountain, on which was portrayed the story of the prodigal son.

10. A gilded silver walking stick which housed a magnifying glass.

11. A large ebony clock decorated with silver.

After these presents came two chamberlains who held in their outstretched hands the credential letters addressed to the Grand Prince and to Patriarch Filaret Nikitich, His Tsarist Majesty's father. Although Filaret had died while we were en route, it was considered prudent to pass the letter on to the Grand Prince. Then came the ambassadors between the pristavs, preceded by two interpreters. Close behind the ambassadors came four lackeys, and after them the young attendants or pages.

Along the way from the ambassadors' house to the audience hall of the Kremlin, a distance of about an eighth of a league, we had to pass between more than two thousand streltsi, closely arrayed on each side. Behind them in all the streets and houses, and on the roofs, stood crowds of people watching our procession. On the way several couriers came to us at full gallop from the Kremlin to advise the pristav that we should ride more rapidly or slowly, or halt completely, so that His Tsarist Majesty should not be obliged to be seated on the audience throne before or after the arrival of the ambassadors.

When we had passed the *Posol'skii Prikaz*, or Chancellery for Foreign Affairs, on the upper square of the Kremlin, our officers and hofjunkers dismounted from their horses and arranged themselves in order. The marshal went ahead of the gifts, and we followed, ahead of the ambassadors. We were conducted to the left through an arched passageway, past a beautiful church (which they call a cathedral), and into the audience hall, located on the right side of the upper square.[5] We were conducted past the church because we are Christians. Turks, Tatars, and Persians are not brought by this way, but directly across the center of the square and up by a broad porch. Before [reaching] the audience hall we passed through a vaulted chamber in which were seated, or standing at the sides, imposing old men with long gray

[5] The audience hall survives in the Kremlin's *Granovitaia Palata* (Palace of Facets).

beards, gilded clothes, and tall sable hats. They are called His Tsarist Majesty's *gosti*, or distinguished merchants. Their clothing belongs to His Tsarist Majesty's treasury; it is distributed for occasions such as this and then returned.

When the ambassadors reached the doors of the antechamber, two boyars in gold robes embroidered with pearls emerged from the audience hall. They received the ambassadors and said that His Tsarist Majesty welcomed them and granted that they and their hofjunkers might appear before him. The presents were left in the antechamber, and the ambassadors, followed by their officers, hofjunkers, and pages, were escorted in to His Tsarist Majesty. As they entered the door the Tsar's chief interpreter, Hans Helmes, then a man of sixty years (in 1654 he was still alive and working at his post), came forward, wished the Great Sovereign Tsar and Grand Prince good fortune and long life, and announced the entry of the Holstein ambassadors. The audience hall was a vaulted, square, stone room, its floor and walls covered with lovely rugs, and its ceiling decorated with Biblical paintings executed in gold and various colors. The throne of the Grand Prince, at the rear of the room by the wall, was three steps above the floor level. It was surrounded by four silver and gilded pillars or columns three inches thick, on which rested a canopy; the pillars and canopy formed a little tower three ells high. At each side of the tower stood a silver eagle with outstretched wings. A still more magnificent throne was being prepared at that time, and 800 pounds of silver and 1,100 ducats had been appropriated for gilt. With all expenses taken into account, the throne was valued at 25,000 thalers. For three years it was worked on by German and Russian craftsmen, notably the Nuremberger Esaias Zinkgraf.

His Tsarist Majesty was seated on the throne attired in a robe set with all sorts of precious stones and embroidered with large pearls. His crown, which he wore over a black sable hat, was encrusted with large diamonds, as was the golden scepter, which, probably because of its weight, he transferred now and then from one hand to the other. Before the throne stood four young and powerful princes, two on each side, in white damask robes, lynx-fur hats, and white boots; crosswise on their breasts hung gold chains. Each held on his shoulder a silver axe at the ready. Along the walls around to the left [and right], and opposite the Tsar, sat over fifty distinguished and splendidly dressed boyars, princes, and state counselors; on their heads were tall black hats of fox fur, which, as is their custom, they did not remove. Five paces to the right of the throne stood a State Chancellor. Beside the Grand Prince's throne on the right was a gold imperial apple as large as a skittle ball, on a sculptured silver pyramid two ells high. Alongside it stood a gold basin and ewer, and a hand towel, so that His Tsarist Majesty could wash his hand after the ambassadors had kissed it.

The Tsar permits only Christians, and not Turks, Persians, or Tatars, to kiss his hand. Possevino, who was very displeased by this handwashing, wrote: "He washes his hands as if to cleanse a sin." This washing was done in the presence of a large number of magnates, confirming their hatred of their fellow Christians. Possevino proposed that other princes point out to the Muscovite the inappropriateness of this custom and give him to understand that they would send him no more ambassadors until he desisted from this disgraceful washing. One may read of this in Possevino's *De rebus Moscoviticis*, p. 2.[6]

After the ambassadors had entered respectfully, they were brought immediately to a point ten paces opposite His Tsarist Majesty. Behind them stood their most important aides, and to the right, two of our noblemen, still holding aloft the credential letters. Hans Helmes stood on the ambassadors' left. The Tsar signaled the State Chancellor to tell the ambassadors that he permitted them to kiss his hand. As each of them approached, His Tsarist Majesty took the scepter in his left hand and, with a friendly smile, extended his right hand to be kissed; but he did not permit the ambassadors' hands to touch his. Then the State Chancellor said, "Let the ambassadors state their business." Philip Crusius conveyed to His Tsarist Majesty the greetings of His Princely Excellence, our gracious Prince and Lord, and expressed sorrow at the death of the Patriarch. His Princely Excellence had expected that God would preserve Filaret's life for a long time yet and accordingly had sent him a letter, which the ambassadors wished respectfully to transmit with the one addressed to His Tsarist Majesty. Then they took the credential letters and passed them to His Tsarist Majesty, who signaled the State Chancellor to take them.

[6] Antonio Possevino, an Italian Jesuit who was sent twice by the Pope to the court of Ivan IV, wrote an important account of Russia published in 1586. See Adelung, I, 321–49. Reports dis-

When the ambassadors stepped back again, His Tsarist Majesty signaled to the State Chancellor to reply. The Chancellor took five steps from the throne toward the ambassadors and [read from a paper]: "The Great Sovereign Tsar and Grand Prince, etc., wishes to advise you, Ambassador Philip Crusius, and you, Ambassador Otto Brüggemann, that he has accepted the letter from your prince, Duke Frederick, and that he will have it translated into Russian, will give an answer through a boyar, and will write to Duke Frederick in due course." The Chancellor had bared his head while reading the titles of the Grand Prince and His Princely Excellence, but immediately afterward replaced his hat. Behind the ambassadors was placed a bench covered with a rug, upon which, at His Tsarist Majesty's request, the ambassadors sat. Then the Chancellor said, "His Tsarist Majesty also grants to the ambassadors' chief aides and hofjunkers permission to kiss his hand." When that was done, His Tsarist Majesty raised himself a little on the throne, and he himself asked the ambassadors, "Is Prince Frederick still in good health?" To this they replied: "Thanks be to God, at our departure we left His Princely Excellence in good health and prosperity. May God grant His Tsarist Majesty and His Princely Excellence continuing health and a happy reign."

Then the Grand Prince's major domo read the list of presents, and these were immediately carried in and held up to view until the Chancellor signaled that they were to be taken away. The Chancellor then said, "The Tsar and Grand Prince of all Russia grants permission to the ambassadors to speak further." Having in view the accord on Persian affairs concluded between His Royal Swedish Majesty and His Princely Excellence of Schleswig-Holstein, the ambassadors requested that they and the Swedish ambassadors be granted a secret audience. At that His Tsarist Majesty had the ambassadors asked about their health and advised that he granted them dinner that day from his table. Then the ambassadors were escorted out by the two boyars who earlier had ushered them in. With the pristavs and streltsi, we rode home again in the order in which we had come.

The Grand Prince's chamberlain, a stately prince magnificently attired, arrived shortly afterward on a beautifully bedecked horse. After him came many Russians who were to entertain the ambassadors

---

agree on whether the hand-washing practice was stopped in the last half of the seventeenth century. See Kliuchevskii, *Skazaniia inostrantsev*, p. 61.

in the name of His Tsarist Majesty. Some of these people covered the table with a long white cloth and placed on it a silver saltcellar with fine salt, two silver vessels of vinegar, several large goblets, three gold cups and two silver ones—each one and a half quartiers in diameter—for mead, and a long knife and fork.

The Grand Prince's deputy sat at the head of the table and asked the ambassadors to sit beside him. Our hofjunkers waited on the table. The deputy ordered three large goblets, filled with Alicante wine, Rhine wine, and mead, to be placed before the ambassadors. He then ordered from His Tsarist Majesty's table 38 large dishes—most of them silver, but not especially clean—containing various stewed, roasted, and baked foods. When the table became crowded, what had been brought earlier was taken away to make room. When the last dish had been placed on the table, the prince rose, stood before the table, signaled the ambassadors to come before the table, and said: "Here is the food that His Tsarist Majesty has ordered, through me, to be given to the Grand Ambassadors of Holstein. May it please them." Then he took a large gold cup filled with a very sweet and delicious raspberry mead, and drank it before the ambassadors to His Tsarist Majesty's health. Following that, he handed the ambassadors and each of us a vessel of liquor, which we were supposed to drink in one draught. Because of the number of people around the prince, one of our group who was standing some distance from him was unable to secure a cup from his hand and asked that it be passed across the table. The prince would not permit that, however, and motioning our companion to come out from behind the table he said: "This table now symbolizes the table of the Russian Emperor. No one dares to stand behind it; you must stand before it."

After the first toast followed one to His Princely Excellence, our most gracious Prince and Sovereign, in these words: "May God preserve Prince Frederick in health for a long time, and grant that he and His Tsarist Majesty shall forever live in amity and friendship." Finally, a round was drunk to the health of the young prince, His Tsarist Majesty's heir. Then we again sat down at the table and drank several more cups of cherry and blackberry mead. After that, the ambassadors presented the deputy with a gilded goblet weighing 54 *loths*.[7] He

[7] A loth (*lot* in Russian) equals half an ounce in weight.

had it carried before him and rode off to the Kremlin, where he showed
the Grand Prince what he had received; for it is their custom that all
presents received from foreigners on such occasions, even including
those given to envoys sent to foreign rulers, must be shown to the Grand
Prince. The tyrannical Grand Prince Ivan Vasil'evich sometimes even
appropriated such gifts and kept them for himself, as Herberstein reports in his *Rerum Moscoviticarum commentarii.*

On August 20th our pristavs came to us again and advised that His
Tsarist Majesty granted us permission to go out: the city was open to
us. If we wished them, horses would be provided. We were also permitted to visit and receive the Swedish ambassadors and their party.
This was a great surprise, for customarily neither ambassadors nor
their attendants were allowed to go out alone while they resided in
Moscow.[8] If they had some business to transact outside of the house,
a musketeer had to accompany them. We and the Swedes received as a
special privilege the right to go out unaccompanied by the streltsi.
Three days later, when the Russians heard that our ambassadors
wished to visit the Swedish ambassadors, the pristavs and the Grand
Prince's Master of the Stable brought them six of His Tsarist Majesty's
horses and conducted them to the Swedish diplomats' residence. We
subsequently got together often, with no opposition from the Russians.

On the 23d the ambassadors invited to dinner several of the German
residents who were our good friends, including the court physician and
His Tsarist Majesty's apothecary. However, when the latter two requested permission from the Chancellor, it was refused, and they were
forbidden to visit us for three days. The Russians had not yet had time
to assess the value of the Prince's presents as they usually do, and the
doctor and the apothecary [were not allowed to see us because they]
would be involved in the evaluation of the chemical-apothecary apparatus.

On the 24th Arend Spiring, mentioned above, the Swedish official
in charge of levies on commerce in Livonia, reached Moscow. At first
the Russians would not usher him in in the splendid way usually vouch-
safed to ambassadors; but since the other Swedish ambassadors took

---

8 Indeed the surveillance had been so oppressive that some envoys complained of being treated
more like prisoners than ambassadors. See, for example, Giles Fletcher's account in Bond, pp.
343–44. Olearius correctly recognizes that the Holsteiners and Swedes received a special privilege.

offence and began to object, the Russians at last sent a pristav out of the city to receive him and usher him in.

On September 1st the Russians solemnly celebrated their New Year. They reckon their years from the creation of the world, and are of the opinion, as are some ancient Hebrew and Greek writers (and some German writers as well), that the world was created in the autumn. I do not intend to go into the reasons for this belief. . . .[9] The [new] year was 7142 (1634 A.D.). Just as they adopted their religion from the Greeks, so the Russians emulate them in reckoning years.[10] The Greek and Eastern Churches declare that they follow the chronology of Nikifor. But whereas Nikifor counts only 5,500 years from the beginning of the world to the birth of Christ, they count 5,508. If one adds to this the number of years since the birth of Christ, i.e. 1,634, one gets 7142. Thus the current year, 1654, is written 7162 by the Russians and the Greek Christians.[11] We, on the other hand, in accord with the true Bible story of the creation of the world 3,949 years before the birth of Christ, reckon this year as 5603.

The procession the Russians organized for the holiday's celebration was very impressive. More than twenty thousand people, young and old, gathered on the Kremlin Square. The Patriarch came out on the upper square with all the clergy—almost four hundred priests—who wore ecclesiastical vestments and carried many banners, ikons, and open ancient books. They came out of the church that is on the right as one ascends to the square. His Tsarist Majesty, with his state counselors, boyars, and princes, entered from the left side of the square. The Grand Prince, with his head bared, and the Patriarch, in the episcopal miter, approached and kissed one another on the mouth. The Patriarch also held out for His Tsarist Majesty to kiss, a cross a span in length, encrusted with large diamonds and other precious stones. Then he bestowed a lengthy blessing upon His Tsarist Majesty and the whole

[9] Here Olearius cites some sources on this topic.

[10] The Russians defended their system on the basis of its agreement with the methods of the Egyptians, the Hebrews, and the Greeks, and with the old chronicles of many European peoples. See Tsvetaev, *Protestantstvo i protestanty*, p. 623.

[11] Nikifor (Nicephoras) was Patriarch of Constantinople in the early ninth century; he wrote a work on historical chronology called *Chronologia compendiara*.

Olearius calculates first from the year when he learned of this system in Russia, and then from the year when he was preparing the second edition of his work. The Greek church added eight years to the 5,500 Nicephoras reckoned from the creation to the birth of Christ. See Paul of Aleppo, I, 304.

community, and wished everyone happiness in the New Year. The people standing by answered, "Amen!" Many of them who had been holding aloft petitions, then threw them toward the Grand Prince with tumultuous shouts. The petitions were collected and taken to the Tsar's chamber. Afterward, everyone in the procession withdrew.

On September 3d three of the Swedish ambassadors, Messrs. Gyllenstierne, Bureus, and Spiring, whose mission corresponded to ours (the other ambassadors, Mr. Philip Scheiding and Colonel Henrik Fleming, had been sent on business pertaining to the Swedish crown alone),[12] were given a public audience as ceremonious as ours. They asked to have a secret audience, jointly with us, and we were granted it. Thus, on the 5th we proceeded to the Kremlin together, in the usual manner. We were escorted across the upper Kremlin Square to [a building on] the left (through a room which, as on the day of the public audience, was filled with stately old men in gilded clothes and tall hats), into the secret audience room. In this room sat four men who had been commissioned to give us a secret audience, two boyars and two chancellors (*d'iaki*) all attired in magnificent clothes.[13] Their robes, made of gold brocade, were set with many very large pearls and other precious stones, and large gold chains hung crosswise on their breasts. Each boyar wore on his head a little hat (something like our skullcap) sewn all over with large pearls, and with a gem at the center. The chancellors wore the usual tall, black, fox hats. The ambassadors were cordially received and invited to sit near their hosts. The boyars sat in the superior place, at the rear of the room near a window, where the side benches joined in the corner. The ambassadors were seated with their backs to the wall, and the two chancellors sat opposite the ambassadors, on a bench without a back (such as are widely used in Russia). In the center of the room stood His Tsarist Majesty's interpreter for secret affairs, Hans Helmes.[14] Except for two secretaries and two interpret-

---

[12] On Scheiding and Fleming's mission, see Forsten, II, 438ff.

[13] The "chancellors" were the chief and vice-chief of the Posol'skii Prikaz, which was instituted in the middle of the sixteenth century (although it was not so named until later) and which was charged with the conduct of diplomatic affairs. Previously negotiations with foreign envoys had been handled by *ad hoc* commissions composed of a few boyars and a few d'iaki chosen at random; the commission reported to the Tsar and the Boyar Duma and received further instructions from them. While the newer system had distinct advantages over the old, it is apparent that vestiges of the old persisted into the seventeenth century. See Belokurov, *O Posol'skom Prikaze*, pp. 1–12, 23–36.

[14] It is ironical that because of its lack of skilled linguists the highly secretive Muscovite state had to employ foreigners as interpreters in its most secret business. It sought to ensure their

ers, who with the Russian scribe were to write the protocol, our attendants had to retire to the antechamber with the pristavs who had escorted the ambassadors into the room.

They had hardly been seated when the senior boyar asked if the ambassadors were adequately provided with food and drink and other necessities. When thanks had been expressed for the fine entertainment and the ampleness of everything, all rose and bared their heads, and the [senior boyar] spoke: "The Sovereign Tsar and Grand Prince, etc. (when the full title had been read [the ambassadors] sat down), has instructed that you be told, ambassadors of the King and of the Prince, that he has had your letters translated into Russian, that he has read them, and that he heard your speeches in public audience." Then the second boyar stood (as his predecessor had done) and spoke: "The Great Sovereign, etc., wishes the King of Sweden and the Prince of Holstein prosperity and victory over their foes, and wishes you to know that the King's and Prince's letters have been carefully read and their intention understood."

The third said, with similar ceremony, that the Great Sovereign, etc., understood from the letters that what the ambassadors said was to be trusted. Their word would be trusted, and His Tsarist Majesty would reply. The fourth said that His Tsarist Majesty had commissioned them to receive the ambassadors' proposals and requests. Then he read the names of those whom His Tsarist Majesty had appointed to participate in the secret audience. They were Prince Boris Mikhailovich Lykov Obolenskoi, Namestnik of Tver; Vasilii Ivanovich Streshnev, Namestnik of Torzhok; and two State Chancellors (*dumnye d'iaki*), namely Ivan Tarasovich Gramotin, Keeper of the Seal and Chancellor [or Chief Secretary],[15] and Ivan Afanas'evich Gavrenev, Undersecretary [*pod'iak*].

After these names had been read everyone again rose, and a Swedish ambassador, Mr. Erik Gyllenstierne, in the name of His Royal Swedish Majesty, thanked His Tsarist Majesty, in German, for granting a secret audience. He then read a proposal from a paper. Our message was some-

loyalty by compensating them generously with salaries, provisions, and land grants. See Liubimenko, "Trud inozemtsev," p. 61. It was doubtless the awkwardness of this situation that had led Boris Godunov to send a number of young Russians abroad for training in foreign languages, but none of the students returned. See Arsen'ev and Golitsyn.

[15] As dumnyi d'iak at the Posol'skii Prikaz, a position approximating secretary of state for foreign affairs, Gramotin participated in the secret audience as a matter of course.

what longer, and when [one of the ambassadors] began to read it, the counselors, not wishing to take the time to hear it out, asked that the written proposals be handed over, and carried them off to His Tsarist Majesty. In the meantime the ambassadors remained in the secret audience room, and our pristavs and some of our retinue rejoined them. In half an hour the Undersecretary came back alone with word that nothing further was to be done for the time being, so we could retire. The proposals would be translated right away, and an answer would then be given. With that we withdrew.[16]

On the 12th three Tatar ambassadors came, with no special ceremony, to present themselves. They were sent by the Cherkassian prince, a vassal of His Tsarist Majesty. After them ran 16 servants. They came [to the Kremlin] in red robes of coarse cloth, but returned thence in red and yellow silk damask robes, given them as presents by the Grand Prince. Such embassies are sent annually by the Cherkassian Tatars, as well as others, even though they bring no important proposals. They come chiefly for the sake of the presents, which they know they will receive.[17]

On the 15th the pristavs came and announced that on the preceding day the Grand Princess had given birth to a daughter, who had already been baptized and named Sophia. Russian infants generally are not left unbaptized for long, nor are great ceremonies and celebrations arranged on the occasion of baptisms, as in Germany. The Patriarch is said to have acted as godfather, as he had done for the rest of the Grand Prince's children. We participated in the general elation, for our provisions for the day were doubled.

On the 17th a Turkish ambassador approached Moscow. He was met with great pomp by sixteen thousand cavalrymen. In this great army, only six standards were evident. The first, belonging to the life-guards, was made of white satin, on which was shown a two-headed

---

[16] As Olearius makes plain hereafter, this was but the first in a series of secret audiences. The negotiations demonstrated that Holstein had blundered in asking for Swedish support, since that only aroused the suspicion of the Russians, who were unalterably opposed to Swedish participation in the Holstein scheme. After that matter had been settled, Holstein was at last awarded the privilege it had requested, but for a financial consideration 50 per cent higher than that initially offered. See Kieksee, pp. 67–69.

[17] One may well wonder why the Tsar should dispense presents to the aides of a vassal rather than receive tribute from them. The vassal in question governed the area around Tersk, in the northern Caucasus. The Tsar gave him a hereditary title and other favors because he collaborated with Russia in its policy vis-à-vis other peoples of this area. *Ocherki istorii . . . XVII v.*, p. 914.

eagle with three crowns, surrounded by a laurel wreath, and the motto: "Through valour, I prevail." Then there were three of blue and white, one depicting a griffin, another a snail, and the third a hand grasping a sword. Then came one of red damask, showing a two-faced Janus; and finally a plain red banner. We supposed that these emblems were made according to specifications provided by the German officers who had been at Smolensk, for the Russians themselves are very unskilled in the portrayal of such things. Ahead of each standard went pipers and drummers, and in front of the guards' standard, six trumpeters, who played in a spirited fashion. Some of the Russian princes rode on stately Persian, Polish, and German horses, which were finely groomed and decorated. Among these horses were ten of the Grand Prince's, on which were hung the large silver chains we noticed at our entry. Some of us, together with the Swedes, organized a company of 50 persons, and with the Swedish marshal, the noble Wolf Sparr, at our head, rode out a league to see the Turk. While we were observing him, he saw us and looked at us intently. We rode a good while alongside him and examined his suite. . . .[18]

When they were only a fourth of a league from the city and the ambassador was advised that the Russians who were to meet them were not far off, he got down from the carriage and mounted a fine Arabian steed. When he had gone on a musket shot's distance, two pristavs, as usual, came to meet him with the Grand Prince's horses. They remained on their horses until the ambassador dismounted. Then, although the Russians doffed their hats in speaking the Grand Prince's name, the Turks kept on their turbans, as is the custom in their country, and indeed they showed no sign of respect whatever.

After receiving the envoy, the Russians quickly mounted their horses again. Although the Turk did not tarry and in fact tried to mount before or at least simultaneously with them, he had been given a very tall and spirited horse, with a high Russian saddle, so that he was at some pains to climb up. When at last, and not without some danger (the horse several times kicked out at him), he mounted the horse, the pristavs escorted him between them to the recently rebuilt ambassadors' residence. Having installed the envoy, they locked the door securely

---

[18] Half a page describing the procession is omitted.

and posted a strong guard. At this time our ambassadors would gladly have visited the Swedes, who had invited them, for the ambassadors' residence was so near the Swedish quarters that one could see into the Turk's courtyard. However, the State Chancellor asked the gentlemen, for certain reasons, to be so good as to remain inside for this one day.

On the 19th, together with the royal Swedish ambassadors, we had a second secret audience. On September 23d the Turkish ambassador was escorted to a public audience. . . .[19]

Our ambassadors had brought to His Tsarist Majesty a letter from His Excellency, the Elector of Saxony. As it was thought desirable to present this letter in public audience, the Russians designated St. Michael's Day for the purpose. On that day the noble Johann Christoph von Uchterits carried the letter before the ambassadors on a yellow and black taffeta [pillow]. The Grand Prince received the letter cordially and asked, "How is the Elector Johann-Georg?" After being informed of His Excellency the Elector's health, he said that he granted the ambassadors food from his table. Then we were conducted home. We waited to receive the food, postponing our dinner until 2 o'clock in the afternoon, but to no avail. We were obliged to order our customary dishes served. About 3 o'clock the Russians came, in the usual order, bringing us a double measure of drink, but excusing themselves with regard to the food, which [they said] could not be prepared so rapidly. They asked if we might not prefer to receive money instead. Since we declined, on the following day a double portion of unprepared food was provided. The Tsar had heard, one of our good friends reported to us, that the first time we were favored we had sent many dishes to others that very day. It must be said, however, that when it is impossible to eat on the same day all that has been granted, it is quite common to send some to good friends so that they too may share the [Tsar's] favor.

On October 1st, a great holiday for the Russians, His Tsarist Majesty with his courtiers and the Patriarch with all the clergy entered the skillfully constructed Church of the Trinity—the Germans call it the Jerusalem—that stands before the Kremlin.[20] On the right side of the

[19] A page describing the procession is omitted.

[20] The actual name of this famous church, which has come to symbolize Moscow, was the Church of the Entry into Jerusalem. It is also known as the Pokrovskii Cathedral, and most popularly as Vasilii Blazhennyi (Vasilii the Blessed).

square in front of the Kremlin is a fenced-off area like a circular stage, on which stand two very large metal guns, one of them an ell in diameter.[21] When the procession reached the stage, the Grand Prince and the Patriarch went up onto it. The Patriarch held out to the Tsar a book with a silver binding on which was an ikon in relief. The Tsar reverently bowed to the ikon and touched his head to it while the priests were reading. After that the patriarch again approached the Tsar, extended to him a gold, diamond-studded cross a good hand long, which the Tsar kissed and pressed to his forehead and both his temples. Then both proceeded to the church and continued their praying. The Greeks also went into the church. Since the Russians are of the Greek faith, they readily admit Greeks to their churches, but not people of other creeds.[22] Great numbers of people were present at the procession, manifesting their reverence with bows and signs of the cross.

On October 8th we and the Swedish ambassadors had a third secret audience, which lasted two hours. On the 12th His Tsarist Majesty, accompanied by a suite of a thousand boyars, princes, and soldiers, went on a pilgrimage to a church half a league from the city. The Grand Prince rode alone, carrying a knout; after him came the boyars and princes, ten in a line, producing a gorgeous spectacle. Then the Grand Princess followed with the young prince and princess, in a large wooden carriage decorated with carvings, covered above with a red cloth, hung on the sides with yellow taffeta, and drawn by 16 white horses. Behind her came the Tsaritsa's female retinue in 22 wooden carriages that were painted green and covered with red cloth, as was the horses' harness as well. The carriages were tightly shut so that no one inside could be seen, unless by chance the wind raised one of the curtains. (By such good fortune, once when her carriage was passing, I saw Her Royal Majesty's face and her elegant clothing.) Along the sides of the procession walked more than a hundred streltsi, carrying white staffs with which they drove off the people who came running from everywhere.

---

[21] This "stage" is the famous *lobnoe mesto,* from which important declarations were made by state and church authorities. The Tsar appeared here before his people once a year. Popular legend to the contrary notwithstanding, executions were carried out not on this platform but in the adjacent Red Square, which then was called *Lobnaia Ploshchad'*. See N. Snegirev.

[22] Actually the Russians for a time had also been wary of contact with the Greeks, because they were associated with the infidel Turks. According to Paul of Aleppo (I, 382), Greek clerics had been forbidden to perform mass in Russian churches, and Greek merchants had not even been admitted.

The people, who greatly love and respect their rulers, repeatedly wished them happiness and blessed their journey.

On the 23d, together with the Swedes, we had a fourth secret audience, at which most matters were resolved. On the 28th all the Swedish ambassadors had a public audience, at which they received their final dismissal. By their order, their attendants publicly carried before them their credential letters as they left the palace. They left Moscow in three parties, on November 7th and 10th, for Livonia and Sweden.

On November 19th we had a fifth and final secret audience. There the ambassadors were advised that, after ample discussion, and in keeping with existing treaties, His Tsarist Majesty had at last declared and resolved, out of special love, to grant His Princely Excellence, Duke Frederick of Schleswig-Holstein, etc., his friend, uncle, and brother-in-law,[23] what heretofore had been refused to many sovereigns: permission for his ambassadors to travel across Russia to Persia and back. However, this was granted on condition that they first return to Holstein and bring back from His Princely Grace a letter ratifying the treaty that had been negotiated.[24] Having achieved this success after many difficulties and much effort, we allowed ourselves all sorts of amusement in the company of several good friends. The ambassadors and some of the rest of us went to the Swedish resident's for a baptism, and to the house of Dr. Wendelin, the Tsar's court physician, for the wedding of our dear former fellow traveler on the journey, Mr. Gar-

---

[23] The degree of consanguinity between the two houses is exaggerated, although they were in fact related through the marriage of Duke Magnus of Holstein to the niece of Ivan the Terrible.

[24] The text of the treaty is in *Akty istoricheskie*, Vol. III, No. 181. The treaty laid down the conditions for relations between the Tsar and a Holstein trading company, which might include up to 30 persons and maintain an agent in Moscow. The company was granted unimpeded passage through Russia to Persia and back, free of payment of duties, and the exclusive right to purchase from Persia raw silk and a few other specified commodities in which Russian merchants did not deal. It was forbidden to trade in dyed silk and a long list of other wares. The company was permitted to build ships in Russia for its use, employing Russian laborers whom they were to teach the craft of shipbuilding. It was allowed to have as many as 400 soldiers and ten armored ships, since the Tsar took no responsibility for the security of the enterprise. The company might maintain houses in various towns, as necessary, and divine worship was permitted in these. It was not to take Catholics into its service.

For these privileges, which were granted for a ten-year period, the company agreed to pay 600,000 reichsthalers in each of the first five years and 800,000 in each remaining year. Half was to be paid in the first half of the year, the rest before the year was out. The Tsar had the right to purchase from the company, at cost, any items it had acquired in Persia that he might desire. Goods from Holstein or Persia were generally not to be sold within Russia; but if sold to Russian merchants a duty was to be paid. At the termination of the ten-year period, the treaty might be renewed, at the Tsar's pleasure, for another ten years. In that case the company would pay thereafter 1,000,000 reichsthalers each year for the privilege.

leff Lüders. The latter subsequently became tutor to the Duke's daughter at the Holstein court in Gottorp. Finally, we also were treated to a grand feast given by David Ruts, a notable Dutch merchant.[25]

On October 22d the Russians held an impressive procession to a church situated in the city, near the ambassadors' residence. The Patriarch and the Grand Prince took part. The way from the Kremlin to the church was covered with planks. In the lead went many candle vendors and several people sweeping the streets with brooms. Then came the procession itself. . . .[26] The church had been built, and annual processions were made to it, because an ikon of the Virgin Mary had been found in the ground at this place.

On December 12th we saw 72 Tatars, all of whom called themselves ambassadors, going to the Kremlin. The Grand Prince spent three full hours with them and personally heard their requests. In the audience hall they disposed themselves on the floor, as is their custom, and each of them—so we were told—was given a cup of mead. Then the two most notable were presented with gold brocade robes, the others with scarlet robes, and so on in declining order, along with sable and other kinds of hats. As they left the Kremlin, they wore the gifts draped over their own clothes. These cruel and malevolent people live in villages scattered over an extensive area south of Moscow. They cause great harm on the Grand Prince's borders, especially near Tula, by pillaging and kidnapping. It is true that Tsar Feodor Ivanovich cut down the forest there, dug a ditch, and built a wall more than a hundred leagues long for defense. However, that helps little now. The Tatars often send embassies to Moscow, but only to obtain gifts. His Tsarist Majesty does not mind the cost if only he [can] buy peace.[27] But the Tatars preserve the peace only so long as it is to their advantage.

On December 16th, with great ceremony, we were brought to another public audience. The magnates rode in sleighs rather than on

[25] Although Dutch by birth, Ruts was in the Danish service. He had purchased Russian grain for Denmark in 1627–28 and was designated the King of Denmark's agent in Moscow in 1634. He continued to serve the King in Moscow for several decades, and was a leading member of the Protestant community in Moscow. See Kurts, *Sostoianie Rossii*, p. 37; Shcherbachev, Nos. 118, 120, and *passim*; and Tsvetaev, *Protestantstvo i protestanty*, pp. 67, 68, 399. Olearius implies later in the book that Ruts also performed commercial services for the Duke of Holstein.

[26] The description of the procession is omitted.

[27] The presents may be regarded as a form of tribute, which Russia's rulers paid to certain groups of Tatars long after the Tatar domination of Russia had ended. Only in the reign of Peter the Great were tribute payments terminated. See Sumner, pp. 15–16, 22, 77.

horseback, as is their custom when there is snow and frost. The ambassadors were brought two finely fitted-out sleighs. One of them was upholstered with red velvet, the other with red damask; at the back they were spread with white bearskins, and over the bearskins lay beautiful Turkish blankets. The horses' collars were gilded and hung with many foxtails (which the notables consider the height of decoration— they ornament even the sleighs of the Grand Prince).

Each of the pristavs went in a separate sleigh, to the right of one of the ambassadors. As before, two magnates met us in front of the audience hall. They escorted the ambassadors to His Tsarist Majesty, who first had the State Chancellor ask if the ambassadors were well. After they answered appropriately, a bench was placed behind them, upon which they were asked to sit. Then the Chancellor said: "The Great Sovereign Tsar and Grand Prince, Mikhail Feodorovich, Autocrat of all Russia, etc., wishes to advise you that you were sent by His Princely Grace, Duke Frederick of Holstein, to His Tsarist Majesty with letters which were well received, and you also were heard, in keeping with your wishes, by the Tsar's boyars, Prince Boris Mikhailovich Lykov, Vasilii Ivanovich Streshnev, and the State Chancellors Ivan Tarasovich [Gramotin] and Ivan Gavrenev. Following that, a treaty concerning certain matters was prepared, and was signed by you. Likewise His Tsarist Majesty received through you a letter from Johann-Georg, Elector of Saxony, and heard its contents. Now you are to receive the Tsar's letters to Prince Frederick of Holstein, etc., and also to Elector Johann-Georg."

With these words the Chancellor passed the letters before the Tsar's throne to the ambassadors, who accepted them in the prescribed manner. Then the Grand Prince bowed and said, "When the ambassadors see His Excellence, Johann-Georg, the Elector of Saxony, and His Princely Grace, Duke Frederick, give them my compliments." Then he made known through the Chancellor that he again granted permission to the ambassadors, their higher officers, and their hofjunkers to kiss his hand. When this was done, we were informed once again that His Tsarist Majesty granted us food from his table. The ambassadors gave thanks in the usual fashion for the kindnesses rendered them by the Tsar and for his good wishes; they wished His Tsarist Majesty long life and a happy and peaceful reign, and good fortune to all the Grand Prince's house. Then they took their leave and returned home.

An hour later the Grand Prince's food and drink arrived. The food consisted of 46 dishes: chiefly fish, boiled, roasted in oil, or baked, some vegetables and baked foods, but no meat, for it was a fast time which they annually keep before the Christmas holiday. This dinner was presented to us by Prince Ivan L'vov, and in all particulars was like that which followed the first audience. Then the Grand Prince's Master of the Horse and the Keeper of the Cellar, as well as those who regularly furnished food and drink in the ambassadors' residence, came to us and asked for gifts. The Master of the Stable, the Keeper of the Cellar, and the Prince were each given a goblet, and the other people (16 in number), 32 rubles.

The next day the pristav came with two translators, namely Hans Helmes, who was employed by His Tsarist Majesty and his boyars in our secret negotiations, and Andrei Angeler, who always attended us in our dealings with the pristavs. They asked how many horses we needed for the return trip (a count of 80 wagons or free horses was made). The interpreters, too, each received a large goblet, as did the senior scribe in the chancellery. Goblets were also sent to some of the magnates who had helped us in our affairs and been good friends to us.

On the 21st our pristavs introduced to us a new pristav, Bogdan Sergeevich Khomutov, who was to conduct us back to the Swedish border. On the next day, having sent 80 wagons to the ambassadors' residence, the pristavs came with a scribe from the [Tsar's] treasury and 12 other Russians, bringing the ambassadors and their party presents from His Tsarist Majesty, namely several timbers of sables, each consisting of 20 pairs. The ambassadors were given in all 11 timbers of fine sables. The officers, hofjunkers, chamber pages, quartermasters, cook, and coachman were each given a timber of lined sables. Other lesser servants were given one or two pairs. The scribe who brought the sables was given a goblet, and the other Russians 30 rubles.

In view of the impending Christmas holiday and the very severe frost, His Tsarist Majesty inquired whether the ambassadors wished to remain in Moscow a few days longer—even though he had dismissed them, they might stay on. Since the ambassadors were anxious to depart, however, we prepared ourselves for the journey. The ambassadors and some others among us bought our own sleighs, the best of which cost no more than three, or at most four, thalers.

In anticipation of the future journey to Persia, the ambassadors sent the skipper Michael Cordes, with six assistants, to Nizhnii [i.e. Nizhnii Novgorod], 100 leagues beyond Moscow, to build a vessel suitable for sailing on the Volga and the Caspian Sea. Then, on December 24th, we readied ourselves for the return trip. Around midday the pristavs and some streltsi came with the two sleighs in which the ambassadors had ridden to the audience. The ambassadors again rode in good order to the outskirts of the city, where we bade farewell to the pristavs, the Germans, and other good friends who had accompanied us an eighth of a league. Then each got into his own sleigh, and we set off.

We traveled all that day and night to Klin, a village 18 leagues from Moscow. The next afternoon, after celebrating our Christmas with a sermon, we continued our journey, traveling all night; toward the morning of the 26th we arrived in the town of Tver. Here, at the first coach station, we obtained fresh horses, which we harnessed in the evening. We traveled 12 leagues through the night to Torzhok. Thence, in four days, or six days after our departure from Moscow, i.e. December 31st [actually the 30th], we reached Novgorod, which is reckoned 110 leagues from Moscow. In winter with one feeding, Russian horses can trot continuously ten to twelve leagues. However, in Russia, the road is level almost everywhere.

[*The last part of Book I, which deals with the return trip to Holstein by land, completed on April 6th, is omitted.*]

BOOK II

The Second Journey to Moscow

WHEN HIS PRINCELY EXCELLENCE was informed that the Grand Prince of Moscow would allow passage through his realm to Persia, he decided to spare no expense in advancing his high aim, and published an order directing that an embassy to the Shah of Persia be carefully prepared and that the new journey be undertaken as soon as possible. Accordingly, all sorts of objects and precious gifts for presentation to the Shah were quickly collected. The retinue was reinforced and luxuriously equipped. Meanwhile His Princely Excellence sent me on a mission to the Cardinal Infant [Ferdinand, brother of Philip IV of Spain] in Brabant. On the return trip I became so ill that our doctor in Hamburg gave me up for dead. During the illness I was given excellent care in Brüggemann's house by him and his household. This I write in his honor, for later, recalling the benevolence I had experienced, I bore with patience many abuses from him. The other members of the suite were also entertained at Ambassador Brüggemann's house, and each one was well treated, according to his quality and station. (Here, as afterward during the journey, horns were blown [when the meat was brought to] the table.)

In accord with the custom of the Prince's court, the people of the retinue were assigned various responsibilities and titles. . . .[1] Some of these people departed with us from Germany and some joined us on the way. In Moscow we added 30 of the Grand Prince's soldiers and

---

[1] The list of the 88 persons, their places of origin, and their positions is omitted. Among them were a doctor, a pastor, an interpreter, musicians, kitchen personnel, and craftsmen, such as carpenters, shoemakers, and a blacksmith. Olearius, having been promoted, is listed as counselor as well as secretary. Michael Cordes and a group of ship's people had been dispatched directly to Nizhnii Novgorod from Moscow when the rest of the first embassy began its homeward journey.

officers and four Russian servants.² Thus, including the ambassadors, a party of 126 [actually 124] persons made the journey to Persia.

When all was fully ready, the ambassadors and their company left Hamburg in good order on October 22d, 1635, and arrived in Lübeck October 24th. There we rested two days, while our baggage and 12 riding horses were transported to the boat in Travemünde. On the 27th the ambassadors followed, and around midday most of the people were aboard the ship. Our vessel was completely new and had never been under sail.

We had just put out from shore and were bringing the ship out of the harbor when a strong and unusual current suddenly began to run from the sea into the Trave River, despite the fact that the wind was from the land to the sea. This phenomenon greatly surprised some of the seamen. In consequence our vessel was carried toward two other large ships that lay in the harbor, not only endangering them but also becoming so entangled with them, that it took more than three hours of arduous labor to free it and guide it out of the harbor and into the road. Some took this as an evil omen for the journey we were just beginning; and, unfortunately, the dismal outcome proved them right.

One of us sent from the ship to a good friend in Leipzig the following farewell poem:

> O Germany! You draw away your sheltering hands
> As you see me lured off to foreign lands.
> Now mother, good night. I shall not wet with tears
> The lap where happily I lay these many years.
> Of myself I leave with you indeed the better part.
> Look after him my friend, let Fortune be his guard,
> And elevate him to honors of high degree,
> Which virtue unsurpassed has earned abundantly.
> Farewell to you, dear friend. With Phoebus's blessed folk
> You will remain secure, while I with savages must walk.
> The loved one's bosom will afford you warmth
> While Thetis grips me in her cold, white arms.

² Holstein was permitted, under its treaty with Russia, to engage as many as 400 soldiers to provide security for a caravan of as many as ten ships laden with valuable cargoes; a much smaller number was employed because the Holsteiners' mission on this occasion was primarily diplomatic.

While care and sorrow your abode pass by,
On cruel boards, in fear and trembling, I must lie.
On you a gentle breath will play from tender lips,
While lashing winds and storms may wreck this feeble ship.
Yet He who rules all things and guards your night
Will still watch over me and, through His might,
When this ordeal is past, a bright new day will make.
Then I to you and Him my humble offerings will take.

[Above, in referring to "the dismal outcome," Olearius may have had in mind the ultimate failure of the Duke of Holstein's scheme; but he could also have been thinking of the extraordinary difficulties the ship encountered in the first two weeks. On October 28th it ran aground. However, when after much difficulty it was dislodged, the ship proved to be still seaworthy. In the succeeding days it was buffeted by severe storms, and two of its masts were shattered. After having repeatedly been given up as lost, the ship was finally wrecked on November 12th on the coast of the island of Hochland, in the Gulf of Finland. The members of the embassy reached the mainland a week or two later and assembled at Revel. Olearius's account of these adventures, a poem he composed about the shipwreck, and a section on Gotland, an island in the Baltic, are omitted.]

When the ambassadors had collected their entire suite at Revel, they ordered read the princely decree on conduct which had been received [at the Duke's court] at Gottorp. It went as follows.

WE, FREDERICK, by God's grace Heir to Norway, Duke of Schleswig, Holstein, Stormarn, and Ditmars, Count of Oldenburg and Delmenhorst, etc., in witness of our favor to the embassy we are now dispatching to Moscow and Persia, do declare:

Inasmuch as we, for important reasons, have chosen and appointed our esteemed, brave, and learned counselors Philip Crusius, Licentiate in Law, and Otto Brüggemann, as our ambassadors to the Grand Prince of Moscow, Mikhail Feodorovich, our beloved lord, uncle, and brother-in-law, and to the Persian Shah, and have furnished them with a distinguished suite, we deem it right that the suite should accord to the ambassadors the necessary respect for the princely honor we have entrusted to them, and thus render all due honor, respect, and obedience to us. To that end there has been devised the following court code, in accord with which all must live.

1. Most important, everyone in our ambassadorial suite is instructed, out of respect for us, to render to both of our above-named counselors all due honor, obedience, and service. Whatever they or their designated marshal may order, determine, or resolve is to be carried out without contradiction or protest; they must always be properly obeyed. We give our ambassadors authority and power to judge strictly, in accordance with the nature of the case, all insubordinate and disobedient [persons] and to punish them.

2. Since fear of God must be the beginning, middle, and end of all things, and since everyone must be responsive to it, especially on such long journeys, everyone in the suite is ordered to be guided in his actions by true fear of God, to attend regularly the sermons and worship services, and to pray to all-powerful God for the success of our important enterprise. Everyone must eschew swearing, cursing, blasphemy, and other coarse vices, or risk our disfavor and such punishments as our ambassadors may prescribe, according to the nature of the offense, and irrespective of persons.

3. Likewise we strictly forbid the indecent expenditure of time in gluttony, drunkenness, and other excesses, whence all sorts of disorders generally arise.

4. In particular, everyone in our embassy must strive for harmony. Each according to his station is obliged to live in amity with his comrades, and each must render friendship, love, and support to the others. It is essential to avoid quarrels, arguments, unnecessary coarseness, abusiveness, and fights. In the case of a misunderstanding, one should not be arbitrary. If someone has a complaint against another, he should report it to the marshal, who either will himself attempt to settle the argument or, if he cannot, will with the proper respect bring the matter to the attention of our ambassadors, who have the capacity to render a final decision by which all must abide. We strictly forbid willful challenges, brawls, and duels in our embassy and in the suite, for such might easily damage our high princely honor, particularly in the eyes of other nations. In this prohibition we definitely include the high-ranking officers, as well as the simple serving people.

5. In order that our ambassadors' suite should be in the best condi-

tion, and in order to avoid every kind of confusion and the disgrace arising therefrom, the marshal appointed by our ambassadors shall keep surveillance over all, both en route and at halting places.

6. In the course of the journey, when our ambassadors designate a time for departure, the marshal is obliged to have everyone under his jurisdiction ready to carry baggage and do whatever else is necessary, with energy and attention, so that our ambassadors shall have no reason for dissatisfaction because of delays.

7. Similarly, the marshal must give instructions to each and all so that everything shall be done in a spirit of amity, and with the proper decorum, without indecent bustle.

8. At stops, the marshal must see to it that the hofjunkers, pages, lackeys, and other servants who are designated to attend our ambassadors serve them and carry out their wishes diligently.

9. Inasmuch as the maintenance of our high princely honor especially requires that our ambassadors be attentively served, the hofjunkers, pages, lackeys and other servants, in keeping with the regime our ambassadors shall establish, must be obedient, industrious, and painstaking in their daily service, must be at the disposal of our ambassadors in the event that they are visited by foreigners, and in general [must conduct themselves] so that everything takes place in a completely worthy manner.

10. If the marshal, in the name of the ambassadors, orders or directs a subordinate [to do something], that person must obey without demur, failing which he may be punished. The marshal is also empowered to advise our ambassadors of the offenses of those not subject to his authority, and they will show the appropriate severity. We, too, for our part, decisively serve notice to all who conduct themselves in an unworthy manner that we shall inflict special punishment and show our disfavor.

11. If our ambassadors wish to send messengers to administrators, governors, magistrates, or other officials in fortresses, towns, or other places by which they shall pass, then those whom they find worthy in the suite must fulfill the tasks entrusted to them, with diligence, proper respect, and loyalty and without demur, and must give a true reply to our ambassadors. Since our ambassadors best understand who is capable of fulfilling such tasks most ably, the preference shown to one or another person should cause neither open nor secret rivalries.

12. In the course of the journey or at stopping places, no one shall insult or ridicule foreign peoples. Rather everyone must treat them with courtesy and friendliness, so that they will have reason to want to render to our people all good services and needed help.[3] Therefore, the marshal shall forthwith severely punish every particular incident of mischief and all inappropriate acts that come to his attention; for it is his duty to oversee conduct and to make full use of his authority.

13. All those in the suite must remain with our ambassadors for the entire journey and must not transfer to the service of any other without their knowledge. As we have released and dispatched our personal physician, Hartmann Gramann, to the ambassadors for this journey, he must remain with them during the trip and must return with them to us.

14. As it is impossible to anticipate in this order every possible circumstance, all that are not provided for herein will be handled at the discretion of our ambassadors, who are empowered to maintain an orderly regime, and to increase the number of articles of this code in accordance with [the requirements] of time, place, and circumstances. Whatever may be prescribed or directed by our ambassadors, personally or through others, for the sake of the maintenance of good order and our high princely honor, even though it is not covered in this code, must be submitted to and obeyed completely by all, without exception, just as though it were exactly so written and included in our code.

15. In order that each shall know his place and station en route, seated, at table, on the journey, and generally in all circumstances, we have drawn up for our suite, as is the custom at our princely court, a definite order [of precedence].[4]

We graciously advise that this our order and all further orders and directives of our ambassadors are to be obeyed by everyone, so that in no manner or degree shall conduct be contrary to them and so that everything shall be done in such a way as to avoid our disfavor and punishment. Rather, may we have reason, at the successful completion of the journey, to grant to each our princely favor. Such is our firm resolve. In confirmation we affix our princely seal of the Secret Chamber

---

[3] This instruction is similar to one issued by Sebastian Cabot to the Willoughby-Chancellor expedition that opened up the northern sea route to Russia in 1553. See Hakluyt, I, 237.

[4] I have omitted the list, which is printed earlier in Book II of the original. It is described in Note 1 above.

and our personal signature. Given at our court, in the princely residence of Gottorp, on the 1st day of October, 1635.

FREDERICK

Since the ambassadors noticed that some of our people had ceased to observe these strictly prescribed rules and procedures, preferring to live by their own wit and will, and that in consequence there had very noticeably crept in every sort of godlessness, insolence, and licentiousness, they considered it extremely necessary to zealously oppose these disturbances and to assure that in the course of such a long and distant journey we should conduct ourselves and live in a manner pleasing to God and to men. Therefore, they drew up the following additional order, and announced it also at Revel.

[*An extended section setting forth the ambassadors' regulations, which were similar to those of the Duke, is omitted. A lengthy section that describes the towns of Revel and Narva and the characteristics of the non-German populations of Livonia is also omitted.*]

On March 7th we left Narva and in the evening arrived at Lilienhagen, seven leagues away. On the 8th we went six leagues to Zarech'e. By midday on the 9th we made four leagues, arriving at the Swedish village of Orlino, where our interpreter, whom we had sent ahead, reported that the pristav awaited us at the border.

The ambassadors called together the leading people of their suite and reminded them, in a friendly way, that out of respect for His Princely Excellence they must render the ambassadors proper honor. Everyone would be obliged to conduct himself as his position required; for the Russians, whose border we were about to cross, pay particular attention to the esteem shown ambassadors by their suite. Out of duty and willingness, we promised to do so, but at the same time we asked that each of us be treated politely and in accordance with his quality and rights, and that we not be indiscriminately abused (as we sometimes seemed to be). When this was promised us, we went forward cheerfully to meet the pristav, whom we came upon a league beyond Orlino, halted in the snowy forest under the open sky, with 24 streltsi and 90 sleighs. Seeing the ambassadors climb out of their sleighs, the pristav, Konstantin Ivanovich Arbuzov, got out of his own.

He was dressed in a green silk robe, hung with gold chains, and over the robe was a long cloak lined with marten. When the ambassadors went toward him, he came several paces to meet them, with the words, "Ambassadors, remove your hats!" Since the ambassadors had already grasped their hats, they answered through their interpreter, "Dear pristav, it is already done." Then the pristav began to read from a paper. By order of the Great Sovereign Tsar and Grand Prince, Mikhail Feodorovich, Autocrat of all Russia, etc., the voevoda of Novgorod, Prince Petr Aleksandrovich Repnin, had sent him to receive Ambassadors Philip Crusius and Otto Brüggemann, to furnish wagons and provisions, and to accompany them to Novgorod and Moscow. When the ambassadors had thanked him, the pristav for the first time extended his hand to them and inquired about their health and the ease of their journey. The horses were then hitched to our sleighs, and on the same day we went another six leagues, to the village of Zverinka.

We arrived at Tesovo at noon on March 10th and reached the village of Mokritsy, eight leagues from Zverinka, toward evening. On the 11th we reached Great Novgorod. As we were entering the city, the pristav attempted to push himself into the front rank with the ambassadors, and in spite of their opposition held his own. When we arrived at his quarters, however, through our interpreter he begged the ambassadors' pardon for his rudeness to them, explaining that he did it not on his own initiative but at the order of the voevoda. If he had not fulfilled the order, he would have been reported and would have incurred the Grand Prince's wrath.

Great Novgorod is reckoned 40 leagues from Narva. There I calculated the elevation of the pole to be 58° 23'. Londorpium, in *Sleidanus continuatus*, fixes it at 62°, and Jovius at 64°, which is too far north.[5] Jovius writes in his book *De legatione Muscovitarum* "Novgorod is oppressed by the gloom of extremely long nights, as if it were constantly winter, for the north pole there is a full 64° from the horizon." At noon on March 15th, I exactly determined the elevation of the sun and found its distance from the horizon to be 33° 45'. Since

5 Johannes Sleidanus (1507–1556) and Michael Lundorp (1580–1629) were German historians. Paolo Giovio (Jovius), an Italian bishop, wrote in 1537 an account of Russia that was based, for the most part, on information he obtained from Dmitri Gerasimov, a Russian envoy to Rome. His work is published in Russian in *Biblioteka inostrannykh pisatelei,* under the name Paulo Jovii.

it was leap year, the declination of the sun at a longitude of approximately $55°$ [$5°$] must be taken as $2° 8'$. If one then subtracts that from the elevation of the sun, the position of the equator is found to be $31° 37'$. Subtracting that from $90°$, we obtain for the elevation of the pole $58° 23'$. The former Swedish ambassador, Andreas Bureus, an industrious scholar extremely learned in mathematics, agrees with this calculation; he locates Novgorod in the same way on his map of Sweden and Russia, placing it even $10'$ lower.

The city of Novgorod is very large, having a circumference of a league. Formerly it was even larger, however, as is evident from the old walls, and the churches and monasteries outside, many of which are falling into ruins. From a distance, owing to the many monasteries, churches, and cupolas, the city makes a fine appearance; but like most cities all over Russia the houses, as well as the city walls and fortifications, are built of spruce timbers or logs. The city lies on a plain by the Volkhov, a river that abounds in fish, particularly large, fat, and delicious perch, which can be bought very cheaply. On the surrounding plains there is much good pasture land. A great deal of hemp, linen, mead, and wax is produced here. Fine Russian leather, an important item of trade, is also made here. The city is very well situated for trade, since the Volkhov River, which flows through it, is navigable. The river flows [north] from Lake Il'men, half a league below the city, into Lake Ladoga. At Nöteburg, Lake Ladoga forms the Neva River, which empties into the Gulf of Finland and the Baltic Sea.

Formerly Livonians, Lithuanians, Poles, Swedes, Danes, Germans, and Flemings carried on a lively trade with Novgorod, with the result that the city became extremely wealthy and powerful. It was once the chief city of all Russia; the residence of a prince, and [the capital] of the whole province [of Novgorod], a great domain that extended all the way to Torzhok; a separate principality, independent of the tsar, with its own princes and coinage. A proud motto was composed, which boasted of the city's large population, wealth, and power: "Who can stand against God and Great Novgorod?" But as Seneca says, "There is nothing so great that it cannot perish." Powerful and invincible though Novgorod seemed, it suffered disaster more than once. For example, in 1427 a Polish army led by Vitovt pressed the city so hard that the Novgorodians were forced to come to them with prayers and expensive gifts, asking for peace, as is related by Solomon Neugebauer in Book Five of his *Historia Rerum Polonicarum*: "Vitovt and the Polish army waged war against the free people of Novgorod, taking as a pretext a boundary dispute. Having overcome the difficulties of the route [of advance], against the Novgorodians' expectations, he laid siege to Opochka. In answer to their humble pleas, and after great tributes had been brought to him, Vitovt agreed to grant them peace."[6]

In 1477, after a war lasting seven years, the tyrant Ivan Vasil'evich overcame them, with the connivance of their own archbishop, Feofil.[7] Ivan entered the city with an army on the pretext of bringing back into obedience to the Greek church some inhabitants who appeared to be partisans of the Roman church. He seized the property of all the merchants and the foremost citizens, appropriated all the archbishop's gold and silver, and made off with more than three hundred wagons loaded with gold, silver, pearls, and other precious things. He also carried off to Moscow [the leading Novgorodians], and transplanted to the city in their stead other persons, who were obliged to pay heavy yearly taxes. This is related in detail by Baron Sigismund von Herberstein, in whose lifetime this event occurred, and by Alessandro Guagnino.[8]

It is known that in 1569, because Ivan IV suspected (falsely) that his stepbrother[9] (who later was poisoned at his order) and the Novgorodians had hatched a plot against him and had appealed to the King of Poland for support, that ferocious monster fell upon Novgorod with an army. He and his soldiers slaughtered everyone they came upon in and around the city, hacked many people to pieces, drove a great crowd onto a long bridge and hurled them into the river, and caused a slaughter the like of which had never before been known in Russia. In this massacre 2,770 notable citizens perished, not counting women, children, and the common people. In the Novgorod district the tyrant sacked or burned 175 monasteries. The monks were murdered and the

---

[6] Olearius's source confuses two of Vitovt's compaigns, as is evident from Vernadsky, *The Mongols and Russia*, p. 295.

[7] The Muscovite ruler was not "the tyrant" Ivan IV, but Ivan III Vasil'evich.

[8] Herberstein could not have witnessed these events, since he was born in 1486. Guagnino served as an officer in the Polish army in sixteenth-century campaigns against the Russians. Further information on Guagnino and his writings is provided in Adelung, I, 10–11, 226–30. A more accurate account of Ivan III's relations with Novgorod is given in Fennell, pp. 35–60. The exile of many Novgorodians and their replacement by other Russians foreshadowed Ivan IV's *oprichnina*.

[9] The reference is probably to Ivan IV's cousin, Prince Vladimir Andreevich.

tyrant seized whatever property was not burned up, as Guagnino reports in his *Descriptio Moscoviae*. The Danish nobleman Jakob [Ulfeldt][10] whom King Frederick II of Denmark sent as ambassador to this tyrannical Grand Prince, relates in his *Hodoeporicon Ruthenicum* that the Volkhov River was so filled with the corpses of the thousands so pitifully slain that its proper flow was impeded. It overflowed its banks and ran through the fields. Since these events occurred only eight years before the ambassador's arrival, he was able to obtain reliable reports from the Novgorod inhabitants with whom he stayed for over a month. In the description of his journey, he says: "Although it may appear improbable that everything actually occurred in just this way, I learned of it from trustworthy people in Russia, i.e. people who still live in Novgorod under the Muscovite power. Otherwise I would not have included the story in my account." He goes on to say that at the time of his visit the area around Novgorod was so bare, as a result of the ravages visited upon it, that if the pristav had not brought a supply of provisions from elsewhere, they would have starved to death.

Although I have already described Ivan Vasil'evich's cruel oppression of Great Novgorod, I deem it well to present two other horrible examples, given by Guagnino, of the events of that time. After the tyrannical Grand Prince had committed the above-mentioned inhuman massacre, the frightened archbishop who governed in the city invited him to dinner, in order to ingratiate himself. The tyrant did not refuse, and at the appointed hour he appeared with his armed bodyguards and suite. During the meal, he sent [his men] to sack the Church of St. Sophia, which was rich in gold and silver (the notables stored their valuables there, considering it a safe place). After dinner, he robbed the archbishop of all his costly vestments, episcopal ornaments, and finery, and said: "Now you are no longer fit to be an archbishop. You would do better as a bagpiper, leading a bear about and making him dance for money. You shall take a wife whom I have sought out and designated." To the abbots and prioresses, who had fled from the monasteries into the city and were present at the dinner,

[10] Olearius frequently uses this source, referring to its author as "the Danish nobleman Jakob," since the author's identity was unknown. Ulfeldt went on missions to Russia in 1575 and 1578. See Adelung, I, 273–83. A Russian edition of Ulfeldt's Latin account is *Puteshestvie v Rossiiu datskogo poslannika Iakova Ul'fel'da v XVI veke.*

he said: "You all must appear at the archbishop's wedding. I hereby invite you, but you must bring good wedding presents." He then ordered each of them to pay a certain sum, depending upon his estimate of their substance, and by threats forced them to comply. They did it the more willingly, thinking it would go to the denuded archbishop. However, the tsar took the money himself, ordered a white mare in foal for the archbishop, and pointing to it with his finger said: "Look, here is your wife. Sit on her and ride to Moscow. There I will order that you be registered in the pipers' guild, so that you can play for a dancing bear." The poor wretch was forced to mount the horse, in a coarse cloth robe, and his legs were tied under the horse's stomach; on his neck they hung a lyre, a zither, and pipes, and thus he had to ride through Novgorod, playing on the pipes. Since he had never learned to play, it may well be imagined how the music sounded. With this humiliation the tyrant let the archbishop escape. But the abbots and monks he executed in various horrible ways. Most of them were hacked to pieces with axes, others were driven at spearpoint into the river, where they drowned.

Then came the turn of one of the foremost wealthy citizens, Feodor Syrkov. He was brought to a camp not far from Novgorod, a rope was tied around his body, and he was ordered to pull the rope across the Volkhov. When the tyrant observed that the man was drowning, he ordered him pulled out and asked him what good things he had seen under the water. Syrkov replied: "Grand Prince! I saw all the devils of this river, of Lake Ladoga, and other neighboring bodies of water gathered waiting for your soul, to carry it to the pit of Hell." To that the tyrant answered: "Good! You saw well, and I shall reward you for the description." Then he ordered that Feodor be set up to the knees in a cauldron full of boiling water and that his legs be cooked until he revealed where his gold and treasure were hidden (for he was a very rich man, who had built and maintained at his own expense 12 monasteries). After the tormented man ordered 30,000 silver guilders brought, the tyrant ordered him and his brother Aleksei to be hacked to pieces and cast into the river.

Such were the horrible massacres inflicted on the people of Novgorod and such was the fall of that good city, which saw how poorly it could stand against any power. Its people also well remember its cap-

ture in 1611 by the Swedish colonel Jakob de la Gardie, which proved
once more the baselessness of the motto about its great might.[11] Now
a voevoda and a metropolitan, appointed by the Grand Prince of
Moscow, reside there in a palace situated beside the river and surrounded by a strong stone wall. Through these people the Grand
Prince governs the city and the whole province in both secular and
ecclesiastical affairs.

The Novgorodians, when they were still pagans, had an idol called
Perun, the god of fire (the Russians call a flame *perun*).[12] At the place
where the idol once stood they built a monastery, which preserves
the god's name, for it is called Perun Monastery. The idol was in the
form of a man holding in his hands a flint that looked like a thunder-
bolt or an arrow. In honor of this god they burned oak wood day and
night; if the attendant negligently allowed the flame to go out, he
paid with his life. When the Novgorodians were baptized as Christians,
they flung the idol into the Volkhov. It is said that the idol floated
against the current; when it came to the bridge a voice said, "Novgorodians, here is something to remember me by," and immediately a
cudgel was thrown up onto the bridge. The voice of Perun was heard
afterward on certain days of the year, and then the inhabitants fled in
panic and beat each other with sticks so cruelly that the voevoda was
hard put to pacify them. According to a reliable witness, Baron von
Herberstein, similar things occurred in his time, too.[13] Nothing of the
sort is heard of any more.

Across the river, opposite the palace, stands the Monastery of St.
Anthony. It is said that St. Anthony himself miraculously caused the
monastery to be built there. The Russians relate, and believe too,
that St. Anthony seated himself on a millstone in Rome and sailed on
it down the Tiber to the sea, around Spain, France, and Denmark,

---

[11] Novgorod remained under Sweden's control until 1617, when by the Treaty of Stolbovo
the Swedes renounced any intention of annexing it. On Swedish policy regarding Novgorod,
1612–18, see Forsten, II, 119ff. John Merrick, the Englishman who helped negotiate the
Treaty of Stolbovo, had earlier plotted to bring northern Russia under English control. See
Lubimenko, *Les Relations commerciales*, pp. 135–43, and "Project for the Acquisition of
Russia."

[12] Actually Perun was the god of thunder and lightning.

[13] This is interesting evidence of the persistence of *dvoeverie*, that is the coexistence of
pagan and Christian beliefs, as late as the sixteenth century. It supports the contention of
Vernadsky that a dual culture persisted into the Moscow period of Russian history. See his
Origins of Russia, pp. 309–16; Chap. 4, *passim*.

through the Sound, the Baltic Sea, and Lake Ladoga, and up the Volkhov River to Great Novgorod, where he came ashore with the stone. When he met some fishermen about to go out for the catch, he contracted to give them a certain sum in return for whatever they got in their first haul. When they brought in their nets, the fishermen pulled onto the shore a large box, in which were found St. Anthony's ecclesiastical vessels, books, and money. According to tradition the saint then built a chapel and settled in it, and when he died was buried there. They say that to the present day you can still see the uncorrupted body, and that great miracles are accomplished for sick people who come here to pray. Strangers and foreigners, however, are not admitted inside the monastery. Some of them are shown the millstone, which leans against the wall. In recognition of this great miracle, and in memory of St. Anthony, this large and splendid monastery was built and furnished with rich revenues.

We stayed in Novgorod until the 15th of March. Once the voevoda ordered a gift of 24 cooked dishes of various kinds and 16 sorts of drinks sent to the ambassadors. The d'iak Bogdan Feodorovich Oboburov, who had been our pristav in the previous embassy, did likewise. The ambassadors, in return, presented the voevoda with a German carriage.

On March 16th, with 129 fresh horses, we set out again in our sleighs, and by evening had gone four leagues, to Bronnitsy, where we again were furnished with horses. The next day we went on and by midday made 40 versts, arriving at Medna; in the afternoon we went another 25 versts, to the coach station of Krestsy. On the 18th we reached Iazhelbitsy, six leagues farther along, and then continued another four leagues to the coach station of Zimogor'e. On the 19th we traveled 50 versts, to Kolomna, and on the 20th five leagues, to the coach station at Vyshnii Volochek.

In this village we met a 12-year-old boy who had been married several weeks before. A marriage of the kind was contracted in Tver for an 11-year-old girl. In Russia, as in Finland, children 12 years old, and even younger, are permitted to marry.[14] Usually these weddings are between widows and boys whose parents have died. In this manner,

---

[14] According to the *Stoglav*, a code drawn up by the church council of 1551, anyone who had reached 12 years of age might marry. Duke Magnus's bride had been but 13. Tsvetaev, *Protestantstvo i protestanty*, pp. 425–26.

they can keep their property, and do not have to depend on friends and guardians.

Before evening we went seven leagues to the village of Vydropusk. Here we were poorly accommodated, for there were not more than three households, and their rooms were like pigpens. Although the smokehouses we met with everywhere in Russian villages were little better, nevertheless they were more suitable than these lodgings. On the 21st we made seven leagues to the town of Torzhok. On the 22d we crossed a stream and went six leagues to Troitska-Mednaia, and then six leagues to the town of Tver. Since the snow had drifted in some places where there were hills, and we could proceed only with great difficulty, that day and the next we traveled on the Volga, which was still solidly frozen, and toward evening we reached the village of Gorodnia, having gained six leagues. On the 24th we shifted back to land, crossed two rivers, passed the village of Zavidovo, and reached Spas'-Zaulki, seven leagues from our last resting place.

During these days we had to cross several rivers. Since the ice was thin, crossing was very troublesome and caused us much annoyance. Beyond the large village of Klin, through which we passed on the 25th, flows a stream named the Sestra; it falls into the Dubna, which, in turn, flows into the Volga. We were obliged to drive strong posts into the bed of the Sestra on the downstream side of our crossing place so that the river would not carry our sleighs away as we went over. On the 26th, half a league from the previous day's crossing, we again encountered the Sestra, which runs a winding course, and had to cross again. That evening we stayed in Peshek, seven leagues from Klin. On the 27th we crossed two streams and before evening went six leagues, to Cherkizovo. On the 28th we went only three leagues, to Nikola-Derebnia, barely two leagues from Moscow. Like other ambassadors who came by way of this place, we had to wait here until our arrival had been announced to the Grand Prince and arrangements had been made for receiving us. . . .[15]

Hardly had we come into Moscow and entered our residence when

---

[15] The next pages, which deal with the embassy's entry into the city and the ambassadors' reception, follow closely the corresponding material in Book I and are therefore omitted. The pristavs assigned to the embassy for the duration of their stay in Moscow were Pavel Ivanovich Salmanov and Andrei Ivanovich Chubarov. Since the ambassadorial residence was occupied by the Persian envoy, who had arrived earlier, the Holsteiners were put up near the Kremlin in a tall stone house that had formerly belonged to the Archbishop of Suzdal.

the Russians appeared with various foods and drinks from the Grand
Prince's kitchen and cellar, and each of the ambassadors and their six
senior aides were provided with special drinks. From this time on, for
the duration of our stay in Moscow, each day our kitchen and cellar
were well stocked. We received daily 62 loaves of bread, each worth
a kopek; a quarter of beef; four sheep, 12 chickens, and two geese; a
hare or a partridge; 50 eggs; ten kopeks for candles, and five kopeks
for the kitchen. In addition, we received weekly a pud ([36] pounds) of
butter, a pud of salt, three buckets of vinegar, two sheep, and a goose.
We daily received 15 tankards for the ambassadors and hofjunkers:
three small ones of vodka, one of Spanish wine, eight of various meads,
and three of beer. In addition, they provided for our attendants one
barrel of beer, a small cask of mead, and another small cask of vodka.

These provisions were furnished in double measure on the day of
our arrival and also on Palm Sunday, Easter, and the young prince's
birthday. We had our own cook fix the food in the German fashion.
We were attended not only by serving people assigned to our household but also by the pristavs, who daily called upon the ambassadors.
While it is true that a *desiatnik*, or corporal, and nine streltsi were set
at the gate of our house, once we had been to a public audience, or as
they say, "had seen the bright eyes of His Tsarist Majesty," we again
enjoyed our former—or even greater—freedom to go in and out, to
extend invitations, and to go visiting.

On April 3d the ambassadors, riding [the Tsar's] horses as usual,
were escorted with the customary pageantry to a public audience. The
procession kept the same order as at our entry into the city, except that
the secretary rode alone ahead of the ambassadors, carrying in his outstretched hand the [Duke's] credential letter on a red satin cloth. The
streltsi and the people stood in great throngs on the streets all the way
from the ambassadors' residence to the Kremlin and the audience hall.
As usual, mounted couriers came frequently and swiftly from the palace to the ambassadors, bringing orders to speed up, to slow down, or
even to halt. This was done so that His Tsarist Majesty might sit
down on the throne for the audience at the proper time. The further
course of the ceremonies corresponded exactly to that of a year before,
at the first audience. From the vaulted antechamber filled with distinguished Russians, two magnates came out to meet the ambassadors, re-

ceive them, and usher them in to His Tsarist Majesty. The Tsar himself asked about His Princely Excellence's health, accepted the credential letter, gave his hand to be kissed, and granted us [food] from his table.

The proposal Ambassador Crusius made at this audience was as follows:

"Most illustrious and most powerful Sovereign Tsar and Grand Prince, Mikhail Feodorovich, Autocrat of all Russia (here the complete title was given). The most illustrious and noble Prince Frederick, Heir to Norway, Duke of Schleswig, Holstein, Stormarn, and Ditmars, Count of Oldenburg and Delmenhorst, our most gracious Prince and Sovereign, sends the greetings of a friend, uncle, and brother-in-law to Your Tsarist Majesty, and heartily wishes you the best of fortune.

"First, His Princely Excellence would be most happy to learn that Your Tsarist Majesty, the young prince and heir, and all of the Tsar's house are in good physical health, reigning happily and peacefully, and prospering in every respect. He wishes with all his heart that The Most High will long preserve all this to Your Tsarist Majesty and all the Tsar's house.

"Further, His Princely Excellence expresses to Your Tsarist Majesty the gratitude of a friend, uncle, and brother-in-law for Your Tsarist Majesty's permission for us, His Princely Excellence's ambassadors, to pass freely through your great realm to Persia and back. In this connection, His Princely Excellence has again sent with us a genuine credential letter, and he has therein ordained that everything earlier negotiated and decided concerning our transit to Persia and back now be exactly confirmed. He also has instructed us to take up some other matters with Your Tsarist Majesty.

"His Princely Excellence now requests Your Tsarist Majesty, as a friend, uncle, brother-in-law, to grant us a secret audience, to hear our plea, and to act upon it favorably. For his part, His Princely Excellence expresses his readiness to extend the services and friendship of an uncle and brother-in-law to Your Tsarist Majesty. Furthermore, with all due respect, we wish to commend ourselves to Your Tsarist Majesty's favor."

After the audience one of the Grand Prince's officials, Prince Semen

Petrovich L'vov, rode up, bringing the food graciously provided by His Tsarist Majesty, 40 dishes in all. Since it was a fast time, they comprised cooked and baked fish, pastries, and vegetables (without meat), and 12 tankards of beverages. When the table was covered and the dishes were ready, the prince personally handed the ambassadors and each of the higher officers of the suite a cup of strong vodka. Then he raised a large gold cup and proposed toasts, in turn, to the health of His Tsarist Majesty, to the young prince, and to His Princely Excellence. The prince was given a large goblet and the bearers some rubles. Then the prince departed.

We sat at the table trying various Russian dishes; some were very well prepared, but most of them contained onion and garlic. What remained was sent to the interpreters and to good friends in the city. Meanwhile the Persian ambassador, whose lodging was near ours, caused drums, pipes, and horns to be played gaily. Since our spirits were already aroused by the toasts, we were inclined to spend the day in revelry and good cheer and were greatly aided in doing so by the splendid drinks which the Grand Prince had provided.

On April 5th we were escorted to the first secret audience. The boyars and magnates in attendance were the same as in the previous year, with the exception of State Chancellor Gramotin, who had retired because of his age. He was replaced by Feodor Feodorovich Likhachev.[16]

While the audience was in progress one of our lackeys, Franz Wilhelm, from Pfalz, died at our residence. Eight days earlier, during the trip, a sleigh had overturned, and Brüggemann's trunk, which was in his charge, had fallen on his chest. We buried the corpse three days later. Since the deceased was of the Reformed faith, the coffin was first taken to the Calvinist church for the funeral oration, and afterward he was buried in the German cemetery.[17] For the funeral procession the Grand Prince sent us a pristav and 15 white horses.

---

[16] Likhachev replaced Gramotin as dumnyi d'iak at the Posol'skii Prikaz in 1635 and held the office until 1643. Belokurov, "O Posol'skom Prikaze," p. 110.

[17] The first Protestant church in Russia was a Lutheran church, established in 1575 or 1576; the first Calvinist church was built in 1629. Although these Protestant prayerhouses were repugnant to the Orthodox Russians (Catholic churches were simply not permitted), tolerance of them was the price the government had to pay to attract foreign technicians and to keep them in its service. The first foreign cemetery dates from the time of Ivan IV; it was situated near Naleika, a section of Moscow that had been inhabited by foreign soldiers in the first quarter of the sixteenth century. See Tsvetaev, *Protestantstvo i protestanty*, pp. 42–45, 66, 115–16.

On April 9th we had another secret audience. On April 10th, Palm Sunday, the Russians celebrated with an impressive procession the festival of Jesus Christ's entry into Jerusalem. The Grand Prince, whose permission to watch the spectacle we had asked on the previous day, sent the ambassadors the usual two white horses and 15 others. We were allotted a wide space opposite the Kremlin gate, and the Russians, more than ten thousand of whom had collected before the Kremlin, were held back so that we could see clearly. Behind us on the stage described earlier stood the Persian ambassador and his suite.

The procession moved from the Kremlin to the Jerusalem Church in the following order. First the Grand Prince and his boyars went into the Church of Holy Mary, where they heard the Mass. Then he emerged from the Kremlin, with the Patriarch, in a solemn procession. In front on a very large, wide, low-slung wagon was carried a tree to which were fastened many apples, figs, and raisins. By the tree sat four boys in white shirts, singing Hosannahs. Behind them came many priests in white choir robes and costly ecclesiastical vestments, carrying banners, crosses, and ikons, on long staffs, and singing in unison. Some of them held censers, which they swung toward the people. Following them were the foremost merchants or gosti, the d'iaki, the scribes, the secretaries, and, last of all, the princes and boyars, some of them carrying palm branches.

The Grand Prince, richly robed and wearing a crown, proceeded arm in arm with two of the most notable state counselors, Prince Ivan Borisovich Cherkasskii and Prince Aleksei Mikhailovich L'vov.[18] He himself led the Patriarch's horse by a long rein. The horse was covered with a cloth, and was adorned with long ears, to make it resemble an ass. The Patriarch sat sidesaddle on the horse. He wore a round white hat set with very large pearls, and a crown. In his right hand was a golden cross embedded with precious stones, with which he blessed the surrounding people. The people bowed their heads very low and crossed themselves toward him and the cross. In line with the Patriarch and behind him went the metropolitans, bishops, and other priests, carrying either books or censers. Fifty boys, mostly dressed in red, also walked before the Grand Prince; some removed their cloaks

---

[18] Olearius refers to the boyars as "state counselors," i.e. members of the Boyar Duma or Council.

and laid them in the path; others, instead of their cloaks, spread vari-colored pieces of cloth (two ells in length) for the Grand Prince and the Patriarch to step on. When the Grand Prince neared the ambassa-dors, and they bowed to him, he halted and sent his senior interpreter, Hans Helmes, to ask about their health. He waited until the interpre-ter returned, and then continued on to the church. After half an hour in the church, they returned in the same order. The Grand Prince again halted near the ambassadors and had them informed that this day they would receive food from his table. Instead, however, we re-ceived a double measure of our usual provisions. For leading his horse, the Patriarch gives the Grand Prince 200 rubles. Palm Sunday cele-brations are held with similar pageantry in other Russian cities; bish-ops or priests take the part of the Patriarch, and the voevoda that of the Grand Prince.

On April 17, Holy Easter Day, there was great rejoicing among the Russians, partly because of the Resurrection of Christ, partly because it was the end of their long fast. That day, and for fourteen days there-after, practically everyone—notables and commoners, young and old —carries colored eggs. In every street a multitude of egg vendors sit, hawking boiled eggs decorated in various colors. When they meet on the street, they greet each other with kisses on the mouth. One says, "*Khristos voskrese*," that is "Christ has risen"; and the other answers, "*Voistinu voskrese*," which means "Indeed He has risen." And no one, neither man nor woman, neither magnate nor commoner, refuses to another a kiss and greeting and an egg. The Grand Prince himself dis-tributes Easter eggs to his courtiers and servants. It was also his cus-tom, the night before Easter, before he went to morning prayer, to visit the prison, open the cells, and give each prisoner (there were always many) an egg and a sheepskin coat, saying: "Let them be happy. For Christ, who died for their sins, has indeed risen." Then he ordered the prison shut again and went off to church.

All during Holy Easter not only did good friends visit [each other] in private homes, but everyone—lay and ecclesiastical people, men and women—avidly patronized simple *kabaki*, that is beer, mead, and vodka houses. They drank so much that frequently people were seen lying here and there in the streets, and some of them had to be thrown onto wagons or sleighs by their relatives and taken home. Under the circumstances, it may be understood why many people, murdered and stripped of their clothing, were found in the morning lying in the streets. Now, thanks to the Patriarch, these great excesses from visits to taverns or pothouses have abated somewhat.

On April 29th Brüggemann, at his own request, had a special secret audience with the boyars. Without his fellow ambassador, he went to the Kremlin accompanied by a few escorts and was conducted to the treasury office, where, in a special room, he was heard for about two hours. As the proposals he made there stemmed not from the [Duke's] order but from his own initiative, the other ambassador, Mr. Crusius, did not have to be informed.[19] On May 6th both ambassadors had their third secret audience, on the 17th a fourth, and on the 27th the fifth and last.

On May 30th, with the permission of the Grand Prince, the young prince's tutor [B. I. Morozov] organized a falcon hunt and invited the ambassadors' chief aides. He sent us his own horses, and conducted us two leagues outside the city to a pleasant meadow, where after we had had good sport, he treated us under a tent to vodka, mead, gingerbread, Astrakhan grapes, and cherry preserves. June 1st was the birthday of the young prince, Ivan Mikhailovich. The Russians celebrated the day with great merriment. So that we could participate in the celebration, our usual provisions were doubled.

On the 3d Brüggemann once again went alone to the Kremlin, and talked in secret to the boyars. On the 4th, the eve of Pentecost, His Tsarist Majesty, with his boyars and counselors, held a public audience and dismissed all the other ambassadors who had been in Moscow simultaneously with us. First of all, the Persian ambassador, who was a *kupchina* or merchant, came to the Kremlin.[20] He returned with a red velvet Russian cloak, lined with beautiful sables, thrown over his shoulders. A similar procedure is followed in Persia on dismissal [of an envoy]. After him the Greeks and Armenians rode into the Krem-

---

[19] Olearius is in error here. This secret audience and that on June 3d, referred to below, dealt with differences that had arisen between the parties to the treaty. The Russian authorities balked at allowing the Holsteiners to proceed to Persia without paying a sizable sum, as stipulated in the treaty. The Holsteiners insisted that since this time they were going to Persia as diplomats, not as merchants, they were not bound to make a payment; the Holsteiners ultimately had their way. See Kieksee, pp. 80–81; and Loviagin, pp. 544, 545.

[20] The Persian ambassador discussed with the Russians the implications of their treaty with Holstein, and hinted at the terms Holstein might expect from Persia. Loviagin, pp. 544–45.

lin, and, finally, some Tatars, who came away with their credentials and gifts openly displayed.

On the 12th our provisioner, Jakob Scheve, arrived in Moscow from Germany. We had left him behind to pick up certain presents for the Shah, which were being made in Danzig. However, he was detained three days outside the city until the chancellor could report to His Tsarist Majesty, who was away on a pilgrimage, and obtain permission for him to enter.

On the 15th the Grand Prince and Princess returned. The Grand Prince was followed by his boyars and courtiers, and the Grand Princess by 36 of her maids and servants in red dresses and white hats, from which long red laces hung down their backs. Around their necks they had white scarves, and all were conspicuously rouged. They rode their horses as men do.

On the 17th I was sent to the chancellery by the ambassadors to transmit something to the State Chancellor. Since he wanted me to be conducted by a pristav, to render me greater honor, I was obliged to stand quite long in the antechamber with ordinary Russians and lackeys, until at last our pristav was found and brought.

The senior and junior chancellors received me cordially and responded favorably to my request. Their window [frames] and table were covered with fine tapestries, and before the chancellor stood a large and beautiful (empty) inkstand. I was told that both the tapestries and the inkstand were set in place just before my arrival and removed afterward. The chancellors' offices are usually not very tidy, and perhaps that was why they had detained me in the antechamber.

On the 20th the pristavs and scribes came to inform the ambassadors, in the name of His Tsarist Majesty, that they could leave for Persia whenever they wished. The embassy would be received by His Tsarist Majesty not now, but upon its return. To do otherwise would be out of order, inasmuch as the embassy was not taking its final leave and returning home. At the final public audience His Tsarist Majesty would deliver credential letters and transmit his compliments to His Princely Excellence, which could not be done now on account of the ambassadors' impending journey to Persia.

Consequently, we prepared to continue the trip, giving instructions to prepare several boats to take us from Moscow to Nizhnii. Since the way was said to be extremely dangerous—we were particularly warned

about Cossacks and brigands on the Volga—the ambassadors, with His
Tsarist Majesty's permission, took into our service for the voyage to
Persia 30 of the Tsar's soldiers and officers.[21] On June 24th and 25th
all these people, along with some metal weapons which we had brought
from Germany, some other stone-firing pieces which we bought in
Moscow, plus our baggage and utensils, were sent ahead to Nizhnii
Novgorod.

On the 26th some Polish ambassadors, or grand couriers as they are
called, came to Moscow and were escorted into the city. When the
ambassadors saw some of us coming out of the city to watch the entry,
they bared their heads, nodded cordially, and greeted us. To the Russian pristavs, however, they gave no notice. To the pristavs' great cha-
grin, they had to dismount from their horses and bare their heads before the ambassadors did. The Poles justified themselves by saying
that they had no desire to honor others; they had come not to receive
but to be received by the Russians.

The ambassadors were not provided with the Grand Prince's horses
for their entry, as is usually done, since recently a Grand Polish Ambassador had declined them, preferring to enter on his own horse. That
Grand Ambassador arrived shortly after the raising of the siege of
Smolensk and the defeat of the Russians there.[22] We were told that he
acted vexatiously toward the Russians in every way. During the public
audience he did not stand, but remained seated while making his
speech; and when he spoke his King's title, and the boyars, as is their
custom, did not remove their hats, he became indignant, spoke some
abusive words, and interrupted his speech until His Tsarist Majesty
signaled to the boyars to bare their heads. Although His Polish Majesty had not ordered gifts to be given, the ambassador personally presented a beautiful carriage to the Grand Prince. But when several timbers of sables were brought to him in return, he declined to accept
them. At that the Grand Prince sent the carriage back.

The ambassador ordered his pristav thrown down the staircase,

---

[21] In keeping with the treaty, these military people were to be paid by Holstein. When they
returned from Persia, they again entered the Tsar's service. *Ibid.*, p. 545.

The list of the soldiers' names is omitted, as are the names of several Russians hired as
servants. All the soldiers were foreigners; the ambassadors evidently lacked confidence in the
quality and reliability of the Russian soldiers. Eight of the hired soldiers died in the course of
the journey.

[22] In 1634.

which greatly angered His Tsarist Majesty. The Tsar caused him to
be asked whether it was done at the King's order, or on his own initiative. If it were by the King's order, His Tsarist Majesty would do
nothing about it for the time being; for victory is in God's hands, and
He gives it to whom He will. This time it had been awarded to His
Royal Majesty, but another time it might be different. If, however,
His Tsarist Majesty learned that the ambassador had acted on his own
initiative, he would write about it to the King, who undoubtedly would
not let such conduct go unpunished. Because the Grand Ambassador
had paid scant attention to the pomp and ceremony at his entry, the
exit arranged for him was more modest.

When we had finished our business in Moscow, we prepared for the
next stage of the journey and received from the Grand Prince the following passport, addressed to his local voevodas and aides and translated by his interpreters. One can observe here the chancellery style.

Passport from His Tsarist Majesty to the Prince of Holstein's Ambassadors

From the Great Sovereign and Grand Prince, Mikhail Feodorovich, of all Russia, from Moscow, to our boyars and voevodas and
d'iaki and all our officials in Kolomna, Pereiaslavl, Riazan, Kasimov,
Murom, Nizhnii Novgorod, Kazan, and Astrakhan.

By our order, Prince Frederick of Holstein's ambassadors and counselors Philip Crusius and Otto Brüggemann, together with their suite
of 85 Holstein Germans and a convoy of 30 of our hired Germans
serving in Moscow, are given leave to proceed from Moscow to Persia, to the Persian Shah, for negotiations on the transit and trade of
the Holstein merchants. Furthermore, they have permission to hire
11 Russian or German volunteers in Nizhnii, or Kazan, or Astrakhan
to reinforce their escort for the voyage to Persia. They also have permission to hire or take on at Nizhnii two pilots who know the way on
the Volga. After they have been to Persia and are on the way back to
Holstein across our Moscow realm, the Holstein ambassadors are permitted to add to these, as they may require, 40 guards or laborers, in
Astrakhan, or Kazan, or wherever convenient, and as many more Russian or German volunteers as they need. The numbers and kinds of
people who, with our permission, are engaged in any city should be

reported by name in that same city, so that these persons may be registered and investigated and for the information of our boyars and voevodas and d'iaki. If they return from Persia in winter, they have permission to engage at their own cost any Russians who wish to hire out and whatever conveyances may be needed for the journey.

As pristav from Moscow to Astrakhan we are sending the Astrakhan nobleman Rodion Gorbatov. When Rodion and the Holstein ambassadors arrive in any given city, you, our boyars, voevodas, and d'iaki, and all our people in authority, are to allow them to pass without any hindrance. And when they have been to Persia and are on the way back to Holstein across our Moscow realm, you will, in keeping with this passport, allow the Holstein ambassadors to hire in Astrakhan, or Kazan, or wherever convenient, as many guards and working hands for the journey on the Volga as they may require. If some of our Russian or German people are hired en route to Persia, the date, the place, and the number engaged are to be reported to you; the names of those hired are to be registered and investigated so that there can be no brigands or runaway slaves among them. If the Holstein ambassadors return from Persia in the winter, you shall allow them to hire at their own expense as many of our Russian people and conveyances as they may require. They are not to be detained as they go from Moscow to Persia and back from Persia to Moscow, and they are likewise not to be deceived. The Holstein ambassadors are to be honored, and every cordiality is to be extended to their suite. Likewise the Holstein ambassadors and their party, on the way to Persia and back, are not to resort to deception, brigandage, or violence with respect to our Russian people, and also are not to seize provisions for themselves and their people. They are obliged to purchase at their own expense, from anyone who wishes to sell, food supplies for themselves, their own people, and those they hire on the way to Persia and back.

Written in Moscow in the Summer of 7144 [1636],
on the 29th of June.
The Tsar and Grand Prince of All Russia
Mikhail Feodorovich.
D'iak Maxim Matiushkin

BOOK III

CHAPTER ONE

The Russian Land

R USSIA, or as some say White Russia, is generally called Muscovy, after the principal and capital city, which lies in the center of the country.[1] One of the outermost parts of Europe, it borders on Asia and is of enormous extent. From west to east, it spans 30° or 450 leagues, from north to south 16° or 240 leagues. When one considers the area now subject to the power of the Tsar, he finds that its northern border reaches beyond the Arctic Circle to the Arctic Ocean, and its eastern border is the great river Ob, which flows across the land of the Nogai Tatars. On its southern borders live the Crimean or Perekop Tatars, and Russia's neighbors on the west are Lithuania, Poland, Livonia, and Sweden.

Russia's territory is divided into various principalities or provinces, most of which are named in the Grand Prince's title. First and foremost among them is the principality of Volodomir, or Vladimir as they now call it, situated between the Volga and the Oka. It still includes the old town and castle of that name. The town was built by Grand Prince Volodomir [Monomakh] in A.D. 928, and he and succeeding grand princes resided there until Grand Prince [Ivan] Danilov[ich] Mikhailovich transferred the capital to Moscow.[2] Other principalities

---

[1] Although one might think that Olearius is confusing Belorussia and Muscovy, in fact toward the end of the fifteenth century and at the beginning of the sixteenth the Poles and the Lithuanians called Muscovite Russia "White" and Belorussia "Black." See Vakar, p. 202. Evidently the practice spread, for the Englishman Clement Adams, writing in the second half of the sixteenth century, called Muscovy "White Russia." See Hakluyt, I, 277. Olearius may have taken this terminology either from Herberstein, or from Adams, whose work he also knew.

[2] The chronicles state that Vladimir Monomakh founded the city in 1108. Ivan Kalita, as he is better known to students of Russian history, established his residence in Moscow rather than Vladimir when he was named Grand Prince by the Mongol Khan in 1328. Rudnitskii and Larin, pp. 6, 18.

formerly had their own princes and sovereigns who governed them, but as a result of wars—most of them waged by the tyrant Ivan Vasil'-evich—now all are subject to the Tsar's scepter and to Muscovy.

Through these territories and provinces flow many fine, long, navigable rivers. I may say, indeed, that the like can hardly be found anywhere in Europe. The chief of these rivers is the Volga, whose length from Nizhnii Novgorod to the Caspian Sea we calculated as 500 leagues; and this does not count its flow from its sources to Nizhnii, which is over a hundred leagues more. The Dnepr or Boristhenes is also an excellent river. It divides Russia from Lithuania and falls into the *Pontus Euxinus,* or Black Sea. Another large river is the Dvina which falls into the White Sea at Archangel. The Oka and the Moscow also are sizable rivers, but somewhat smaller than the other three. Many less important streams, of which we shall not speak, provide a livelihood to those who live along them, both by their convenience for trade and by their bountiful fisheries. It is worth noting that the sources of these rivers are not in mountains or hills, as is usual (for these are lacking throughout the grand princedom), but in fields, swamps, and sandy places.

In Russia there are many large and, in their way, noble cities. Chief among them are Moscow, Great Novgorod, Nizhnii Novgorod, Pskov, and Smolensk. (The latter at first belonged not to Russia but to the Lithuanians and the King of Poland, as one may read in Petrejus's *Muscovitische Chronica.*[3] Then in 1514 the Muscovites took it. In 1611 it was recaptured by King Sigismund of Poland. In 1632 Grand Prince Mikhail Feodorovich besieged it again but was obliged to raise the siege ingloriously and with great losses. Just recently, in 1654, the city was transferred by treaty to the Grand Prince.) Other towns are Archangel, Tver, Torzhok, Riazan, Tula, Kaluga, Rostov, Pereiaslavl, Iaroslavl, Uglich, Vologda, Vladimir, and Staraia Rusa. Some think that Russia acquired its name from the last of these. The cities I have listed are the most notable in Russia, but there are also a great many small towns and hamlets, and innumerable villages. There are fortresses in many cities, and in most cases, like the cities themselves,

---

[3] Peter Petrejus, a Swede, spent four years in Russia's service during the Time of Troubles and subsequently was sent on several missions from Sweden to Russia. His book, *Regni Muscovitici Sciographia,* first published in Stockholm in 1615, is considered one of the most informative reports on Muscovite Russia. See Adelung, II, 238–58.

they are built of timbers and beams laid upon one another, which makes them vulnerable to fire. There are also good towns in Kazan, Astrakhan, and other Tatar lands that have been subjugated to the Grand Prince. However, since these do not belong to Russia proper, we shall examine them in the account of our journey [to Persia].

Since Moscow is the capital and chief city of the whole grand princedom, it is decidedly worth our while to give it more detailed attention. It took its name from the Moscow River, which flows through the southern part of the city and washes the red wall [described below]. Baron von Herberstein writes of having heard from others that the elevation of the pole from the horizon at Moscow is 58°; and on a June 9th, with his own astrolabe, he found the elevation of the sun at high noon to be 58°. Supposing the sun by the new [Gregorian] calendar to be at 18° of Gemini and to have a declination of 23°, when one subtracts the latter from the elevation of the sun he obtains 35° as the elevation of the equator. If one subtracts this figure from a full quadrant of 90°, he obtains a remainder of 55° for the elevation, and not [58°] as Herberstein claimed. Incidentally, even if we count by the old [Julian] calendar the answer still does not accord with his opinion. From repeated investigations I personally found the elevation of the pole to be 55° 36′ latitude. In my first edition, through a typographical error, 56° [rather than 55°] was given. Moscow's longitude is 66°, as far as I could determine at the time of the moon's passage across the meridian.[4]

This city lies in the middle of the country, in its bosom, as it were. The Muscovites calculate that it stands 120 leagues from all its borders, but leagues are not the same everywhere. The circumference of the city is reckoned to be three leagues; earlier it was once again as large. Matthiae a Michovia writes that in his time Moscow was twice as large as Florence in Tuscany, or Prague in Bohemia.[5] However, in

[4] The new calendar, adopted in 1582 by Pope Gregory XIII, differed from the old by ten days. The Catholic countries adopted the new calendar almost immediately, but Protestant countries did not follow suit until the eighteenth century.

Olearius's figure for Moscow's longitude is very different from what one finds on a present-day map, but it must be pointed out that now measurements are made from Greenwich, whereas then longitudinal determinations were made on a different basis.

[5] Matthiae a Michovia, a learned physician of Cracow, visited Russia in 1517 and subsequently published one of the earliest foreign accounts of that land: *Descriptio Sarmatiarum* (Cracow, 1521). On this work, see Adelung, I, 179–81. Giles Fletcher, who was Elizabeth of England's envoy to the Tsar, reported in 1588—just 17 years after the Tatars had destroyed Moscow—that the Russian capital was larger than London. See Bond, p. 17.

1571, the time of the great Crimean Tatar invasion, it was completely burned, up to the Kremlin walls. The same thing happened again in 1611, when the Poles put the torch to it.[6] This is discussed by Helmoldus in his *Chronica [Slavorum]*; by Chytraeus in *Saxonia*, in his account of that year; by Metteranus[7] (under the year 1572); and by Petrejus in *Muscovitische Chronica*, p. 40. We were told that as a result of that fire there are, even now, as many as 40,000 [*sic*] ruined sites.

The homes in the city (except for the stone residences of the boyars, some of the wealthiest merchants, and the Germans) are built of pine and spruce logs laid one on top of another and crosswise [at the ends], as may be seen from some of the drawings. The roofs are shingled and then covered with birch bark or sod. For this reason they often have great fires. Not a month, nor even a week, goes by without some homes —or, if the wind is strong, whole streets—going up in smoke. Several nights while we were there we saw flames rising in three or four places at once. Shortly before our arrival, a third of the city burned down, and we were told that the same thing happened four years earlier. When such disasters occur, the streltsi and special guards are supposed to fight the fires. They never use water, but instead quickly tear down the houses nearest the fire, so that it will lose its force and go out. For that purpose every soldier and guard is obliged to carry an axe with him at night. So that the stone palaces and cellars may be spared from spreading flames, they have very small windows, and these may be sealed by sheet-metal shutters. Those whose houses are destroyed in a fire can quickly obtain new ones. Outside the white wall [treated below] is a special market with many partly assembled houses. One can buy one of these and have it moved to his site and set up at little expense.

The streets are broad, but in the fall and in rainy weather they are a sea of mud. For that reason, most of the streets are covered with round logs, laid parallel to one another, so that one can walk across as readily as on a bridge.

The city is divided into four main districts. The first is called Kitai-

---

[6] This occurred during the Time of Troubles. In March 1611, the people of Moscow rose up against their conquerors, and in an effort to repel the insurgents the Polish occupiers set the city afire. See *Istoriia Moskvy*, I, 334–39. Other great fires occurred in 1626 and 1629. Sytin, pp. 84, 88.

[7] Emanuel van Meteren (1535–1612), a Flemish historian, published *Historia; oder Eigentliche und warhaffte Beschreibung aller furnehmen Kriegshandel* in 1596.

gorod, or "the middle city," since it occupies the most central area, indicated in the map by the letter B.[8] It is surrounded by a thick stone wall which they call "the red wall." On the south side, as already mentioned, the wall is washed by the Moscow River, and on the north by the Neglinnaia, which unites with the Moscow behind the Kremlin. About half of this district is occupied by the Grand Prince's castle, the Kremlin, which itself has the breadth and extent of a respectable city.[9] The castle is surrounded by triple stone walls and a deep moat, and is defended with fine weapons and soldiers. Within are many magnificent stone palaces, churches, and other buildings, which are inhabited or frequented by the Grand Prince, the Patriarch, the foremost state counselors, and magnates. The previous Grand Prince, Mikhail Feodorovich, who was alive at the time of our visit, had fine stone palaces and also built a splendid palace in the Italian style for his son, the present Grand Prince. However, for his health's sake, so they say, he [Mikhail] lived in a wooden dwelling. The present Patriarch also ordered an extremely sumptuous residence built, which is scarcely inferior to the Grand Prince's.[10]

In addition to two cloisters, one inhabited by monks and the other by nuns, there are 50 stone churches here. Of these the foremost and largest are the Troitskaia, the Presviataia Maria, the Mikhail Arkhangelskii (in which the tsars are buried), and the Sviatoi Nikolai. The one to our left as we went to the audience hall has great double doors, which are entirely covered by thick silver leaf. These churches, like the stone churches all over the country, have five white cupolas, each of which is topped by a triple, eight-ended cross. The cupolas of the Kremlin churches are overlaid with a smooth, thick layer of gold leaf which sparkles brilliantly in bright sunshine, and gives the entire city a beautiful appearance from afar. Some of us, on approaching the city, said that it shines like Jerusalem from without but is like Bethlehem inside.

[8] The letters on Olearius's plan of Moscow are not shown in the adaptation included here. See map facing p. 151.

[9] The Kremlin is not usually considered part of Kitaigorod, which became a distinct section of the city much later than the Kremlin—in 1534, when it was enclosed by a wall. *Kitai* means China in Russian, and some suppose that there was a connection between Kitaigorod and China; but the name Kitaigorod derived rather from the old Russian word *kitai*, which refers to the mode of construction of the wall that enclosed it on the north, west, and south. See Tikhomirov, *Rossiia v XVI stoletii*, p. 75.

[10] It was built between 1642 and 1655. See *Istoriia Moskvy*, I, 643. Paul of Aleppo, who was in Russia during the 1650's, describes it in *The Travels of Macarius*, II, 224–26.

In the middle of the Kremlin square stands the highest tower of all, the bell tower of Ivan the Great, which is also covered with gold leaf. Near it stands another tower, in which hangs a very large bell of 356 hundredweight, cast in the reign of Boris Godunov. This bell is rung during great processions, on holidays, and when a Grand Ambassador enters the city or is given a public audience. It is set in motion by 24 or more people who stand below in the square. On either side of the bell tower hang two long ropes, with small ropes attached at the bottom for the many people required to pull. To prevent [excessive] swinging and [consequent] danger to the tower, this bell is rung gently; several people are posted above, by the bell, to help put the tongue in motion.

Within the Kremlin are also located the Grand Prince's treasury, stocks of food, and powder magazines. Outside of the Kremlin in Kitaigorod, to the right of the great Kremlin gates, stands a skillfully constructed church, the Holy Trinity; when it was almost finished, the architect's eyes were put out by the tyrant to render him incapable of making another like it.[11] Near the church, on the ground, lie two great stationary iron guns trained on the great road by which the Tatars are likely to invade the city.

Before the Kremlin is the largest and best market square in the city. All day long it is full of tradespeople, both men and women, and slaves and idlers. Some women usually stand near the stage mentioned above selling linen; others hold in their mouths and offer for sale rings, usually set with turquoise. I heard that along with these they offer something else for sale as well.[12] In the market place and in the neighboring streets, the wares and craft articles are displayed in stalls in particular locations, so that articles of one kind are all found in a single place. Sellers of silk and cloth, goldsmiths, saddlemakers, shoemakers, tailors, furriers, belt- or girdle-makers (*Bundmacher oder Korsner*), hat makers, and others each have their special streets where they sell their wares. This arrangement is very convenient, for every-

---

[11] Although this is an arresting tale, there is no evidence to support it. See V. L. Snegirev, *Pamiatnik arkhitektury*, pp. 30–31. The fact that this story enjoyed wide currency tells something of the popular image of Ivan IV.

[12] Olearius was rightly informed about the character of these women. When another foreign visitor, a Pole named Tanner, asked about them, he was told that they were prostitutes. Kurts, *Sochinenie Kil'burgera*, p. 484.

one knows where to go to find [what he wants].[13] Also near the Kremlin, on a street to the right, is their ikon market, where they sell only
painted pictures of the ancient saints. They do not call it a trade in
ikons [i.e., not buying and selling], but an exchange for money, and
this does not allow for much haggling.

Farther along on the right as one goes from the ambassadors' residence to the Kremlin is a special place where, in good weather, the
Russians sit out in the open, having themselves shaved and their hair
cut. They call it the louse market. The place is so thickly covered with
shorn hair that walking there is like walking on cushions. In this section live most of the gosti or leading merchants, and also some Muscovite princes.

The second district of the city is called Tsargorod or "the Tsar's
city." It is laid out like a half-moon and is surrounded by a strong
stone wall that, because of its color, they call the white wall. The Neglinnaia River flows through its center. Here reside many magnates
and Moscow princes, noblemen, notable citizens, and merchants who
conduct their commerce hither and yon out in the country. Many artisans, especially bakers, also live here. In Tsargorod are located the
bread and flour stalls, the butchers' blocks, the cattle market, and taverns selling beer, mead, and vodka. His Tsarist Majesty's stable is also
in this district. Here as well—at the place on the Neglinnaia that they
call the *Pogannyi prud*,[14] is a casting works where many metal guns
and large bells are made. Hans Falck, a very experienced master from
Nuremberg, works here. Merely by observing him at work some of
the Russians learned casting. By a special method, he made a weapon
from which 26 pounds of iron may be shot with 25 pounds of powder.
On that account he gained such great renown in Holland that he is
mentioned in the Dutch edition of Metteranus's work.

The third district of Moscow, Skorodom, is the outermost part, en-
closing Tsargorod on the east, north, and west.[15] They say that before
the Tatars burned Moscow, Skorodom had a perimeter of five leagues.
A stream called the Iauza flows through it and unites with the Mos-

[13] On the organization of trade in Kitaigorod, see *Istoriia Moskvy*, I, 428–36.

[14] *Pogannyi prud* means polluted or dirty pond. It was later cleaned up and renamed.

[15] After a high earthen wall was built around this part of the city in 1637, it became known
as *Zemlianyi Gorod* (earthen-walled quarter). Kliuchevskii, *Skazaniia inostrantsev*, pp. 229–30.

cow. In this district is located the wood market and the house market mentioned above, where one may purchase a house that can be built in another part of the city in just two days. [Skorodom means quick house.] The logs are already joined together, and one needs only to assemble the parts and to chink [the cracks] with moss.

The fourth section of the city, the *Streletskaia sloboda* [streltsi quarter or suburb] lies to the south of the Moscow River, toward the Tatars, and is surrounded by a barrier of timbers and wooden fortifications. They say that this district was built by Vasilii, the tyrant's father, for the foreign soldiers—Poles, Lithuanians, and Germans—and because of the frequent drinking bouts was called Naleika, from the word "Nalei!," which in their language means "Fill your glasses!" Because the foreigners drank more than the Muscovites, and since it was impossible to expect that this customary, and even inborn, vice could be curtailed, they were allowed [a whole suburb in which] to drink freely. However, in order that this bad example might not take hold among the Russians (who are also extremely inclined to revelry and drinking, but were allowed to drink only on the greatest holidays), the wet brotherhood had to live alone on the other side of the river. One may read of this in Herberstein and in Guagnino. At the present time the streltsi and other common people live in this section.

Within and without the walls surrounding the city of Moscow are many churches, chapels, and monasteries. In the first edition I fixed their number at 1,500, which Mr. Johann Ludwig Gottfried (in his *Archontologia Cosmica,* p. 467) considered very surprising and even unbelievable. As a matter of fact I set the figure too low; for afterward further information was given me, partly by our fellow countrymen who have known the city many years and partly by some Muscovites who came to Holstein last year (to arrest the False Shuiskii,[16] who had been there for some time). I had occasion to see these Russian visitors daily, and they agreed unanimously that there are more than two thousand churches, monasteries, and chapels in Moscow.

At present almost every fifth house is a chapel, since every magnate builds a private chapel and maintains a personal priest at his own expense. Only a magnate and his own household worship God in these

---

[16] The bizarre career of "the false Shuiskii," who was born Timoshka Ankudinov, is treated at length by Olearius. See pp. 191–95.

chapels.[17] By an order of the present Patriarch, in consideration of the frequent fires, most of the wooden chapels have been torn down and replaced by stone ones. Some of the chapels are no more than 15 feet wide on the inside. We have now said enough about Moscow.

Because Archangel is an important commercial city and, so far as I know, has not yet been described anywhere, I shall take some notice of it here.[18] On maps, as well as in the atlas, this city is called St. Michael the Archangel, but the Russians ordinarily call it Arkhangelsk. It lies far to the north in the Dvina country at the place where the Dvina River divides, flowing thence to either side of Pudozhemskii Island and into the White Sea. The city and its harbor are relatively new. Formerly ships entered the left arm of the Dvina by the St. Nicholas Monastery, whence the name St. Nicholas harbor. Sand silting down caused the mouth to become too shallow, however, and since the right arm was deeper it came into wider use, and the city was built there.[19] They say that the city itself is not very large, but it has been made famous by the many foreign merchants who trade there. For every year ships with all kinds of goods come there from the Netherlands, England, and Hamburg. At the same time, merchants from all over Russia, especially the Germans from Moscow, collect there, and in the winter return home with their goods on sleighs.

The present Grand Prince has set up a large customshouse, and duties are collected by the voevoda, who lives in the castle. Since these duties are somewhat burdensome to the merchants, and since His Royal Swedish Majesty asks only a 2 per cent duty on goods imported through Livonia at Narva, it is supposed that the greater part of the commerce will be drawn away from Archangel and directed across the Baltic Sea to Livonia.[20] This route is also much less dangerous.

[17] Many notable families maintained their own chapels because they did not wish to have their womenfolk attend public churches. Rushchinskii, p. 62.

[18] More than two centuries later, B. G. Kurts (*Sochinenie Kil'burgera*, p. 422) credited Olearius with being the first foreigner to describe Archangel. For an interesting account of the trade at Archangel, see Kostomarov, *Ocherk*, pp. 65ff.

[19] In 1584.

[20] Sweden had a decided interest in the transfer of Western trade with Russia to the eastern Baltic ports, which were under her control. Russia opposed such a shift, but she sometimes feigned interest in order to exact better terms from the English and Dutch merchants who profited from the Archangel trade. To bring about the transfer, Sweden reduced duties on goods imported through her eastern Baltic ports; but Russia countered in 1652 by increasing the levies at Novgorod on goods coming there from Swedish territory. Olearius, who evidently was unaware of these maneuvers, was wrong in expecting the Archangel trade to decline in

In a bay on the White Sea, not far from Archangel, are three islands lying close to one another. The largest is Solovka, the others Anzer and Kuzov.[21] On Solovka is a monastery in which a Russian saint was buried. Last year, at the request of the Patriarch, the Grand Prince ordered the saint's coffin dug up and transferred to Moscow, of which more below.[22] Some say that former grand princes hid a great treasure on this island, which is high-lying and rocky, with steep banks, and not easily accessible.[23]

Inasmuch as its many provinces are situated far apart, and even in different climate zones, the character of the air, the weather, and the soil in the grand princedom is not uniform. In the Moscow region and neighboring areas, the air is generally fresh and healthy. As everyone writes, and as the Russians themselves say, little is heard here of epidemic diseases or great plagues; moreover, one meets many very old people. It is therefore very surprising that this year (1654), at the time of the campaign at Smolensk, a great, virulent plague broke out in Moscow. They say that people who leave their houses believing themselves healthy fall down in the streets and die. Therefore Moscow is now closed to entry and departure.[24]

---

the near future. His judgment was probably based upon the marked decrease in the number of English and Dutch ships coming to Archangel, but this was a temporary phenomenon caused by the Anglo-Dutch war of 1652–54.

To be sure, Russia was prepared to countenance a shift of its trade with the West from Archangel to the Baltic, but only if she herself controlled an outlet to that sea. With that in mind, in 1655 she requested that Sweden cede Ingermanland to her. Sweden was no more willing to grant the request than was Russia to shift its Archangel trade to the Baltic so long as Sweden controlled the coast. When Peter the Great succeeded in seizing part of the Baltic coast, he ordered the transfer of Russian trade there. See Kurts, *Sostoianie Rossii*, pp. 48, 173–207, 231–32, and *Sochinenie Kil'burgera*, pp. 422–23.

[21] There are actually six islands in this group.

[22] The reference is to Philip, former abbot of Solovka Monastery and, later, Metropolitan of Moscow, who was exiled by Ivan IV and then slain at his order, for telling the Tsar some bitter truths.

[23] Olearius included in the 1656 edition a map showing the location of Archangel and a sketch of the harbor, which he obtained from a friend who had been there often.

[24] Because of the plague, the Patriarch of Antioch's mission to Moscow was detained for a considerable time in Kolomna. Paul of Aleppo reports that ten thousand families were victims of the plague in Kolomna and that the Tsar counted 480,000 dead in the capital. Paul is not always a reliable source, however, and these figures are doubtless exaggerated. His observations on the measures taken in Kolomna to fight the plague are noteworthy: the priests sprinkled holy water around the town and the people begged for the proclamation of a fast, as another measure of defense. The voevoda took this to heart and ordered that no animals were to be slaughtered and no taverns opened for three days. See Paul of Aleppo, I, 319–20, 328–32.

Generally the winters are so exceedingly cold all over Russia that one can hardly protect himself. Frozen noses, ears, hands, and feet are not uncommon. In 1634, when we were first there, the winter was so cold that the ground of the market place before the Kremlin cracked, leaving a fissure 20 sazhens long and a quarter of an ell wide. None of us could take fifty paces in the street with face uncovered, without feeling as though his nose and ears were frozen. I found completely true the contention of some writers that drops of water and saliva expelled from the mouth froze before they reached the ground.

Although the cold is severe in the winter, nevertheless the grass and foliage come quickly into view in the spring, and during the growing and maturation period, this land is no less productive than our Germany. Since snow always falls in large quantities and to a considerable depth, the soil and shrubs are covered and protected from the extreme cold by a blanket of snow. Because of the frozen ground and the abundant snow all over Russia and Livonia, it is easy to travel in the low Russian sleighs made of bast or linden bark. Some of us lined the sleighs with felt, over which we laid long sheepskins, which could be had very cheaply, and covered the sleighs above with felt or cloth blankets. In this way we stayed warm even in biting cold, and indeed perspired and slept while the peasants drove. For travel the Russians have small, swift horses, which are accustomed on a single feeding to trot eight, ten, and sometimes even twelve leagues, as I twice witnessed in going from Tver to Torzhok. However, like roads all over Russia, the road there has few hills and valleys. Accordingly, one can make a long journey swiftly and very cheaply.[25] Peasants hire out for two to three, or at most four, reichsthalers to take one a full 50 leagues; that was what I once paid to be taken from Revel to Riga, a distance of 50 leagues.

The weather is as hot in the summer as it is cold in the winter. The summer days are oppressive to the traveler not only because of the sun's rays, but also because of the innumerable gnats which the sun

---

[25] Traveling in Russia was not everywhere as easy and rapid as Olearius represents it. Paul of Aleppo, who traveled north to Moscow, wrote of the roads: "To travel on them was a hardship sufficient to turn the hair of young men gray." And when the ground was not covered with snow and frozen, the gyrations of the carriage "were so violent and frequent that our entrails were rent within us, and the backs of our poor horses were all but broken with the strain." *Ibid.*, I, 285, 302.

brings out of the swamps. Indeed all over Russia these pests give you no rest, day or night. Therefore, one must either lie close to the fire at night or, as mentioned above, take refuge under a mosquito netting.

This extensive country here and there is covered with shrubbery and forests of pine, birch, and nut trees; other places are waste or swampy. Nevertheless, because of the good quality of the soil, where it is worked the least bit the land is extremely fruitful (excluding the area a few leagues round about Moscow, where the soil is sandy), so that there is a great abundance of grain and pasture. The Dutch themselves admit that several years ago, at the time of the great inflation of grain prices, Russia helped them much with her grain.[26] One rarely hears of high prices in Russia. In parts of the country where grain has no market, no more land is cultivated than is needed to get through the year; provisions are not stored up, for everyone is confident of a rich annual harvest. Accordingly, they leave many fine, fertile lands uncultivated, as I myself saw in traveling through some regions with fertile black soil, on which grass grew so tall that it reached the horses' stomachs. Since it was so abundant, this grass was not collected and used for the cattle.

One should marvel, too, at what we were told in Narva. There, the soil is much better on the Russian side of the river, and everything grows faster and better than on this side of the Narva in the Allentaken district, even though one side is separated from the other only by the river. In this part of Ingermanland, as well as in Karelia, Russia, and northern Livonia, the ploughman throws the seed onto the ground not more than three weeks before John's Day [June 24th]. Because of the constant heat of the sun (which hardly passes below the horizon at sunset), one witnesses a growth such that in the course of seven weeks, or at most eight, there has been time to sow and reap. If they sowed earlier, the seed would not get started because of frost and cold winds.

[26] Some Dutchmen considered Russia "the Dutch Sicily" [i.e. breadbasket], but this was an exaggeration. Although the Dutch did import large quantities of grain from Russia at various times, they were obliged to compete with other states for this privilege. A few years before the first Holstein mission to Moscow a Dutch embassy to Russia had succeeded in obtaining only one-tenth of the grain it sought to buy. The Tsars used their grain supplies as an instrument of foreign policy during the Thirty Years War, selling it to or withholding it from different powers, as suited their purposes. See Lubimenko, *Les Relations commerciales*, pp. 195–96, 198; Vainshtein, pp. 62–69.

In the matter of the harvest, the Russians have this advantage over the Livonians; they usually can bring their grain into the barns and houses dry, whereas the Livonians are forced to dry their grain by the heat of a fire. In every country estate there is a specially built house called a *riga,* in which the unthreshed grain is placed over the beams. Then a fire is set in a stove something like a bake-oven, and the grain is dried by the rising heat. It often happens that the rigas and the grain go up in smoke. The grain, if it has been a bit too long in such a drying room, is not as good for seed as that which has dried by itself.

In some places, especially in Moscow, there are also fine garden plants, such as apples, pears, cherries, plums, and red currants. Thus the actual situation here is very different from the one depicted by Herberstein, Guagnino, and others, who contend that, because of the extreme cold, there are no fruits or delicious apples to be found in Russia. Among other good apples, there is one kind whose flesh is so tender and white that if you hold it up to the sun you can see the seeds. However, although they are of excellent appearance and taste, they cannot be stored long, unlike German apples, because of their extremely high water content.

They also have all sorts of kitchen vegetables, notably asparagus as thick as a thumb, which I myself sampled in Moscow at the home of a good friend of mine, a Dutch merchant. Besides, they grow good cucumbers, onions, and garlic, in great quantities. The Russians have never planted lettuce or other salad greens; they paid them no attention and not only did not eat them but even laughed at the Germans who did, saying that they ate grass. Now some of them are beginning to try salad.[27] They grow melons everywhere in enormous quantities, thus providing an important article of trade and nutriment. The melons grown here are great not only in number but also in size, and are so delicious and sweet that they may be eaten without sugar. In 1643 a good friend sent me a pud of these melons when I left Moscow.

The Russians have their own special methods of planting and cultivating melons, which are described in part by Herberstein. They soften the seeds in sweet milk, and sometimes in standing rainwater

---

[27] Yet a foreign visitor to Russia in 1678 found the Muscovites still astonished at people who ate salad greens. Kurts, *Sochinenie Kil'burgera,* p. 521.

mixed with old sheep dung. Then they arrange a mixture of horse manure and straw on the ground into a bed two ells deep. On top it is covered with good soil, in which they make small holes about half an ell wide. They plant the seeds in the middle so that they will be warmed not only below, but on all sides, from the collected heat of the sun, which helps them along. At night they cover these mounds against the frost with little roofs made of mica. Occasionally these roofs are left during the day as well. After a while they cut off the shoots that have grown out of the side, and at certain times the ends of shoots also. Thus by their industry and care they assist the growth.

We were told also about an exotic melon, more properly a gourd, which grows beyond Samara between the Volga and the Don. This variety is similar in size and type to ordinary melons, but its shape is that of a lamb. Therefore the Russians call it *baranets*—(lamb).[28] The stem is attached to the hilum [navel], and wherever the fruit turns (for during growth it changes its place insofar as the stem permits), there the grass withers away, or as they say, is consumed by the melon. When the melon ripens, the stem also withers, and the fruit gets a furry skin like that of a lamb. Supposedly, the skin can be dressed and prepared for use against the cold. In Moscow we were shown some pieces of skin, torn from a blanket, which were said to have been from a baranets melon. It was tender and crinkled like the skin of a newborn lamb. [Joseph] Scaliger, in *Exercitationes*, p. 181, mentions this fruit, which, when it is surrounded by various grasses, attains full growth like a lamb in pasture, but when these are wanting, wastes away and perishes. The Russians say that the fruit quickly matures. They also hold to be true what Scaliger further says, *viz.* that no animals but wolves attack this fruit, thanks to which [it may be used] to trap them.

Formerly Moscow had few pretty herbs and flowers. However, soon after we were there, the last Grand Prince ordered that a fine garden be planted and that it be beautified with various costly herbs and flowers. Until then the Russians knew nothing of fine cultivated [double] roses, but were limited to wild roses and eglantine, with which they ornamented their gardens. Some years ago, however, Peter Marselis, a leading merchant, brought there from the garden of my

[28] Herberstein (II, 74–75) also describes this plant, although not just as Olearius does.

most gracious Prince, in Gottorp, the first double and Provence roses, and they were well accepted.[29] In Muscovy there are no walnuts or grapes, but all kinds of wine are imported through Archangel by Dutch and other ships. Now wine is also obtained from Astrakhan, where they have begun to cultivate the vine. We will say more of this below.

From the foregoing it may be inferred that the absence of certain fruits and plants is to be attributed not so much to the soil and air as to the negligence or ignorance of the inhabitants. They have no lack of those fruits of the soil essential for the ordinary nourishment of life. They raise great quantities of flax and linen, which are therefore very cheap. Honey and wax are found in the forests in such abundance that in spite of the amount used in meads—and in wax candles, which they use for their own needs as well as for divine worship—large amounts of both can be exported. Most of these goods are sent abroad by way of Pskov.

Throughout Russia, and in Livonia as well, wherever the forest has not been burned off to prepare fields for cultivation, the land is covered with woods and shrubbery. Therefore, there is much wood and field game. Birds are so plentiful that the Russians do not value them as much as we, who consider them a rarity. The peasants get very little for grouse, heath cocks, hazel hens of all sorts, wild geese, and ducks. Cranes, swans, and small birds like fieldfare, thrushes, larks, and finches—though often encountered—are not considered worth hunting and eating. Storks are not to be seen either here or in Livonia.

The forests also abound with various wild animals, with the exception of deer, which they do not have at all, or which, as others say, they rarely see. Elk, wild boars, and rabbits are very plentiful. In some places, for example throughout Livonia, the rabbits are the usual gray in the summer but snow-white in the winter. It is surprising that in Courland, which is separated from Livonia only by the Dvina, the rabbits remain gray in winter. Whenever the Dvina is frozen over,

[29] This is but one of the many services performed for the Russian crown by this Hamburg merchant who resided in Moscow. In addition to promoting the development of the iron industry in Russia, which is treated below, and other economic enterprises, Marselis frequently served the Tsar on diplomatic missions. He was one of the most influential foreigners in Russia in the seventeenth century. See Amburger's *Die Familie Marselis*, pp. 81–85, on Marselis's relations with the Holstein embassy.

gray rabbits may be taken in Livonia, where they are called refugees from Courland. . . .[30] As well as edible game, one sees also many predatory and inedible beasts, such as bears, wolves, lynx, tigers, foxes, sables, and marten, whose skins are an important item of Russian trade.

Since there are ample pasture lands, they have many horned cattle —cows, oxen, and sheep—which are sold for very little. Once, during our first trip to Ladoga, we bought a fat, though not a large, ox (for in Russia the cattle are generally small) for two thalers, and a sheep for ten kopeks. The flowing waters and the stagnant lakes, of which there are many in Russia, teem with fish of all kinds except carp, which are not found in Livonia either. In Astrakhan, however, we saw many unusually large carp, caught in the Volga, which could be bought for a schilling apiece. They had coarse, tough flesh and were not very tasty.

Among minerals, mica is most important. It is obtained in certain areas where quarrying is done, and is used all over Russia for windows. The country formerly had no mines, but a few years ago one was opened in Tula, on the Tatar frontier, 26 leagues from Moscow.[31] It was brought into operation by some German miners sent here by His Excellence the Elector of Saxony, at His Tsarist Majesty's request. To the present day this mine gives a good yield, especially of iron. One and a half leagues from this mine is an iron forge, built between two hills in a pleasant valley, by a handy brook.[32] Here iron is smelted and forged into ingots, and all sorts of articles are cast. Mr. Peter Marselis manages the forge according to a special contract concluded with the Grand Prince. Every year he furnishes His Tsarist Majesty's arsenal with a certain number of iron bars, some heavy guns, and many thousands of pounds of ball. For that reason, now as in the past he enjoys

[30] I have omitted a paragraph in which Olearius explains, not very persuasively, why some rabbits change color and others do not.

[31] Actually, iron ore was mined and processed in Russia in the last half of the sixteenth century. See *Ocherki istorii . . . Konets XV v.*, pp. 52ff.

[32] The Tula ironworks was established by a Dutch merchant, Andrew Vinius, in 1637, pursuant to a contract made with the Russian government five years before. To help finance the enterprise, Vinius took Marselis and F. Akema into the company. Later Vinius was ousted and the others took charge, expanding their operations and initiating new ones in other areas. Marselis's high standing with the government is apparent from a letter of privilege given him in 1638. See *Sobranie*, Vol. III, No. 109. A 1644 grant of the right to build new iron enterprises, including all terms of the contract, is in *ibid.*, No. 118. The history of the iron enterprises associated with Vinius, Marselis, and Akema is briefly summarized in *Ocherki istorii . . . XVII v.*, pp. 88–90.

the Grand Prince's special favor and respect. He also conducts other big commercial operations in Moscow.

Fifteen years ago, in Tsar Mikhail Feodorovich's lifetime, someone reported a vein of gold somewhere in Russia, but didn't know how to mine it. Accordingly, the discoverer not only did not get rich, as he had anticipated he would, but on the contrary was reduced to poverty. Those who promise to enrich the sovereigns through new discoveries —as often happens in the courts of princes—at the tsar's court secure little gratification or reward. The Grand Prince was pleased to have pointed out to him any new way of increasing his treasury. But in order that the Tsar might avoid losses in case of fraud or failure, the proponent had to carry out the experiment at his own expense. If he had no means, some funds were advanced on the basis of a definite security. If the experiment succeeded he was richly rewarded; but in the opposite case he, and not the Grand Prince, sustained the loss.

In corroboration of this, I can cite the example of the gold miner just mentioned. He was a prominent English merchant and a good friend of mine, whose name I am honor-bound not to reveal. An upright and benevolent person, he had long lived in Moscow, where he carried on a lucrative trade. When, on the basis of the particular qualities of a certain soil, he announced that he hoped to find gold-bearing ore, the Grand Prince was pleased to grant him money, on security, to proceed. However, this good fellow's enterprise miscarried, and the labor and expense were lost. Since his own property did not suffice to repay the sum the Grand Prince had advanced, he was put into the debtors' prison. Later, at the request of some of his guarantors, he was released and allowed to go about asking money of good people, in order to collect enough to satisfy the Grand Prince and his guarantors, and then leave the country. He himself told me very movingly and in great detail about his misfortune and his Russian trial, which took place during my last visit to Moscow [in 1643].

[*The next two chapters of the original, Chapters Three and Four, are omitted, since they digress from the main theme; the first is devoted to the Samoeds, an eccentric tribe of far northern Russia, the second to the people of Greenland.*]

CHAPTER TWO

The Russian People

WE WILL FIRST examine the external features of the Muscovites, that is, their appearance, their build, and their clothing; and then we will turn to their internal or spiritual qualities, their capabilities, and their customs.

Russian men, in the main, are tall, stout, strong people, and their skin is of the same color as that of other Europeans. They place great store by long beards and large stomachs, and those who have them are held in high regard. (His Tsarist Majesty designates merchants who are well endowed in these respects to attend public audiences given ambassadors, supposing that his dignity is thereby enhanced.) Their mustaches droop down over their mouths. The priests wear their hair long, so that it hangs down onto their shoulders; all the others are close cropped. The magnates even have their heads shaved, imagining this to be an ornament. [Saint] Ambrose does not share this opinion. He says: "From trees we may judge wherein the beauty of the human head consists. Take the leaves away from a tree and the whole tree becomes unpleasant to the eye." Perhaps this idea was taken from Ovid, who wrote, "A head without hair is as repulsive/ As a bull without horns, a tree without leaves, a field without grass." However, when anyone transgresses somehow against His Tsarist Majesty or learns that he has fallen into disgrace, he allows his hair to grow long and in disorder for as long as the disgrace endures.[1] They may have adopted this custom from the Greeks, whom they generally strive to imitate. For Plutarch tells (*Quaestiones Romanae*, XIV, 267) that when a great misfortune befell them they went with long, disheveled hair; women in such circumstances sheared their heads.

The women are of average height, are generally well built, and

---

[1] George Turberville, an English visitor to Russia in 1568, wrote a poetic description of this custom: "It is their common use to shave or els to sheare / Their heads, for none in all the land long lolling locks doth weare, / Unlesse perhaps he have his sovereigne prince displeas'd, / For then he never cuts his haire, untill he be appeas'd." Hakluyt, II, 104.

are delicate in face and body. In the towns, however, they all paint
and powder themselves so crudely and obviously that they look as
though someone had thrown a handful of flour at their faces and
colored their cheeks with a paintbrush. They also color their eyebrows
and eyelashes black, or sometimes brown.

Some women who are naturally prettier than rouge can make them
are persuaded by neighbors, or others whose company they keep, to
paint themselves in this fashion, so that their natural beauty should
not give offense to those who require artificial embellishment. Something of the kind occurred while we were there. The wife of one of
the foremost magnates and boyars, Prince Ivan Borisovich Cherkasskii, who had a lovely face, at first declined to rouge herself. However, the wives of other boyars began to harass her for being scorn-
ful of the customs and habits of the country and for shaming other
women by her conduct. They also worked through their husbands
and [eventually] brought it about that this naturally beautiful woman
was obliged to powder and rouge herself and, so to speak, to light a
candle in bright sunshine. Since powdering and rouging is done openly,
a box of rouge is usually among the presents the groom sends his bride
on the eve of the marriage.

Married women roll their hair up under their hats; young ladies
leave it hanging down their backs, plaited into a braid, from the bottom of which hangs a red silk tassel. They cut off the hair of children
under ten years of age, girls as well as boys, leaving only long locks
on either side. To distinguish girls from boys, they hang large silver
or bronze rings in the girls' ears.

The men's clothing is much like the Greeks'. Their shirts are wide,
but short, scarcely covering the seat; the collar is flat and smooth,
without pleats; and the back, from the shoulder down, is covered
with a triangular [piece of cloth] and sewn with red silk. Some have
gussets under the armpits, and also on the sides, made very skillfully
of red satin. The wealthy have their shirt collars (a good thumb in
width), as well as a strip in the front (from top to bottom), and the
places around the cuffs, embroidered with multicolored tied silk, and
sometimes with gold and pearls; such decorative collars extend out
over the cloaks; they are fastened with two large pearls, or with gold
or silver clasps. Their trousers, which are broad at the top, may be
drawn in or opened out by strings. Over the shirt and trousers, they

wear tight cloaks called "kaftans," which are like our jerkins; but theirs hang to the knees, and have long sleeves, which are gathered into folds at the wrists. The collar, which rises behind the head, is a fourth of an ell long and broad, lined on the underside with velvet, and with gold brocade among the wealthy. Over the kaftans some people wear still another garment which reaches down to the calf or below and is called a *feriaz*. Both of these garments are made of cotton, calico (*kindiak*), taffeta, damask, or satin, depending upon what the wearer can afford. The feriaz' is lined with cotton. When they go out, over all these they don ankle-length cloaks, which in most cases are made of violet-blue, brown (the color of tanned leather), or dark green cloth, but sometimes many-colored damask, satin, or gold brocade. Luxurious robes, kept in the Grand Prince's treasury, are distributed among the men who attend public audiences, to increase their splendor.

These outer kaftans, or cloaks, have wide collars; and, in front, from top to bottom, and on the sides, they are drawn together with strings embroidered with gold or with pearls. Sometimes long tassels hang from the strings. The sleeves are of almost the same length as those of the kaftans, but very narrow. They are gathered at the wrists into many folds, so that [in putting one on] one is hardly able to push his hands through. Sometimes when walking, they allow the sleeves to hang free below the hand. Some slaves and rogues carry stones and bludgeons in them, which are difficult to detect. Frequently, especially at night, they attack and murder people with these weapons.

All Russian men wear hats. During public ceremonies the princes, boyars, and state counselors wear hats of black fox or sable, an ell high. Otherwise they wear velvet hats like ours, lined and trimmed with black fox and sable; however, not much fur protrudes. These hats are sewn on both sides with gold or strings of pearls. Ordinary citizens wear hats of white felt in summer and of cloth, lined with some plain fur, in winter.

For the most part, like the Poles, they wear short shoes, made of either ordinary or Persian Morocco leather and pointed in front. They know nothing of cordovan. Women, particularly young women, wear shoes with very high heels, some of them one-fourth of an ell high. The lower part of the backs of these heels are nailed all about with fine nails. In such footgear they cannot run much, because the toes of the slippers hardly reach the ground.

The ladies' attire is much like the men's, except that the outer garment is wider, though of the same cloth. The garments of wealthy women are trimmed in front with fringed braid and other golden laces; others are decorated with strings and tassels, and sometimes with large silver and pewter buttons. The sleeve is not fully sewn above, so that they may thrust their hands through and allow the sleeves to hang. However, they don't wear kaftans, much less square ones that rise up around the back of the neck. The sleeves of their blouses are six, eight, or ten ells long, and, if of light cotton, even longer, but narrow; when worn, these are drawn into small folds. On their heads they wear broad and loose hats of gold brocade, satin, or damask, with gold laces sometimes sewn with gold and pearls, and embellished with beaver fur. They wear these hats so that their hair hangs smoothly halfway down the forehead. Grown women wear large hats of fox fur.

Formerly the Germans, the Dutch, the French, and other foreigners who had come to live among them, either in the service of the Grand Prince or for trade, affected Russian clothes and styles. They were even constrained to do so in order to avoid being insulted and set upon by malicious scoundrels. However, a year ago [1652 or 1653] the present Patriarch put an end to this, on the basis of the following incident. Once during a great procession in the city, in which he himself participated, the Patriarch as usual bestowed a blessing upon the people arrayed about him. Some of the Germans standing among the Russians were not willing to bow and make the sign of the cross to the Patriarch, which he noted with indignation. Upon learning that they were Germans, he said, "It is not right that the unworthy foreigners should thus receive a blessing not intended for them." So that he might thenceforth recognize and distinguish them from the Russians, an order was issued to all the foreigners to divest themselves of Russian clothes forthwith, and to dress, in the future, in the garb of their own country.[2]

Although it appeared dangerous not to obey, some of the foreigners

---

[2] Although mention is made of this decree in other contemporary accounts, I have not found it in any collection of published documents.

were hard put to fulfill the order right away. Many of them could not obtain new clothes at once, not so much because of want of cloth and trimmings as for lack of tailors. Yet, since they were supposed to be present at court daily, they could not absent themselves without damage to their standing. Therefore each made use of whatever he had. While some borrowed clothes from friends, others donned the clothing of their fathers, grandfathers, and great-grandfathers, which had lain in trunks since the time the tyrant had taken many Livonians captive and brought them to Moscow.[3] These clothes occasioned no little laughter, not only because of the antiquated and diverse styles but also because the garments were too big for some and too small for others. Now all foreigners, no matter what their country, must always dress in the clothing of their native land so that they may be distinguished from the Russians.

In Moscow lives a certain prince named Nikita Ivanovich Romanov, who is the foremost and wealthiest person [in the realm], after the Tsar, as well as a close relative [a cousin] of the Tsar. This gay blade is fond of German music, and he not only admires the foreigners, especially the Germans, but is greatly taken also with their dress. Accordingly, he ordered Polish and German clothes made for himself, and sometimes for pleasure went hunting in them, despite the Patriarch's objections to such attire. This boyar also angered the patriarch on occasion over religious questions, by answering him curtly and impertinently. Finally, however, the Patriarch tricked him out of his [foreign] clothes and secured his renunciation of them.[4]

When you observe the spirit, the mores, and the way of life of the Russians, you are bound to number them among the barbarians. Although they preen themselves on their connection with the Greeks, they have adopted neither their language nor their art. Indeed, they have little in common with the Greeks, of whom it was said in ancient

---

[3] During the Livonian Wars, Ivan IV ordered that Livonian captives no longer be sold but instead be transported to Russia, which might then take advantage of their skills. The decree appears in *Dopolnenie*, Vol. I, No. 102. See also Tsvetaev, *Protestantsvo i protestanty*, pp. 32–46.

[4] Tsvetaev (*Protestantsvo i protestanty*, p. 761) questions Olearius's contention, arguing that Nikita was too wealthy and powerful to be done out of his clothes by a ruse and that some other, unknown consideration must have figured.

times that they alone were intelligent and discerning, and the rest, the non-Greeks, were barbarians. For the Russians do not love the liberal arts and the lofty sciences, much less occupy themselves with them. And yet it has been said: "Good instruction in the arts refines the customs and makes them secure against barbarization." Thus they remain untutored and uncouth.[5]

Although they know nothing of them, most Russians express crude and senseless opinions about the elevated natural sciences and arts, when they meet foreigners who do possess such knowledge. Thus, for example, they regard astronomy and astrology as witchcraft. They consider it unnatural for anyone to know and foretell eclipses of the sun and moon, and the movements of the stars.[6] Therefore, when we were returning from Persia, and it became known in Moscow that the Grand Prince had invited me to become his astronomer,[7] some began to say, "A sorcerer in the suite of the Holstein embassy who can tell the future from the stars will soon be back in Moscow." I learned that people were already hostile to me, and this, among other reasons, led me to decline the invitation. Moreover, the Muscovites were perhaps not interested in having me as an astronomer, but wished to keep me in the country because they learned that I had charted and mapped the Volga River and the Persian provinces through which we passed.[8] When later, in 1643, my most gracious Prince again sent me to Moscow, once for amusement I placed a glass lens over a little hole in the wall of a dark room and began to draw in bright colors what was in

[5] On science in pre-Petrine Russia, see Vucinich, Chap. 1.

[6] An Englishman in Peter the Great's service reported the case of a foreigner who, about a hundred years before, had predicted an eclipse: when it occurred, a mob demanded his execution as a sorcerer, and he had to be ushered out of the country under government protection. See Perry, pp. 209–10. Since I have not found this story elsewhere, I suspect that it is a legend inspired by Olearius's own experience and remarks, but distorted almost beyond recognition.

[7] Olearius was invited into the Tsar's service in 1639. The invitation (*Sobranie*, Vol. III, No. 110) refers to reports that "you are very learned and skilled in astronomy and geography, and the movement of the heavens, and the measurement of the earth, and [that you have] other useful skills and knowledge; and such skilled men are wanted by us, the Great Sovereign."

[8] Olearius's reasoning is interesting because it casts doubt on the authenticity of one of the rare instances in Muscovite times when the state seemed to show a concern for learning for its own sake. Other instances also appear to have been connected with utilitarian motives. For example, when Godunov sent a number of Russians abroad to study foreign languages, he evidently intended to use them as translators in the Posol'skii Prikaz. See Golitsyn, Part 3, p. 4. When the same ruler asked the well-known English mathematician, John Dee, to enter the Russian service, the invitation was prompted by Dee's reputation for knowledge of navigation and chart making. Hakluyt, II, 360–62.

the street opposite the window. The chancellor, who came in on me just then, crossed himself and said, "This is truly sorcery, especially since the horses and people are going along upside down."

Although they admire and value physicians and their art, nevertheless they will not employ the means of learning better cures that are generally resorted to in Germany and other countries, such as the dissection of human corpses and the study of skeletons. To everything of the kind they are extremely hostile. Some years ago an experienced barber, a Dutchman of jovial disposition, named Quirinus, was in the Tsar's service. He had a human skeleton hanging on the wall above a table in his room. Once he was sitting before the table playing the lute, as was his habit, when the streltsi who then always guarded the foreign quarter came toward the sound of the music and looked in through the doorway. When they saw the bones hanging on the wall, they were frightened, and especially since they saw the skeleton stir. Accordingly, they left and let it be known that the German barber had a skeleton hanging on his wall, that moved when he played the lute. The rumor reached the Grand Prince and the Patriarch, who sent others with instructions to look into the matter attentively. These people not only confirmed the testimony already given, but added that the corpse danced on the wall to the sound of the lute.

Very astonished at this, the Russians took counsel and decided that the barber must surely be a sorcerer; he and his skeleton would therefore have to be consigned to the flames. When Quirinus learned that such a dreadful end was being planned for him, he sent a leading German merchant who enjoyed the favor of the magnates to Prince Ivan Borisovich Cherkasskii, to give a veracious report and frustrate the design. The merchant said to the boyar: "The barber certainly ought not to be accused of sorcery on account of the skeleton, for in Germany the best doctors and barbers use them. Then, if some living person breaks a leg or is wounded in some part of the body or other, it is easier to know how to go about curing him. The bones moved because the wind blew in through the open window and not because the lute was played." After this the sentence was rescinded. However, Quirinus had to leave the country, and the skeleton was dragged out beyond the Moscow River and burned.

Later on they proposed to work a similar tragedy on a German painter named Johann Deterson. Four years ago, when a great fire broke out in Moscow, the streltsi came to tear down the neighboring houses to extinguish it. In so doing, they came upon an old skull in the painter's house, and would have cast it and the painter both into the fire, had not some of those present declared that German painters customarily used skulls to draw from.

With regard to intelligence, the Russians are indeed distinguished by cleverness and shrewdness. However, they use these qualities not to strive for virtue and glory, but to seek advantage and profit and to indulge their appetites. Therefore, as Jakob [Ulfeldt] says: "They are crafty and clever, stubborn, unbridled, hostile and perverse, not to say shameless, inclined to every sort of wickedness, disposed to place might above right, and divorced—believe me—from all virtue."[9]

Their cleverness and shrewdness are manifested, in their commerce, among other activities; when buying and selling for profit, they resort to any expedient they can think of to cheat a neighbor.[10] And anyone who wants to deceive them has to have a good head. For they shun truth and are so given to lying that they themselves rarely believe anyone else. Anyone who succeeds in deceiving them, they praise and consider a master. To cite an instance, some Moscow merchants invited a certain Dutchman who, in a transaction, had mulcted them of a large sum, to join their company and become their partner in trade; since he was such a master of deception, they hoped through him to have advantageous trade. It is strange that although they do not regard deception as a matter of conscience, but more as a wise and

---

[9] Krizhanich, the Croatian priest who came to Russia in the 1660's, wrote a defense of his fellow Slavs against the charges of foreign writers like Olearius, whom he mentions by name. He labels Olearius a slanderer (*laiatel'*) for, among other things, endorsing Ulfeldt's sweeping denunciation. In a chapter entitled "On the Nature of the Germans," Krizhanich launches a vigorous counterattack. Interestingly enough, he cannot suppress his admiration for certain qualities and attainments of the Germans; but overriding that is his conviction that they are a people steeped in repellent vices, traffickers with the devil, and seducers of other peoples. Fittingly enough, he calls for their expulsion from Russia. Krizhanich I, 158ff.; II, 249ff. and 271.

[10] Herberstein (I, 112–14) describes some of the tricks the Russians resorted to in his time. It is worth noting that, according to Kilburger (Kurts, *Sochinenie Kil'burgera*, p. 88), Russia's inhabitants "from the highest to the lowest, love to traffic, which is why there are more shops in the city of Moscow than in Amsterdam or in some entire kingdoms." He conceded, however, that many Russian shops were very small. In view of this great propensity for trade, one is moved to wonder why capitalism failed to develop in Russia—a question of great moment for Russian cultural history. Kilburger himself presents some interesting thoughts on the matter (*ibid.*, pp. 89–90). Additional light is provided in the interesting article by Kirchner, "Western Businessmen in Russia." It would be incorrect to assume that the foreign merchants were exemplars of honest dealing, as Kostomarov shows (*Ocherk*, especially pp. 29–34, 74–77).

praiseworthy mode of conduct, nevertheless, many of them consider it a sin not to return the excess portion when a person has mistakenly paid too much for something. They say that in such a case the money is given unknowingly and against the will, so that to keep it is theft; whereas the participant in an [ordinary] deal pays voluntarily and in full consciousness of what he is doing. In their opinion, one should trade with intelligence and wit, or not at all.

To demonstrate their craftiness, deceitfulness, and malice to neighbors who have aroused their anger and hate, the following is set forth. As theft is a vice seriously punished among them, they seek an occasion to accuse the other party of it. Thus they may go to a neighbor's to borrow money, leaving in exchange some clothing, baggage, or other things for security; and sometimes they stealthily leave something else in the house or in the neighbor's shoes, where letters, money, knives, and other small articles are usually kept. Then they make an accusation, charging that the things were stolen; when the things are found and recognized, the accused is punished. Because such deceptions and falsehoods became so widespread and generally known, however, on New Year's Day, 1634, while we were there, the Grand Prince had a new order publicly proclaimed: "no one, not even father and son, can lend money to another, give security, or enter into any obligations, without the drawing up of a paper signed by both parties. In the opposite case, all claimants will be considered suspect and may be made to pay damages to the accused." Corrupt judges themselves sometimes secretly instigate their neighbors to commit scoundrelly acts, hoping to gain advantage thereby. We shall explain more of this below.

False witness and deception are so prevalent among them that they threaten not only strangers and neighbors but also brothers and spouses. Plenty of examples of this are known. In the time of Boris Godunov (as the Narva pastor, Mr. Martin Baer,[11] who then lived in Moscow, told us), it once happened that the Grand Prince, extremely afflicted by gout, proclaimed that anyone who could deliver him from

---

[11] Baer came to Russia in 1601 as a church-school teacher and lived there 12 years, becoming a pastor in 1605. Various historians attributed to him a valuable account of Russia from 1584 to 1613, which constitutes Vol. 1 of Ustrialov, *Skazaniia sovremennikov o samozvantse.* A new edition, K. Bussov, *Moskovskaia khronika, 1584–1613,* was published in Moscow in 1961. Konrad Bussow (Bussov), Baer's father-in-law, was in the Russian service for many years. The introductory essay in the new edition demonstrates conclusively that the ac-

this ailment, no matter what his station or creed, would receive great favor and wealth. When a certain boyar's wife whose husband was mistreating her learned of this, she saw an opportunity to avenge herself. She went and reported that her husband had an effective way to help the Grand Prince but chose not to grant him this favor. The boyar was called in to the Grand Prince and questioned, but claimed to be ignorant of medical science, whereupon he was mercilessly knouted and thrown into prison. When he said that his wife had prepared this trap for him to secure revenge, and that he intended to repay her, he was beaten still more severely, and was even threatened with the loss of his life.

They promised to carry out the threat if he failed to cure the Grand Prince in short order. The good boyar was so frightened that he knew not where to begin. Nevertheless, he requested a 14-day delay in order to collect some herbs, with the aid of which he thought to seek his salvation. He wished to prolong his life at least that long, in hopes that something else might meanwhile turn up. When the reprieve was granted, he sent to Serpukhov, two days journey from Moscow on the Oka River, for a whole wagonload of assorted herbs and grasses, which grew luxuriously and abundantly there. He made a bath of these for the Grand Prince, and to the boyar's great joy, the patient's ailment passed, though perhaps not so much from the bath as of itself. The boyar was then whipped still more severely for having possessed such skill and having withheld it from the Grand Prince. At the same time he was rewarded with new clothes, 200 rubles, and 18 peasants as perpetual and hereditary property. He was strictly warned against taking revenge on his wife, and it is said that the two lived peacefully together thereafter.

Formerly, in such cases of hostile and spiteful informing, especially in cases concerning offense to His Majesty, the accused, without inquiry, argument, or reply, was sentenced to punishment and reduced to poverty, or was executed. Not only the lowly suffered, but also persons of high estate, both foreigners and natives. Cases of this sort

count was fundamentally Bussow's, although Baer assisted him in preparing it for publication, and added certain materials. See Ustrialov's Introduction, and Tsvetaev, *Protestantsvo i protestanty*, pp. 52–54, 201–11. Tsvetaev suggests that Baer, who was very hostile to the Russians, also predisposed Olearius to view them unsympathetically. Petrejus, whose work Olearius frequently cites, drew heavily on the Bussow-Baer account, although making no acknowledgement.

among the Russians are countless. Nor were ambassadors of foreign sovereigns spared. This sort of summary trial was given an ambassador of the Holy Roman Emperor, who was convicted and exiled to a far-off region. Later, in despair and in hope of better treatment, he adopted the Russian faith. He was in Moscow while we were there.[12] Something of the kind happened also to the King of France's ambassador, Charles Talleyrand, Prince of Chales [Chalais], against whom secret testimony was given, as is the Russian custom, by his malicious colleague, Jacob Rouchelle [Roussel].[13]

When, however, the authorities recognized that many would unashamedly and groundlessly inform on others solely out of hatred and enmity, it was decided to proceed more cautiously in such cases. It was ordered that henceforth in criminal cases the accuser or informer was also to be put to torture, and to reiterate the complaint under extreme pain.[14] If he adhered to his initial testimony and information, it would then be the turn of the accused [to be tortured]; although sometimes, when the case is very clear, the punishment is prescribed with no further trial. Thus, for example, when we were there, a spiteful wife informed on [her husband] a cavalryman, to the effect that he intended to poison the Grand Prince's horses and, if an opportunity presented itself, the Grand Prince himself. The wife was put to torture, but since she bore the pain and held fast to her testimony, the husband was pronounced guilty and exiled to Siberia. The wife remained in Moscow and received half her husband's annual pay for her support.

[12] The reference is to Adam Dorn, whom Olearius later refers to by name as the translator of a Latin cosmography into Russian. Dorn's arrest was not quite as groundless as Olearius portrays it. He came to Russia ostensibly en route to Persia on a diplomatic mission, but actually to conduct clandestine talks looking to the occupation of the Russian throne by a member of the Hapsburg family. See Vainshtein, pp. 26–27. On Dorn's baptism, see Tsvetaev, *Protestantsvo i protestanty*, p. 414.

[13] Olearius referred to this affair in a section of Book I that I have omitted. Although both were Frenchmen, Roussel and Talleyrand actually were employed by Sweden's King, Gustavus Adolphus, in an incredibly complex diplomatic intrigue directed against the Hapsburgs. In this scheme, Russia was encouraged to wage war against Poland, a *de facto* ally of the Hapsburgs. Roussel, who enjoyed Patriarch Filaret's favor, secured Talleyrand's arrest and exile on the charge that he was a Polish spy, when Talleyrand, officially his subordinate, endeavored to act independently in the negotiations with Russia. In spite of the French government's intervention on his behalf, Talleyrand was obliged to spend three years in Siberian exile, and was released only after Filaret's death. On this affair, which long baffled diplomatic historians, see Vainshtein, pp. 111–16, 119–20, 123ff., 135–36, and *passim;* and Rambaud, pp. 33–36.

[14] A student of judicial procedures in Muscovy has shown that Olearius here overstates the case. While torture was frequently resorted to in the investigative process, it was not "a constant and indispensable feature." This writer cites five situations in which torture was employed, all of them cases in which there was reason to doubt the trustworthiness of the witness. See Tel'berg, pp. 144–46.

Since the Russians resort to craftiness and treachery in many things, and do not keep faith with one another, it may be imagined how they feel about foreigners, and how difficult it is to trust them. If they offer friendship, they do so not out of love of virtue (which they do not respect, even though the philosopher says that it ought to be our cynosure and goal) but for advantage and profit. Therefore, one can justly say of them, "The rabble befriend you only in expectation of gain."

The Russians, and particularly those who through fortune, wealth, offices, or honors have risen above the station of the common people, are very arrogant. Far from concealing this, they openly demonstrate it by their facial expressions, words, and deeds, especially in their relations with foreigners. Just as they have less regard for foreigners than their own countrymen, similarly they consider no ruler in the world comparable to theirs in wealth, power, greatness, distinction, and virtue. They refuse any letter addressed to His Tsarist Majesty if the slightest detail of his title is omitted, or [if anything included] is strange to them.

When, a year ago, two Russian ambassadors were sent to the government of Holstein,[15] it was laughable to see how they declined to accept His Princely Excellence's letter to His Tsarist Majesty because of the superscription "uncle and brother-in-law"—the customary address to prior grand princes—until these words were eliminated. They said that they would have to answer with their lives for it, since they consider His Tsarist Majesty too lofty to be called brother-in-law by any foreign ruler. Great pains were taken to inform them of Duke Magnus of Holstein's (my most gracious Sovereign's cousin) relationship with the Tsar's forebears, in justification of the inclusion of these words. Their attitude was rather like that of the Persians with respect to Ali, their great saint and patron, of whom they say that "although not God, he is a very close relative."

The Russians are crudely self-regarding and ready to speak sharply if anyone fails to respect and treat them as they wish. The pristavs whom His Tsarist Majesty sends as his agents to receive foreign am-

---

[15] They were sent to negotiate the extradition of Timoshka Ankudinov, the false Shuiski, referred to in an earlier note. After Holstein renounced its treaty with Russia in 1640, Duke Frederick requested the return of all papers relating to it. Russia refused to comply pending payment of the sums due it under the treaty. In 1653, however, the documents were returned to Holstein as a *quid pro quo* for Ankudinov's extradition. See Kurts, *Sostoianie Rossii,* p. 129; Shcherbachev, No. 51.

bassadors are not ashamed openly to ask the ambassadors to remove their hats and dismount before the Russians. They push themselves forward in order to ride or walk ahead of the ambassadors, and perpetrate many other rude violations of courtesy. They contend that it would entail great damage to their ruler and the whole nation if they showed some civility and deference to foreign guests and the ambassadors of great sovereigns. Yet, in the words of Frederick de Merseler, in his work *Legatos,* these ambassadors "are in the image of their sovereigns and must be considered worthy of the honor accorded sovereigns."

Even the foremost Russians use crude and indiscreet terms in their letters to foreigners, but they are quite put out if we respond in kind. Nevertheless, we met some few who treated us with courtesy and kindness. It is said that formerly they were even more impolite but have been somewhat softened as a result of communication with foreigners. The above-mentioned Nikita [Romanov] surpassed them all not only in intelligence but in honesty and urbanity. He is a most valuable person and an ornament that the Russians should treasure, as will be seen from the anecdotes below.

So arrogant are the Russians that they yield nothing even to one another; they constantly strive for place and, on that account, often become involved in altercations. Something of the kind occurred once in the course of our journey, at Nizhnii Novgorod. On July 14th the state chancellor's major domo in Moscow, a notable man, came to have a look at our newly constructed ship and to greet the ambassadors. When he was invited to dinner along with the pristav, there began a bitter quarrel over precedence. *Bledin syn, sukin syn, butzfui matir* [son of a whore, son of a bitch, fuck your mother] and other vile words were the choice terms with which they vehemently belabored each other. The major domo said that since he was a nobleman and the other was of the common people, he had the right to sit in the superior place. The pristav replied that he was an official of the Grand Prince, and in deference to his master, the better place by right belonged to him. We got fed up with this and embarrassed to hear such swearing and abuse, which went on for almost half an hour; but they continued uninhibitedly until the ambassadors interfered and said, "We thought you came as friends, bringing comradeship, not trouble, and we re-

quest you to refrain from dishonoring each other in our presence."
They asked the guests to be friendly and cheerful, so that their presence would be more pleasing to us. After that they quieted down and,
when they had drunk amply, even became confidential with each
other.

The Russians are in general a very quarrelsome people who assail
each other like dogs, with fierce, harsh words. Again and again on the
streets one sees such quarrels; the old women shout with such fury
that he who is unaccustomed to it expects them at any moment to seize
each other's hair. They very rarely come to blows, however; but when
they do, they strike with their fists, beating one another with all their
might on the sides and genitals. No one has ever seen Russians chal-
lenge one another to an exchange of saber blows or bullets, as Germans
and other Europeans do. Still, there are cases when the foremost magnates, and even princes, fiercely lash at one another with knouts, while
mounted on horses. We heard reliable testimony of this, and we ourselves saw two noblemen so engaged at the entry of the Turkish ambassador.

When their indignation flares and they use swearwords, they do not
resort to imprecations involving the sacraments—as unfortunately is
often the case with us—consigning to the devil, abusing as a scoundrel,
etc. Instead they use many vile and loathsome words, which, if the
historical record did not demand it, I should not impart to chaste
ears. They have nothing on their tongue more often than "son of a
whore," "son of a bitch," "cur," "I fuck your mother," to which they
add "into the grave," and similar scandalous speech. Not only adults
and old people behave thus, but also little children who do not yet
know the name of God, or father, or mother, already have on their
lips "fuck you," and say it as well to their parents as their parents to
them.

Recently, by a public order, this foul and shameful swearing and
abuse was severely and strictly forbidden, upon pain of knouting. Certain secretly appointed people were sent to mix with the crowd on the
streets and in the markets and, with the help of streltsi and executioners assigned to them, were to seize swearers and punish them on the
spot by beating, as an object of public disgust. This habitual and deeply
rooted swearing demanded more surveillance than could be provided,

however, and caused the observers, judges, and executioners such an intolerable burden of work that they tired of spying out and punishing that which they themselves could not refrain from, and gave it up as a bad job.

However, so that swearing, abuse, and dishonor might not be leveled indiscriminately at the notables and commoners alike, the authorities ordered that anyone, Russian or foreign, who strikes or otherwise dishonors a notable or his wife, or one of the Grand Prince's aides, must pay a very heavy fine, which they call "paying for dishonoring" (*zaplatit' beschest'e*).[16] The amount of the beschest'e varies according to the quality, office, or title of the person dishonored and is called *oklad*.[17] In accordance with a special census, everyone is assigned a particular oklad. Depending upon his ancestry and worth, a boyar who has been reviled is paid 2,000, 1,500, or 1,000 thalers, or less. An official of the Tsar is awarded the amount of his annual salary. Thus, for example, since a physician earns 600 thalers (not counting his additional weekly allowance), a calumniator, on being sentenced by the court, must pay him that amount. If the physician's wife and children are insulted, the wife must be paid double, each daughter 1,800 thalers, and each son 600 thalers. If, further, the slanderer also abuses his victim's parents, grandfathers, and grandmothers—as often happens when some frivolous rascal is in a rage—he is obliged to pay equally for dishonoring them, even though they may be long since dead.[18] If it is impossible for the offender to pay what is due with all the money or proper-

---

[16] The concept of *beschest'e* goes back at least as far as Kievan times, when it was invoked in cases both of physical and of verbal abuse. Grekov, *Kiev Rus,* p. 165. In the law code of 1649, the *Ulozhenie,* a large number of the articles of Chapter Ten are devoted to beschest'e. A good recent edition of the 1649 code is Tikhomirov and Epifanov.

[17] In the *Ulozhenie,* as in old Russian usage generally, the word *oklad* does not have this connotation, but refers instead to monetary and land compensation for services. The fine itself frequently was called a beschest'e; sometimes it was simply stipulated that a given sum be paid for a beschest'e. Olearius's error can doubtless be explained by the fact that the amount of the fine, as he himself points out below, was often stated in terms of the annual salary (*oklad*) of the offended party.

[18] An examination of the *Ulozhenie* shows the beschest'e system to be more complex than Olearius makes it, although his description is essentially correct. In certain cases, prison terms and corporal punishment were prescribed, rather than fines; in others, the fine was to be set by the Tsar; and in still others, the fine was not based on annual salary. Art. 99, Chap. Ten, which deals with insults to wives and children, stipulates for offended daughters a fine not three but four times that for the father. In view of the inferior position of women in Russian society, it is curious that the preservation of their honor was taken more seriously than that of their husbands and fathers. There seems to be no ground for Olearius's assertion concerning payment for dishonoring deceased persons.

ty he possesses, then he himself is sent to the house of the injured party, who may do with him as he pleases. Accordingly, offenders are often held as serfs, or are ordered publicly knouted.

This method of dealing with slanderers and people who dishonor others applies to the Germans and other foreigners as well as to the Russians.[19] But though it is widespread among the Russians, it is seldom met with among the foreigners—I know of only two cases involving them.[20] In Grand Prince Mikhail Feodorovich's time, an old Englishman, John Barnesley, was obliged to pay a beschest'e to Dr. Dee, another Englishman and the Tsar's physician. Somewhat later the young Colonel Bockehoffen demanded a beschest'e of Captain de la Coste, a Frenchman. However, Colonel Bockehoffen himself had been condemned to pay a fine to the Frenchman Anton de Gron (as will be related below, he was subsequently rebaptized).[21] As de Gron was a good friend of the captain the quarrel was settled by mediation, one fine canceling the other, and the affair ended amicably.

One should not seek great courtesy and good manners among the Russians, for neither is much in evidence. After a meal, they do not refrain, in the presence and hearing of all, from releasing what nature produces, fore and aft. Since they eat a great deal of garlic and onion, it is rather trying to be in their company. Perhaps against their will, these good people fart and belch noisily—as indeed they did intermittently during the secret audiences with us.

Just as they are ignorant of the praiseworthy sciences, they are little interested in memorable events or the history of their fathers and forefathers, and they care little to find out the qualities of foreign peoples. One hears nothing of these subjects in their gatherings. I am not speaking here, however, of the carouses of the great boyars. Most of their

[19] Certain articles of the *Ulozhenie* applied to foreigners as well as Russians. One of the distinctive features of the *Ulozhenie* as compared with its predecessor, the *Sudebnik* of 1589, is its frequent reference to foreigners, a circumstance that points up the increasing prominence of these people in the seventeenth century.

[20] According to a Soviet writer, S. K. Bogoiavlenskii (p. 231), the foreigners had frequent recourse to the courts. But it may well be that they were only rarely involved in beschest'e suits, and almost never among themselves.

[21] The Frenchman is more commonly known by the name Jean rather than Anton, and his last name is sometimes spelled Groen. A brother came to Russia with him and was also rebaptized. Jean submitted to the government a grandiose scheme for economic development, which probably influenced the rise of mercantilism in Russia. See Kurts, *Sostoianie Rossii*, pp. 67–68, 69, 79–81; and Baklanova. Although neither Kurts nor Baklanova was aware of it, De Gron's scheme was published, though wrongly identified, in Viskovatov, pp. 165–70.

conversation is directed to the side of things toward which their nature and base way of life incline: they speak of debauchery, of vile depravity, of lasciviousness, and of immoral conduct committed by themselves and by others. They tell all sorts of shameless fables, and he who can relate the coarsest obscenities and indecencies, accompanied by the most wanton mimicry, is accounted the best companion and is the most sought after. Their dances have the same character, often including voluptuous movements of the body. They say that roving comedians bare their backsides, and I know not what else. The Danish ambassador [Ulfeldt] was entertained by such shameless dances when he was there. He tells in his *Hodoeporicon* (p. 17) of seeing Russian women assume strange poses and make strange signs at the windows of their houses.

So given are they to the lusts of the flesh and fornication that some are addicted to the vile depravity we call sodomy; and not only with boys (as Curtius [*De Rebus Gestis*] tells) but also with men and horses. Such antics provide matter for conversation at their carouses. People caught in such obscene acts are not severely punished. Tavern musicians often sing of such loathsome things, too, in the open streets, while some show them to young people in puppet shows. Their dancing-bear impresarios have comedians with them, who, among other things, arrange farces employing puppets. These comedians tie a blanket around their bodies and spread it above their heads, thus creating a portable theater or stage with which they can run about the streets, and on top of which they can give puppet shows.

"They have divested themselves of every trace of shame and restraint," says Jakob [Ulfeldt]. In Moscow we ourselves several times saw men and women come out of public baths to cool off, and, as naked as God created them, approach us and call obscenely in broken German to our young people. Idleness strongly prompts them to this kind of dissolute behavior. Daily you can see hundreds of idlers standing about or strolling in the market place or in the Kremlin. And they are more addicted to drunkenness than any nation in the world. Hieronymus [St. Jerome] said, "A stomach filled with wine craves immediate sexual satisfaction." After drinking wine to excess they are like unbridled animals, following wherever their passions lead. I recall in this connection what the Grand Prince's interpreter told me at Great Novgorod: "Every year there is a great pilgrimage to Novgorod [to the Khutynskii Monastery]. At that time a tavern keeper, for a consideration given the Metropolitan, is permitted to set up several tents around the tavern; beginning at daybreak, the pilgrim brothers and sisters, as well as the local people, gather to toss off several cups of vodka before the service of worship. Many of them stay all day and drown their pilgrim devotion in wine. On one such day it happened that a drunken woman came out of the tavern, collapsed in the street nearby, and fell asleep. Another drunken Russian came by, and seeing the partly exposed woman lying there, was inflamed with passion, and lay down with her to quench it, caring not that it was broad daylight and on a well-peopled street. He remained lying by her and fell asleep there. Many youngsters gathered in a circle around this bestial pair and laughed and joked about them for a long time, until an old man came up and threw a robe over them to cover their shame."

The vice of drunkenness is prevalent among this people in all classes, both secular and ecclesiastical, high and low, men and women, young and old.[22] To see them lying here and there in the streets, wallowing in filth, is so common that no notice is taken of it. If a coachman comes across any such drunken swine whom he knows, he throws them aboard his wagon and takes them home, where he is paid for the trip. None of them anywhere, anytime, or under any circumstance lets pass an opportunity to have a draught or a drinking bout. They drink mainly vodka, and at get-togethers, or when one person visits another, respect is rendered by serving one or two "cups of wine," that is, vodka. The common people, slaves, and peasants are so faithful to the custom that if one of them receives a third cup and a fourth, or even more, from the hand of a gentleman, he continues to drink up, believing that he dare not refuse, until he falls to the ground—and sometimes the soul is given up with the draught. We met with such situations while

[22] Samuel Collins (p. 24), an Englishman who served as physician to Tsar Aleksei Mikhailovich for nine years, remarked that drunkenness was "the epidemic distemper not only of Russia but of England also." Montaigne (p. 41) observed that French envoys to Germany found it necessary to get drunk, i.e. to honor the native custom, if they were to get their business done. These observations provide some needed perspective for the student of seventeenth-century Russia. Nevertheless, the fact that foreigners were impelled to dwell so much on drunkenness among the Russians suggests that they conspicuously outstripped others in this regard.

we were there, for our people were very generous and obliging to the Russians. Not only the common people, I affirm, but also the leading lords—even the Tsar's Grand Ambassadors, who are bound to uphold the honor of their sovereign in foreign countries—are without restraint when strong drink is offered them. If something they rather like is put before them, they pour it out like water, until they begin to behave like people robbed of reason, and finally must be picked up as though they were dead. A case of this sort involving the Grand Ambassador sent to His Majesty King Charles IX of Sweden occurred in 1608. He became so intoxicated by the strongest vodka—even though he had been warned of its fiery power—that on the day he was to have been brought to an audience he was found dead in bed.

While we were there, taverns and pothouses were everywhere, and anyone who cared to could go in and sit and drink his fill. The common people would bring all their earnings into the tavern and sit there until, having emptied their purses, they gave away their clothing, and even their nightshirts, to the keeper, and then went home as naked as they had come into the world. When, in 1643, I stopped at the Lübeck house in Novgorod, I saw such besotted and naked brethren come out of the nearby tavern, some bareheaded, some barefooted, and others only in their nightshirts. One of them had drunk away his cloak and emerged from the tavern in his nightshirt; when he met a friend who was on his way to the same tavern, he went in again. Several hours later he came out without his nightshirt, wearing only a pair of under-drawers. I had him called to ask what had become of his nightshirt, who had stolen it? He answered, with the customary "Fuck your mother," that it was the tavern keeper, and that the drawers might as well go where the cloak and nightshirt had gone. With that, he re-turned to the tavern, and later came out entirely naked. Taking a hand-ful of dog fennel that grew near the tavern, he held it over his private parts, and went home singing gaily.

It is true that recently these public taverns, some of which belonged to the Tsar and some to the boyars, have been abolished, because they drew people away from work and gave them an opportunity to drink up their earnings. Now one can no longer buy two or three kopeks worth of vodka. Instead, His Tsarist Majesty ordered that each town have one *kruzhechnyi dvor,* which sells vodka only by the jug or tankard.[23] The people who are appointed managers of these establishments have taken a special oath, and they annually supply an unbelievable sum of money to His Tsarist Majesty's treasury. However, daily drunkenness has hardly diminished as a result of this measure, for several neighbors pool their funds to buy a tankard or more, and do not disperse until they have emptied it to the dregs. Some of them also buy up large quantities and secretly sell it by the cup. It is true that now fewer people are seen naked, although the number of drunkards wandering about and wallowing in the gutters is not much reduced.

Women do not consider it disgraceful to themselves to get intoxicated and collapse along with the men. From my inn in Narva, the Niehoff House, I saw an amusing spectacle. Several women came with their husbands to a carouse, sat with them, and drank amply. When the men had got drunk, they wanted to go home. The women demurred, and though their ears were boxed, nevertheless, they declined to get up. When at last the men fell to the ground and went to sleep, the women sat astride them and continued toasting one another with vodka until they, too, became dead drunk. Our host in Narva, Jakob von Köllen, related that just such a comedy took place at his wedding. After they got drunk, the men struck their wives for the pleasure of it, and then proceeded to tipple with them again. Finally the women, sitting astride their sleeping husbands, drank to each other until they toppled over alongside them and slept. One may easily imagine the peril to honor and modesty, and its frequent ruin, under such conditions of life.

I said that the clergy is not anxious to rid itself of this vice either. One is as apt to meet a drunken priest or monk as a layman or peasant. It is true that in the monasteries they drink no wine, vodka, mead, or

[23] The private operation of taverns was banned, and a single kruzhechnyi dvor per town authorized, in 1651 and 1652—not in 1634, as Olearius asserts farther on. The decrees were not obeyed, however, and presently the government gave way and tolerated the existence of something rather like the old system. See Pryzhov, Chap. 12. It has been plausibly argued that the reduction of the number of taverns was chiefly motivated by fiscal considerations, for the Russian government profited more from the sale of grain abroad than from its conversion into alcohol for sale in taverns. Basilevich, "Elementy merkantilizma," pp. 14–15. However, this view is inadequate taken by itself, for numerous regulations emanating from the church in the 1640's and 1650's expressed a genuine movement for reform of pernicious practices among both laymen and clergy.

strong beer, but only *kvas*, that is weak beer or small beer.[24] Nevertheless, when the monks go out and are guests of good friends, they not only feel that they cannot refuse a good draught, but even demand it; and they drink greedily, taking such delight in it that they may be distinguished from lay drunkards by nothing but their clothing.

When we passed through Novgorod, during the second embassy, I saw a priest in a robe or underwear (he had undoubtedly pawned his cloak in a tavern) staggering along the streets. When he came opposite my inn, he wanted to bestow the customary blessing upon the streltsi who were standing guard. When he extended his hand while endeavoring to bend over somewhat, his head proved too heavy, and he pitched over into the mud. After the streltsi picked him up, he blessed them anyway with his besmeared fingers. Since such spectacles may be seen daily, none of the Russians are astonished by them.

The Russians also greatly love tobacco, and formerly everyone carried some with him. The poor man gave his kopek as readily for tobacco as for bread. However, it was presently remarked that people got no good whatever from it, but, on the contrary, appreciable ill. Servants and slaves lost much time from their work; many houses went up in smoke because of carelessness with the flame and sparks; and before the ikons, which were supposed to be honored during church services with reverence and pleasant-scented things, the worshippers emitted an evil odor. Therefore, in 1634, at the suggestion of the Patriarch, the Grand Prince banned the sale and use of tobacco along with the sale by private taverns of vodka and beer. Offenders are punished very severely—by slitting of the nostrils, and the knout.[25] We saw marks of such punishment on both men and women, of which more when we discuss their system of justice.

---

[24] Olearius was misinformed on this, as is apparent from the numerous decrees banning intoxicating liquors in the monasteries. See for examples *Akty sobrannye*, Vol. IV, Nos. 37, 322, 325, 328. These and other, similar decrees also disprove Olearius's allegation regarding lack of concern about drunkenness among the clergy. Like his predecessor, Iosif, in whose patriarchate these decrees were published, Nikon was an implacable foe of this ill. He assigned agents to apprehend culprits, who were severely punished. Paul of Aleppo, p. 410; Pascal, pp. 163–65 and *passim*.

[25] In the *Ulozhenie*, Art. 10–21 of the last chapter deal with the sale and use of tobacco. The *ukaz* of 1634, and Art. 11 of the *Ulozhenie* after it, prescribed even the death penalty. Tikhomirov and Epifanov, p. 298. In practice, however, tobacco was made available to Russian soldiers, and enforcement of the ban, in general, became increasingly lax. Kurts, *Sochinenie Kil'burgera*, pp. 322–23. Peter the Great later repealed the ban, when he sold a monopoly of the tobacco trade with Russia to an English nobleman. See Schuyler, I, 303.

Since the Russians are by nature cruel and fit only for slavery, they must constantly be kept under a cruel and harsh yoke of restraint, and be driven to work with cudgels and whips. They scarcely show displeasure with this, since their condition requires it and they are accustomed to it. Now and then young bastards get together and strike each other, in order to make such treatment a habit—part of their second nature—so that they may bear it more easily.

They are all serfs and slaves. It is their custom and manner to be servile and to make a show of their slavish disposition. They bow to the ground to notables, and even throw themselves at their feet. They give thanks for beatings and punishments. All subjects, whether of high or low condition, call themselves and must count themselves the Tsar's *kholopi,* that is slaves and serfs. Just as the magnates and nobles have their own slaves, serfs, and peasants, the princes and the magnates are obliged to acknowledge their slavery and their insignificance in relation to the Tsar. They sign their letters and petitions with the diminutive form of their names, such as Ivashka instead of Ivan, or "*Petrushka, tvoi kholop* [your slave]." Also, when the Grand Prince speaks to anyone, he employs diminutive names. One can judge of the boyars' slavery, too, by the barbaric punishments meted out to them for offenses.[26] The Russians [appropriately] declare that everything they have belongs to God and the Grand Prince. Foreigners in the Grand Prince's service must also acknowledge their servility and accept whatever pleasure and pain goes with it.[27] Although the Tsar has a gracious eye for the most important of them, they can very easily make a mistake and fall into disgrace.

It was formerly very dangerous to be the Tsar's physician, for if some medicine did not produce the desired effect, or if the patient died while under care, the doctors fell into the greatest disfavor and were treated as slaves.[28] The story of Grand Prince Boris Godunov and his

[26] As Kliuchevski (*Skazaniia inostrantsev,* pp. 73–77, 81–82) remarks, foreign observers were deeply impressed by the Russian nobility's subservience to the Tsar; since many were themselves members of the upper classes, they were especially sensitive to the contrast between their own status and that of the Russians who were ostensibly their counterparts. The Croat Krizhanich also was outraged by the indignities suffered by the Russian nobles. Petrovich, p. 84.

[27] They, too, in addressing the sovereign, called themselves his slaves. For example, the Tsar's physician, Dr. Belau, spoke of himself as "Ivashka, thy slave." See *Akty istoricheskie* Vol. III, No. 225.

[28] The situation had been even worse than Olearius portrays it. Lakhtin (pp. 8–9) states that the first two pioneers of rational medicine in Russia were slain when their royal patients died.

doctors is well known. When in 1602 Duke Johann, brother of King Christian IV of Denmark, came to marry the Grand Prince's daughter, and suddenly fell ill, the Grand Prince demanded, with harsh threats, that the doctors demonstrate their greatest skill on the Duke and not permit him to die. When no medicine helped, and the Duke died, the doctors were forced to hide and not show themselves for a long time.[29]

This Grand Prince had among his physicians one from northern Germany whom he himself had made a doctor. When the latter once asked leave to enroll in a German university and take a doctor's degree, the Grand Prince asked him what it meant to obtain a degree and how it was done. He was told that one had to pass an examination in the art of healing, to determine whether he was qualified; if he passed, he was declared a doctor and given a certificate with the medical faculty's signature and seal. To that the Grand Prince objected: "You can save the trip and the expense. I have recognized your skill (not long before, this physician had in fact relieved him of the pain he suffered from gout), and I myself will make you a doctor and give you a certificate larger than any you would receive abroad!" And so it was done.[30]

After the death of Duke Johann, the Grand Prince had this Muscovite doctor called when he again had an attack of gout. The doctor, believing his life to be in danger, appeared in torn, cut-up, old clothing, with his hair hanging shaggily and in disorder around his head and face. He crawled in through the door on all fours, saying that so long as he was in disgrace he was not fit to live, much less to see the bright eyes of His Tsarist Majesty. A boyar standing nearby, thinking to earn the Tsar's love, kicked the doctor with the end of his shoe, wounding him in the head, and called him a dog. However, the doctor, observing a kind expression on the Tsar's face, sought to make capital of this insult, and continued in a lamenting voice: "Oh great Tsar, I am your slave and no other's. I have gravely offended you, and deserve death, and would gladly die by your hand. But I am insulted that this slave of yours reviles me; for I know that you do not wish another to

---

[29] An extended and moving account of the Duke's death is given in Tsvetaev, *Protestantstvo i protestanty*, pp. 215–18, 443–54.

[30] This may have been the first case of the sort, but it was not the last. See Lakhtin, pp. 27–28.

perpetrate violence upon me, your servant." This meek speech turned the anger of the Grand Prince into mercy. The physician received 500 rubles as a gift, the other physicians were delivered from disgrace, and corporal punishment was inflicted on the boyar.

The slaves and servants of the magnates and other lords are countless. Many have more than fifty, and some even more than a hundred, on their estates or in their households.[31] Most of those in Moscow, instead of being fed in the households, are given a subsistence allowance, though it is so small as hardly to sustain life. That is why there are so many thieves and murderers in Moscow. When we were there, scarcely a night went by that houses were not broken into and robbed. Moreover, often the master of the house was barricaded in his room and obliged to watch passively, if he were not strong enough to deal with the thieves or did not wish to put his life in danger and have the house burned down around him. For that reason, special guards are hired at the households of notables, who are supposed to make their presence known every hour by striking a hanging board—like a drum—with a baton. However, it often happened that such hirelings kept guard not so much for the lords as for the thieves, arranged a safe path for the latter, helped them to rob the place, and then ran off. Therefore, no one is hired nowadays either as a guard or servant (for, besides slaves, hired servants may be had) without references from well-known inhabitants. Especially in Moscow, slaves make the streets very unsafe, so that unless one has good weapons and companions he cannot escape attack, as we had occasion to learn. Returning late at night from a party at a good friend's, one of our members who advanced far ahead of the rest of us was assailed by two Russian street robbers. When he cried out to signal that he was in danger, we sped to his assistance, whereupon one of the thieves hid himself, and the other was beaten so severely that he could hardly drag himself away.

On another occasion, when our ambassadors and their suite were returning from a notable's house where they had been guests, our cook, who lagged behind and was accompanied home by the host's cook, was

---

[31] One contemporary account asserts that a boyar might possess from 200 to 1,000 serfs. See Kotoshikhin, p. 131. Magnates such as Nikita Romanov and Boris Morozov undoubtedly had even more.

shot. One night shortly afterward some robbers slew the steward of
the Swedish ambassador Arend Spiring when he was on his way home
from a good friend's. His waistcoat, still smeared with blood, was put
up for sale eight days later. The same thing happened to our Lieu-
tenant Johann Kit. After we returned from Persia, he attended a German wedding in my company. While returning home alone a little
before me, he was so badly beaten by Russian bandits that, after lying
unconscious for a day and a night, he gave up the ghost.

Other cases, involving the Russians alone, are legion. Not a night
went by without leaving assorted dead, who were discovered on the
streets the following morning. Murders were numerous on their great
holidays, but especially during Butter-week, a period of eight days
before Ash Wednesday, when they get drunk daily. On December 11th
while we were there, 15 dead were counted before the *Zemskii Dvor*,
the place to which the slain are dragged in the morning so that people
whose relatives had failed to come home at night may seek them out.
Those who are not recognized and taken away are buried without ceremony. The slaves and robbers were not even afraid in broad daylight
to fall upon His Tsarist Majesty's physician, Mr. Hartmann Gramann.[32] Several of them forced him to the ground and wanted to cut
off the finger on which he wore a signet ring. It would have been done
had not a good friend of the doctor, a prince near whose gate this
occurred, sent his servants out to seize him from the hands of the
brigands.

In the face of such danger at night, the burghers showed no pity. If
they heard someone suffering at the hands of robbers and murderers
beneath their window, they would not even look out, much less come
to his assistance. I am told that a better regime has now been introduced, involving the posting at night of a strong guard of streltsi and
soldiers at all crossings. And no one, whether on foot, on a horse, or
in a carriage, is permitted to appear on the streets without a lantern
or other light. Everyone is also questioned about why he is on the
street. Those who are caught without a light are detained and brought
to the *Streletskii Prikaz*, where, on the following day, they are inter-

---

[32] Gramann, a German from Thuringia, studied medicine at Jena, Leipzig, and Wittenberg, and practiced in Halle. In 1633 he was engaged as the Holstein embassy's doctor. He
entered the Tsar's service in 1639 and remained in Russia for many years after. See Rikhter,
II, 67–72.

Frontispiece of the 1669 English edition of Olearius's work, which was bound with Von Mandelslo's account of the East Indies.

Tsar Mikhail Feodorovich.

The seal of Tsar Mikhail Feodorovich.

The Patriarch and the Tsar in a religious ceremony at the so-called *lobnoe mesto* in the great square before the Kremlin. In the background is the church of Vasilii Blazhennyi (St. Basil).

The Holstein embassy at a public audience granted by Tsar Mikhail Feodorovich.

The ceremony of Christ's entry into Jerusalem.

Varied costumes worn by Muscovite men and women.

The Posol'skii Dvor, Court of the Chancellery of Foreign Affairs.

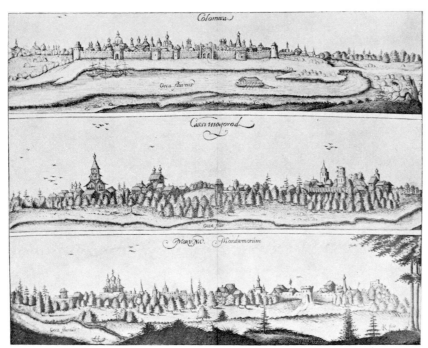

Three towns on the Holstein embassy's route: Kolomna, Kasimovgorod, and Murom.

The Holstein embassy's ship, the *Friedrich*, before Nizhnii Novgorod.

Ceremonies performed before Pentecost in memory of deceased relatives and friends.

Kissing an ikon in a Russian court.

A Russian debauch.

A bridal carriage.

Russian amusements. In the center a puppeteer.

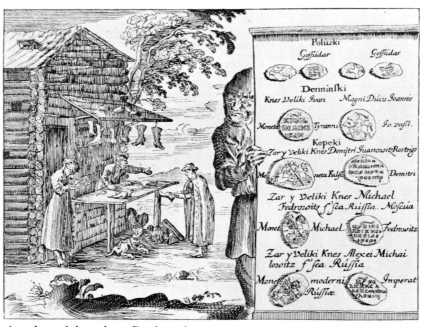

A craftsman's boot shop. Russian coins.

The title page of the first edition of Olearius's work.

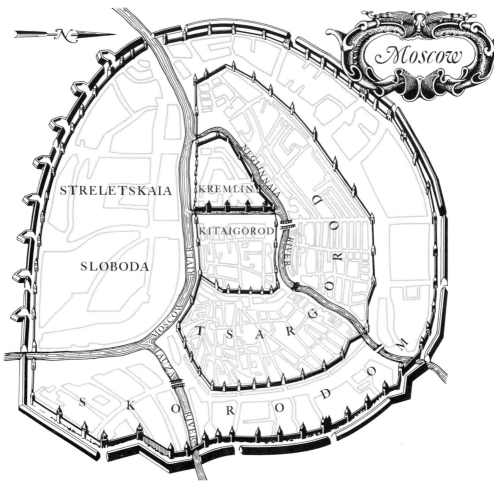

A plan of the city of Moscow based on an engraving by Olearius. Although in the text Olearius speaks of the Kremlin as part of Kitaigorod, on his map he shows them as distinct sections of the city. Tsargorod, because it was surrounded by a white wall, was also called Belyi Gorod. After 1637, Skorodom was known as Zemlianyi Gorod. In the mid-seventeenth century, the area that Olearius calls Streletskaia sloboda was considered a part of Zemlianyi Gorod. Many streltsi were stationed there, but they were located in other parts of Zemlianyi Gorod as well. Olearius's map is discussed in Sytin, pp. 96–98.

rogated; after the matter has been clarified, they are either freed or put to torture.

In August, the haying season, the slaves make the road 20 leagues this side of Moscow extremely dangerous. The boyars have their own hayfields, and they send the servants there to work. In this place is an eminence from which they can detect travelers far off, and here many have been plundered, and even murdered and buried in the sand. Although complaints were registered against these rogues, their masters, who scarcely provide covering for their people's skins, looked between their fingers at the matter.

When, as a consequence of the death or generosity of their master, the slaves and servants of some lord receive their freedom, they soon sell themselves again. Since they have no way to support themselves, they neither value freedom nor know how to use it. Their nature is such that, as the wise Aristotle said of the barbarians, "they cannot and shall not live other than in slavery." To them applies also what Aristotle said of the peoples of Asia Minor, who are called Ionians because they derived from the Greeks: "They are miserable in freedom and comfortable in slavery."

A lord is completely free to sell or give his slaves to another. The relation of fathers and children to slavery that prevails is as follows. Fathers are forbidden to sell their sons, and no one does it. They are even unwilling to give a son as a servant to a notable, preferring to put up with hunger at home. They so comport themselves both because they are magnanimous and because they consider such an arrangement shameful. However, when someone falls into debt and is unable to pay, he has the right to mortgage his children or give them into the service of the creditor for a certain term of years to discharge the debt. A son is delivered for five rubles a year, a daughter for four, until they have served out the debt, after which the creditor must set them free. If a son or daughter is unwilling to be mortgaged and the father is taken to court for not being able to pay, then, according to Russian law, the children must pay the debts of the parents. In that case the children may give the father's creditor a *kabal*, or certificate of obligation, binding them to become his serfs.[33]

---

[33] The contracting of debts and punishment for non-payment are covered in the *Ulozhenie*, Chap. Ten, Art. 254ff. Art. 266 orders debtors who cannot pay to become the servants of their

As a result of slavery and their crude, grim way of life, the Russians are the more easily brought to war and employed in it. When it comes to that, they are sometimes brave and bold soldiers. The ancient Romans, in keeping with the laws of Emperors Gratian/Valentinian and Theodosius, would not permit bondsmen, dissolute scamps, and persons of uncertain origin or character to serve in their wars. But in those days, men who enlisted and were used as soldiers had a different aim (that is, glory and worldly happiness) than most have today (plunder, robbery, and enrichment). Nowadays it is commonly said, as [Coroebus] did in Virgil: "Craft or courage are equally acceptable when a foe must be beaten." Why then trouble, as the Romans did, to pick and choose among those who wish to enlist?

[Yet] the Russian slaves are steadfastly loyal to their lords and military commanders; if they have good, well-trained foreign colonels and leaders (of whom they are short), then they show great manliness and courage. But they are much better suited to the defense of fortresses than to the field,[34] as the example cited of the two Russians at the surrender of Nöteburg shows. A similar conclusion may be drawn from the campaign of 1579 against the Poles. At the Suckol castle, which the Poles put to the torch, they did not quit opposing the enemy before them even when the clothes on their backs began to burn. One may read of this in Henning's *Liefflländische Chronica.* In the same place, mention is made of the surrender of the Padis Abbey in Livonia [1580], where the Russians besieged in the fortress were so weakened by hunger that they were unable to come out to meet the conquering Swedes at the gates. And Henning adds in wonder, "In a fortress give me soldiers like these, who are ready to venture whatever their commander asks of them."

But in field engagements and in the siege of cities and fortresses, the Russians do not fare as well, although they do what is asked of them. Usually they came off second best in clashes with the Poles, Lithuanians, and Swedes, and they sometimes proved more ready to flee than

---

creditors and to work off the debt at the rate of five rubles per year; nothing is said of mortgaging children, though that was in fact done. Kliuchevskii (*Istoriia soslovii,* pp. 107–9) discusses various forms of servitude.

[34] This view was widely shared by foreign commentators on the Russians. See Kliuchevskii, *Skazaniia inostrantsev,* pp. 105–7.

to pursue the enemy.[35] The fact that in the past year they occupied the city of Smolensk with an army numbering more than 200,000 men can no more be attributed to their great bravery than their full retreat from Smolensk with great losses and dishonor in 1632 can be considered a mark of cowardice.[36] For on both occasions suspicious circumstances were involved. The first time it was a matter of General Shein; this time there were some extraneous factors, unknown before.

Although the Russians, especially the common people, in their slavery and with their heavy yoke, can bear a great deal for love of their ruler, if matters go beyond a certain point, it may be said of them: "Try patience often enough, and madness at last ensues." Then the affair ends with a dangerous mutiny, the fury of which is aimed not so much against the topmost officials as against the lower. This is most apt to occur if the inhabitants are subjected to severe persecution by their fellow citizens and obtain no relief from the authorities. Once they are aroused, they are difficult to pacify; notwithstanding the danger that may threaten them, they resort to every kind of violence, and rage like madmen.

Grand Prince Mikhail Feodorovich knew this very well. When the soldiers, returning in miserable condition from Smolensk, began to complain bitterly about the treachery of General Shein (regarding whom a superior official was also suspicious, and not without cause), the court was dilatory about taking strong measures against the accused.[37] But when the authorities perceived that a general uprising threatened, to appease the people they ordered that Shein be beheaded. So that he should submit, and thus spare danger to others, the following stratagem was resorted to. Shein was persuaded that he was being taken out only for show, only to let the people see the Grand Prince's intention, and that he would not be executed; as soon as he had lain down, a stay would come, followed by clemency, and the people would be satisfied.

[35] As Herberstein (I, 97) put it, their motto in the field seemed to be, "If you do not flee, we must."

[36] In 1654, during the war between Russia and Poland over the Ukraine, Russia gained control of Smolensk for the first time since having lost it in the Time of Troubles.

[37] Nineteenth-century historians were not of one mind in regard to Shein's alleged treachery. After examining the matter closely, the Soviet historian Vainshtein (pp. 169–86) finds Shein guilty of mismanagement of the Smolensk campaign, but acquits him of treason against the Tsar.

Comforted, and full of hope that was reinforced by the assurances from the Patriarch, Shein came forward and lay prostrate on the ground. The executioner was then given the signal to strike forthwith, which he did, and with several blows, he cut off Shein's head.

Later in the same day, Shein's son, who also had been at Smolensk, was beaten to death with the knout, at the people's demand. The general's friends were speedily exiled to Siberia. With that the people were satisfied, and the mutiny ended. These events occurred in June 1633. [Paul] Piasecius described this war with Poland in his *Chronica memorabilium in Europa,* but not with full details. One may find it in his account of the years 1633 and 1634.

Further examples of the Russian people's disposition to be extremely long-suffering and then to become infuriated and to mutiny will be presented below. In the description of their police administration, we will adduce two frightful mutinies and rebellions that occurred in Russia a few years ago.

CHAPTER THREE

Households and Social Life

THE DOMESTIC ARRANGEMENTS of the Russians vary according to their station. Generally they live meagerly and spend little on their homes. The magnates and the rich merchants, it is true, now live in costly palaces. These were built only in the last thirty years, however, and before that they too lived in wretched dwellings. The majority, and especially the common people, live on extremely little. Their houses are shoddy and cheap, and the interiors have few furnishings and utensils. Most have not more than three or four earthen pots and as many clay and wooden dishes. Few pewter and even fewer silver dishes, let alone cups for vodka or mead, are seen. These people are not in the habit of expending much effort on cleaning and polishing their vessels. Even the Grand Prince's pewter and silver plate, with which the ambassadors were entertained, was black and repulsive, as were some of our lazy hosts' tankards, which had not been washed for a year or more. None of the houses, whether rich or poor, display vessels as ornaments; the walls are bare, except in the houses of the wealthy, where they are hung with mats and some ikons. Very few people have feather beds, in lieu of which they lie on benches covered with cushions, straw, mats, or their clothes; in winter they sleep on flat-topped stoves, like bake-ovens, as the non-German people in Livonia do. Side by side lie men, women, and children, as well as servants, both male and female. In some places, we found chickens and pigs under the benches and stoves.

They are not accustomed to tender dishes and dainty morsels. Their daily food consists of groats, beets, cabbages, cucumbers, and fresh or salt fish. In Moscow, they use coarse salt fish, which sometimes stinks because they are thrifty with the salt. Nevertheless, they like to eat it.[1] One can detect a fish market by the odor well before he sees or comes upon it. Because of their excellent pastures, they have good lamb, veal, and pork, but they spend little on meat; for their religion prescribes as many fast days as meat-eating days, and therefore they have become used to coarse and wretched food. They know how to prepare so many dishes of fish, pastry, and vegetables that one may forget about meat. As I have already mentioned, on one fast day the Tsar granted us 40 such dishes. They have a special kind of pastry, much eaten in Butter-week, which they call a *pirog*. It is like a pie or, more exactly, a fritter, though somewhat longer; it is filled with minced fish or meat and onion, and is baked in butter, or during fasts, in vegetable oil. The taste is not unpleasant. Everyone treats a guest with these, if he means to receive him well.

They have a very common food which they call *ikra*, made of the roe of large fish, especially sturgeon and whitefish. They expel the roe from the membrane in which it is contained, salt it, and after it has stood for six to eight days, mix it with pepper and finely chopped onions. Some also add vinegar and country butter before serving it. It is not a bad dish. If one pours a bit of lemon juice over it, instead of vinegar, it gives a good appetite, and has a restorative effect. Ikra is salted on the Volga, chiefly at Astrakhan. Some of it is dried in the sun. They fill hundreds of barrels with it and then send it to other countries, especially to Italy, where it is considered a delicacy and is called *caviaro*. Certain people lease the trade from the Grand Prince for a certain sum of money.[2]

The Russians prepare a special dish when they have a hangover or feel uncomfortable. They cut cold baked lamb into small pieces, like cubes, but thinner and broader, mix them with peppers and cucumbers similarly cut, and pour over them a mixture of equal parts of vinegar and cucumber juice. They eat this with a spoon, and afterwards a drink tastes good again. They generally prepare their food with garlic and

---

[1] Stung by this charge, Krizhanich retorted that he himself had seen the Germans eat worm-ridden cheese with relish. See Petrovich, p. 85.

[2] Many grants of monopoly trade rights were made to foreigners in the seventeenth century. In 1649 a certain John Osborne held a six-year caviar concession. In 1675, it was granted to a Hamburg merchant named Belkins. Iakubov, p. 450; *Polnoe sobranie zakonov*, Vol. I, No. 596.

onion, so all their rooms and houses, including the sumptuous chambers of the Grand Prince's palace in the Kremlin, give off an odor offensive to us Germans. So do the Russians themselves (as one notices in speaking to them), and all the places they frequent even a little.

The drink of the common people is *kvas*—comparable to weak beer or small beer—and also beer, mead, and vodka. Every dinner must begin with vodka, and in the course of the meal other drinks are served as well. In addition to good beer, the tables of the magnates offer Spanish, Rhenish, and French wines, various kinds of mead, and double vodka. They have good beer, which the Germans in particular know how to brew and preserve, doing so in the spring. They prepare ice-cellars, in the bottom of which they place snow and ice, and above that a row of kegs; then another layer of snow, and again kegs, and so forth. Over the top they lay straw and boards, since the cellar has no roof. Thus they can bring one keg after another into use, and they may have fresh and delicious beer throughout the summer—which is quite hot. They import wine by way of Archangel. The Russians, who prefer vodka, do not like wine as well as the Germans do.

They brew excellent and very tasty mead from raspberries, black-berries, cherries, and other fruits. We enjoyed raspberry mead best of all for its bouquet and taste. They taught me how to brew it, as follows. First of all, ripe raspberries are placed in a cask. Water is poured over them, and they are left for a day or two, until the flavor and the color pass from the raspberries to the water. Then the water is decanted from the berries and mixed with pure honey (separated from the wax), one tankard of honey to two or three of the water, depending on whether one wants sweet or strong mead. Small pieces of toasted bread, spread on both sides with a little yeast, are thrown in. When fermentation has begun, the bread is removed so that the mead will not get its taste, and then it is allowed to ferment another four or five days. Some who wish to give the mead a spicy taste and aroma suspend cardamom and cin-namon, wrapped up in scraps of cloth, inside the barrel. When the mead stands in a warm place it ferments for as long as eight days; therefore, once the mead has fermented a certain period of time, the cask must be put in a cool place and the yeast withdrawn. Sometimes they pour ill-tasting vodka over raspberries, mix it, and after it has stood a day and a night, decant it and mix it with honey mead. They say that this makes a very pleasant drink. Since the vodka is counteracted by the raspberry juice, they say that its taste is no longer sensed in this drink.

They sometimes arrange banquets, at which they demonstrate their grandeur by the variety of food and drink served. However, when the magnates have feasts and invite people beneath them in rank, it is certain that they are seeking something other than their good company. Their largess serves as a baited hook, with which they gain more than they expend. For, according to their custom, guests are supposed to bring the host valuable gifts. Formerly, when a German merchant received such attentions and an invitation, he was already sensible of what this honor would cost him. It is said that the voevodas in the cities, especially those where a lively trade is carried on, show their liberality once, twice, or three times a year, by inviting the rich merchants to banquets of this sort.

The highest mark of respect and friendship they show a guest at a feast or in the course of a visit, to convey that he is welcome and that they approve of him, is as follows. After the guest has been fed, the Russian has his wife, richly dressed, brought out to the guest to present him with a cup of vodka from her own hand. Occasionally, as a mark of particular favor to the guest, he is permitted to kiss her on the mouth. This great honor was rendered me personally by Count Lev Aleksandrovich Shliakhovskii, when I was last in Moscow, in 1643.

After a sumptuous dinner he called me away from the table and the other guests. He ushered me into another room and said that the greatest honor and favor anyone can be given in Russia is for the mistress of the house to come out and render homage to the guest as to the master. Since I, as an aide of His Excellency the Prince of Holstein, was dear to him, to show his respect and reverence for the many kindnesses the prince had extended him at the time of his persecution and migration (of which more below), he wanted to do me this honor. Then his wife came forth. She had a very lovely, but berouged face, and was dressed in her wedding costume. She was accompanied by a maid who carried a bottle of vodka and a cup. Upon her entry she bowed her head first to her husband and then to me. Then she ordered a cup of vodka poured out, took a sip, and handed it to me to drink, repeating this procedure three times. Then the count invited me to kiss her. Since I was unaccustomed to such honors, I kissed only her hand, but he insisted that I kiss her mouth. Accordingly, out of respect to a higher ranking personage, I was obliged to adapt myself to their custom and accept this honor.[3] Finally, she handed me a white satin handkerchief, embroidered with gold and silver, and embellished with a long fringe. The wives and daughters of the magnates present such handkerchiefs to a bride on her wedding day. Attached to the one given me was a little paper on which was inscribed the name of Streshnev, the uncle of the Grand Princess.

The boyars and magnates, of course, spend large sums to support their luxurious and extensive households. This they can do because they receive large salaries and have great estates worked by peasants, which provide them with large annual incomes. The merchants and artisans obtain their daily bread and income from the practice of their occupations. The merchants are shrewd and eager for profit. Within the country they trade in all varieties of goods essential for daily life. Those who have the Tsar's permission travel to neighboring countries, like Livonia, Sweden, Poland, and Persia, where they trade principally in sables and other furs, linen, flax, and Russian leather.[4] They often buy cloth from English merchants, who carry on a great commerce in Moscow,[5] at four thalers per ell, and resell it, unchanged, for three or three and a half thalers, and still make a profit. It is done in this way. They buy one or several pieces of cloth at the quoted price, engaging to pay in six months or a year. Then they sell the cloth to shopkeepers (who measure out the cloth), for cash, with which they then purchase other

[3] Tsvetaev (*Protestantstvo i protestanty*, p. 416) implies that the guest's obligation to kiss his host's wife was an invention of Shliakhovskii. However, a contemporary Russian account supports Olearius's contention that the embrace was an established custom. See Kotoshikhin, pp. 122–23.

[4] Most of Russia's foreign trade was carried on on Russian soil, particularly in border towns —Novgorod, Pskov, Archangel, and Astrakhan—and in Moscow. Russian merchants were rarely seen abroad, but foreign merchants were conspicuous in Russia. Some of them acted as the Tsar's commercial agents for his trade with West European countries.

[5] Even in 1647, when Olearius's first edition was published, this would have put the matter too strongly; in 1656, when the second edition appeared, it was simply untrue. From the time of Chancellor's discovery of the northern route to Russia in 1553, English commerce in Russia prospered. But during and after the Time of Troubles, the English steadily lost ground, and the Dutch gained the upper hand. In 1649 the English merchants were forbidden henceforth to trade in Moscow. A convenient pretext was found in the beheading of King Charles II of England, but the pressure came from Russian merchants, who persistently sought to minimize or destroy foreign competition in the Russian market. On the history of the English Muscovy Company, see Lubimenko, *Les Relations commerciales*, and Willan. On Russian mercantilism, see Basilevich, "*Elementy merkantilizma.*" The order expelling the English merchants from Moscow to Archangel appears in *Polnoe sobranie zakonov*, No. 9.

goods. And thus they can profit, on the average, three times or more from the turnover of their money.[6]

Since they require little for their wretched existence, in such a large community the artisans can earn enough with the labor of their hands for their food and vodka and the support of their relatives. They are very receptive and can readily imitate what they see the Germans do. In just a few years they have learned and adopted from them a great deal of which they were formerly ignorant. With such technological improvement, they sell their manufactured goods at higher prices than before. I was especially astonished by the goldsmiths, who can now produce a silver vessel as deep and tall, and quite as well shaped, as any German can make.

He who wishes to retain for himself any special knowledge or technique does not allow the Russians to observe him at work. Hans Falck, the famous gun caster, at first managed things in this way: when he made the molds for or cast his finest weapons, his Russian assistants had to leave. But it is said that now they themselves know how to cast large guns and bells.[7] I was told by several Germans from Moscow and some Russians that in the past year, in the Kremlin near the tower of Ivan the Great, an apprentice designated by Hans Falck cast a great bell, which, after being cleaned, weighed 7,700 puds, that is [277,200] pounds. However, after this bell had been hung in an especially prepared housing and was rung, it cracked. They say that before this happened, it had an excellent tone. Now it has been broken up, and His Tsarist Majesty wants another great bell cast at the same spot and

---

[6] The economic historian Basilevich credits Olearius with correctly representing the relationship between the foreign merchants and the small Russian traders. By these dealings, foreign merchants were able to evade the government restriction that forbade them to engage in retail selling. The small Russian merchants, whose livelihood depended upon foreign credit, also frequently acted as agents of foreign merchants in forestalling goods from small producers for shipment abroad. The relationship that foreign merchants thus established with small and medium Russian merchants benefitted both, but militated against the interests of the large Russian merchants. The latter repeatedly sent petitions to the government, ostensibly on behalf of the whole merchant class, designed to destroy or reduce the power of the foreign merchants by forbidding them to trade within the country. These representations eventually culminated in the enactment of the New Trade Charter of 1667, which, with some exceptions, expelled the foreign merchants to the country's periphery. See Basilevich, "Kollektivnye chelobit'ia" and "Novotorgovyi ustav"; and Muliukin, *Ocherki*, Chap. 3.

[7] Foreign artisans who entered the Russian service were usually bound by contract to teach their skills to their Russian aides. Tsvetaev (*Protestantstvo i protestanty*, pp. 397–401) adduces evidence that Marselis and Akema, for whom Falck worked, conspired to conceal the arts of metallurgy from the Russians, thus violating the terms of their contract.

hung as an eternal monument to his name. It is said that the works for the casting and the mold have already been built, at great expense.[8]

Russians of high and low estate are in the habit of resting and sleeping after the noon meal. Accordingly, most of the best shops are closed at noon, and the shopkeepers and their young helpers lie down to sleep outside them. This midday rest rules out conversations with any of the magnates or merchants at that time.

The Russians determined that False Dmitri was not the Grand Prince's son, nor even a Russian by birth, because he did not take an afternoon nap like other Russians. They inferred the same from the fact that he did not often go to the bath, as the Russians do. For they attach great importance to bathing, considering it—especially at the time of marriage, after the first night—an indispensable practice. Therefore, in all towns and villages, they have many public and private baths, in which they may often be found.

To see personally how they bathe, I went incognito into a bath in Astrakhan.[9] The bath was partitioned by planks, so that the men and women could sit separately; but they entered and left through the same door, and they wore no aprons. Some held a birch branch in front of them until they sat down in their places, others nothing at all. The women sometimes came out naked, with no timidity before others, to talk to their husbands.

They can stand great heat, for they lie on the sweating-benches and drive the heat onto their bodies with branches and leafy twigs (which was unbearable for me). When they have turned completely red and are so weakened by the heat that they can no longer bear it, they dash out, naked, and pour cold water on themselves—or in winter, wallow in the snow and rub their skins with it, exactly as if it were soap—and then go back into the warm bath. As the bathhouses are usually located at water sites and near brooks, they are able to rush from the hot bath into the cold. If some German youth plunged into the water with the women to bathe, they were not so dismayed and indignant, as were

---

[8] The Russian passion for building great bells continued unabated for some time. The largest bell in the world, cast between 1733 and 1735, is still on exhibition in the Kremlin.

[9] Olearius's description of the Russian bath may be compared with the shorter but equally vivid account attributed in the ancient chronicle to the apostle St. Andrew. See Cross *The Russian Primary Chronicle*, p. 139.

Diana and her playmates, as to splash water on him and transform him into a deer—even if they had the power to do so. In Astrakhan it once happened that four young women came out of a bath to cool off, and plunged into an inlet of the Volga that has a flat bottom and forms a pleasant place for cold bathing. When one of our soldiers also dived into the water, they began jokingly to splash water on one another. One of them who went out too deep stepped into quicksand and began to sink. When her friends became aware of the danger, they cried out and rushed to the soldier, who was swimming by himself, and begged him to save her. Easily persuaded, the soldier sped toward her, seized her around the waist and raised her up so that she could take hold of him, and swam in with her. The women showered praise on the German and said that an angel had sent him.

We saw bathing of this kind not only in Russia but also in Livonia and Ingermanland, where the common people, and especially the Finns, in the most severe winter weather, dashed from the bathhouses into the street, rubbed themselves with snow, and then ran back again into the heat. This rapid change from hot to cold was not dangerous for them since they had been conditioned to it from their youth. Therefore, the Finns and Latvians, as well as the Russians, are people of toughness, strength, and endurance, who can bear well extremes of heat and cold. In Narva I saw with amazement how Russian and Finnish boys eight, nine, or ten years of age, dressed in their plain, light, linen cloaks, walked and stood barefooted in the snow, for half an hour, just like geese, as if they were unaware of the unbearable frost.

In general, people in Russia are healthy and long-lived. They are rarely sick, but if someone is confined to bed, the best cure among the common people, even if there is high fever, is vodka and garlic. It should be added that nowadays the great lords sometimes ask the German doctors for advice and proper medicines.[10]

We encountered good baths built inside dwellings among the Germans in Moscow, as well as among the Livonians. In these baths there were arched stone ovens in which, on an elevated grill, lie many stones.

---

[10] Ordinarily they could not apply directly to the doctors, all of whom were in the Tsar's service, under the direction of a department of the government, the Aptekarskii Prikaz. They were obliged, instead, to petition the Tsar for the privilege of obtaining professional medical attention.

There is an aperture from the stove into the bathroom, which they close with a cover and cow dung or clay. Outside there is another aperture, smaller than the first, through which the smoke escapes. When the stones are sufficiently heated, the inner aperture is opened and the outer shut. Then, depending upon how much [steam] one wants, a certain quantity of water, sometimes infused with herbs, is poured onto the stones. In the baths, sweat- and wash-up-benches are arranged around the walls, one above the other, covered with linen cloths and cushions, stuffed with hay, and strewn with flowers and various aromatic grasses, with which the windows are also adorned. Scattered on the floor lie small finely chopped shrubs, which give off a very pleasant odor. A woman or girl is assigned to attend the bathers. When an acquaintance or a cherished guest bathes with them, he is looked after attentively, waited on, and cared for. The mistress of the house or her daughter usually brings or sends into the bath some pieces of radish sprinkled with salt, and also a well-prepared, cool drink. If this is omitted, it is considered a great fault and the mark of a bad reception. After the bath they treat the guest, according to his worthiness, with all sorts of pleasure-giving refreshments.

Such honorable hospitality and cleanliness, however, are not to be sought among the arrogant, self-interested, and dirty Russians, among whom everything is done in a slovenly and swinish fashion. One of the members of our suite, having observed the ways of the Muscovites, their life and character, recently described them in brief in the following verses:

> Churches, ikons, crosses, bells,
> Painted whores and garlic smells,
> Vice and vodka everyplace—
> This is Moscow's daily face.

> To loiter in the market air,
> To bathe in common, bodies bare,
> To sleep by day and gorge by night,
> To belch and fart is their delight.

> Thieving, murdering, fornication
> Are so common in this nation,
> No one thinks a brow to raise—
> Such are Moscow's sordid days.

Although the unseemly game of Venus is very widespread among the Russians, nevertheless they do not have public houses with prostitutes, from which the authorities receive income, as they unfortunately do in Persia and some other countries. They have ordinary marriages, and a man is permitted to have just one wife. If his wife dies, he may take another, and may even wed a third time, but he may not obtain permission for a fourth. If a priest weds people who have no right to marry, he must abandon his calling. Priests who serve at the altar absolutely must be married; but if the wife of such a priest dies, he may not remarry unless he renounces his priestly office, discards his headdress, and takes up trade or some other occupation. In arranging marriages they take into account the degree of consanguinity and do not allow weddings of close blood relatives. They also avoid connections between relatives by marriage, and do not permit the wedding of two brothers to two sisters, or even of two godparents of the same child. Their marriages are conducted in public churches with special ceremonies, and at the wedding they observe the following customs.

Young men and women are not permitted to become acquainted on their own, much less to discuss marriage together or to become engaged. Rather, in most cases, when parents have grown children whom they wish to be married, the father of the girl approaches someone whom he considers appropriate for his child, speaks either to him personally or to his parents and friends, and expresses his disposition, intention, and opinion concerning the marriage. If the offer is well received and someone wishes to see the daughter, the request is not refused, especially if the daughter is pretty. The mother or a female friend of the groom is given permission to see her. If she has no visible blemish, that is if she is neither blind nor lame, then final negotiations between the parents and friends of the two young people are initiated concerning the dowry, or *pridanoe*, as they call it, and the celebration of the marriage.

Generally, even the lesser notables raise their daughters in closed-off rooms, hidden from other people, and the groom does not see the bride before he receives her in the marriage bedroom. Thus some are deceived, and instead of a beautiful bride are given an ugly and sickly one; sometimes, instead of the daughter, some friend, or even a maid-servant is substituted.[11] Such cases are known [even] among high-ranking personages. Under the circumstances, one should not be surprised that husbands and wives often live together like cats and dogs, and that wife-beating is so common in Russia.

Their weddings are elaborate, and the bride is conveyed to her new home with special pageantry. Among the progeny of leading princes and boyars these ceremonies are performed in the following manner. Two women (called *svakhi*) are assigned to the bride and groom. They serve as stewardesses, who arrange one thing and another in the wedding house. On the wedding day, the bride's svakha prepares the marriage bed in the groom's house. She is accompanied by about one hundred servants dressed in kaftans, each carrying on his head something required for the marriage bed or for decorating the wedding room. The marriage bed is prepared on 40 sheaves of rye, laid alongside of each other and interlaced. The groom must arrange these in advance, and set near them some vessels or casks full of wheat, barley, and oats. These are supposed to symbolize bountifulness and assist in assuring that the pair will have abundant food and provisions during their wedded life.

Late in the evening, when everything is in readiness and order, the groom and his friends set out for the bride's house. The priest who has been engaged to perform the marriage ceremony rides in the lead. The bride's friends have already gathered and they cordially receive the groom and his companions. The groom's best and closest friends are invited to the table, which bears three dishes of food, but no one eats. The head of the table is reserved for the groom; but while he remains standing, talking to the bride's friends, the place is occupied by a boy. The groom must persuade him to yield it with a gift. When the groom has taken his place, the veiled bride, magnificently dressed, is seated beside him. To prevent their seeing one another, a piece of red satin is stretched between them and held by two boys. Then the bride's svakha comes, combs her hair, parts it, plaits it into two braids, places a crown and other ornaments on her head, and then allows her to sit

---

[11] One interesting case was reported in which the prospective groom was permitted a look at the young lady from a hidden nook. Taking advantage of his limited visibility, the parents exposed the sound side of their one-eyed daughter to view, after which the marriage papers were drawn up. See Collins, p. 37.

with her face uncovered. The crown is made of finely beaten gold or silver plate and is lined with cloth; near the ears it is somewhat curved, and from it are suspended four, six, or more strands of large pearls, which reach down well below the breast. The sleeves (which are three ells in width) and front of her outer garment are thickly studded with large pearls; so is the collar of her robe (three fingers wide and not unlike a dog's collar), which fits snugly around her neck. Such a dress costs well over a thousand thalers.

The svakha also combs the bridegroom's hair. During this time the women stand on benches and sing all sorts of obscenities. Then two handsomely dressed young people bring forth, on a tray decked with sables, a very large round cheese and several loaves. These people, who come from the bride's house, are called *korovainiki* [carriers of the loaves]. The priest blesses them, and also the cheese and bread, which then are carried to the church. Next, on the table is placed a large silver dish containing square pieces of velvet and satin [large] enough for a small purse, flat square pieces of silver, and hops, barley, and oats, all mixed together. One of the svakhi covers the bride's face again, and scatters the dish's contents over the boyars and the other men. While a song is sung, the guests may help themselves to pieces of velvet and silver. Then the fathers of the bride and groom stand up and exchange the rings of the couple to be married.

After these ceremonies, the svakha ushers the bride out, seats her in a sleigh, and conducts her, with her face covered, to the church. The horse drawing the sleigh is decorated with many foxtails at his neck and under the shaft. The groom follows immediately behind with his friends and the priest. It sometimes happens that the priest has already managed so well to taste the wedding beverages that he has to be supported on both sides on the way, to keep him from falling off the horse, and also during the church service. The sleighs are accompanied by some good friends and many slaves, and many coarse indecencies are bandied about.

In the church the part of the floor where the marriage is to be performed is covered with red satin, and on top of this is placed a special piece on which the bride and groom stand. When the marriage ceremony begins, the priest first of all asks for food offerings, such as pirogs, pies, and pastries. Then large ikons are held over the heads of the bride and groom, and they are blessed. The priest then takes into his hands the groom's right hand and the bride's left, and thrice asks them if they wish to have one another and to live together [in peace]. When they answer "Yes," he leads them around in a circle, while singing the 128th Psalm. They sing the verses after him and dance. After the dance, pretty garlands are placed on their heads. If they are a widower and a widow, the garlands are placed not on their heads but on their shoulders. Then the priest says, "Be fruitful and multiply," and unites them with the words, "Whom God has joined together let no man part," and so forth. Throughout this ceremony all the guests in the church burn small candles. The priest is given a gilded wooden cup or a drinking glass of red wine. He drinks some of it in honor of the married couple, and the groom and bride must drink three draughts. Then the groom throws the glass to the ground and he and the bride trample it into little bits, saying, "Thus let any who wish to arouse enmity and hatred between us fall under our feet and be trampled." The women then shower them with flax and hemp seed and wish them happiness. They also pull and push the newly married bride, as if to separate her from the groom, but the two hold fast to each other. When these ceremonies are over, the groom escorts the bride to the sleigh and mounts his horse again. Six wax candles are carried alongside the sleigh, as it proceeds to the bride's new home, and again coarse jokes are told.

When they come to the wedding house, that is, to the bridegroom's house, the groom and the guests sit down at the table to eat, drink, and be merry. Meanwhile the bride quickly undresses down to her shift and gets into bed. The groom scarcely has begun to eat when he is summoned to the bride. Before him go six or eight boys with burning torches. When she learns of the groom's arrival, the bride gets out of bed, puts on a fur coat lined with sable, and welcomes her beloved with a bow of her head. The boys insert the burning torches into the casks of wheat and barley placed there earlier by the groom; then each is given a pair of sables, and they depart. The groom sits down at a covered table with the bride, whose face he now sees for the first time. They are served, among other foods, a roasted hen. The groom tears it apart, throws over his shoulder whatever breaks off first, be it a leg or a wing, and eats the rest. After the meal, which does not last long, he gets into bed with the bride. No one else is present, except for an old attendant who walks back and forth outside the room. Meanwhile the parents and friends busy themselves with all manner of tricks and charms to ensure the couple a happy wedded life. The attendant who guards the room must ask from time to time whether the deed is done. When the groom replies affirmatively, it is announced to all with trumpets and drums. The drumsticks have been poised above the drums, and now the musicians play gaily. A bathroom is then heated, wherein the bride and groom bathe in turn a few hours later. Here they are washed with water, honey, and wine; and then the groom receives as a gift from the young wife a bathrobe, embroidered at the collar with pearls, and a complete set of new and costly clothes.

The next two days are spent in great and extravagant eating, drinking, dancing, and every manner of amusement they can think of. They also have all sorts of music, employing among other instruments one called a psalter, which is very like a dulcimer. It is held on the lap and, like a harp, is plucked with the fingers. Inasmuch as many of the women, when unguarded by their drunken husbands, are apt to permit considerable liberties to the young men and the husbands of others, the men take advantage of such occasions to amuse themselves freely. This is our account of the marriage ceremonies and customs among the present-day boyars in Moscow.

When common people and burghers wish to celebrate a marriage, a day before the wedding the groom sends his bride new clothing, a hat, and a pair of shoes, as well as a little box containing rouge, a comb, and a mirror. On the next day, when the marriage is to take place, the priest comes with a silver cross, accompanied by two boys carrying burning wax candles. The priest blesses the boys, and then the guests, with the cross. The bride and groom then sit down at the table, and a red satin cloth is held between them. When the bride has been all prepared by the svakha, she presses her cheek to the bridegroom's, while both look into a single mirror and smile cordially to each other. Meanwhile, the svakhi approach and shower them and the guests with hops. After these ceremonies they set off for the church, where the wedding is performed in the manner described above.

After the wedding, the women are secluded in their chambers and rarely appear in company. They are more often visited by their friends than permitted to visit them.

Since the daughters of the magnates and merchants receive little or no training in housekeeping, when they are married they occupy themselves with it scarcely at all. Instead, they merely sit and sew beautiful handkerchiefs of white satin and pure linen, embroidering them with gold and silver, and make little purses for money, and the like. They may not take part in the slaughter or cooking of chickens or other animals, for they suppose that this would defile them. Therefore, they leave all such work to the servants. Because they are mistrusted, they are rarely allowed out of the house, even to go to church. These customs, however, are not strictly observed among the common people. At home the women go poorly attired except when they appear, at the order of their husbands, to render honor to a strange guest by sipping a cup of vodka to him, or when they go through the streets, to church, for example; then they are supposed to be dressed gorgeously, with their faces and throats heavily made up.

The wives of princes, boyars, and the foremost people ride in the summer in closed carriages lined with red satin, with which they also decorate their sleighs in the winter. They sit pompously in their sleighs, as if they were goddesses, with a slave girl at their feet. Alongside of it run many servants and slaves, sometimes as many as 30 or 40. The horse that draws the carriage or sleigh, like that which conveys a bride, is hung with long foxtails, producing an extremely odd sight. We saw similar ornaments on the sleighs of the great magnates, indeed even on the Grand Prince's sleigh, which sometimes displays fine black sables instead of foxtails.

Since they so rarely appear in company and are little involved in housework, young wives are idle much of the time. Occasionally they arrange recreation with their maids, for example riding on swings, which they especially like. Sometimes they lay a board over a block, and one person stands on each end; then they rock and propel one another high into the air. Sometimes they use ropes, by which they can swing themselves very high. The common people in the suburbs and villages often play such games in the streets. They also have public swings [primitive Ferris wheels], which are built in the form of a gallows, with moving parts perpendicular to it, on which two, three, or more people can ride simultaneously. They indulge in such amuse-ments especially on holidays. Then certain youths keep seats and other essential parts in readiness and lend them out for several kopeks to anyone who wants to swing. Husbands are very willing to allow their wives such pleasures, and sometimes even help them at it.

The animosity and brawls that often arise between spouses are caused by indecent or abusive words—which come easily to their lips—ad-dressed by the wife to the husband; or because she gets drunk more often than the husband; or because she arouses his suspicion by unusual friendliness with other married men and young swains. Often all three provocations occur at once. When, as a result, the wife is beaten with the knout or a stick, she does not take it too ill, for she is aware of her guilt, and also she sees that her neighbors and sisters who indulge in the same vices get off no better. However, I did not find that Russian wives regard frequent blows and beatings as a sign of intense love and their absence as a mark of their husbands' indifference and dissatisfac-tion with them, as is contended by some writers who follow Petrejus's *Russian Chronicle* (and Petrejus undoubtedly borrowed this from Herberstein or from Barclajus's work, *Icon Animorum*). Indeed, I cannot imagine their wanting what every creature naturally dreads, or their taking as a mark of love what is in fact a mark of anger and hos-tility. In my opinion, the well-known proverb, "Blows do not make friends," applies as well to them as to others. No person in his right mind will hate and torment his own flesh without reason. Perhaps some wives said to their husbands in jest [such things as Herberstein wrote of]....[12]

They do not punish adultery by death; indeed they do not even call it adultery but simply fornication if a married man spends a night with another's wife. They only call him an adulterer who takes another's wife in marriage. If a married woman commits fornication, and it is reported and proved, she is punished with the knout and must spend several days in a monastery living on bread and water. Then she is sent home, where the master of the house beats her again for having neglected the housework.

---

[12] Olearius finally concludes that although what Herberstein wrote might have been true in some cases, it can hardly be made the basis of a sound generalization.

If a pair have become tired of each other and no longer can live together in peace and harmony, the way out is for one or the other to enter a monastery. If the husband does so, leaving his wife out of reverence for God, and his wife takes another husband, then the first may be consecrated as a priest, even though he might earlier have been a shoemaker or a tailor. A husband also has the freedom to consign his wife to a monastery if she is childless, and may marry another after six weeks. Some of the Grand Princes who were unable to obtain a male heir from their wives dispatched them to monasteries and married others. The tyrant Ivan Vasil'evich [properly, Vasilii III Ivanovich] forcibly installed his wife Solomonia in a monastery, after 21 years of married life with her, because he could have no children by her. He then married another, Elena, the daughter of Mikhail [properly, Vasilii] Glinskii. Soon afterward, however, his first wife gave birth to a son in the monastery, an event that is related by Tilmannus Bredenbachius [*De Armeniorum moribus*, etc.] (on p. 251) and by Herberstein, in greater detail (on p. 19).[13]

Likewise, if a husband can prove his wife guilty of something dishonorable, she must allow herself to be shorn and sent to a monastery. This being the case, many a husband acts more out of caprice than according to right. If he becomes angry with his wife on mere suspicion, or for some other unworthy reason, he bribes a pair of rogues, who will go to court with him and accuse the wife, testifying that they caught her in some misconduct or harlotry. Thus it comes to pass— and especially where kopeks help the plot along—that a good woman, before she knows what is afoot, must don a nun's habit and, against her will, go to a monastery, where she must remain for the rest of her life. For anyone who has once accepted this condition, and had the scissors applied to her head, may no longer leave the monastery and contract a marriage.

While we were there, a great misfortune befell a certain Pole who

---

[13] Solomonia was installed in the Pokrovskii Monastery in Suzdal in 1525. The story of her having given birth to a son is apocryphal. In 1934, excavations at the monastery turned up a child's grave beside Solomonia's. Within it, however, was found not the skeleton of a child but a richly attired doll. Voronin, pp. 235–36.

Vasilii's action in divorcing his wife caused considerable controversy among the clergy, with the Josephites sustaining the ruler and the supporters of Nils Sorskii opposing him. Solomonia was later canonized, according to Pascal, p. 101.

had adopted the Orthodox faith and married a beautiful young Russian. When he had to go off on urgent business and stayed away more than a year, the good woman, probably because her bed was cold, shared it with another, and presently delivered a baby. Hearing of her husband's impending return, she felt uncertain that she could give a satisfactory account of her housekeeping, fled to a monastery, and was shorn. When her husband arrived home and learned what had occurred, he was aggrieved most of all by the fact that his wife had let herself be consecrated a nun. He would willingly have forgiven her and taken her back, and she would have returned to him, but they could not be reunited no matter how much they wished it. In the eyes of the Patriarch and the nuns, it would have been a sin against the Holy Ghost that could never be forgiven.

Although the Russians are greatly addicted to sexual intercourse, both in and out of wedlock, still they consider it sinful and defiling. Therefore, during coitus they temporarily lay aside the little cross that they are given upon baptism and that they wear around the neck. Moreover, since coitus is not supposed to take place in the presence of holy ikons, they are carefully covered.[14] One who has engaged in sexual intercourse is not supposed to enter the church on that day unless he has washed himself well and put on clean clothes.[15] The very pious even then will not enter the church but instead remain in the porch to pray. After a priest has been with his wife, he must wash well above and below the navel before he may enter the church, and he may not go to the altar. Women are considered more unclean than men; accordingly, they are not fully admitted when mass is celebrated, and usually stay at the rear, near the doors of the church.

[14] According to a contemporary account, *The Reporte of a Bloudie and Terrible Massacre in the Citty of Mosco* (London, 1607), p. 23, one of the charges against False Dmitri was that he had had intimate relations with his wife in the presence of an uncovered ikon of the Virgin Mary. The author of this account, which was published anonymously, is identified in the British Museum as William Russell.

[15] Rushchinskii (p. 102) writes that a couple was not admitted to church after having had sexual intercourse, but had to wait outside until given absolution by the priest.

The Tsar and His Powers

THE RUSSIAN SYSTEM of government, as the preceding chapters sug-
gest, is what the political thinkers call "a dominating and despotic
monarchy."[1] After he inherits the crown, the Tsar, or Grand Prince,
alone rules the whole country; all his subjects, the noblemen and
princes as well as the common people, townsmen, and peasants, are his
serfs and slaves, whom he treats as the master of the house does his
servants. This mode of rule is very like that which Aristotle describes
in the following words: "There is also another kind of monarchy,
found in the kingdoms of some of the barbarian peoples, which stands
closest of all to tyranny." If one keeps in mind the basic distinction
between a legitimate and a tyrannical order, that the first subserves
the welfare of the subjects and the second the personal wants of the
sovereign, then the Russian government must be considered closely
related to tyranny.

In addressing the Tsar the magnates must unashamedly not only
write their names in the diminutive form, but also call themselves
slaves, and they are treated as such. Formerly the gosti and magnates,
who were supposed to turn out at public audiences in sumptuous dress,
were beaten on the bare back with the knout, like slaves, if they failed
to appear without good reason. Now, however, they get off with a two-
or three-day confinement in prison, depending upon [the influence of]
their patrons and intercessors at court.

---

[1] West European visitors to Muscovite Russia often described it as an oriental despotism.
Comparisons with the government of the Ottoman Empire were especially frequent. Kliuchevskii,
Skazaniia inostrantsev, p. 81. See also Wittfogel and Baron. Though there was much truth in
their characterization of Russia's governmental system, Western observers were apt to exag-
gerate the Tsar's power somewhat. Olearius was no exception, as subsequent notes will show.
For a critique of Fletcher's account of the Muscovite government, which has some relevance for
Olearius, see Seredonin, especially pp. 217–26.

They call the Grand Prince, their ruler, "Tsar" or "His Tsarist Majesty," and some trace the title's origin to the word Caesar.[2] Like the Holy Roman Emperor, he has an imperial coat of arms and a seal depicting a two-headed eagle with its wings hanging downward. Formerly one crown was shown above the eagle's head, but now there are three, to represent, in addition to the Russian realm, the two Tatar kingdoms of Astrakhan and Kazan. On the eagle's breast hangs a shield showing a horseman plunging a spear into a dragon. This eagle was first introduced by the tyrant Ivan Vasil'evich, for his glorification, for he prided himself on being descended from the Roman emperors.[3] The Tsar's interpreters and some of the German merchants call him "Emperor." However, since the Russians also call King David "Tsar," the word is much closer in meaning to king. Perhaps it derives from the Hebrew *zarah*, which means balsam, or a scented oil (as is evident from the First Book of Moses, Chapter 37, and Jeremiah, Chapter 51), and connotes the anointed, because in ancient times the kings were anointed.

The Russians exalt their Tsar very highly, pronouncing his name with the greatest reverence at assemblies, and they fear him exceedingly, even more than God. One may say of them, too, what [the Persian poet] Saadi said of the king's timid servant in *The Rose Garden:* "If you honored and feared God as the king / You would appear before us as an angel incarnate." Beginning very early, they teach their children to speak of His Tsarist Majesty as of God, and to consider him equally lofty. Thus they often say, "God and the Grand Prince [alone] know that." The same idea is expressed in others of their bywords: they speak of appearing before the Grand Prince as "seeing his bright eyes." To demonstrate their great humility and sense of duty, they say that everything they have belongs not so much to them as to God and the Grand Prince. They came to use such expressions partly in consequence of the violent acts perpetrated by the tyrant Ivan Vasil'evich and partly because they and their property indeed are in that condition. So that they might remain tranquil in slavery and terror,

---

[2] According to Vernadsky (*Russia at the Dawn of the Modern Age*, p. 166), the term "Caesar" was applied in the Byzantine Empire to an office of the second rank. The Russian word "Tsar" was a translation of "Basileus," the title of the Byzantine Emperor.

[3] The two-headed eagle was introduced not by Ivan the Terrible but by Ivan III.

they are forbidden, on pain of corporal punishment, to travel out of the country on their own initiative [for they might then] tell [their countrymen] of the free institutions that exist in foreign lands. Likewise, no merchant may cross the border and carry on trade abroad without the Tsar's permission.

Ten years ago, through the special favor of the Grand Prince, the old German translator Hans Helmes (who died at the age of 97) was allowed to send his son, who had been born in Moscow, to a German university to study medicine; [the son was expected] afterward to serve the Tsar.[4] He was so successful that he obtained the medical degree with great honor, and at Oxford University in England was considered almost a marvel. But once having escaped from Muscovite slavery, he had no wish to return. Later the Novgorod merchant Petr Mikliaev, an intelligent and knowledgeable man who was ambassador to our country a year ago and who then asked me to instruct his son in Latin and German, was unable to obtain permission [for his son to leave] from either the Patriarch or the Grand Prince.[5]

Although they possess the same power, the most recent grand princes have not emulated the former tyrants, who violently assaulted their subjects and their subjects' property. Yet some [of our contemporaries] hold to the contrary view, perhaps basing themselves on old writers such as Herberstein, Jovius, Guagnino, etc., who depicted the Russians' miserable condition under the tyrants' iron scepter. In general, a great deal is written about the Russians which no longer applies, undoubtedly because of general changes in time, regime, and people. The present Grand Prince is a very pious ruler who, like his father, does not wish a single one of his peasants to be impoverished. If one of them, whether a boyar's serf or his own, is stricken by misfortune as a

---

[4] Foreigners generally entered the Russian service either for a given term or for life. In the latter case, the document that granted entry used the phrase *na gosuderego imia* (in the sovereign's name). "Akty o vyezdakh," p. v. In such instances the service obligation applied also to sons, and they could leave for study or other purposes only with the Tsar's permission. Helmes would never have been entrusted with the post he held had he not entered the service for life. Published documents show that permission to study abroad, particularly medicine, were readily granted, from which it may be inferred that those who went generally did return. For a discussion of the history and significance of entering the service "in the sovereign's name," see Muliukin, *Priezd inostrantsev,* pp. 144–53.

[5] Perhaps because of the unfortunate outcome of Godunov's experiment in sending more than a dozen Russian youths abroad to study: none of them returned. Foreigners, especially medical men, may have been more trustworthy because of the special favor and high rewards the Tsar granted them.

result of a bad harvest or some other untoward occurrence, the prikaz to whose jurisdiction he is subject gives him assistance and, in general, keeps an eye on his activity so that he may recover, pay his debt, and fulfill his obligations to the authorities.[6] And if someone is sent in disgrace to Siberia for having abused His Majesty or for some other serious offense—which seldom happens nowadays—even this disfavor is mitigated by providing the exile with a tolerable livelihood, in keeping with his personal condition and worth. Magnates are given money, scribes positions in the chancelleries of Siberian cities; streltsi and soldiers are given places as soldiers, which yield an annual salary and a decent living. The most oppressive aspect for most of them is that they are banished from His Majesty's countenance and deprived of the right to see his bright eyes. Moreover, there have been instances in which such disgrace worked a great advantage, namely when the exiles' professions or trades were more fruitfully pursued [in Siberia] than in Moscow; some prospered so well that, if they had their wives and children with them, they did not wish to return to Moscow even when released.

The Tsar is understandably concerned about his majesty and quality, and enjoys the rights of majesty as other monarchs and absolute rulers do. He is not subject to the law and may, as he desires and deems fit, publish and establish laws and orders. These are accepted and fulfilled by all, whatever their station, without any contradiction and as obediently as if they had been given out by God himself. As Chytraeus justly remarks (*Saxonia*, Book I), the Russians imagine that the Grand Prince does everything according to the will of God. To signify the infallible truth and justice of his actions, they have a proverb: "One may not alter the word of God and the Tsar, but must obey it without fail."

The Grand Prince appoints and removes officials, and even expels and executes them as he pleases.[7] Thus they have precisely the same customs that, according to the prophet Daniel, prevailed in the reign of Nebuchadnezzar, who slew, had beaten, elevated, or humbled

---

[6] The latter consideration makes it plain that the Tsar's concern was not entirely altruistic. Data supporting this view may be found in Zaozerskii, p. 155.

[7] Actually, in the matter of appointments, the Tsar was limited by the *mestnichestvo* system. It obliged him to give precedence, on the basis of seniority, to certain families and individuals, when filling high offices. The system was weakening, however, and was abolished in 1682.

whomsoever he wished. In all the provinces and cities, the Grand Prince appoints the voevodas, namestniks, and administrators, who, with the clerks and d'iaki, or scribes, are supposed to hold court and dispense justice. The decisions they hand down the [Grand Prince's] court considers just, and there is no appeal from their verdict to the court. In the administration of the provinces and towns the Tsar follows the system that Kleobul, in Barclajus's work, praises and commends to the King of Sicily, that is, he does not leave a voevoda or chief official in one place for more than two or three years unless there is a compelling reason. This practice is followed, on the one hand, so that a locality may not be subjected too long to an unjust administration, and, on the other, so that the namestnik may not become too friendly with the inhabitants and be tempted to neglect his duty.

The Grand Prince alone has the right to declare war on foreign nations and may conduct it as he sees fit. He does consult with the boyars and counselors about this, but in the manner of Xerxes, the Persian Emperor, who assembled the Asian princes not so much to secure their advice on the proposed war with the Greeks as to personally declare his will to the princes and prove that he was a monarch.[8] He said then that he had, in truth, assembled them in order that he not do everything at his own discretion, but at the same time they were to understand that their business was more a matter of listening than of advising.

The Grand Prince also distributes titles and honors, making princes of those who have rendered services to him or to the country, or whom, in general, he considers worthy of his favor. Some grand princes who heard that in Germany a monarch may confer doctors' degrees have imitated that right, too. Some of them, as already pointed out, have given such titles to their physicians, and some even to their barbers.

The Tsar coins his own money of pure silver, and sometimes of gold, in four cities of the realm: Moscow, Novgorod, Tver, and Pskov. The coins are as small as Danish sechslings, smaller than the German pfennig; some of them are round and some oblong. On one side there is usually shown a horseman plunging a spear into a rampant dragon

---

[8] The Boyar Duma in fact had more authority than Olearius allows. Besides, he was unaware of another body, the *Zemskii Sobor* (Assembly of the Land), which, though irregularly convened, sometimes exercised considerable influence.

(they say that this was earlier the coat of arms of Novgorod alone);
on the other side, the name of the Grand Prince and the city where the
money was coined are inscribed in Russian letters. This kind of coin is
called a den'ga or kopek,[9] and each is equal in worth to a Dutch stuiver
or, almost, a Meissen groschen or a Holstein schilling. There are 50 of
them to a reichsthaler. They have still smaller coins, half-kopeks and
quarter-kopeks, which they call polushkas and moskovkas.[10] They are
difficult to use in commerce, for they are so small that they easily slip
between the fingers. Therefore, the Russians have acquired the habit
of putting as many as 50 kopeks in their mouths when they are occupied in examining or measuring some good, and continuing to talk and
bargain unhindered, so that an observer cannot notice. One may say
that the Russians transform the mouth into a pocket. In business dealings they count by altyns, grivnas, and rubles, even though these coins
do not exist as such. They reckon them in terms of certain numbers of
kopeks, thus: three kopeks equal one altyn, ten a grivna, and 100 a
ruble. They also use our reichsthalers, which they call efimki (from the
word Joachimsthaler),[11] and gladly exchange them for 50 kopeks
apiece. Then they trade them to the mint and gain on the transaction,
since a ruble or 100 kopeks weighs one-half a loth less than two reichsthalers.[12] Gold coins are not much in evidence. The Grand Prince orders them struck only for distribution to the soldiers to celebrate a victory over an enemy or for other special occasions.

---

[9] The den'ga was not a kopek but a half-kopek. The equivalents Olearius states are correct
for kopeks (fifty to the reichsthaler, three to the altyn, ten to the grivna, and one hundred
to the ruble), but should be doubled in each case for den'gas. See Kurts, *Sochinenie Kil'burgera*,
p. 154.
[10] The polushka was not a half-kopek but a quarter-kopek. Moskovka seems to have been
another name for den'ga. *Ibid.*; and Kliuchevskii, *Skazaniia inostrantsev*, pp. 304–6.
[11] Joachimsthal is the German name for the Bohemian town of Jachymov, the location of a
silver mine and the place where reichsthalers were first coined. The word "efimki" is evidently
a corruption of "iakhimki" (coins from Jachymov).
[12] Because of this advantage and because the tsars were perennially short of silver for coinage,
the government assiduously strove to obtain efimki and framed its commercial policies accordingly. One of the relevant regulations required that Russian merchants who obtained efimki in
trade operations with foreigners turn them over to the treasury and receive Russian coins in
exchange. In 1662 a government effort to corner all the silver in the country and leave only
copper coins in circulation touched off a serious uprising, the so-called copper rebellion. Although it retreated thereafter, the government's continuing preoccupation with the problem is
evident in the New Trade Charter of 1667, under which foreign merchants were obliged to
pay customs duties in gold of efimki. See Basilevich, "Elementy merkantilizma," pp. 11–12,
16ff; and "Novotorgovyi ustav," pp. 612–13.

The Grand Prince also levies heavy customs duties from time to time. Today both Russian and foreign merchants must pay a 5 per cent tax at Archangel and Astrakhan, which brings in a great profit in a year.[18]

The Tsar sometimes sends costly embassies to the Holy Roman Emperor, the Danish, Swedish, and Persian kings, and other monarchs. The most important persons sent are called Grand Ambassadors, and the less important, *poslanniki*. Sometimes he sends great gifts, consisting entirely of furs. I know, from a trustworthy witness, of a memorable instance of the kind. In 1595 Grand Prince Feodor Ivanovich sent with an important embassy to Emperor Rudolf II the following: 1,003 timbers of sable, 519 timbers of marten, 120 black fox, 337,000 fox, 3,000 beaver, 1,000 wolfskins, and 74 elk hides. Sometimes when they do not bring gifts from the Grand Prince, the ambassadors, and especially the poslanniki, themselves present sables, expecting something in return. If the latter is not forthcoming straightway, they do not shrink from offering reminders.

Almost every year the Grand Prince sends to the Persian Shah poslanniki who, since they have only minor missions to perform, also engage in trade (over and above these, the Grand Prince sends his own merchants).[14] Their dealings are particularly advantageous inasmuch as the Shah provides full maintenance for them while they are in his country. Because the Tsar quite often sends his ambassadors to foreign monarchs, he is frequently visited by ambassadors from foreign courts. It often happens that two, three, or more ambassadors are in Moscow at once, and then the settling of their affairs and their dismissal go very slowly. Some foreign rulers maintain in Moscow legates, permanent consuls, or residents, who live in their own special compounds.[15] Comfortable houses and residences have been built in Moscow for

---

[18] In response to the pressures of Russian merchants, the government obliged foreign merchants to pay additional duties if they transported their goods into the country for sale. Basilevich, "Elementy merkantilizma," p. 11.

[14] Except for periods when they granted concessions to foreign trading companies, the tsars claimed a monopoly of the Persian silk trade, which was carried on by their agents.

[15] At different times in the seventeenth century, England, Sweden, Denmark, Poland, and the Ottoman Empire had representatives in Moscow. Few such residents or embassies were permanent, however. The expulsion of the English merchants from Moscow in 1649 destroyed the basis for a permanent English resident. And when Pommerening, the Swedish agent, left Russia in 1651, the Tsar refused to accredit his successor, Rodes. See Kurts, *Sostoianie Rossii*, pp. 7–8.

visiting envoys. There are no beds in these houses, however, and anyone who does not care to sleep on straw and hard benches must bring
his own bed with him. The gates of the ambassadors' houses are posted
with strong guards, and formerly they strictly saw to it that none of an
ambassador's suite went out, and that no strangers entered. The ambassadors were guarded as though under arrest. Now, however, after
the first public audience, anyone can go where he pleases. The inhabitants told us at the time of the first embassy that we were the first lega-
tion to have the right to go out freely.[16]

So long as they remain in the country, the ambassadors and their
suites are very amply maintained.[17] They are regularly visited by two
pristavs who have been assigned to serve them. The pristavs usually
ask the ambassadors various questions. Why have they come to the
Grand Prince? Do they know the contents of the letter to the Tsar?
Do they have gifts to present to His Tsarist Majesty and how many?
Do they have anything for the pristavs personally? Soon after the
presents have been handed over, on the second or third day, the Tsar
orders certain people to determine their value.

Formerly, after having been granted a public audience, the ambassadors were always invited to dine in the Grand Prince's chambers,
sometimes at his own table.[18] Now the food and drink graciously
granted are usually furnished at the ambassadors' residences. If they
have presented gifts from their sovereigns or on behalf of themselves,
upon their departure the ambassadors and their aides carry away fine
presents in the form of sables and other furs. So long as they bring a
friendly dispatch from foreign sovereigns, ambassadors generally are
given a timber of 20 pairs of sable, which cost 100 thalers or more in
Moscow.

To facilitate the travel of ambassadors and couriers, a good system
has been established on the highways. In various places there reside

---

[16] Olearius was overly sanguine if he thought a new era had begun, for, as Kliuchevskii
(*Skazaniia inostrantsev*, pp. 54–56) points out, indignities continued to be visited upon foreign
envoys after this time.

[17] Krizhanich (I, 372) castigated foreign diplomatic representatives who stayed long and
at great expense, and, after their departure, were wont to write insulting books "in which all
our laws, and gifts, and entertainments are snapped at and subjected to ridicule."

[18] For example, Herberstein and Jenkinson, the English ambassador to Ivan the Terrible,
were so honored. Herberstein, II, 126; Morgan and Coote, I, 31–32.

certain peasants who must daily have ready in the village 40, 50, or more horses so that upon receipt of the Grand Prince's order they may quickly harness up the horses and speed them on their way. The pristav either goes ahead himself or he sends someone else to advise of the courier's approach. When the courier arrives, whether by day or at night, and blows a whistle, the coachmen turn out right away with their horses. Consequently it is easily possible to cover the distance from Novgorod to Moscow, which is reckoned 120 leagues, in six or seven days, and in the winter, by sleigh, faster yet. For this service each peasant receives an annual wage of 30 rubles and is granted land by the Grand Prince, free of any levies and other obligations. When they turn out, the pristav is supposed to give each of them an altyn or two (this they call "buttering the bread"). This employment is very advantageous for the peasants, and many strive to become coachmen.

In order better to explain the essence of the Russian system of police and administration, I propose to make a digression from [the account of] my journey to tell briefly of some of the grand princes and of the remarkable events of their times that are related to our subject.[19] I shall begin with the cruel tyrant and continue to the present ruler, Aleksei Mikhailovich.

The tyrant Ivan Vasil'evich ascended the throne in 1540 A.D., and waged terrible and cruel wars against his neighbors. He brought many German Livonians and other captives to Moscow, where their descendants live as slaves even now. He raged and tyrannized cruelly and inhumanly, not to say in an unchristian manner, equally against Christians, even his own subjects, and Turks, Tatars, and pagans. Some examples have already been adduced above in the description of Great Novgorod, and it was shown very clearly, in fact, how unjust is Jovius's glorification of him in the first book of his history, where he calls him "an outstanding zealot of the Christian religion." Probably such a superficial impression was received because he dared to perform the duty of chief priest, resolved disputes in spiritual affairs, sacrilegiously

---

[19] This brief survey may give some indication of the quality of historical understanding in the seventeenth century, but it has little or no value as a source for the period it treats. For that reason, no attempt has been made to annotate or to correct errors in this portion of the work.

served mass himself, sang, and executed other church ceremonies, as if he were a priest or monk. Frequently, at table, he gaily chanted the Athanasian Creed.

He had several wives, one after another. By the first, he sired two sons: Ivan, whom he himself slew with a staff, and Feodor, who succeeded him. By his last wife, he fathered his son Dmitri, whom Boris Godunov had murdered, as will be told here shortly. The tyrant died on March 28, 1584, at the age of 55. He suffered a horrible death, and expired with a pitiful groan. His body, which had begun to decay while he was still alive, emitted an unbearable stench for several days before he died, as well as after.

Feodor Ivanovich

Ivan's son Feodor was crowned Grand Prince on July 31st of the same year, at the age of 22. Since he was young and his wit not as quick and active as was needed, given the then troubled condition of the country (his chief pleasure and vocation was to ring the bell before and after the worship services, as Solomon Henning tells in his *Liefländische Chronica*, p. 150), it was deemed proper that Boris Godunov, the state Master of the Horse and the brother of the Grand Princess, should help him rule.

This Boris Godunov, with his intelligent judgment and careful administration, gained such great respect and love in the country that it was generally agreed, in the event of the death of Grand Prince Feodor Ivanovich and also of the young prince Dmitri, no one would be better suited to govern than he. Boris took note of this, and in order that the wishes of the Russians might sooner be fulfilled, he had the young prince Dmitri murdered at Uglich in his tenth year. It was done by hirelings, to whom the court servitors had made great promises. The deed accomplished, the murderers merrily returned to Moscow, hoping to be well rewarded by Boris for a service so willingly rendered. Instead, Boris ordered the murderers slain at once in order that the treachery might remain secret. He also secretly set fires in various parts of Moscow so that the Muscovites might not mourn Dmitri's death so much as the destruction of their own homes and hearths, and thanks to their own misfortune, would have reason to forget another's. He himself acted extremely grieved and indignant at the murder, sent many Uglich inhabitants into miserable exile, and razed the castle as a place defiled by murder. Grand Prince Feodor Ivanovich, after ruling for 12 years, contracted a short-term sickness and died in 1597.

Boris Godunov

Since Feodor Ivanovich left no heir, and his brother was dead, the magnates took counsel to decide who should be the sovereign. "Although there were in the country many distinguished magnates from among whom a ruler might be chosen [they thought], no one was as wise and cautious as Boris Godunov. Moreover, he was already accustomed to governing, and therefore he, and no one else, must be Grand Prince." When Boris was offered this high honor, he disclaimed all intention of accepting, because [the office] brought trouble, annoyance, hostility, and enmity. He declared that he should rather wear the cowl of a simple monk than a crown and scepter, and went off to a monastery. Nevertheless, he conducted an intrigue with certain magnates and good friends to the end that no one but him should be chosen; his refusal notwithstanding, he was to be importuned until he agreed. Everything was done according to his wishes. When the Russians heard that he was going with his sister to a monastery, they came to him in great crowds, fell to the ground weeping, and pleaded with him not to be shorn too hastily, for they wished to choose him as Grand Prince. At last their tears and the pleas of his sister softened him, and he accepted the crown that he had already coveted for a goodly time, and which he would not have yielded to anyone for anything. In this way, Boris Godunov became Grand Prince in 1597.

During his reign, a commotion was caused by a Russian monk named Grishka Otrep'ev, who was born in Iaroslavl to a minor noble family. He had been sent to a monastery as a check on his insolence and effrontery. He declared himself to be Dmitri, the tyrant Ivan Vasil'evich's son, and succeeded in having himself recognized as such and crowned Grand Prince. The affair began in the following way. At the instigation of a crafty, old, rich monk, this intelligent young man went secretly to Lithuania, entered the service of Prince Adam Wishnowetski, and by his faithful service won his favor. Once when his lord was angered by some offense or other, he called Grishka a "son of a bitch" in the usual abusive way, and struck him on the neck. Grishka began to cry bitterly

and said, "Lord, if you knew who I am, you would not have called me
a son of a bitch and would not have treated me this way!" When the
Prince wished to know who he was, he answered that he was the son
of Grand Prince Ivan Vasil'evich. Boris Godunov had wanted to kill
him, but instead had murdered a priest's son of his age and appearance.
With the aid of kind folk, he had been saved and brought to a monastery. Then he presented a gold cross studded with precious stones,
which he said had been hung around his neck at his baptism. He explained that he had not wished earlier to reveal who he was out of fear
of Boris Godunov. Then he fell on his knees before the Prince and
entreated him to take him under his protection. As this fugitive monk
was able to recount all the circumstances, in which he had been well
versed, and accompanied the tale with winning facial expressions, he
moved his lord to believe the story. He was forthwith granted magnificent clothing and horses and was accorded honor fully in keeping
with the station of a Grand Prince's son.

Little by little, it became known in Russia that the true heir to the
grand-princely throne, miraculously saved by God from his foes, had
been found. They believed the story the more willingly in that Boris,
disturbed by the rumors, promised estates and much money to whomsoever should deliver the supposed Dmitri into his hands. Meanwhile,
for safety's sake, Dmitri went to Poland, where he was well received by
the voevoda of Sandomierz. He was promised assistance in regaining
his ancestral throne as soon as possible, if, on his side, he agreed to establish the Catholic religion in Moscow after he recovered the throne.
Dmitri not only agreed to all this, but even secretly embraced the Roman Catholic religion himself and promised besides to wed the voevoda's daughter and to make her Grand Princess. The voevoda was
greatly pleased with this proposition. [The pretender] was presented
at the court of the King of Poland, where, because it was believed that
he was Ivan Vasil'evich's son, he was sumptuously received and entertained. Seduced by the prospect of obtaining such a distinguished husband for his daughter, and desiring to spread his religion, the voevoda
threw all his energy into this enterprise. With other Polish magnates
he mobilized a great army, with which Grishka appeared in Russia and
openly launched a bloody conflict against the reigning Grand Prince.
In the campaign, he succeeded in occupying one house and town after

another and gained many adherents, including some military commanders whom Boris had sent against him. All this so shocked the Grand Prince that he died suddenly and unexpectedly on April 13, 1605.

Feodor Borisovich

The magnates in Moscow now elected as sovereign the late Grand Prince Boris's son, the still very young Feodor Borisovich. However, when they saw that Dmitri's power was waxing as time went on, they discerned in this a harbinger of trouble for themselves, took counsel, and came to an agreement that the one with whom they had to deal was the real Dmitri, although they had formerly considered him to have been slain at Uglich. Thence they arrived at the conclusion that there was no basis for fighting the country's [true] sovereign. When these views were made known to the community, [the Muscovites], a people of fickle disposition, were easily persuaded to this opinion and began to cry aloud, "May God grant happiness to Dmitri, the country's true heir, and may He eradicate all [his] enemies!" They ran into the Kremlin, seized the recently elected Grand Prince, and imprisoned him. Then they plundered and exiled all of Boris Godunov's remaining kin. They sent to Dmitri, requesting that he come and occupy his father's throne, and asked forgiveness for their long resistance, which had been called forth partly by ignorance, partly by the instigation of the Godunovs. They advised at the same time that they had already opened the road for him. Feodor Borisovich and his mother and sister were in captivity, and they were ready to give them and all their family into his power. False Dmitri had awaited this news a long time. Even before his entry into the capital city of Moscow, he sent ahead the scribe Ivan Bogdanov to murder Feodor and his mother and then to announce that they had poisoned themselves. Accordingly, the young Grand Prince Feodor Borisovich was strangled in the second month of his rule, to be precise, on June 10, 1605.

False Dmitri

On June 16th, False Dmitri with all his forces at last entered Moscow. Muscovites of high and low estate went to meet him, bearing magnificent gifts, and congratulated him upon his arrival. On July 29th he was crowned with great pomp. Then, so that the deception might be less noticed and he might more readily be taken for the true Dmitri, he had the true Dmitri's mother, whom Boris Godunov had sent to a distant monastery, brought to Moscow. He went out to meet her with a magnificent suite and cordially escorted her into the city. He arranged a royal table for her in the Kremlin, visited her daily, and showed her such great respect as only a son could render to his own mother. The good woman, who knew that her own son had in fact been killed and that this other could not be her own, nevertheless lent herself to the [realization of the] scheme, partly out of fear, partly out of a desire to enjoy such reverence and pleasures after the great grief and sorrow she had suffered. She contradicted no one.

Dmitri began to arrange and observe court procedures, a governing system, and customs and usages different from those of other Russians and [previous] grand princes. He wedded a Polish Catholic girl, the daughter of the Sandomierz voevoda, after taking a great amount of money and other wealth from the treasury and sending it to Poland for the sumptuous outfitting of his bride. The marriage was celebrated more in the Polish than the Muscovite manner, and on the day immediately following the wedding the new Grand Princess doffed her Muscovite clothes and donned Polish ones. Dmitri himself ordered the cook to prepare veal and other dishes that the Russians, who consider them loathsome, do not eat. In the course of the entire wedding celebration, he never once went to the bath, even though it was daily prepared for him. He went unwashed to church, followed by a pack of dogs, which defiled its sanctity. He did not bow sufficiently low to the ikons and generally did many things that greatly upset the Russians. Thus it dawned on them that they had been deceived.

Vasilii Ivanovich Shuiskii, one of the most notable of the country's prince's, secretly held discussions with other magnates and priests about this, and pointed out to them the great danger to which their religion, country, and people were exposed by this Grand Prince. [Then they said], "Evidently he is not the Grand Prince's son by birth and not the true father of the country, but a traitor." And they decided to rid themselves of Dmitri. However, the secret plot became known to him, and he ordered many of the Russians burned to death. Shuiskii, the head of the conspiracy, was tortured, beaten with the knout, and condemned to death. But when they brought him to the place of execution, and the axe was already poised above his neck, the Grand Prince ordered that he be granted mercy, and pardoned him of the crime of lèse majesté. In this way, he reasoned, he would show himself to be a severe and a just ruler, depending on the circumstances, and he would inspire both fear of involvement in plots and love for himself.

For some time afterward, the Russians were tranquil and submissive to him, and thus led him to feel entirely secure—until the day of the wedding, which was celebrated on May 8th, 1606. When, together with the bride, many heavily armed Poles and other foreigners entered the city, the Russians' eyes were opened again. Once more Prince Vasilii Shuiskii secretly called the city's notables to his residence, repeated the great danger the present Grand Prince posed to the country, and said that to leave the administration of the government in his hands any longer would undoubtedly lead to its final ruin. [He said] that he himself had already risked his life once for the Greek religion and the welfare of the country, and he was prepared to do it again and to seek means of avoiding disaster, if they would only help him. Without reflecting long, the others promised, and vowed with him to sacrifice their property and their lives if he would proceed with what was wanted.

They kept this decision secret and awaited an opportunity, which they found in the last days of the wedding celebration. On the night of May 17th, the ninth day of the wedding festivities, while Dmitri and his intimates lay in a drunken sleep, the Russians arose, gave the signal by ringing all the bells, burst into his bedchamber, and pillaged and plundered everything. The Grand Prince, who tried, with the aid of the remaining guards, to escape to the square through the window, was seized, unmercifully beaten, and returned to the bedroom with much taunting.

When his supposed mother learned of this and was asked by Shuiskii, to the kissing of the cross, whether Dmitri was truly her son, she immediately answered in the negative; she had had but one son, who in his youth was perfidiously slain. After that Dmitri was shot with a pistol. Then the servants, wedding guests, and other foreigners, including some jewelers who had brought to Moscow many very precious ornaments—in all 1,700 people—were mercilessly slaughtered. The Grand Princess, her brother, and her father, the voevoda, as well as the Polish King's ambassadors who had been sent for the wedding celebration, were imprisoned and badly treated. For example, the noblewomen were forcefully thrown to the ground and dishonored. The naked body of Dmitri was dragged through the square before the Kremlin and left lying three days on a table, so that everyone might see and damn the imposter. They then buried him, but soon afterward the corpse was disinterred and burned.

Prince Vasilii Ivanovich Shuiskii

Since all of this came about strictly in accord with the intentions of the Russians, they made their leader, Vasilii Ivanovich Shuiskii, Grand Prince, and crowned him on June 1, 1606. His reign had hardly commenced when a new pretender appeared. [This adventurer], named Grigorii Shakhovskoi, thought to make use of the stratagem of the previous Dmitri. During the tumult in the Kremlin, he secured the Grand Prince's seal, and went off with it, in the company of two Poles, to Poland. On the way he spread the rumor at all the inns that he was Dmitri, and, thanks to his cleverness, he had escaped from the Russians. As the affair had occurred at night, someone else was mistaken for him and was killed on the spot. Now he wanted to get to Poland to raise a new army and revenge himself upon the Muscovites for the shame and losses he had suffered. Everywhere he distributed generous gifts to the innkeepers. Those who had not been in Moscow believed him and communicated [the news] to Moscow. These rumors again called forth no little disturbance. So the Russians had to wage a great war against this imposter, and still another, a third pretender. The latter also called himself Dmitri, the natural son of Ivan Vasil'evich, but actually he had been a simple scribe in Moscow. As he was very witty and eloquent, he gained a considerable number of adherents, not only among fugitives but also in the great cities. They were joined by the Polish magnates, who helped him no little in order to get revenge on the Muscovites for the shame they had sustained. When the Russians several times suffered severely from these foes, they began to blame Prince Shuiskii, holding that he was unsuccessful in his rule, inasmuch as victory eluded him and inclined to the side of the enemy. The bloodletting in Russia would not end, they thought, so long as he remained in power. Therefore, put up to it by three Moscow lords, namely Zakharii Liapunov, Mikhail Molchanov, and Ivan Rzhevskii, they deprived Shuiskii, in the third year of his rule, of his scepter and crown, and dispatched him to a monastery. There, against his will, he was shorn as a monk. Then they decided not to take a ruler from among themselves but instead to have someone of a foreign lineage, born of royal or princely parents. With regard to stature, similarity of language, manners, and clothing, etc., they knew of no more suitable candidate than Vladislav, the son of the King of Poland. Accordingly, they made a proposal to the Polish King, who accepted on certain conditions. This occurred in 1610.

Then the Russians brought their Grand Prince, Vasilii Shuiskii, out of the monastery, and sent him, along with his brother Dmitri Shuiskii, a Russian colonel, and a third brother and some other lords of the Shuiskii clan, to Smolensk, as hostages to the Polish King. While under the power of the Polish King, Vasilii died. He was buried, so they say, near the road between Warsaw and Thurn.

Vladislav, Son of Sigismund, King of Poland

The Polish King ordered his colonel Stanislav Zolkiewski, who at that time was threatening Moscow with his army, that when an armistice had been concluded, he was to take the oath in the name of Vladislav, to begin to manage affairs, and to remain in Moscow until Vladislav himself should arrive. The Russians agreed to this, swore allegiance to the colonel representing Vladislav, and in turn accepted his vow. They conducted Zolkiewski with a thousand persons into the grand-princely palace in the capital, and welcomed him with all sorts of luxurious presents and entertainments. Meanwhile, the Polish army stood peacefully outside the city. Between the Muscovite and Polish camps there was great friendship; each day they fraternized and exchanged things. The Poles began to enter the city individually, seeking shelter with the townsmen. Ultimately, there were 6,000 persons in and around the Kremlin. They became very burdensome to the Russians in their homes and churches and on the streets, and the burghers preferred to have no dealings with them, particularly since the time of arrival of the Grand Prince was somewhat drawn out. It seemed too long to them, and the whole affair began to appear suspicious. Therefore, on January 26, 1611, thousands of Muscovites gathered in the square before the Kremlin, and began to complain bitterly at the great violence and the dissolute behavior of the soldiers with respect to their daughters and wives, and especially to their ikons, at which the Poles fired their pistols. Besides, the daily provisioning of 6,000 men in the city cost a great deal. They also complained that they were being hindered in all their affairs and were exhausted by the exactions. Further, they did not know what to think of the newly elected Grand Prince's failure to appear. Therefore, they could bear no more, and [the soldiers] had to resort to other means to secure their well-being.

Although the Polish colonel tried to pacify them with kind words, and even ordered severe punishments for some of the criminals among his soldiers, the Russians were not satisfied. Fearing a general uprising, the Poles set a strong guard, occupied all the streets and gates, and forbade the Russians to go about with deadly weapons in their hands. This embittered the Russians all the more. They collected in crowds in different parts of the city so that the Poles should have to divide up in order to fight them. The Poles set fires in various parts of the city, and the Russians were obliged to flee if they were not to allow their wives, children, and everything dear to them to perish in the flames. Out of this came such a colossal fire that the whole great city of Moscow, except for the Kremlin and the stone churches, was reduced to ashes in two days. More than two thousand Muscovites perished, and the rest were forced to flee the city. Afterward the Kremlin, the grand-princely treasury, the churches, and the monasteries were pillaged, and unbelievable wealth, in the form of gold, silver, pearls, precious stones, and other valuable things, was seized and sent to Poland. As Petrejus tells, for amusement the soldiers loaded large single pearls into their firearms and shot them into the air. Even now the Russians complain of that monstrous plundering and, among other things, about the loss of a large unicorn embellished with large diamonds and other precious stones.

Fourteen days after the turmoil, Zakharii Liapunov (who earlier, with two accomplices, had secured Shuiskii's exile and the election of the Polish King's son as Grand Prince) came up to Moscow with several thousand people whom he had collected in the country, besieged the Poles in the Kremlin, and, since they had been noticeably weakened in the earlier fighting, inflicted such great damage upon them that the Poles asked for peace, surrendered the Kremlin, and once again left the country.

Mikhail Feodorovich

When the Russians again became masters of their country, they selected and crowned Mikhail Feodorovich as Grand Prince. This occurred in 1613. His father was Feodor Nikitich, a relative of the tyrant, Ivan Vasil'evich. When the father abandoned the wedded state and entered the priestly calling, he was chosen Patriarch. He then changed his name and was called Filaret Nikitich. Like him, his son was very pious and God-fearing. Through his entire life, he showed great respect and filial obedience to his father. When the envoys of foreign sovereigns were to come in public audience before His Tsarist Majesty, his father and the clergy, by his wish, sat at his right hand. Patriarch Filaret died in 1633, shortly before our arrival in Moscow.

Upon taking the throne, Grand Prince Mikhail Feodorovich found great disorders in the country. He tried to conclude peace with the neighboring rulers as soon as possible, ruled modestly, and dealt graciously with foreigners and natives alike. Everyone said that the Russians had never in a full hundred years had such a benevolent tsar. He died suddenly on July 12, 1645, in his 49th year, after a reign lasting 33 years. Eight days later his wife, the Grand Princess, died. His son, Prince Aleksei Mikhailovich succeeded, and rules at present.

Before continuing with a description of Aleksei Mikhailovich's reign and my observations on the condition of Russia, I wish to take notice of another pretender who, before the death of the last ruler and the accession of the present one, resorted to a deception of the sort [perpetrated by] the False Dmitri and gave himself out as the lawful heir to the throne.

A certain Russian named Johannes Sinensis claimed that in Sarmatian his name translated as Ivan Shuiskii. After fleeing Moscow, where he had committed certain crimes, he represented himself in foreign lands as the son of the former Grand Prince Vasilii Ivanovich Shuiskii. At great expense the present ruler, Aleksei Mikhailovich, had him sought out. He was captured and was executed in Moscow last year.

As he was known in a number of foreign countries, to some extent personally, to some extent by rumor, and many—including even great sovereigns—were ignorant of the truth about him (indeed there were many very erroneous ideas current), I wish briefly to tell the whole truth, as I reliably learned it not only from the Russians but also from the Germans living in Moscow, who were well acquainted with him.

His true name was Timoshka Ankudinov. He was born in the town of Vologda, in the district of the same name, of humble parents. His father, whose name was Demka or Dementii Ankudinov, traded in flax. As his father observed in him good qualities and a notable intelligence, he made it possible for him to go to school. There he studied so diligently that he learned to read and to write a fine hand. It appears that he attained a degree of education that the Russians have not yet surpassed. Besides, it turned out that he had a fine singing voice—he could sing the church liturgy beautifully—and therefore Nektarii, the Archbishop of Vologda and Velikoperm, befriended him, took him into his home, and engaged him in the service of the church. He conducted himself so well that the archbishop gave him in marriage the daughter he had fathered before assuming the spiritual dignity of archbishop. Timoshka now began to be arrogant and sometimes spoke of himself in letters as the grandson of the Vologda and Velikoperm governor. After the archbishop's death, having squandered his wife's property, he went with his wife and child to Moscow, where he was taken in by Ivan Patrikeev, a former friend at the archbishop's court and now a clerk at the Novaia Chetvert' Prikaz, who secured him a position as scribe in the same prikaz.

Here, too, he did so well that he was entrusted with the collection and disbursement of money. This prikaz managed the revenues received from the Grand Prince's taverns and saloons. For a time he fulfilled his duty conscientiously, but at last he got mixed up with bad company, began to drink and gamble, and, in the course of things, appropriated the Grand Prince's money. When he saw that in the next audit he would be short 100 rubles, he resorted to every kind of ruse and fabrication in order to make up the stolen money (for at the Moscow court such audits are done very strictly, and everyone involved is kept in a state of fear). For one thing, he went to a scribe in the same prikaz, Vasilii Grigor'evich Shpil'kin, who was his godparent (a matter of great significance in Muscovy) and had often treated him kindly. He told him that a good friend, a notable merchant, had come from

Vologda, and he [Timoshka] had invited him to his home on the following day. In order that his wife might be more richly dressed than
usual when, as is the custom, she toasted the guest with vodka, he asked
his godparent and good friend to lend him his wife's pearl necklace and
[other] ornaments. He promised to return them to his home promptly
and in good condition.

Suspecting no deception, Shpil'kin willingly fulfilled his request, and
asked no security, even though the jewels cost more than a thousand
thalers. Timoshka not only forgot to return the things but, when
Shpil'kin reminded him of it, he denied having received anything and
demanded proof. Shpil'kin then took Timoshka to court, and in the
face of his continued denial, had him imprisoned. As the accused could
not be convicted, he was released on bond. Meanwhile, he could not
return the embezzled money. At this point, Timoshka's own wife, with
whom he was not getting along well, began to accuse him of this crime
and also of practicing pederasty, at which he was often caught. Timoshka began to fear that his wife might tell everything, and all his evildoing become known. In order to suppress the matter, he resolved on an
even greater crime. He took his son to his good friend Ivan Peskov, at
the Razboinyi Prikaz, and that night came back to his home on Tverskaia Street, near the Swedish Resident's house, locked his wife in her
room, ignited a fire, and burned down the house with his wife inside.
Then he fled to Poland; so for a long time it was not known if he were
alive or if he had perished in the fire. This occurred in 1643.

When some Muscovite ambassadors came to Poland two years later
and learned that a Russian was there, Timoshka, fearing that they
would begin asking about him, fled to the Cossack Hetman, Khmelnitskii. He complained to him that he was being persecuted because he
was of the grand-princely line. By flattering speeches he won the favor
of Khmelnitskii, who treated him well. Two years afterward, an ambassador of the Tsar, named Iakov Kozlov, was sent on a mission to
Khmelnitskii. He saw Timoshka there, recognized him, and by kind
words tried to persuade him to give up his fugitive existence and return
to Moscow, [arguing that] the mistake with the Grand Prince's funds
might easily be forgiven through the intervention of good friends. At
that time it was not yet known that he had given himself out as the son

of Grand Prince Shuiskii. However, Timoshka did not believe his friend, and as his guilty conscience drove him further, he disappeared again, and in 1648 fled to Turkey. There he allowed himself to be circumcised, and adopted the Muslim faith.

His lecherous conduct here placed his head in jeopardy, so he secretly fled to Italy, to Rome, and there he adopted the Roman Catholic faith. Thence he went to Vienna, in Austria, and from there, in 1650, to Prince Rakoczy in Transylvania, or Semigrade. The Prince took him in, believed his clever avowals, greatly pitied him, and in accord with his persuasive plea, released him with recommendations to other rulers. Then he went to Sweden, where, thanks to Prince Rakoczy's letter of recommendation, [Queen] Christina rendered him every kindness and dismissed him with fine gifts. Meanwhile, some Russian merchants in Stockholm advised Moscow of the presence of a person [of his description]. Tsar Aleksei had the scribe Kozlov immediately sent to His Royal Swedish Majesty with a letter, the gist of which was as follows: "It has come to the attention of His Tsarist Majesty that, to his great detriment, there has appeared in Stockholm a certain Russian who calls himself the son of Vasilii Ivanovich Shuiskii (who left no male progeny) and gives his name as Johannes Sinensis. For the sake of our neighborly friendship, it is desirable that the said False Shuiskii be turned over to our ambassador."

However, even before the arrival of the messenger, the said Shuiskii managed to decamp and got to Livonia. His servant Kost'ka, that is Konstantin, who stayed behind, was caught, shackled with many chains, and sent to Moscow. In response to a search letter sent by His Royal Swedish Majesty, Timoshka himself was imprisoned under guard at Revel, but he escaped and fled. At this point, simply because a plot was suspected, Timoshka's mother and everyone who had been friendly to the fugitive were imprisoned and tortured, and some of them died. Leaving Livonia, Timoshka went to Brabant and stayed, as he writes, at Archduke Leopold's. Thence he went to Leipzig and Wittenberg, with a Pole named Stephan Lipovski, where he embraced Protestantism and received the Eucharist, as may be seen from his confession (which was written in Latin and accompanied by his own signature and seal, and which to the present time is located in Wittenberg University). At last he came to Neustadt in Holstein, where he was caught and locked up under the guard of a Russian merchant named Petr Mikliaev, of Novgorod, who had been sent with the Tsar's search letters to the German princes and kings. In accord with a most polite request by the Russian, and also by a notable Lübeck merchant, he was brought from Neustadt to the princely residence in Gottorp and held there until the Tsar sent special letters and messengers to His Princely Highness of Schleswig-Holstein.

Because of this Timoshka, His Tsarist Majesty from time to time had sent ambassadors and messengers with search letters to the European kings, princes, and rulers, so that the fugitive should feel secure nowhere and should be captured wherever he might be. Therefore, as soon as he learned from the ambassador in Sweden that Timoshka had been caught in Neustadt in Holstein, he sent two messengers, one after another, with identical letters, to His Princely Highness.

[*The next pages, omitted here, give the letter, which goes over much the same ground Olearius has already covered, and the details of Timoshka's interrogation, torture, and execution.*]

On July 12th, 1645, Mikhail Feodorovich, Grand Prince of all Russia, died. On the next day, July 13th, his 16-year-old son, Aleksei Mikhailovich, was proclaimed Tsar and Grand Prince of all Russia. And on the same day, by unanimous consent of the boyars, the magnates, and the whole community, he was crowned and the oath of allegiance to him was taken. At the instance of Boris Ivanovich Morozov, the young sovereign's former major domo and tutor, the coronation for certain reasons had to be performed so soon that not everyone in the country who wished to attend was able to.

The crowning of the Muscovite grand princes is traditionally carried out as follows. To Moscow are called all of the metropolitans, archbishops and other bishops, and abbots; the princes, voevodas, and other officials; as well as the leading merchants of all Russia and all the provinces subject to the Grand Prince's power. When the coronation is to begin, the Patriarch, with the metropolitan and the rest of the clergy, proceeds into the great Kremlin church.[20] After them comes the new Grand Prince, with the state counselors, the boyars, and the officials.

20 The Uspenskii Sobor.

In the church is a raised platform three steps high and covered with costly rugs. Three chairs covered with gold brocade stand on it, one for the Grand Prince, another for the Patriarch; on the third lies a hat set with precious stones and large pearls. From the crown of the hat hangs a tassel, to which is attached a little golden crown set with diamonds. By the hat lies a sumptuous gold brocade robe embellished all about with pearls and precious stones and lined with very black sables. They say that a grand prince named Dmitri [properly, Vladimir] Monomakh obtained it from Kaffa in a war with the Tatars, and designated it for the coronation of the grand princes.

When the Tsar and the boyars enter the church, the priests begin to sing. The Patriarch reads a prayer, bidding God, St. Nicholas, and other saints to be present at the coronation. The foremost state counselor then comes forward with the Grand Prince-elect, advises the Patriarch that they have accepted as Tsar the nearest heir to the throne of the Russian state, and asks the Patriarch to bless and crown him. The Patriarch then escorts the candidate up onto the stage, seats him on the chair, presses to his forehead a gold cross encrusted with gorgeous precious stones, and blesses him. Then one of the metropolitans reads the following prayer, as set down by Petrejus in his Russian chronicle.

"Our Lord God, King of kings, Thou who through Thy prophet Samuel chose Thy servant David and anointed him King of the people of Israel, hear now the prayer that we unworthy ones make to Thee. From Thy sacred height, look down upon Thy faithful servant who now sits on the throne and whom Thou hast raised to be King of Thy people, saved by the blood of Thy Holy Son. Anoint him with the oil of gladness, preserve him by Thy might, set on his head a crown embellished with precious stones, give him long life, and place in his hand a kingly scepter. Seat him on the throne of justice, and subjugate to him all who speak in barbarian tongues; let his heart and mind always be in fear of Thee so that he will be obedient to Thy commandments all his life; teach him to defend and preserve against heresy and error all that the holy Greek Church prescribes and wishes. [Let him] govern Thy people with justice, and give alms to the poor that they may enter into life everlasting." The Patriarch ends the prayer with a loud exclamation: "Thine is the kingdom, and the power, and the glory, and may God the Father, God the Son, and God the Holy Ghost be with you."

After the prayer two bishops take the robe and hat from the chair and hold them, and the Patriarch instructs the boyars who have mounted the platform to dress the Grand Prince. Meanwhile he blesses him again. He then passes the hat with the crown to the boyars, instructs them to put it on the Grand Prince, and saying, "In the name of God the Father, God the Son, and God the Holy Ghost," blesses him a third time. The Patriarch then calls each member of the clergy in the church to approach and bless the Grand Prince with his hand. When that is done, the Patriarch and the Grand Prince sit down on the chairs, but soon rise again. The priests then begin to sing the litany, "Gospodi pomilui" (Lord have mercy). At every third word, they say the Grand Prince's name. When they all sit down again, one of the metropolitans goes up to the altar and says aloud, "May God preserve our Tsar and Grand Prince of all Russia, whom He loves and has given to us, in good health and long life." The other priests and magnates in attendance or standing outside of the church repeat this wish, and cries of jubilation go up. All the magnates then beat their heads to the ground before His Tsarist Majesty and kiss his hand. Then the Patriarch alone goes before the Grand Prince and pronounces the following exhortation: "Since now, by God's will, he is chosen and crowned Grand Prince of all Russia by the governmental, secular, and ecclesiastical estates, and to him is entrusted the important task of governing the lands subject to him, therefore let him love God, abide by His laws, and dispense justice in accordance with them, and let him also defend and propagate the true Greek faith."

Afterward, the Grand Prince is blessed once more and then goes into the church across the way, named Mikhail Archangel. At this time money is scattered among the people. In the church, the litany is sung again. From there the Grand Prince goes to the church of St. Nicholas and then, in the company of the state counselors, into the great hall, where the ecclesiastical and secular magnates are given a sumptuous banquet. At this affair they get so drunk that many of them do not know how to get home.

The title the Russians at present give their Grand Prince is as follows: "Great sovereign Tsar and Grand Prince Aleksei Mikhailovich of all Great and Little Russia, Autocrat of Moscow, Kiev, Vladimir, and Novgorod, Tsar of Kazan, Tsar of Astrakhan, Tsar of Siberia, Lord of Pskov, and Grand Prince of Tver, Iugra, Perm, Viatka, Bolgaria, and others; Lord and Grand Prince of Nizhnii Novgorod, Chernigov, Riazan, Rostov, Iaroslavl, Beloozero, Udora, Obdorsk, Kondinsk, and all the northern lands; Lord of the Iversk country, of the Kartalinsk and Georgian kings, of the Kabardian land, of the Cherkass and Gorsk princes, and Sovereign and Lord of many other eastern, western, and northern states and lands, to the father, grandfather, and heir [i.e. for many generations]."

The places included in the Tsar's title, and many other lands, provinces, and cities, bring a large annual revenue into His Tsarist Majesty's treasury, something on the order of several millions. The revenues come from taxes, imposts, customs duties, taverns, trade, and landed estates. Although His Tsarist Majesty's subjects generally do not pay heavy taxes, nevertheless, owing to the large number of lands and peoples under his sway, large sums are taken in. When a war must be waged, the townsmen, merchants, and traders make heavy supplementary contributions. Under the preceding grand prince, when war was to be waged at Smolensk, they had to give a *piatina*, a fifth of the value of their property.[21] The present tsar has taken only a tenth. Boyars and magnates, according to the number of their estates, must maintain a certain number of foot soldiers and cavalrymen. Noblemen themselves must go into the field with their servants. The monasteries, too, must furnish and maintain a given number of soldiers, depending upon the number of villages and peasants they possess. The customs the Tsar collects at the borders and in the chief commercial towns also bring him great revenue. A leading German merchant in Moscow told me that the important trading city of Archangel once, in the course of a year, turned in the unbelievable sum of 300,000 rubles, that is six tons of gold.[22] The pothouses, saloons, and taverns, or *kruzhechnye dvory* as they are now called, bring the Grand Prince—who now owns all of them throughout the country — an extraordinary amount of money, since the Russians know no restraint in drinking vodka. For-

---

[21] The piatina was levied by the Zemskii Sobor of 1632.

[22] The figure is unbelievable—and wrong. Either the foreign merchant was misinformed or Olearius misunderstood him. The figure quoted may have been the amount the treasury took in from the Tsar's own trading operations at Archangel, which were extensive—for example, the ruler reserved for himself a monopoly on sales of grain to foreign states. The customs collected at Archangel ran from 22,000 to 33,000 rubles annually, between 1640 and 1646. The take ranged from 51,000 to 91,000 in the 1650's. See Kurts, *Sochinenie Kil'burgera*, pp. 396–400. The Tsar also had a monopoly of the trade in silk, rhubarb, and caviar. Kurts, *Sostoianie Rossii*, pp. 151–53, 157–59.

merly the boyars and magnates had their own taverns in various places, which they leased to different individuals, as the Grand Prince did also. However the boyars raised the rental charge so high that many of the lessees were ruined. Now the boyars and magnates are forbidden to maintain taverns, for all have been taken over by the Grand Prince. In each town a particular house has been designated where vodka, mead, and beer can be obtained, and the receipts go exclusively to His Tsarist Majesty's treasury. In Novgorod there had always been three taverns, each of which turned in 2,000 rubles for a total of 6,000; under the new order, the sum is greater yet. There are around a thousand such taverns in the country, though not all are as profitable.

The Tsar also receives great income from sables and other furs provided him by the northern lands. He carries on a lively trade in these and other goods, both within and without the country, employing the services of certain persons to whom he entrusts both the goods and large sums of cash.[23] He sends them to neighboring countries, especially Persia and Turkey, to engage in trade on behalf of his treasury. In Persia we met one of these factors or agents of Grand Prince Mikhail, named Savel,[24] who had been sent out with 4,000 thalers. Since he employed his talent badly, in the three years he spent there, he lost all the money. The envoy Aleksei Savinovich Romanchukov,[25] who had been sent to Persia with us, received orders to put this disloyal merchant in chains and bring him back. He did in fact meet Savel in Shemakha in Media; but, since his interpreter died about then, he employed the merchant in his stead. He did not disclose the Grand Prince's order, treated the merchant very generously, and took him along to the Persian Shah, calculating that with kind words he might lure him to the border. Savel saw through the ruse, however, and when the ambassador wanted to set off on the return trip, he fled to Ispahan [the site of a Muslim religious refuge], had himself circumcised, adopted the Moslem faith, and remained in Persia.

The Tsar has here and there rich landed estates, which he leases in return for large sums.[26] He also obtains a good return from the iron mines at Tula, referred to above. But though his income is great, his

---

[23] The "certain persons" were the *gosti*. On the Tsar's involvement in the fur trade, see Fisher, Chaps. 4, 5, 7, 8, 10, and 11.

[24] His name was Savka Arapov. Zevakin, p. 8.

[25] Romanchukov is treated in a note in Book IV.

[26] Abundant information on the Tsar's enterprises is given in Zaozerskii.

expenditures are not small. He must spend a great deal annually for the support of the streltsi, of whom there are many on the borders, because of hostile relations with neighbors, and in the cities. In Moscow alone there are 16,000 and in Kazan district 6,000, all of whom receive fields and lands as salary. All told, in the provinces there are many more than a hundred thousand of them.[27]

The far-off Tatars, who are expected to make frequent attacks,[28] each year send embassies to secure money, and the Tsar is put in the position of having to buy peace. The wars he wages cost much, for he must put a large army into the field and maintain the officers, mostly Germans, at high salaries.[29] He must always pay salaries promptly, and may even give several months' in advance to some who request it. For this reason people from all over flock to enter his service.[30]

Large means go for the embassies of foreign rulers that often visit him. Sometimes two, three, or more such embassies are in Moscow for an extended period, and so long as they remain within Russia's borders they are maintained free of charge. He also has a large and numerous court establishment, and apart from his own costly table, he daily feeds, in and outside the Kremlin, up to a thousand people.

The Tsar dines in the following manner. When dinner time comes, it is not announced with trumpets as at other courts, but someone runs to the kitchen and cellar, and calls out at the top of his voice, "The

[27] Olearius probably has confused the number of streltsi with the total number of military men in the country. According to Fletcher and Margeret, the streltsi in the late sixteenth and early seventeenth centuries numbered between 12,000 and 18,000. Meyerberg, an ambassador of the Holy Roman Emperor, who visited Russia in 1661, gives a figure of 40,000 for the whole country. See Kliuchevskii, *Skazaniia inostrantsev,* pp. 89–96 for further discussion of the size of the armed forces.

[28] The Tatars made several devastating raids in 1637–38. Kostomarov, *Russkaia istoriia,* p. 43.

[29] The foreign officers received higher pay than their Russian counterparts. Kliuchevskii, *Skazaniia inostrantsev,* pp. 122–23. Olearius is mistaken in describing the officers as predominantly German. Germans predominated among the foreign officers to be sure. But although the foreign officers were numerous in the higher ranks, they could hardly have been a majority of the total number of officers. For example, serving on the southern frontier in 1639 were 316 foreign and 428 Russian officers. Chernov, p. 150.

[30] This was especially true in Olearius's time, when lulls in the Thirty Years War—and then its termination—released large numbers of men who had no other profession than that of soldier. Serving in the Tsar's army was far from an unmixed blessing, however. Salaries were in fact paid irregularly. And the most capable high-ranking officers found it impossible or next to impossible to secure their release, even though they had enlisted for a definite and limited term. For the cases of the Danish General Bauman and the better-known Patrick Gordon, see *Dopolnenie,* Vol. V, No. 23; and Brikner, *Patrik Gordon i ego dnevnik,* pp. 14–15, 19, 36, 50–51.

Sovereign's dinner." Immediately dinner is brought. His Tsarist Majesty sits at a separate table, and if the Patriarch and other magnates are invited to dine with him, special tables are set by his. There are usually 50 or more dishes, but not all are brought to the Grand Prince's table. The servants bring them up and show them to the *stol'nik*, who directs to the Grand Prince's table only the things he likes. As a mark of favor, other dishes are sent to various lords and aides, the Germans as well as the Russians, and especially to the Tsar's doctors, physicians, and healers.

At present the Tsar has only one physician, Mr. Hartmann Gramann, who went to Persia with us. He is very well versed in hermetic medicine and always had greater success than others in curing ills. Therefore he is in high favor, and not with His Tsarist Majesty alone, for the boyars, princes, and magnates also greatly admire and respect him and bring him gifts. He receives a monthly salary of 62 rubles, besides an annual sum of 300, for a total of 1,044 rubles, in addition to bread, grain, malt, honey, and other things for the household.[31] When he has to bleed someone or give other medical treatment, he receives an extra payment of 50 rubles in cash, and also a piece of satin or damask, a timber of sables, and the like. The physicians rarely receive cash payment from the boyars, princes, and other magnates, but are given sables, bacon, vodka, or other provisions instead. They must appear at the court daily and beat their heads to the magnates, especially to their superior, the inspector of the Tsar's apothecary (which, incidentally, is very well supplied).[32]

His Tsarist Majesty employs, at great expense, many interpreters of various languages, and also many other aides, both Germans and other foreigners. There is a particularly large number of foreigners among the high military officers, some of whom have abandoned their

[31] Foreign doctors were the highest paid people in the Tsar's service around the middle of the seventeenth century. Prince Cherkasskii, the highest paid Russian, received 850 rubles a year. Lakhtin, p. 24. Of course, Cherkasskii's income was greatly increased by what his estates produced. Foreign officers with the rank of colonel received a monthly salary of 30 to 40 rubles. Kliuchevskii, *Skazaniia instrantsev*, pp. 122–23.

[32] There was no private medical practice in Russia before about 1677–81, when retiring foreign doctors were first permitted to remain in the country and continue their practice, free of the jurisdiction and control of the Aptekarskii Prikaz. Muliukin, *Priezd inostrantsev*, pp. 88–91. According to Rikhter (II, 300–4, 378–83), the Tsar's apothecary had been founded by an Englishman named James Frencham, in the late sixteenth century. Lakhtin (p. 83), who wrote almost a century later, considered this less certain.

religion and been rebaptized. They receive high salaries even in peace-time. Among his other interpreters, His Tsarist Majesty has an excellent person named Johann Böcker von Delden, of Copenhagen. He received a good university education, traveled widely, and learned many languages. A man of this sort has not before been in Moscow [in the Tsar's service]. He serves as interpreter-general and is usually sent with ambassadors on the most important missions. For example, he recently went to the court of His Imperial Majesty at Vienna, in the company of two of the Tsar's envoys, Ivan Ivanovich Baklanovskii, a nobleman, and Ivan Polikarpovich Mikhailov, a d'iak. In recognition of von Delden's outstanding qualities, His Imperial Majesty, as a special favor and on his own initiative, granted him a patent of nobility, as I learned in a letter from a good friend in Vienna, who sent me a copy.[33]

Among the Grand Prince's aides and courtiers, particularly the Russians, one can observe many of the same phenomena as at the majority of princely courts. In all, virtue battles with vice, and the latter frequently gets the upper hand. Those who have more easy and frequent access to the ruler than others are also the more irascible, selfish, coarse, and censorious. To win them over, one must approach them obsequiously, greet them with a deep bow of the head and a greatly lowered hand, and frequently give them presents, not because they have done anything benevolent, but to keep them from doing something malicious. Thus, a sorry situation prevailed in Moscow some years ago. With presents (which they call *posuly*), one could accomplish anything and obtain anything; if he wished, he might even tear away from another an unquestionable right, or have a guilty party in a most unsavory affair declared innocent.

[Along this line], soon after Grand Prince Aleksei's wedding, some of his new relatives, and some of the old magnates as well, contrived abuses that led to an extraordinarily violent mutiny. After this, some of them were found with bloody heads, and others with no heads at all, as will be related in the next chapter.

---

[33] A brief biographical article is Amburger's "Johann Böcker von Delden."

The Rebellions in Moscow and Pskov[1]

AFTER GRAND PRINCE ALEKSEI MIKHAILOVICH ascended the throne, and while he was still a very young ruler, his former major domo and tutor, Morozov, remained with him; and it was in accord with his will and wishes that the Grand Prince and the entire administration operated.[2] First of all he drew to his side those who could most assist his design. His Tsarist Majesty's relatives who aspired to influence, especially those on the side of his mother, the former Grand Princess, he exiled from the court, appointing them to posts as voevodas and other important positions.[3] He wished, in the manner of Lycogenes in Barclajus (Book 1, p. 2), to people the court with his partisans and to distribute the chief posts among friends, who in turn would be obligated to him. None of the magnates could surpass him in zealous service and readiness to attend the young Tsar. To distract his attention from the other magnates, who might trouble him with affairs of state that he was still too young to manage, Morozov very often took him

---

[1] The treatment of the Moscow rebellion of 1648 that follows, although not an eyewitness account, long figured as one of the principal sources on that affair. See, for example, Kostomarov, *Russkaia istoriia*, pp. 106–11. Later studies, however, have revealed various errors, chronological and other, in Olearius's account, some of which will be pointed out hereafter. In general, his treatment highlights the more obvious and sensational aspects but does not sufficiently clarify either the underlying causes of the disturbances or the character of the chief social forces involved.

In 1888, on the basis of a newly found document, S. F. Platonov rearranged the events into their proper chronological order. In 1913, P. P. Smirnov cast new light on the uprising by drawing attention to the attitude of the military servitors and by disclosing the connection between the Moscow riots and the convocation of the Zemskii Sobor that produced the *Ulozhenie*. Subsequently, S. V. Bakhrushin and Smirnov published much more thorough studies. See Platonov, "Moskovskie volnenie"; Smirnov, "O nachale" and *Posadskie liudi*; and Bakhrushin. Loewenson's brief bibliographical article in English reproduces one of the key contemporary documents.

[2] Morozov took charge of four departments of government, which made him something like a prime minister. The more important of them were the treasury and the departments that controlled the streltsi and the foreign troops. See Bakhrushin, pp. 61–62.

[3] This activity led to conflicts, of which Olearius was unaware, between new and displaced courtiers. Bakhrushin sees the Tsar's cousin Nikita Romanov and Prince Iakov K. Cherkasskii as aggrieved parties who tried to turn the 1648 disturbances to their own advantage. *Ibid.*, pp. 63–64.

hunting or to other recreations. To maintain the favor of His Tsarist Majesty, he strove to enter into a close kinship with him. He advised him to marry soon, and so that the choice should fall on a person of the middling nobility, to which Morozov himself belonged, he proposed a nobleman's daughter whose sister Morozov himself thought of marrying.

At the time there was a certain nobleman named Il'ia Danilovich Miloslavskii, who had two beautiful daughters but no sons. This Il'ia frequently came to Morozov, who then was factotum at the court, as they say, and assiduously wooed him, so that Morozov came to admire him not only for the sake of his lovely daughters but also for his complaisance. Once, at an opportune time, Morozov praised the beauty of the sisters so highly that he awakened in the young prince a keen desire to see them. Both sisters were brought [to court] ostensibly to visit the Tsar's sisters. When His Tsarist Majesty glimpsed them, he fell in love with the older one. Miloslavskii was informed of the Tsar's favor and that he would become His Tsarist Majesty's father-in-law. He lost no time in giving his consent and expressing his gratitude for the high honor. Then, since he was not particularly wealthy, a large sum of money and various costly things were sent to him so that he could fit out himself and his people. Soon after, on the 70th day before Easter, 1647, in the bride's 22d year, the nuptials took place. They were carried out quietly, without the special pomp that usually accompanies [such] weddings so that neither the bride nor the groom might be harmed by sorcery, which the Russians fear greatly.[4] Eight days after the Tsar's wedding, Boris Ivanovich Morozov celebrated his marriage to the sister of the young Grand Princess and thus became the Grand Prince's brother-in-law.

After Il'ia Danilovich Miloslavskii became the Tsar's father-in-law, he was very powerful. He was given a house in the Kremlin, near His Tsarist Majesty's residence, where he was to live with his wife. He had it torn down forthwith and a magnificent palace built from the ground up. One after another, the old aides [at the court] were obliged to depart, and Miloslavskii's relatives were installed in their places. Since

---

[4] Tsar Aleksei was moved rather by the pleas of his confessor, Stefan Vonifat'ev, to celebrate the marriage without the usual revelry and in keeping with the spirit of Christian piety. See Kapterev, pp. 103–4.

[the new aides] all had had occasion to go hungry, they proved very greedy and voracious. One of them (who especially distinguished himself in this regard) was Levontii Stepanovich Pleshcheev, who was appointed chief judge of the *Zemskii Dvor* or town hall.[5] He fleeced and exploited the common people beyond measure, and it was impossible to satiate him with presents. When contending parties came to him in the chancellery he cleaned them out to the marrow of their bones so that both sides were reduced to beggary. He hired unscrupulous rogues to inform falsely against honest people who had some resources and to accuse them of anything from theft to murder, or other evildoing. Then the poor people were clapped into prison, treated tyrannically, and held for several months, which brought them to the brink of despair. Meanwhile his godless minions were supposed to negotiate with friends of the arrested and secretly give them wise counsel on how to secure their friends' release. Through such thieving assistants, he haggled over how much had to be delivered to him. He himself would not receive any of the accused or their friends.

Among other such godless officials was a certain Petr Tikhonovich Trakhaniotov, Pleshcheev's brother-in-law (Pleshcheev was married to his sister). He was already an *okol'nichii*, one rank removed from that of boyar or state counselor. He had been appointed head of the *Pushkarskii Prikaz,* and had under his jurisdiction the ammunition and the gunsmiths, cannoneers, and all who served in the arsenal. He dealt with them very harshly and held back what was coming to them for their work. In Moscow, by the Grand Prince's order all his officials and artisans are paid their salaries promptly each month; the money is even brought to some at their homes. Trakhaniotov, however, let people wait several months; and when after great importuning they were paid only half, or even less, they were obliged to give a receipt for the whole salary.

Various restraints were placed on trade and many monopolies established.[6] Whoever brought the most presents to Morozov returned home cheerfully with a letter of privilege. Another [official] had mea-

---

[5] Although the Zemskii Dvor, or Zemskii Prikaz, was concerned with the affairs of the city of Moscow, it was actually one of the departments of the central government.

[6] Small traders were important among the turbulent populace in 1648, and the gosti, the privileged merchants who were apt to receive monopoly rights, were victimized by the mobs. The small traders had other grievances as well. Bakhrushin, pp. 69–71, 87.

suring rods made with an eagle stamped on each. Afterward, anyone
wanting to use such an instrument had to buy one of this kind for one
reichsthaler, though it actually was worth only ten kopeks. The old
measures were prohibited under penalty of heavy fines. This regulation, which was put into effect in all the provinces, brought an income
of many thousands of thalers.

Still another who wanted to render a service to the Tsar's treasury
and win favor for himself proposed that the price of salt, which stood
at two grivnas a pud, be increased by one grivna.[7] He calculated that
many thousands would be taken into His Tsarist Majesty's treasury
annually by such a tax. A year later, however, it was necessary to calculate how many thousands had been lost on salted fish—used as food
in Russia more than meat—that spoiled because it was not properly
preserved, owing to the high price of salt. Besides, much less salt was
sold than before, and remaining in the packing houses, it turned into
brine and dribbled away.

The common people became resentful at these great burdens and
intolerable actions.[8] Morning and evening, crowds gathered at the
churches to discuss what to do about their plight. It was clear that the
people closest to the Tsar did not wish to hear any complaints, still less
to abolish the burdens. Therefore they all decided to seek an opportunity, whenever His Tsarist Majesty rode out or went in procession
from the Kremlin to the city church, to make certain requests of the
sovereign himself, in the name of the whole community. They proposed to complain of Levontii Stepanovich Pleshcheev's injustices and

---

[7] This and the regulation described in the preceding paragraph call attention to an important cause of the Moscow disturbances—fiscal policy in the first years of Aleksei Mikhailovich's reign. With a view to putting the government on a sound financial basis, salaries of the
military forces were cut, and new indirect taxes, such as the one on salt, were levied. The new
taxes were more burdensome than the direct taxes they replaced, and the salary reduction
weakened the military's loyalty to the government. Since these policies emanated from the
treasury department, it is not surprising that Morozov, its head, and Nazarii Chistyi, Morozov's
chief aide and the promoter of the salt tax, should have been singled out for attack during
the troubles. *Ibid.*, pp. 49, 74.

[8] Although elements of the lower strata undoubtedly participated in the rioting and pillaging that followed, the disturbances involved primarily the middle layers of the city population,
reinforced by disaffected military men. Smirnov ("O nachale," pp. 45ff) first showed the importance of the lesser servitors (*dvoriane* and *deti boyarskie*), who had come to Moscow for a
muster, in pressuring the government to institute changes and to convoke a sobor. Bakhrushin
shows that they also supported the demands of the traders. But well before these servitors
appeared on the scene, the streltsi had gone over to the rebels, thus putting the government in
a precarious position. Bakhrushin, pp. 72–76, 77–78.

of the unscrupulous acts he daily perpetrated, and to ask that he be dismissed and an honest person put in his place. Although several such attempts were made, each time the boyars who customarily accompanied His Tsarist Majesty took the petitions. Since he did not read them himself, but only had something of their substance reported to him, the oppressed population's requirements were not properly represented to the Tsar, and nothing was done to satisfy them. Accordingly, the common people became more and more embittered, collected in crowds before the churches with great lamentations, and resolved to bring their wants and grievances to His Tsarist Majesty orally when an opportunity arose.

It happened that on July 6, 1648, a traditional holiday was being celebrated, for which His Tsarist Majesty, with all his boyars and magnates, proceeded to the Sretenskii Monastery, within the city. An innumerable crowd of common people gathered on the great market square and along all the streets by which the procession passed. After the service, when he was returning, the common people forcibly broke through to him, seized his horse by the bridle, and asked to be heard. They complained and cried out against Pleshcheev and his injustices, insistently demanding that he be dismissed and replaced by an honest man of good conscience, failing which the common people would perish. Frightened by the unexpected appeal and by such melancholy complaints from the whole people, His Tsarist Majesty spoke to them in a friendly way, suggested that they calm down, and promised to look into the matter and to give them satisfaction. Pacified by this gracious pledge, they thanked him and wished him good health and a long life, and with that he rode on. But then, some of the boyars favorable to Pleshcheev came by and rebuked the people and beat them on the head with knouts, knocking some of them to the ground.

Seizing whatever came to hand, the people collected stones and heaved them at the perpetrators of this outrage. The boyars, unaccustomed to such heavy hail on their backs, fled and hastened to the Tsar at the Kremlin. Since the people wandering in the courtyard there received them in the same manner, they sprang from their horses and barely managed to get up the great stairway leading to His Tsarist Majesty's chamber, for the enraged people furiously pursued them. The streltsi, who daily stood guard on the stairway, restrained the people long enough for the fugitives to escape into the Grand Prince's chamber.[9] Then the crowd began to rave and storm like madmen, and to cry that Pleshcheev be turned over to them. Thereupon Boris Ivanovich Morozov came out on the upper porch and began, in the name of His Tsarist Majesty, to dissuade them from making such demands, at which shouts went up, "Yes, and we must have you too!" To save himself from the threatening danger, Morozov had to depart quickly. After this the mob fell upon Morozov's house, a splendid palace located within the Kremlin, broke open the gate and door, plundered, and robbed whatever they found, and destroyed everything that they could not take away with them. One of Morozov's chief aides, who attempted to resist them, was thrown out of the window of an upper room and lay dead where he landed.

Although they found Morozov's wife at home, they caused her no bodily harm, but only said, "Were you not the sister of the Grand Princess, we would hack you to bits." They were so furious that they spared not even the holy ikons, which they usually venerate so highly; they tore from them the pearls and precious stones with which they were embellished and then flung them into the square. They wrecked, among other valuable things, a carriage that was covered inside and out with gold brocade and lined with costly sables. On this carriage, the rims of the wheels and all the parts usually made of iron were of silver. It is said that His Tsarist Majesty had presented it to Morozov as a wedding carriage. Some of the mob broke into the cellar to the barrels of mead and vodka, drank their fill, and smashing the barrels they were unable to drink up, they waded knee-deep in liquor. When the fire that had been set in the house reached the cellar, they were burned along with the building.

After this pillage, the mob separated into several bands. Some went after Pleshcheev, others after Tikhonovich [Trakhaniotov], still others after the State Chancellor [Chistyi], and some after others whom they considered suspicious—even the scribes and, in general, anyone who in any degree had been friendly to or associated with the hated ones. They

---

[9] The streltsi later proved unreliable both because their salaries had been cut and because many of them, who doubled as petty traders, were linked in interest with the city's other small merchants. The strength that their support conferred soon led opposing high-level factions to curry their favor. *Ibid.*, pp. 65–67.

plundered their households, robbing or destroying whatever came to hand. They seized costly things and great wealth, especially at Morozov's house. They measured out pearls by the handful, selling a whole hatful for 30 thalers, and selling a black fox skin and a pair of fine sables for half a thaler. They sliced up gold brocade with knives and divided it among themselves.

Scarcely three days before this event, State Chancellor Nazarii Ivanovich Chistoma [Chistyi, who had inspired the salt tax], while riding home from the Kremlin, was thrown from his horse, which was frightened by an enraged cow, and was carried home half dead. As a result, he was confined to bed. But when he learned that the people had plundered Morozov's house and reasoned that they might well decide also to visit him and settle scores, he dragged himself out of bed, crept across the floor, and concealed himself underneath a bath broom (made of birch foliage bound together). He also ordered his boy servant to lay several pieces of smoked lard over him. However, the boy betrayed his master and gave him away, took several hundred ducats, and set out for Nizhnii Novgorod. The maddened people threw themselves upon the house, dragged Nazarii out from under the twigs and then, by his feet, down the stairway and into the courtyard, where they beat him to death with cudgels. His head was so battered that he could no longer be recognized. Then he was cast into a manure pit, and boxes and trunks were thrown on top of him. When we were in Moscow, even we had occasion to experience this Nazarii's iniquitous and malicious disposition.[10] Since he counted for much with the foremost figures at court, and since he did not forthwith receive from us the presents he desired, he greatly hindered us in our enterprises.

While the pillage was occurring on the outside, the Kremlin was locked. Early on the next morning, July 7th, all the German officers were secretly told to assemble, well armed, and to appear immediately in the Kremlin, for the insurgent mob continued to go into and out of the Kremlin from time to time. When the Germans had gathered a considerable force in fulfillment of this order, they were surprised that the rioters very readily made way for them and even addressed them

---

[10] In February 1639, the Holstein ambassadors lodged a complaint against Chistyi, who they claimed had extorted a large bribe from them. See Loviagin's Introduction, p. xi; also Amburger, *Die Familie Marselis*, p. 83.

cordially: "You are honest Germans, who do us no harm. We are your friends and have no intention ever to do you any harm." Previously, they very often quarreled with the Germans and were hostile.[11]

The Kremlin gates were opened, the Germans entered, and for the security of the castle, they were immediately dispersed to certain posts and put on guard. Then the Tsar sent out his cousin, the great and praiseworthy lord Nikita Ivanovich Romanov, whom the people loved for his kindness. He was to endeavor to assuage enraged tempers and restore peace. With bared head he came out to the people (who greeted him very deferentially and called him their father) and movingly told how pained His Tsarist Majesty was by the trouble. On the preceding day he had promised them to look assiduously into these affairs and to give them most favorable satisfaction. His Tsarist Majesty wished, through him, to have these words repeated to the people and would, without fail, keep his promise. Therefore they could be calm and peaceful. To this the people answered that they were very satisfied with His Tsarist Majesty. They wanted very much to quiet down, but not before those responsible for their misery, namely Boris Ivanovich Morozov, Levontii Stepanovich Pleshcheev, and Petr Tikhonovich Trakhaniotov, were turned over to them so that, before the people's eyes, these men could have inflicted upon them the punishment they deserved. Nikita thanked them for the answer and for their continued loyalty to His Tsarist Majesty, and agreed to convey properly their demands in regard to the three. However, he swore to them that Morozov and Petr Tikhonovich had taken to their heels and were no longer in the Kremlin. They asked then, if that were the case, that Pleshcheev be turned over to them at once. Nikita then bade the people farewell and rode back to the Kremlin.

Soon after, word was received from the Kremlin that His Tsarist Majesty had decided to surrender Pleshcheev without delay, and had agreed to his execution before the people's eyes. Moreover, if the others were found, they would be treated as justice demanded.[12] The execu-

---

11 The streltsi, at least, were hostile to them even at this time, for the foreigners were paid a good deal more than their Russian counterparts. Bakhrushin, p. 74. Contingents of foreign troops repeatedly played a critical role during times of disorder in the seventeenth century. On their involvement in the crises of 1662 and 1689, see Brikner, *Patrik Gordon i ego dnevnik*, pp. 20–21, 70–73.

12 Bakhrushin argues persuasively that the popular agitation against Morozov and his creatures presented Nikita Romanov and Prince Cherkasskii an opportunity to displace their

tioner was ordered to appear, and the people immediately brought him and his assistants to the gates, where they were at once admitted. Meanwhile the people took counsel among themselves and decided that those among them who had horses should patrol the roads outside the city to seek out the fugitives and return them.

The executioner had not been in the Kremlin more than a quarter of an hour when he emerged, bringing Pleshcheev with him. When the infuriated people set eyes on him, they were unable to wait until he was brought to the place of execution, to hear the sentence read and to have it carried out. Instead, they fell upon him, and while in the hands of the executioner, Pleshcheev was clubbed to death. His head was beaten to such a pulp that his brains splattered over his face. His clothing was torn off and the naked body dragged through the dirt around the market place, while they cried: "Thus will all such scoundrels and thieves be treated. God preserve His Tsarist Majesty's health for many years!" The corpse was left lying in the dirt and was trampled on. Finally a monk came and chopped the remnants of the head from the trunk, saying, "This is because he once had me cudgeled, even though I was innocent."

True to Nikita's words, Boris Ivanovich Morozov had sought salvation in flight, but the cartsmen and coachmen who barred the way saw him and drove him back. To his great fortune, however, he escaped and got into the Kremlin by a secret way, so none of the pursuers observed him. To demonstrate to the people that he seriously wished to apprehend the fugitives, however, His Tsarist Majesty sent Prince Semen Pozharskii and some others to look for Petr Tikhonovich. They found him at the Troitskoe Monastery, 12 leagues from Moscow, and on July 8th brought him back, but to the town hall rather than to the Kremlin. As soon as His Tsarist Majesty was informed, he ordered the executioner to bring him forthwith to the market square. A wooden block was placed beneath his neck, and his head was cut off with an axe.

---

opponents in the seats of power. When the Tsar's chief aides came under fire, it was undoubtedly Nikita who advised Aleksei to appease the populace by surrendering to it, or ousting, those against whom the people raged. At the height of the crisis, Cherkasskii was given charge of the four departments Morozov had been administering, and Nikita Romanov took over the direction of the Boyar Duma. However, this arrangement did not last. Thanks to the Tsar's favor and to his own suppleness—Morozov presently showed himself more willing than Nikita to meet the socioeconomic demands of the turbulent elements—the Tsar's brother-in-law and his followers regained power. This was signaled by the transfer of Cherkasskii's posts to Il'ia Miloslavskii, Morozov's father-in-law and henchman. Bakhrushin, pp. 63–68.

This measure again helped to cool heated tempers. All thanked His Tsarist Majesty for good justice, wished him long life, and demanded that Morozov be dealt with in the same manner. They knew that the cartsmen had seen Morozov on the road and that he had fled. As they did not know where he had taken refuge, however, they could not ask that he be surrendered immediately. Therefore they contented themselves with a statement that their demands should be met as soon as he was found. This was promised them. After that the rabble calmed down and quiet was attained.

These events occurred shortly before noon [on July 8th]. Shortly after noon fires broke out in the Dmitrovka and Tverskaia quarters, and in various other places.[13] The virulent mob hurried there more to plunder than to help. It was an extremely serious blaze, consuming everything within the white wall up to the Neglinnaia River. It crossed the Neglinnaia bridge and entered the red walled-section of the city near the Grand Prince's largest and best tavern. As a result, the whole city, including the Kremlin, was placed in the greatest jeopardy. Not a person wanted to escape or could, since all were as drunk as could be from the vodka they had pillaged from the cellars during the fire. They knocked the bottoms out of the barrels that were too large to take out, drew off the vodka into hats, caps, shoes, and gloves, and got so drunk that the blackened streets were covered with them. Many who completely lost consciousness were suffocated by the smoke and fumes, and burned up.

Around 11 o'clock at night, while several Germans were standing and watching in horror as the Grand Prince's tavern went up in flames, they became aware of a monk dressed in black, coming toward them, who moaned and groaned as he dragged behind him a heavy burden. When he drew closer, he cried aloud for help and said, "This frightful fire will not end until the godless Pleshcheev's accursed body (which he was dragging) is cast into the flames and burns." When they refused to assist him, he began to berate them soundly. Then, however, several young men came up and helped him drag the corpse to the blaze and throw it in. As soon as the body began to burn, the flames began dying down before the eyes of the astounded spectators, and went out.

---

13 It was later rumored that Morozov had instigated the firing of the city in order to throw the insurgent forces into disarray. *Ibid.*, p. 77.

A few days later, His Tsarist Majesty feasted the streltsi who made up his bodyguard with vodka and mead. His father-in-law, Il'ia Danilovich Miloslavskii, showed cordiality and kindness to the leading townsmen; he daily invited various of the guildsmen to his house, treated them well, and tried to win the favor of the most important of them.[14] The Patriarch ordered the priests to soothe the still indignant temper of the people. His Tsarist Majesty also filled the vacated offices and places with wise and pious men who enjoyed popular sympathy.

When he saw that this highly distressing cloudburst and storm had quite subsided, and supposed everything was now ready for a peaceful amelioration of the situation, on the day of a procession His Tsarist Majesty had the people called to the stage outside the Kremlin, where, with Nikita Ivanovich Romanov, he appeared before them. He expressed great regret that they, without his knowledge, had suffered such oppression at the hands of the godless Pleshcheev and Tikhonovich, who now had received their just deserts. He further said that he had appointed to their places pious men who would govern with mildness and justice and promote the people's well-being, under the watchful eye of the Tsar himself. He announced that the heavy tax on salt would be immediately repealed,[15] and promised, at the first opportunity, to recover the monopoly charters he had distributed, and to restore the [popular] privileges and benefits to their former condition. He added that in all things he would be the father of the country, remaining graciously disposed to his subjects. Then the people bowed their heads low to him and wished him long life.

Then the Tsar continued that he had no desire to whitewash Boris Ivanovich Morozov, whom he had also promised to hand over to them, but neither could he find him entirely guilty. He wanted the assurance of the people, of whom he never before had asked anything, that they would comply with his first request and forgive Morozov this time. He

[14] The streltsi were given money as well as feasts, in an effort to regain their support for the government. Miloslavskii's activities were aimed not so much at "the leading townsmen," some of whom were victimized in the rioting, but to a group active in the disorders, the middle strata of traders and "guildsmen." *Ibid.*, pp. 69–71, 73, 87–88. Olearius was unaware of the role of the provincial military servitors, whose support of the agitation contributed to its success. They, at the same time, secured satisfaction of their own demands for increased salaries and landholdings and for the convocation of a Zemskii Sobor—measures which the great magnates opposed. See Smirnov, "O nachale," pp. 45ff; Bakhrushin, pp. 75–76.

[15] Olearius was mistaken, for the salt tax had actually been repealed in December 1647, months before the outbreak of the disturbances. However, the government did offer redress of other grievances.

himself guaranteed that Morozov would henceforth render them only loyalty, love, and all good. If they wished him no longer to occupy the position of state counselor, then he would relieve him of it, but only on condition that he who was like a second father to the Tsar, who had educated and raised him, should not have to give up his head. He could not bear that, and hoped that in the future they should make no such demand of him. When, in token of his great love for Morozov, tears came to His Tsarist Majesty's eyes, bringing his speech to a close, the people took counsel and began to shout aloud: "May God give His Tsarist Majesty long life! Let be what God and His Tsarist Majesty request!"

The Tsar was as gladdened at that as he formerly had been saddened by the demand for Morozov's head. He thanked the people for this decision, asked them to be peaceful and obedient, and swore that he would be faithful forever to the promise he had just made. After this, His Tsarist Majesty and his party peacefully proceeded back to the Kremlin. Not long afterward, the Tsar went to the Holy Trinity Monastery, and with him went Morozov, to whom the people on both sides of his horse bowed very low in reverence. Subsequently, no one who submitted a petition or request to His Tsarist Majesty through him was refused, if it was at all possible to comply.[16] It is also reliably reported that Morozov has now become a great patron and benefactor of the Germans as well as the Russians.

The welfare of the young ruler and his subjects had been exposed to such grave danger at this time because unjust and grasping officials had been given too free a rein. And in spite of the Russians' slavish temperament, they react [violently] when greatly oppressed. I wish also to recount the case of a mutiny that occurred at Pskov, wherein one can witness similar conduct on the part of self-seeking officials and infuriated common people.

In 1649 His Tsarist Majesty sent to Her Royal Swedish Majesty, Christina, a distinguished embassy headed by the okol'nichii Boris Ivanovich Pushkin. The embassy was supposed to settle, among other

---

[16] This may have been true, but Morozov no longer held key state offices. Also, continued opposition to Morozov was reported as late as April 1649. See Iakubov, pp. 445, 447.

important affairs, a great quarrel that had been going on for 32 years
over subjects who had fled from one side of the border to the other.
An accord was reached under which no claims were to be made regarding those who had crossed in the first 30 years (for they were widely
dispersed, and many had died); but anyone who had done so in the last
two years was to be returned. Since it turned out that many more
Swedes [actually Russians subject to the Swedish crown] had fled to
the Russian side than Russians [i.e. Swedes subject to the Russian
crown] to the Swedish,[17] it was arranged that His Tsarist Majesty
should pay a sum of 190,000 rubles, partly in cash and partly in rye,
in the spring of 1650. At the appointed time, the Swedish agent, Mr.
Johann de Rodes,[18] arrived in Moscow and received 150,000 rubles
in kopeks and ducats. The remaining 40,000 rubles were to be paid in
rye.

To that end, His Tsarist Majesty commissioned a Russian merchant
in Pskov, named Feodor Emel'ianov, to buy this quantity of rye. A
coarse and self-interested person, he widened the intent of his commission much further than was proper and permitted no one else to
buy as much as a *chetverik* of rye, unless he was friendly with him or
was paid a sufficiently high price.[19] He also made it known that practically everything he collected was to be sent to the Swedish crown, in
settlement of His Tsarist Majesty's debt. This made Sweden anathema
to the Pskov community, and the people began to arrange meetings
in the taverns, charging Russia's ambassador Pushkin with treason
for contracting to pay so great a sum. Some wanted to implicate Morozov in the affair, too, for they had not yet forgotten what had occurred
in Moscow two years before.

Supposing that all this had taken place unbeknown to His Tsarist
Majesty, they informed the people of Great Norgorod and so zealously

---

[17] The Treaty of Stolbovo (1617) drew a boundary between Sweden and Russia that left
many Russians on the Swedish side. Patriotic sentiment, as well as religious pressure from
Swedish Lutherans induced many of them to flee back to Russian territory. See Solov'ev, V, 492;
Tsvetaev, *Protestantstvo i protestanty*, pp. 593–94. According to Pascal (p. 166), the Tsar's
desire to keep the Orthodox Russians from being returned to Swedish jurisdiction was inspired
by the church reform movement (the so-called Zealots of Piety) with which he was affiliated.

[18] Rodes's dispatches from Moscow offer important testimony not only on Swedish-Russian
relations at the time but on many other matters, including the Pskov uprising. A modern study
of this disorder, Tikhomirov's *Pskovskoe vosstanie 1650 g.*, portrays it as a class conflict; an
abbreviated account by the same author appears in *Ocherki istorii . . . XVII v.*, pp. 249–56.

[19] A chetverik was a measure of dry weight, equivalent to about 22½ pounds.

incited the most important of them to mutiny that the voevoda [Feodor Khilkov] had much trouble restraining them from fulfilling their evil design. They also decided not to permit the money to leave the country when it was brought; nor would they permit the purchase of rye for payment to the Swedes, since that had raised the price of their bread. They sent three emissaries to Moscow—a merchant, a Cossack, and a musketeer—to determine whether the Tsar knew what was being done. At the same time, as they had decided, they went to Emel'ianov's house, broke in, and since he himself had fled, seized his wife and tortured her to make her reveal where her husband kept his money. They took everything away and plundered the house. No doubt Emel'ianov would not have escaped alive if they had caught him. They expelled the voevoda [Nikifor Sobakin], who had tried to assert his authority and power over them, from the city; then they called all the noblemen living around Pskov into the city and forced them to vow to act in accord with the people.

When the three honorable Pskov emissaries arrived at Novgorod, through which they had to pass, the voevoda ordered their legs chained, and they were sent thus to the Grand Prince. Both the fugitive Feodor Emel'ianov and the voevoda brought word to Moscow of what had happened. Immediately afterward another messenger came with the news that [the Pskovians] had taken several thousand reichsthalers from the leading Swedish merchant of Narva, Levin Nummers, had beaten him, shaken him up, set him on rolling beer kegs that had been placed one on top of another, abused him, and committed every sort of outrage against him. Consequently, the Tsar sent a notable lord and a boyar there to investigate the matter and to pacify the people.[20] The people, however, at first refused to let them through, locked the gates, and selected a headman from among themselves. They eventually admitted the voevoda and the boyar, but immediately imprisoned the voevoda. When the boyar began to talk to them harshly in His Tsarist Majesty's name, they attacked and beat him in a most horrible manner. When he tried to hide in a monastery close by, they broke in the door, dragged him out, and treated him so [roughly] that it was long doubtful whether he would survive.

---

20 The lord was the new voevoda Vasilii Petrovich L'vov, the boyar, Prince F. F. Volkonskii. The headman chosen was Gavrilo Demidov.

Meanwhile, so that the payment of the agreed upon debt should not fall short, the 40,000 rubles was also paid in cash and not in rye. The Swedish agent, carrying the money, was escorted by a strong convoy of streltsi across the Russian border and onto Swedish soil. His Tsarist Majesty dealt severely with the insurgent Pskovians. He designated Prince [Ivan] Nikitovich Khovanskii[21] as commander, assigned him a large force of mounted men of the lesser nobility, and sent them off. They were joined by two other colonels, Munce Carmichael and Hamilton, who were stationed at Onega near the Swedish border with 4,000 infantrymen.[22] These men were sent without fanfare to Pskov. When the Pskovians realized that it was a serious affair, their spirits fell. They tried to resist at first, but then threw themselves on His Tsarist Majesty's mercy, admitted their guilt, and begged for clemency. Some of the instigators were executed, some were sent to Siberia. Thus this dangerous uprising, too, was quelled.

[21] Khovanskii, as is apparent from the following chapter, was one of the Tsar's boyars. A. L. Ordyn-Nashchokin, who was destined to become one of Russia's greatest statesmen, performed his first important service by helping to pacify the rebellion in his native Pskov without resort to force. Khovanskii, under whom he served, recommended him highly to the Tsar and thus undoubtedly contributed to the advancement of his career. Later the two became foes. See the article on Ordyn-Nashchokin in *Russkii Biograficheskii slovar'*, Vol. XI.

[22] Carmichael and Alexander Hamilton were Scottish colonels in the Tsar's service.

The Officials and the Administration

A T PRESENT THE RUSSIAN government and civil order are established somewhat better, and the courts and administration of justice have different forms, than before. Although Miloslavskii and Morozov have great influence, and the Patriarch introduces one innovation after another, nevertheless the other magnates, according to their status and duties, have definite realms of state and private [royal household] affairs to administer.

There are now usually 30 boyars, or state counselors, at court,[1] but sometimes there are [one or] two more or less. In Shuiskii's time, they say, there were 70 boyars. Last year [1654], when a campaign at Smolensk was about to begin, there were 29 boyars, whose names follow:

Boris Ivanovich Morozov
Boris Nikita Ivanovich Romanov[2]
Ivan Vasil'evich Morozov
Prince Ivan Andreevich Golitsyn
Prince Nikita Ivanovich Odoevskii
Prince Iakov Kudenetovich Cherkasskii
Aleksei Nikitovich Trubetskoi
Gleb Ivanovich Morozov
Vasilii Petrovich Sheremetev
Prince Boris Aleksandrovich Repnin
Mikhail Mikhailovich Saltykov
Vasilii Ivanovich Streshnev
Prince Vasilii Semenovich Prozorovskii
Prince Feodor Semenovich Kurakin
Prince Grigorii Semenovich Kurakin

Prince Iurii Petrovich
   Buinosov-Rostovskii
Ivan Ivanovich Saltykov
Grigorii Vasil'evich Pushkin
Prince Feodor Feodorovich Volkonskii
Lavrentii Dmitrievich Saltykov
Prince Iurii Alekseevich Dolgorukii
Il'ia Danilovich Miloslavskii
Vasilii Vasil'evich Buturlin
Prince Mikhail Petrovich Pronskii
Prince Ivan Petrovich Pronskii
Prince Ivan Nikitovich Khovanskii
Prince Feodor Iur'evich Khvorostinin
Vasilii Borisovich Sheremetev
Nikita Alekseevich Ziuzin

---

[1] Although Olearius uses boyars and state counselors interchangeably, the practice is not entirely justified. In addition to the boyars, the okol'nichie and the dumnye dvoriane were also members of the Duma or Council. See Kliuchevskii, *Istoriia soslovii*, p. 98.

[2] Romanov's first name was Nikita, not Boris.

Below them are the okol'nichie, from whose ranks the boyars are selected.

Prince Andrei Feodorovich
  Litvinov-Masal'skoi
Prince Ivan Feodorovich Khilkov
Nikifor Sergeevich Sobakin
Prince Dmitrii Petrovich L'vov
Prince Vasilii Petrovich L'vov
Prince Semen Petrovich L'vov
Prince Ivan Ivanovich Romodanovskii
Prince Vasilii Grigor'evich
  Romodanovskii
Stepan Gavrilovich Pushkin
Prince Semen Romanovich Pozharskii
Bogdan Matveevich Khitrovo
Petr Petrovich Golovin

Ivan Andreevich Miloslavskii
Prince Ivan Ivanovich
  Lobanov-Rostovskii
Prince Dmitrii Alekseevich Dolgorukii
Prince Petr Alekseevich Dolgorukii
Semen Luk'ianovich Streshnev
Ivan Feodorovich Bol'shoi Streshnev
Mikhail Alekseevich Rtishchev
Prokofii Feodorovich Sokovnin
Prince Boris Ivanovich Troekurov
Aleksei Dmitrievich Kolychev
Vasilii Aleksandrovich Choglokov
Ivan Vasil'evich Olfer'ev

After these come six *dumnye dvoriane,* whom they call *deti boyarskie* (lesser noblemen).[3] They are like hofjunkers.

Ivan Afanas'evich Gavrenev
Feodor Kuz'mich Elizarov
Bogdan Feodorovich Narbekov

Zhdan Vasil'evich Kondyrev
Vasilii Feodorovich Ianov
Afanasii Osipovich Pronchishchev

There are three dumnye d'iaki:[4] Almaz Ivanovich, Semen Ivanovich Zaborovskii, and Larion Dmitrievich Pronchishchev.

These are the people who at present are foremost at the Tsar's court, and who conduct all court, government, and private affairs, high and low, in secret and ordinary councils, and in the chancelleries. They divide the offices and ranks among themselves in the following way. Formerly the position of Master of the Horse was considered the highest place and the closest to His Tsarist Majesty. Since the time of Grand Prince Shuiskii, this post has remained unfilled.[5] Then follows the office of major domo (*dvoretskii*), which now is highest of all. The major

---

[3] The deti boyarskie were lower-ranking members of the military servitor class. They might be called provincial dvoriane but not dumnye dvoriane, to whom they were inferior in rank and function. *Ibid.*, pp. 98–100.

[4] The non-aristocratic heads of important state chancelleries, who, as their title suggests, also participated in sessions of the Duma.

[5] Perhaps because Boris Godunov, who had last held that position, was suspected of having used the influence it conferred on him to usurp the throne.

domo has charge of everything relating to court management and the court establishment, and especially everything relating to the Tsar's table. The third place is occupied by the *oruzhnichii* or Chief of the Arsenal, who has under his control all the Tsar's personal weapons and arms, and also the horses, finery, and equipment for decoration and for processions. Then follow the boyars, the okol'nichie, the dumnye d'iaki or state chancellors; the *postel'nichie* (makers of the royal bed), the keeper of the keys, the chamberlain, the *kravchii* or carver and cup-bearer, the *stol'niki* (the noblemen who serve the table); the *striapchie*, that is the mounted hofjunkers, who are obliged to go everywhere with His Tsarist Majesty; the dvoriane [moskovskie] or ordinary noble-men; the *zhil'tsy* or pages; the d'iaki or chancellery secretaries, whom they usually call vice-chancellors, and the *pod'iachie* or scribes in the prikazi or chancelleries.[6]

A large proportion of the state counselors and other court officials are princes and rich lords, who own extensive lands and many serfs. They may not reside on and manage these lands personally but must delegate the administration to their stewards, servitors, and agents. They them-selves are obliged to live in Moscow and, even though they may have no business, must appear daily at court, and beat their heads to the Tsar.[7] Matters are thus arranged so that they will not hatch plots against His Tsarist Majesty, as they might if they resided on their lands among their dependents.

These lords live in sumptuous houses and palaces, in grand style, and they appear on the streets dressed in costly clothes and with great pomp, while alongside their horses or sleighs run many servants and slaves. When they ride they have at the saddle horn a small drum, a little more than a fourth of an ell in diameter, which they beat with their whip handle to signal the people swarming in the streets, and in the marketplace before the Kremlin, to make way for them.

Some of the princes who reside in villages have far too little to main-

[6] Kotoshikhin's contemporary account (Chap. 2) gives a fuller description of the hierarchy of officialdom. Kliuchevskii's explanation (*Istoriia soslovii*, pp. 133–42) is clearer. The names stol'nik, striapchii, etc. had once referred to offices at the court, but in the seventeenth century they generally signified ranks rather than particular offices. The dvoriane moskovskie, who served in the capital, were distinct both from the dumnye dvoriane and the provincial dvoriane.

[7] As Paul of Aleppo (I, 263) noted with some astonishment, "to beat one's head to the Tsar" was not a symbolic phrase but an actual description of what was expected and done. The boyars and others bowed their heads to the floor before the Tsar.

tain a style of life in keeping with their rank and live much more poorly, so it is often difficult to distinguish them from the peasants.[8] For instance, during our first journey, when our translator asked in Budovo about the prince living there, it turned out that he had unwittingly put the question to the prince himself, who, in the manner of a peasant, was looking through the window of a smokehouse. When the prince gave him to understand that he did not take this error kindly, the translator had to apologize for having mistaken the prince for a peasant.

It is said that the Russian princes trace their origin from Volodomir, a point treated in detail by [Martin] Cromer in *Polonicae Res*, Vol. II, Book 3, p. 439.

When they have important state business to discuss, the boyars and [other] state counselors hold their counsels in the Kremlin, after midnight, assembling around 1 or 2 o'clock and adjourning toward midday, at 9 or 10 o'clock. His Tsarist Majesty does not personally sign any of the decisions, opinions, orders, treaties, appointments, and so forth that are published in his name. All are signed by the boyars and state chancellors, and are only confirmed with the Tsar's seal. If a peace or a treaty with a neighboring ruler is concluded and the Grand Prince must ratify the agreement, this is done by an oath and the kissing of the cross.[9]

The state counselors or boyars are employed not only at the [Grand Prince's] court but also in the departments for civil affairs and the administration of justice. There are, in Moscow, 33[10] of these chancelleries, which the Russians call prikazi. I shall list them here and also name the persons now in charge.

1. The *Posol'skii Prikaz*, which deals with [foreign] affairs, the business of ambassadors and couriers, and the affairs of foreign mer-

[8] The offspring of princes, except for the eldest son, did not inherit the title, although many used it anyway. So large was their number that many counted for nothing, and some were so poor that they were glad to serve a commoner for five or six rubles a year. Fletcher, in Bond, p. 117.

[9] This practice, which goes back at least to A.D. 911, is discussed in Fedotov, pp. 284–95. See also *Sobornoe Ulozhenie Tsaria Alekseia Mikhailovicha*, p. 194.

[10] According to Kotoshikhin, there were 42 prikazi, although he himself listed only 37. Olearius speaks of 33 but actually lists only 32, since he skips from number six to eight. When the lists are compared, we find that Kotoshikhin names nine prikazi not included in Olearius's list, which produces a total of 41. The nine are: *Prikaz Tainikh Del* (Secret affairs); *Streletskoi Prikaz* (Affairs of the streltsi)—it is curious that Olearius does not include this one in his roster, for he refers to it in passing in Book III, Chap. Two; *Prikaz Maloi Rossii* (the Ukraine); *Khlebnoi Prikaz* (receives and disposes of taxes in kind); *Schetnoi Prikaz* (an accounting office); *Pechatnoi Prikaz* (Keeper of the Seal); *Tsarskaia Masterskaia Palata* (the Tsar's clothier); *Tsaritsynaia Masterskaia Palata* (clothier of the Tsaritsa and the royal children); *Panafidnoi Prikaz* (conducts services in honor of Russia's past rulers). The titles given the various prikazi by Olearius and Kotoshikhin do not always correspond exactly.

chants. The dumnyi d'iak or State Chancellor here is Almaz Ivanovich.[11]

2. The *Razriadyni Prikaz,* in which the names and families of the boyars and dvoriane are registered, and the profits and losses incurred in time of war recorded. Its director is the dumnyi d'iak [properly dumnyi dvorianin], Ivan Afanas'evich Gavrenev.

3. The *Pomestnyi Prikaz,* which keeps records of the hereditary and landed estates, settles controversies concerning them, and upon their sale receives the taxes. The chief is Feodor Kuzmich Elizarov.

4. The *Kazanskii Prikaz,* and 5. the *Sibirskii Prikaz,* which hear and deal with affairs concerning the kingdoms of Kazan and Siberia, respectively. Here also [tributes of] sables and other furs are received and dispensed. The chief is Prince Aleksei Nikit[ov]ich Trubetskoi.

6. The *Dvortsovoi Prikaz,* which conducts all business relating to the court and its maintenance. The chief is the boyar [Vasilii] Vasil'-evich Buturlin.

8. The *Inozemskoi Prikaz,* to which all the foreign military officers are subject in matters of justice, and whence they receive orders in peacetime. Il'ia Danilovich Miloslavskii, the Tsar's father-in-law, directs this department.

9. The *Reitarskii Prikaz,* to which all native men recruited into the cavalry are subject for judicial purposes, and from which their orders and salaries are issued in peacetime. These cavalrymen, who are all from the poor nobility and have feudal holdings, receive 30 rubles a year. This prikaz is also under Il'ia's direction.

10. The *Bol'shoi Prikhod,* to which all collectors of revenue throughout Russia must give an annual accounting. This prikaz sees to the dispensation of proper weights of wheat and rye in relation to the prices charged, and to the proper measure and price of various foreign wines sold from the wine cellars. From this prikaz, all foreigners in His Tsarist Majesty's court or military service punctually receive their monthly salaries, as well as their annual salary, payable around Christmas. Here the head is the boyar Prince Mikhail Petrovich Pronskii.

---

[11] One might well wonder why the Posol'skii Prikaz, one of the most important departments of government, should have been entrusted to someone relatively low in the official hierarchy. According to Kliuchevskii (*Skazaniia inostrantsev,* pp. 152–53), dumnyi d'iaki rather than boyars were sometimes put in charge of this and one or two other of the most important prikazi just because the most knowledgeable and experienced people available were wanted for these posts. Olearius subsequently praises the qualities of Almaz Ivanovich.

11. The *Sudnoi Volodomirskoi Prikaz,* to which all the boyars and Moscow magnates are subject for judicial purposes. Anyone who wishes to make a complaint against one of them must do so here. Here also cases of a private character are tried. The boyar Prince Feodor Semenovich Kurakin directs this prikaz.

12. The *Sudnoi Moskovskoi Prikaz,* which dispenses justice to the stol'niki, striapchie, dvoriane, and zhil'tsy, that is the dvoriane who serve the Tsar at table or on the road, the ordinary [Moscow] dvoriane, and pages. The same boyar is their judge.

13. The *Razboinyi Prikaz,* which handles complaints, conducts investigations, administers torture, and renders sentences in keeping with the nature of the case for street robberies, murders, thievery, and violence, within and without the city. The chief figure in the prikaz is the boyar Prince Boris Aleksandrovich Repnin.

14. The *Pushkarskii Prikaz,* in whose jurisdiction are all those occupied with the casting of guns and bells or concerned generally with military armaments. These casters, blacksmiths, armourers, cannon makers, musket makers, arms and pistol makers obtain here not only justice but also their salaries. In place of the godless Petr Tikhonovich, the boyar Prince Iurii Alekseevich Dolgorukii was made chief here.

15. The *Iamskoi Prikaz,* in whose jurisdiction are all the Tsar's couriers and conveyances, as well as the coachmen, whom they call *iamshchiki.* These people are paid here. Also, those who travel on His Tsarist Majesty's business are here equipped and furnished with funds in accordance with the stipulations set forth in the passports graciously granted to them. The head is the okol'nichii Ivan Andreevich Miloslavskii.

16. The *Chelobitnyi Prikaz,* which receives complaints against all d'iaki, secretaries, scribes, elders, and doorkeepers of the prikazi and brings them to trial. Its chief is the okol'nichii Petr Petrovich Golovin.

17. The *Zemskii Dvor* or *Zemskii Prikaz,* where all the burghers and the common people of Moscow may make complaints of injustice against one another. The same prikaz registers and levies taxes on all lots and houses bought and sold in Moscow. Each year the taxes on houses, the bridge and gate tolls, and the revenues for the maintenance of the city walls are brought in and paid here. The chief is the okol'nichii Bogdan Matveevich Khitrovo.

18. The *Kholopii Prikaz,* which draws up special letters, called *kabaly,* concerning people who enter into bondage to someone else. The director is Stepan Ivanovich Islenev.

19. The *Bol'shoi Kazny Prikaz,* which controls the gold and silver brocade, the velvets and silks, the cloths and various stuffs needed for the Tsar's wardrobe and for presents, such as welcoming gifts from His Tsarist Majesty to newly appointed officials, or favors to other persons. Under this prikaz is what is usually called in German "der grosse Schatshof" [the grand treasury]. It is housed in a building in the Kremlin which has many large, deep cellars and stone vaults, in which the state treasury and the income from the cities, the customs duties, and the annual surpluses from the prikazi are collected and stored. All this is managed by the Tsar's father-in-law, Il'ia Danilovich Miloslavskii.

20. The *Kazennoi Prikaz,* which adjudicates matters concerning the gosti and the most important Russian merchants and traders. Il'ia is chief here, too.

21. The *Monastyrskii Prikaz,* where the affairs of the monks, nuns, priests, and other clerics are administered, and where court cases involving ecclesiastics are tried. The okol'nichii Ivan Vasil'evich Khilkov presides over this prikaz.

22. The *Kamennyi Prikaz,* the chancellery where all of the carpenters, stonemasons, and building workers receive justice, punishment, and their salaries. This is a large establishment, which always has on hand a great supply of all materials essential for the Tsar's construction projects, such as lumber, stone, lime, iron, and so forth. The lord and overseer is the dvorianin Iakov Ivanovich Zagriazhskoi.

23. The *Novgorodskaia Chetvert',* to which is brought and computed all the income of Great Novgorod and Nizhnii Novgorod. Here the problems of these cities, and sometimes the litigation of their citizens, are examined and settled. Although, as related above, no appeal from the provincial court of a voevoda to [a higher] court is permitted, nevertheless, they resort to subterfuge to get around this. If, having begun a suit in the local offices, they observe that the case is going badly, they do not allow it to come to a verdict, but take the affair to the appropriate prikaz in Moscow. The chief of this prikaz is the dumnyi d'iak Almaz Ivanovich.

24. The *Galitsko-Volodomirskii Prikaz,* which receives the income

from the provinces of Galich and Volodomir and hears the needs and requests of these provinces. The chief is the okol'nichii Petr Petrovich Golovin.

25. The *Novaia Chetvert'*, to which all the taverns, saloons, and pothouses of all the provinces submit their incomes and accounts. Thence the *kruzhechnye dvory* or saloons are supplied with vodka and other beverages. Also any Russian accused of secretly selling vodka or tobacco is charged and punished here. For, as related above, the Russians are forbidden, on pain of severe punishment, to sell or "drink" tobacco. Offenders who are caught are punished, depending on their rank, by high fines or the knout, or by exile in Siberia. However, the Germans are allowed to smoke tobacco freely and to sell it to one another. The head of this prikaz is Bogdan Matveevich Khitrovo.

26. The *Kostromskii Prikaz*, which manages the income and the judicial affairs of Kostroma, Iaroslavl, and the adjoining towns. The boyar and Chief of the Arsenal, Grigorii Gavrilovich Pushkin, presides over this prikaz.

27. The *Ustiuzhskii Prikaz*, which handles the income and judicial affairs of Ustiug and Kholmogory. Here the head is the okol'nichii Prince Dmitri Vasil'evich L'vov.

28. The *Zolotoi i Almaznoi Prikaz*, which prepares, stores, and dispenses precious stones, and costly gold and silver articles made by the German gold- and silversmiths. The smiths also are under its judicial authority. Grigorii Pushkin is chief here, too.

29. The *[O]ruzhennyi Prikaz*, which keeps all the Tsar's armaments and weapons of war, as well as various ornaments for processions and ceremonial occasions. It also embraces the arsenal or armory [*oruzhennaia palata*]. Those who have dealings with things of this kind are subject to justice in this prikaz. The same Pushkin administers it.

30. The *Aptekarskii Prikaz*, which includes the Tsar's apothecary. The court physicians, barbers, apothecaries, distillers, and all concerned with these affairs, must appear here daily to inquire if something is needed of them. They must also beat their heads to the chief of this institution, Il'ia Danilovich Miloslavskii.

31. The *Tamozhennyi Prikaz*, the customs department, managed by one of the gosti, with several helpers, who receives customs on all goods.

At the end of the year, he renders an accounting to another prikaz, the Bol'shoi Prikhod, and then another gost' is appointed in his place.

32. The *Sbor Desiatoi Den'gi Prikaz,* to which is sent the one-tenth penny [the tithe] agreed upon as a war contribution [from the merchants]. This prikaz is now under the boyar Mikhail Petrovich Pronskii, and beneath him is the okol'nichii Ivan Vasil'evich Olfer'ev.

33. The *Sysknoi Prikaz,* where all unusual new business not in the jurisdiction of other departments is brought and dealt with. Here the chief is Iurii Alekseevich Dolgorukii.

These, then, are His Tsarist Majesty's chancelleries, the business they concern themselves with, and their chiefs. In addition, the Patriarch has three special prikazi: the *Razriad*[*nyi*], in which the ecclesiastical possessions are registered and recorded, and the archives kept; the *Sudnyi,* in which the Patriarch holds his ecclesiastical court and metes out punishment; the *Kazennyi,* in which the patriarchal treasury and annual revenues are stored and guarded. Over these prikazi he has placed certain people in ecclesiastical orders who report everything to him, keep accounts, and execute his orders and judgments.

In all of the Tsar's and Patriarch's prikazi there are very many scribes who, as well as writing a good hand, are quite well tutored in their method of arithmetic. Instead of a counter, they use plum pits, which each always carries with him in a little purse.

Although the taking of bribes is forbidden under threat of punishment with the knout, nevertheless it occurs surreptitiously.[12] The scribes in particular are ready to accept pledges or presents, so one may often learn about the most secret affairs. Sometimes they even approach those concerned in a given affair and offer to make a disclosure for a certain sum. But in so doing, they often perpetrate crude deceptions conveying something fabricated instead of the truth, partly for fear of the consequences to themselves in the event of discovery, partly out of ignorance. Just this happened, for example, in 1643, when I received in Moscow a letter from the Tsar addressed to His Princely Excellence, my most gracious sovereign. At that time an important agent there desired to know the letter's contents. In greatest secrecy he was given a copy, which I too was permitted to transcribe, since I was a

---

[12] For further discussion of corruption among Russian officials, see Kliuchevskii, *Skazaniia inostrantsev,* pp. 155–58.

good friend of the agent. When, however, the original letter was translated, in its proper place, it turned out to be quite different from the copy secretly passed.

Acts, trials, protocols, and other chancellery business are set down not in books, but on long paper scrolls. To make them, they cut up whole sheets of paper in long strips, glue the narrow edges together, and roll them up. Some of the scrolls are 20, 30, and even 60 or more ells long. One can see very many of them in the chancelleries, piled one on top of another.

The administration of justice is carried out in the chancelleries just described. Each boyar or other person designated as a judge has under him a d'iak, or secretary, and also several assessors. Contending parties come before them, are interrogated, and sentenced. Formerly there were very few written laws and customs,[13] which had been established by different grand princes, and these dealt only with traitors to the country, criminals who offended His Majesty, thieves, murderers, and debtors. For the rest, they acted in the main on their own discretion, and sometimes rendered a verdict according as they were well or ill disposed toward the person in the dock. A few years ago, however, in 1647 to be exact,[14] upon His Tsarist Majesty's order the wisest heads of all stations were gathered together to compose and set down certain laws and statutes, which His Majesty and the boyars then confirmed, and these were subsequently published. This book, in folio, is a good two fingers thick and is called the *Sobornoe Ulozhenie*, which means the unanimously approved collected law. Now they render judgments, or at any rate are supposed to, in accordance with this law. As all of this is done

[13] This appears to be a misunderstanding. Actually a good many of the statutes in the *Ulozhenie* (1649) had been promulgated before. Though it also included some new legislation, the *Ulozhenie* in the main represented a codification of preexistent laws.

[14] The Zemskii Sobor that produced the *Ulozhenie* was not called in 1647, but in July 1648. It convened on September 1st of that year, and remained in session into 1649, when the *Ulozhenie* was published. Olearius, who was not in Russia at the time, was unaware of the connection between the Moscow uprising of 1648 and the convening of the sobor that drew up the *Ulozhenie*. (Indeed, as observant as he was, he apparently did not know of the existence of the Zemskii Sobor as an institution of the Russian state. This is all the more surprising because four sobors were convened in the 1630's, the period of the Holstein embassies.) The relationship between these events was clearly established by Smirnov in "O nachale." His key conclusion (p. 54) reads: "It may be said that the Zemskii Sobor of 1648–1649 and its *Sobornoe Ulozhenie* was born of the June revolution in Moscow and represented a concession exacted from the authorities, who turned out to be powerless and defenseless when the streltsi and the dvorianin army went over to the turbulent throng."

in His Tsarist Majesty's name, it is incontrovertible, and no appeal is permitted.

Formerly the trial of litigants proceeded as follows. If one accused another and could prove nothing, the judge prescribed that the affair be settled by oath. Then the accused, to whom the choice belonged, was asked: "Will you take an oath upon your soul or do you wish to place the burden upon the soul of the accuser?" Each week, for three consecutive weeks, whichever party proposed to take the oath had to be brought to the court and instructed and admonished as to what a great and dangerous thing it was to take an oath, and in every way was warned against going through with it. If, nevertheless, he took the oath, then, even though the oath were true, everyone round about spat in his face, he was driven from the church in which he had executed the oath, and was thereafter held in contempt and constantly pointed to; he was no longer permitted to enter the church, much less to take communion, unless he were seized by a grave illness and showed genuine signs of imminent death. Only in that case could he be given communion.

More recently the following manner of disposing of a case was instituted. He who wishes to take an oath is asked before a sacred ikon if he wants to swear upon his soul and his salvation. If he replies affirmatively, a cross a span in length is held before him. He first makes the sign of the cross and then kisses the cross. Then they take an ikon off the wall and hold it out to him to kiss. If he has sworn truly, he is permitted to receive communion after three years, and they treat him quite rudely.[15] If it becomes known that he took a false oath, he is stripped and beaten with a knout, and then sent in disgrace to Siberia. In this case he is not given communion though he be breathing his last. This is why the Russians loath to take an oath, much less a second or third, and why only foolhardy and dissolute persons are apt to do it. Still, when they are gathered together, or when they are engaged in buying and selling, it is very common for them to persuade one another with a

---

15 Olearius was so carried away by the indignities visited upon those who kissed the cross that he neglected to say how such civil cases were resolved. Actually, if one of the litigants agreed to kiss the cross, the case was forthwith decided in his favor. If both kissed the cross, and the evidence did not clearly indicate which was in the right, the case was decided by casting lots. Fletcher (in Bond, p. 66), who provides this information, also stresses the seriousness imputed to taking an oath but says nothing of ostracism suffered by those who swore truly. Possibly Olearius was wrongly informed on this point; if rightly, the motives for ostracizing those who took an oath remain obscure.

facile "by the cross," at which, as is their fashion, they make the sign of the cross with their fingers. This sort of thing, however, is not always to be trusted.

They use various horrible methods of torture to force out the truth. One of them involves tying the hands behind the back, drawing them up high, and hanging a heavy beam on the feet. The executioner jumps on the beam, thus severely stretching the limbs of the offender from one another. Besides, beneath the victim they set a fire, the heat of which torments the feet, and the smoke the face. Sometimes they shear a bald place on top of the head and allow cold water to fall on it a drop at a time. This is said to be an unbearable torture. Depending on the nature of the case, some may, in addition, be beaten with the knout, after which a red-hot iron is applied to their wounds.

If a case of brawling is being tried, usually the one who struck first is considered guilty, and he who first brings a complaint is considered in the right. One who commits a murder not in self-defense (they consider the opposite justified), but with premeditation, is thrown into prison, where he must repent under severe conditions for six weeks. Then he is given communion and decapitated.

If someone is accused of robbery and convicted, he is put to torture all the same [to determine] if he has stolen something besides. If he admits nothing more, and this is the first offense, he is beaten with the knout all along the road from the Kremlin to the great square. Here the executioner cuts off one of his ears, and he is put into a dungeon for two years. If he is caught a second time, then, in the manner described above, he has the other ear cut off and is installed in his previous lodging, where he remains until other birds of the kind are found, whereupon they are all sent together to Siberia. However, no one pays with his life for robbery, unless a murder is committed along with it. If, under torture, the thief names those to whom he sold stolen goods, the buyers are brought to court and ordered to make restoration to the complainant. They call such payment *vyt'*,[16] and on its account many are constrained against purchasing suspicious things.

Cases involving debts and debtors are more numerous than any other kind. He who will not or cannot pay is obliged to sit locked up in the

---

[16] In its general sense, the word *vyt'* signified a measure or quantity. Here, the value of the stolen goods was the gauge by which the fine was determined.

house of a servant of the court, just as in cases of arrest and detention among us. If the debt is not paid in the period of grace allowed, the debtor, no matter who he may be, Russian or foreigner, man or woman, merchant or artisan, priest, monk, or nun, is placed in the debtors' prison. Every day he is brought to an open place before the chancellery and is beaten on the shinbones for a whole hour with a supple stick of about a small finger's thickness, which frequently causes the victim to shriek aloud with pain. However, if the beater has received a bribe or a present, he beats lightly and amiss. Some also place heavy sheet-metal or long wooden strips in their boots, so that these will absorb the blows. After having borne these torments and humiliations, the debtor either is returned to prison or must furnish guarantors [to promise] that he will appear on the following day to be beaten again. They call this form of punishment *stavit' na pravezh*. If the debtor is entirely without means to pay, he becomes the slave of the creditor and must serve him.

Other common punishments inflicted upon criminals include slitting the nostrils, beating with cudgels, and beating with the knout on the bare back. A person's nostrils are slit if he has used snuff. We had occasion to see several who had been punished in this manner. Every master may use a cudgel on his servants or anyone over whom he has the least authority. A criminal must take off his cloak and other clothes, down to his nightshirt, and then lie down with his stomach to the ground. Two people then sit astride him, one on his head, the other on his legs, and he is beaten on the back with a supple rod. The spectacle produced resembles that of a furrier flaying a hide. This kind of punishment was often resorted to among the Russians who accompanied us on our journey.

In our opinion, beating with the knout is a barbaric punishment. On September 24, 1634, I saw this form of punishment inflicted upon eight men and a woman, who, in violation of the Grand Prince's order, had sold tobacco and vodka. Before the chancellery called the Novaia Chetvert', they had to bare their bodies down to the waist. Then each in turn was obliged to place his stomach to the back of one of the executioner's servants, while holding him around the neck. The legs of the offender were bound together, and a special person held them down with a rope, so that the one being punished could move neither up nor down. The executioner retired a good three paces behind the offender and flailed as hard as he could with a long thick knout, making the blood gush forth freely after each stroke. To the end of this knout were attached three thongs made of hard, tanned elk hide, each the length of a finger, which cut like knives. (In this manner some persons whose crimes were great were beaten to death.) A servant of the court stood by and read from a paper the number of strokes each was to receive. When the prescribed number had been fulfilled, he cried, *Pol'no!*, that is, "Enough!" Each was given from 20 to 26 strokes, and the woman 16, after which she fell unconscious. Their backs retained not so much as a finger's thickness of skin intact. They looked like animals whose skin had been flayed. After this, each of the tobacco sellers had a paper of tobacco hung around his neck, and the traders in vodka a bottle. They were joined by twos, the arms of a pair bound together, and driven, with lashes, out of the city and then back to the Kremlin.

It is said that the friends of some of the whipped apply warm, freshly cut lamb's skin to the lacerated back to help it heal.[17] Formerly, those subjected to such punishment were afterward treated as well as anyone else; others spoke, ate, and drank with them as they pleased. Now, however, these people are considered somewhat disgraced.

The Russians, in the course of time, are in many respects changing for the better because they imitate the Germans a good deal and have been influenced by them in the matter of glory and shame. For example, they formerly did not consider the office of executioner as infamous and dishonorable as they do now. Now no honest or notable person has friendly relations with someone who has been whipped unless false witness was given against him, or unless he was wrongly punished because of the judge's enmity toward him. In the latter case, he is more pitied than shunned, and to prove his innocence good people fearlessly have traffic with him.

Honest people nowadays avoid the company of knouters and executioners. Although the latter may take up other business or trades, they are loath to do so, since executioners receive a large income. For each punishment they receive money not only from the authorities but also from the criminals (if they have money, and he is not too hard on

---

[17] A century and a half later the same treatment was still administered to victims of unusually severe knoutings. Aksakov, p. 58.

them). Besides they sell vodka—secretly of course—to the arrested persons, of whom there are many every day, and thus acquire a goodly sum each year. For this reason, some purchase these offices with gifts. However, the resale of these offices is now forbidden. When there is a shortage of such people and it is necessary to carry out a large number of executions, the butchers' guild is obliged to assign several executioners from its ranks.

Religion

IN TURNING TO THE RELIGION of the Russians, I may properly begin with the question that was examined in public disputations by Dr. Bodfidius, court minister to Gustav[us Adolphus], the late King of Sweden, and then by Magister Heinrich Staahl, superintendent at Narva, in Livonia, namely, "Are the Russians Christians?"[1] When Russians are asked this, they answer that it is indeed they who are rightly baptized and the best Christians in the world, while we, at best, are besprinkled Christians.[2] Therefore, if a foreign Christian wishes to adopt their faith, he is obliged to be baptized anew.[3] In fact, we may agree with the above-mentioned persons that there can be found among the Russians the *essentiala christianismi*, or the most important articles of Christianity. These are the true Word of God and the Holy Sacraments.

They have the Holy Bible—the Old Testament, with 70 Greek commentaries, and the New Testament, translated and published in the Slavonic and Russian languages.[4] Strangely, though, they never allow the whole Bible into their churches, holding that there are many loath-

---

[1] Tsvetaev (*Protestantstvo i protestanty*, pp. 687–89) briefly treats Bodfidius's work, as well as the works of other foreign theologians who considered the question. The theologians, few of whom had observed Russian religion at first hand, generally answered the question affirmatively, though with reservations. Some of the lay foreigners who visited Russia came to the opposite conclusion. One such was M. Shaum, a German who served in the Swedish forces during the Time of Troubles and subsequently wrote an account of False Dmitri's fortunes. *Ibid.*, pp. 588–89.

[2] An allusion to the Russian belief in total immersion.

[3] This rule was established during the reign of Ivan IV, but it applied only to Protestants for several decades, since the Orthodox church considered Roman Catholic baptismal procedure acceptable. However, after the Time of Troubles, which greatly intensified anti-Catholic feeling, the rule was enforced upon Protestant and Catholics alike. *Ibid.*, pp. 344–50. During his visit to Russia in the 1650's, Patriarch Macarius of Antioch was instrumental in securing the abrogation of the requirement for Catholics. See Paul of Aleppo, II, 296–97. A church council of 1667 ratified the decision. Tsvetaev, *Protestantstvo i protestanty*, pp. 388–90.

[4] According to Zenkovsky (p. 7), the full text of the Bible was not published in Russian until well after the 1630's.

some and unchaste things in the Old Testament, which would defile their holy church.[5]

Thus they admit only the New Testament and some writings of the prophets. They do, however, permit the possession and reading of the entire Bible at home. They have, along with the Bible, [the writings of] several ancient church fathers and teachers, such as Cyril, the Archbishop of Jerusalem who composed a catechism under the Emperor Theodosius (see Baronius, *Annales Ecclesiastici*, IV, 459, or *Bibliotheca patrum*, Colon., Vol. XII, p. 1003); John Damascene; Gregory Bogoslov (this is probably Gregory Nazianzus); Ivan Zlatoust, that is John Chrysostom (whom they call "him of the golden mouth"); and Ephrem the Syrian. They hold—and this view is maintained by Gerard Fossius of Leiden, in the dedication of the book that he translated into Latin—that Ephrem received from an angel a book written in gold letters, which no one but he could open. Soon afterward, he began to speak and write in an exalted manner.

They have, besides these personages, their own Russian holy teacher, named Nicholas the Wonder Worker. He wrote sacred words that they diligently study. They say that he performed a great miracle, and for that reason a carved bust of him was placed in a chapel on the great street that leads to [Moscow's] Tver gates, and wax candles were burned before it daily. During the recent uprising, however, the great fire that broke out reduced it to ashes, or as the Russians say, carried it off to heaven.

They also acknowledge the Athanasian creed[6] and believe that God, who created everything, is one in His essence and threefold in manifestation; that Christ suffered for all humanity; and that the Holy Ghost, coming from the Father through the Son, sanctifies us and enables us to do good works. Thus it cannot be doubted that their faith, or the substance of their belief (*Fides, quae creditur*), is Christian; but, as they say in the schools, the way they express this belief (*Fides, qua creditur*) is questionable, and it turns out, in fact, to be very poor. They have recourse to the evangelists, the apostles, the prophets, and many other

---

[5] Giles Fletcher (in Bond, p. 126) explained the matter somewhat differently: the Russians considered the Books of Moses, especially the last four, to be superseded and without force since the birth of Christ.

[6] They in fact did not profess the Athanasian creed, which, though it prevailed in the Western church, had been rejected by the Eastern church.

saints, as well as the Lord Christ—and not just as intercessors, as the most learned say, but as agents of salvation, as the majority believe. Moreover, they daily render to painted pictures representing their saints the honor that is due to God alone, of which more below. As regards the expression and verification of their Christian faith through good works and love of neighbors, there was little evidence of this in their lives and in the episodes recounted above. They take good works to consist in the endowment and building of churches and monasteries, actually assigning to these [acts] a much greater significance than is warranted.

They call themselves members of the Greek church, although they do not follow its rules very exactly; they make many slips, and on their own initiative, have introduced many supplementary teachings. In their chronicles they write that the Christian faith penetrated Russia in the time of the apostles: the apostle Andrew, of Greece, came up the Dnepr River and crossed Lake Ladoga to Novgorod, where he preached Christ's evangel, established the true worship, and ordered the building of churches and monasteries.[7] However, after a long while, in the course of many wars carried to Russia by the Tatars and pagans, the true Christian faith was for the most part suppressed or extinguished, and paganism and idol worship introduced. Thus matters remained until the time of Grand Prince Volodomir, who himself was at first a pagan. When, with auspicious arms, he subjugated Russia and most of Sarmatia, he came to enjoy such great prestige among the foreign Christian princes that they began to send impressive embassies to court his friendship. As he was well pleased by these offers of friendship and seemed amenable to their wishes, they endeavored to draw him away from pagan idol worship to the Christian faith. Subsequently, Volodomir sent ambassadors and couriers to various places in Christendom, in order to obtain accurate information about their creeds. Since he was best pleased with the Greek faith—which had earlier existed in Russia and even then survived in some, though not many, places—he decided to adopt it. . . .[8]

---

[7] In Book II, apropos of his discussion of the town of Novgorod, Olearius presented a different and more accurate account of St. Andrew's travels as rendered in the chronicle.

[8] The myth of the apostolic conversion of Russia was an adaptation of an earlier myth about the conversion of Constantinople. The Constantinople See was supposed to have been founded by St. Andrew, one of Christ's apostles and a brother of St. Peter. The myth arose toward the end of the sixth century, after Andrew's bones had been moved from Rome to Constantinople. Subsequently taken over and appropriately altered, the myth appeared in the Russian Primary Chronicle;

From that time on there has been a close friendship between the Greeks and the Russians. The Russians consider the Greeks more holy and pious than themselves[9] and annually spend great sums on them. As Possevino writes, formerly the Muscovites each year sent the Greek church 500 ducats in alms; but this has been discontinued. Instead, Greek monks sent by the Constantinople or Jerusalem patriarchs appear two or three times every year, bringing gilded bones of the saints and various other relics and ikons, in exchange for which they receive and carry off as gifts sums of money far surpassing what was formerly given.[10]

Six years ago, in 1649, the Jerusalem Patriarch, Paisii by name, came to Moscow with several Greeks,[11] bringing some earth from the Lord's grave (which, however, is made of stone) and sanctified water from the Jordan. He was magnificently received, brought to the Tsar and Patriarch with great ceremony, and given—so trustworthy friends have written me—a gift of more than 50,000 ducats. However, on the homeward journey, the Turks took away all the gold, money, sables, and silk he was carrying with him, leaving him only the sacred articles and books.

In all the provinces the Russians have but one religion and [religious] practice, and none but they have it. Their religion ends at their borders, unless one counts a few who have settled in Narva, just across the Swedish frontier.[12] The majority, especially the common people,

---

however, it was not added to and fully exploited until later, when the expanding Moscow state endeavored to provide itself and its religious establishment with an ancient pedigree. See Dvornik, Chap. 4, pp. 263–64.

An extended passage treating the discussions of commentators on the origins of Russian Christianity is omitted.

[9] Actually, some Russians did, while others did not. Differences of opinion about the propriety of altering Russian church practices and religious texts to make them conform to the Greek precipitated a schism in the Russian church about the time of Olearius's second edition.

[10] It was such a mission, involving the Patriarch of Antioch rather than prelates of Constantinople or Jerusalem, that provided the occasion for Paul of Aleppo's visit to Russia, which he described at length in *The Travels of Macarius*. Frequently, more was involved than just the transfer of relics, for Russia strove to turn its connections with branches of the Orthodox church in foreign lands to political advantage. According to Vainshtein (pp. 116–17), foreign delegations seeking alms were sent away empty-handed if they did not bring political intelligence of interest to the Tsar. Vainshtein describes (pp. 115–19) how Kyrill Lukaris, Patriarch of Constantinople in the 1620's and 1630's, rendered valuable political services to Russia and received lavish gifts in return.

[11] One of these was Arsenius, whom, further on, Olearius associates with the Latin-Greek school in Moscow. See Kapterev, p. 98.

[12] This is not entirely accurate. Under the Treaty of Stolbovo with Sweden in 1617, a considerable area inhabited by Russians was ceded to Sweden. The treaty conceded to the Metropolitan of Novgorod ecclesiastical jurisdiction over these Russians. Although the Swedes put intense

can explain and answer very little about the articles of their faith. Their situation is just as Herberstein and Possevino found it in their times; like the Athenians, who thought that whatever suited their king was a right enough religion for them, they accept whatever the Tsar and Patriarch prescribe. They are given no sermons and are not instructed [in their creed].[13] Also the Patriarch neither permits much discussion of matters of faith nor allows disputations with foreigners.[14] Accordingly, they all hold one and the same opinion.

Not long before our arrival at Nizhnii Novgorod, a Russian monk had several conversations on matters of faith with a Protestant pastor who lived there, and who told me of them. In the course of the talks, the monk learned a number of sound things. When the Patriarch heard of this, he ordered the monk seized and brought to Moscow. There he was asked how he dared to speak frequently to a Protestant pastor and to dispute about religion. The monk cleverly replied that the German pastor wanted to embrace the Orthodox faith. Accordingly, he had instructed him, and the affair was going so well that he hoped soon to win him over completely. At that, the monk was released.

The Russians received their alphabet and script from the Greeks simultaneously with their religion, but they somewhat altered these and also increased the number of letters with special Slavonic characters. They use the letters and script in both printed and handwritten books.

---

pressure on the Russians to adopt Lutheranism, in 1630 the Russians still had 48 of their own churches in the Swedish zone. Tsvetaev, *Protestantstvo i protestanty*, pp. 590–94. Olearius also forgot certain areas of the Ukraine, where the prevailing religion was substantially the same as the Russians', and which, even after 1654, remained outside the Tsar's control.

[13] Although this was generally so, in the first part of Aleksei Mikhailovich's reign, a group intent on religious and moral reform, the "Zealots of Piety," resorted to preaching as a means of attaining their ends. Sparked by the Tsar's confessor, Stefan Vonifat'ev, and numbering among its leaders Ivan Neronov, Login of Murom, and Avvakum, the movement enjoyed the Tsar's support. Neronov, Login, and Avvakum subsequently fell out with Patriarch Nikon; but when the church schism developed, Neronov, unlike the other two, was reconciled with the official church. See Kapterev, Chap. 5.

[14] This too was true in the main, but there were some notable exceptions. Ivan IV engaged in religious disputations with the Protestant Jan Rokita and the Catholic Possevino. Materials relevant to these disputes appear in "Otvet Tsaria Ioanna Vasil'evicha Groznago Ianu Rokite" and *Pamiatniki diplomaticheskikh snoshenii*, X, 296–308.

Moreover, in Olearius's time, a notable religious disputation took place in Moscow. Extending from April 1644 to July 1645, it was intended to persuade Count Waldemar of Denmark, a Protestant, to embrace the Russian faith. Tsar Mikhail Feodorovich wished the Count to marry his daughter, Irina, but there was no question of permitting this unless he first abjured his religion. Although Waldemar and his supporters were permitted to bring counter-arguments, obviously this was no disinterested investigation of the relative merits of the religions involved. On the disputation, see Tsvetaev, *Protestantstvo i protestanty*, pp. 650ff.

Although their language differs from the Slavonic and the Polish, it is still so closely related to these that anyone familiar with one of them can easily understand the others. This language has nothing in common with Greek except for some few words which were borrowed from the Greek and are commonly used in church services and as [titles of religious] offices. Since in the schools the Russians learn to read and write only their own language,[15] or at most Slavonic as well (of which more hereafter), no Russian, whether ecclesiastic or layman, of high rank or low, understands a word of Greek or Latin.[16]

At present, and this is to be wondered at, the Patriarch and the Grand Prince are striving to make their youth study the Greek and Latin languages. Very close to the Patriarch's palace they have already built a Latin and Greek school, which is under the supervision and direction of a Greek named Arsenius.[17] If this enterprise is crowned with success and they become able to read and understand the writings of the Holy Fathers and other Orthodox [writers] in the originals, it may be hoped that with God's help they will arrive at a better understanding of their own religion. They have no lack of good heads for learning, and indeed one meets among them extremely talented people, gifted with good minds and memories. The present State Chancellor in the Posol'skii Prikaz, Almaz Ivanovich, was in Persia and Turkey once during his youth, and in a short while he learned the languages well enough that he can even now speak to persons from these countries without an interpreter.[18] Owing to his good mind and conscientious performance of

---

[15] Olearius tells us little of education and literacy, believing no doubt that it was insignificant in quantity and quality. A much cited author, A. I. Sobolevskii, though admitting that education above the elementary level was non-existent before the mid-seventeenth century, has argued that literacy was much more widespread than is generally thought. Some of his evidence for literacy is unconvincing; nevertheless, it is impressive to learn that 9,600 copies of a primer were published between 1647 and 1651. See Sobolevskii, *Obrazovannost'*.

[16] Many foreign visitors were struck by the Russians' ignorance of foreign languages. The authorities seem to have viewed their study as subversive, probably because it opened to the student a new world of ideas, religious and other. This would explain why, some decades earlier, the boyar Golovin, who was deeply interested in foreign languages, feared to have it become known. Therefore he had a German and a Pole come to him secretly, in Russian dress, to read German and Latin books with him behind locked doors. See Tsvetaev, *Protestantstvo i protestanty*, pp. 754–55.

[17] There have been sharp disagreements among historians about who Arsenius was, when the school was founded, and what its relation was to the later, well-known Slavonic-Greek-Latin Academy. These matters were settled in Belokurov's *Adam Olearii*. Belokurov placed the school's establishment in 1652–53 and considered it a forerunner of the better-known Academy. He identified Arsenius as one of the Greeks who had come to Russia with Paisii, the Patriarch of Jerusalem, a few years earlier. However, in the Soviet work, *Ocherki istorii . . . XVII v*, p. 563, the person in question is identified as a Ukrainian teacher named Arsenius Satanovskii.

[18] Further on, Olearius mentions the notable success of the pristav Romanchukov, who accompanied the embassy to Persia, in studying and learning Latin.

duty, he repeatedly participated in grand embassies and then became a dumnyi d'iak or state secretary, or as they now call them here, a State Chancellor.

The above-mentioned secret translator Johann Böcker von Delden, who knows many languages, gave them the opportunity to read about unfamiliar things in books that he translated from Latin and French; as did Adam Dorn, former ambassador of the Holy Roman Emperor, who also has been mentioned above. The latter composed a brief cosmography or description of the world, and the former, among other things, translated a history of the Great Mogul into Russian.[19] Once in a while, nowadays, some of the notables take such books into their hands.

The principal manifestations of their Christianity and present-day worship are: the practice of holy baptism, the reading of God's word in their churches, the taking of communion; revering God and dead saints, respecting and bowing to ikons, making processions and pilgrimages to the graves of their saints, fasting at designated times, confessing, taking Holy Sacraments, and administering the last anointment.

They consider baptism absolutely essential for acceptance into the Christian church and for the attainment of eternal bliss. They believe and confess that they were conceived and born in sin, and that Christ established the bath of rebirth and purification to wash away original sin (which they consider to be both corporal and spiritual). Therefore, as soon as a child is born, they baptize it without delay. If the newborn child is somewhat weak, he is baptized at home, though not in the room where he was born—for they consider it completely defiled. If the baby is healthy, it is brought to the church by the two people invited to be godparents. The priest meets them at the door, makes the sign of the cross with his fingers on the child's forehead, and blesses him with the words, "May God watch over your coming in and going out, now and forever."

The godparents give the priest nine wax candles, which he lights

---

[19] In Sobolevskii's *Perevodnaia literatura,* p. 60, Dorn is identified as a collaborator in the translation of Mercator's *Cosmography* from Latin into Russian. But neither Sobolevskii nor Amburger, whose article on Böcker von Delden has been cited, credits him with the translation of a work on the Great Mogul. For that matter, they list no translations by him. Parenthetically, Sobolevskii (pp. 73–74) records that Olearius's book was translated into Russian toward the end of the seventeenth century, but not published.

and then fixes in the shape of a cross to the tub filled with water, which stands in the middle of the church. Then he censes the tub and the god-parents with incense and myrrh, and with much ceremony blesses the water. After this the godparents, holding the burning candles, and the priest, reading from a book, go three times around the tub, behind a deacon bearing an ikon of John [the Baptist]. Then, as at our baptisms, certain questions are put to the godparents, for example, "How shall the child be named?" A paper on which the name is written is then passed to the priest. He places it on an ikon, holds the ikon on the child's breast, and prays. Then he asks, "Does the child believe in God the Father, the Son, and the Holy Ghost?" When the godparents answer affirmatively, they and the priest turn about, with their backs to the font. Then he asks, "Does the child reject the devil and all his angels and works, and does he intend to remain in the pure Greek religion all his life?" In answering each such question, the godparents and the priest are supposed to spit forcefully on the ground. Then they turn again to the font, and the driving out of the demons takes place. Laying his hands [on the child] the priest says, "Impure spirit, leave this child and make way for the Holy Ghost." He three times makes the sign of the cross on the child by blowing across him, and thus, supposedly, ex-pels the devil. For they believe that before baptism the impure spirit dwells in the child. I was told that the exorcism of Satan nowadays takes place outside the church doors so that the unclean spirit may not defile the church.

The priest takes a scissors, cuts some hairs crosswise off the baby's head, and lays them in a book. Then he asks, "Does the infant wish to be baptized?" And, taking the naked child from the godparents with both hands, he immerses it completely in the water three times and says, "I baptize you in the name of God the Father, the Son, and the Holy Ghost."

He then puts a little salt in the baby's mouth, anoints his forehead, chest, hands, and back, crosswise, with sanctified oil; dresses him in a clean white shirt, and says, "Now you are pure and white, and cleansed of original sin." Around the infant's neck is hung a little cross of silver, gold, or lead (according to the substance of the parents), which he must wear all his life, as witness that he is a Christian. If anyone is found dead in the street without such a cross, he is not buried [in hallowed ground?]. The priest also assigns the infant a saint and gives him his picture. His whole life long, the baptized must appeal to this saint and revere its ikon above all others. After the ceremony of baptism, the priest fondles and kisses the baby, as do the godparents. He admonishes the latter to be as genuine parents to the child and to refrain from wedding one another, for marriages of this sort are strictly forbidden.

If two or three children are brought simultaneously for baptism, the bath of rebirth is fixed anew for each; [this is done] even if there are a hundred of them. Once water has been used to cleanse of original sin, it must be poured out in a special place, so no one may defile himself with it. For they consider that the baptismal water cleanses not only spiritual sins and impurities of the soul, but also bodily sins. They generally bathe and cleanse themselves in the same pharisaical manner at wedding time, and after copulation, nocturnal emissions, or urination, washing the members employed. Many of them think that such external washing is adequate for cleansing the filth of their sins, which they regard as a material essence adhering to them.

Water used in baptism is never warmed by fire. In winter, they simply allow it to stand for a while in a warm place. Adults who are to be baptized (for example, converts to their religion, and also, formerly, the Chaldeans) are taken to a river, in which in winter time a hole is cut in the ice. Here, with the usual ceremonies, they are totally immersed three times.

Chaldeans was the name given, when we were there, to certain dissolute people who each year received the Patriarch's permission, for a period from eight days before Christmas until the Day of the Three Saintly Kings [Epiphany], to run about the streets with special fireworks. They often burned the beards of passersby, especially the peasants. While we were there, they burned up a peasant's load of hay, and when he began to resist them, they burned his beard and the hair on his head. Whoever wanted to be spared had to pay a kopek. They were dressed as carnival revelers, wearing on their heads painted wooden hats, and their beards were smeared with honey to prevent their being burned by the fire they were casting about. They were called Chaldeans in memory of those servants in King Nebuchadnezzar's time who, as the legend has it, started a fire in an oven wherein they intended to burn Shadrach, Meshach, and Abednego. Perhaps, in former times, they also meant to commemorate a miracle that was supposed to have occurred at their conversion. They make the fire with a special powder which they pound out of a plant or herb that they call *plaun'*. These flames are marvelous and enjoyable to watch, especially when they are thrown at night or in the dark, and one can get much amusement from it.[20]

During their escapades the Chaldeans were considered pagans, and impure. It was even thought that if they should die during these days they would be damned. Therefore, on the Day of the Three Saintly Kings, a day of great general consecration, they all were baptized anew, to cleanse them of their godless impurity and join them once again to the church. After receiving baptism they were again [considered] as pure and holy as the others. Some of these people had been baptized ten times and more. Since these hoodlums committed many grievances and much mischief against the peasants and common people, as well as against pregnant women, and since their playing with fire had caused no little danger besides, the Patriarch has entirely abolished their ridiculous games and masked running about.

Foreign and apostate Christians as well as Tatars and pagans who embrace the Russian faith and wish to be baptized must first spend six weeks in a monastery, where the monks instruct them in the religion —principally, their mode of prayer, the acknowledgment of the saints, and their manner of bowing to their ikons and crossing themselves. Then they are brought for baptism to a river, where they must three times spit upon their former religion as heretical and accursed, and vow never again to embrace it. After baptism they are dressed in new Russian clothes given them by the Grand Prince or other magnates [who serve as] their godfathers, and they are given maintenance, according to their status.[21]

At the present time, there are many such apostates in Moscow. Not only at the conclusion of the war at Smolensk 22 years ago, but in the last five years as well, many soldiers, especially Frenchmen, have had

---

[20] Olearius says more of this plant and its uses toward the end of Book IV, where he tells of a display of fireworks seen at Ardebil in Persia.

[21] Numerous documents have been published regarding the conversion of foreigners to the Orthodox faith and setting forth the rewards granted them. See for example, "Akty o vyezdakh," pp. 205–34; and Tsvetaev, *Pamiatniki*, pp. 42–66. A foreign visitor to Russia in the 1670's reported the existence of a section of Moscow (the Basmannaia) where many rebaptized foreigners lived. See Reitenfels, "Skazaniia o Moskovii," p. 93.

themselves rebaptized in order to remain in the country and obtain maintenance from the Grand Prince—even though they understand nothing of either the language or religion of the Russians. It is especially surprising that even some notable and intelligent people, for base profit, agreed to apostatize and embrace the Russian religion:[22] for example, the French nobleman Pierre de Remont, Count Shliakhovskii and, more recently, Anton de Gron, Colonel Alexander Lesly of Scotland, and others.

This Count Shliakhovskii, of whom I spoke above, came to Holstein and Denmark in 1640 and touchingly complained to His Princely Excellence and His Royal Danish Majesty, Christian IV, that because he, who came from a family of counts, the von Slicks, was of the Protestant faith, he had been persecuted by the Catholics. He recounted his affairs so plausibly that these sovereigns were moved to pity. They did him every sort of favor, and agreed to his plaintive request that he be given a recommendation to His Tsarist Majesty in Moscow. When, in accord with the King's request, he was well received in Moscow, he spoke very candidly of having come to the country to adopt the Russian faith and to remain with His Tsarist Majesty. The Russians were very pleased with this, not only because of his high rank, which they greatly value, but also because he understood the Latin and Polish languages. Gladly accepted, he was baptized, made a prince, named Prince Lev Aleksandrovich Shlik, and given a monthly salary of 200 reichsthalers in cash.

Some thought he hoped to wed the Grand Prince's daughter, Irina Mikhailovna. When he learned that negotiations were afoot to wed her to a foreign count, for which purpose two embassies had already been sent from Moscow to Denmark, he was greatly upset. In the end, however, he was content to be given the daughter of a leading, wealthy boyar. In time, His Royal Danish Majesty learned that Slick was not of high rank, but had been simply an underling of Count Caspar von Dehnhoff in Poland, and had used the recommendation only in order to get across [the border]. He wrote the Grand Prince the truth, and begged his pardon for the recommendation, which had been obtained

---

[22] Though it is plain that the Russian authorities encouraged foreigners to embrace the Orthodox faith, Krizhanich (I, 373) attacked the apostates as self-seeking and untrustworthy. Tsvetaev (*Protestantstvo i protestanty*, pp. 343–44), while conceding that material considerations frequently led foreigners to have themselves rebaptized, insists on the force and attractiveness of the religion itself as a cause of conversions.

by deception. The Grand Prince was most displeased to learn of this, but did not wish to take back the favor he had granted. He left Slick the title of prince and the salary, which is still paid, but severely took him to task for having given himself out as Count von Slick. After that, and to the present day, he still writes his name as Prince Lev Aleksandrovich Shliakhovskii, and is reckoned among the Tsar's dvoriane or hofjunkers.[23]

Colonel Lesly was led astray by misfortunes. After he had served in the Smolensk campaign,[24] Tsar Mikhail awarded him a large sum of money, which he took out of Muscovy; but later on, under Tsar Aleksei, he wished to reenter the service. Therefore, he came to Moscow again some years ago with a grand embassy from Sweden (headed by a nobleman and state counselor, Erik Gyllenstierne) and offered his services to the Russians. Since the latter did not anticipate war at that time and did not wish to expend money needlessly, the colonel suggested that he would be satisfied with a landed estate and peasants, instead of cash—to which they agreed.[25] He was given a fine estate on the shores of the Volga and the peasants who belonged there.

Subsequently, his wife and children came to Russia, and they settled on this estate. The colonel's wife, an intelligent and conscientious housekeeper, apparently burdened the Russian peasant women with more work than they were accustomed to. They became discontented and said they no longer could serve her; for she gave them meat to eat on fast days, in violation of the Russian faith; kept them with difficult work from attending church, and did not permit them enough time in the morning to make the proper reverences to God and their ikons. Besides, she was said to have beaten the people and, what was most reprehensible of all, to have taken an ikon from the wall and thrown it into a glowing oven, where it was consumed. For the Russians, the latter was a great and terrible accusation. After this the colonel, with his wife and children and all the household servants, was brought to Moscow, and the complainants and the accused were heard in the presence of one another.

---

23 Further information on Shliakhovskii is presented in *ibid.*, pp. 355–70.

24 Colonel Lesly recruited a large contingent of foreign soldiers for the campaign at Smolensk in 1632. The order authorizing him to do so is reprinted in *Sobranie*, Vol. III, No. 81.

25 At least as early as the time of Boris Godunov, foreigners in Russia's service frequently were paid, in part, by land grants; the labor of the peasants furnished revenues. See Borodin, p. 188; Muliukin, *Ocherki*, pp. 160–66. Their right to hold estates is clearly confirmed in the *Ulozhenie*, where foreigners are grouped with other landholding elements in Chap. 16, Art. 3, 13, 16, 30–32. In this respect, the foreigners were treated in the same manner as native servants of the state.

The colonel's wife did not deny that she had required strict fulfillment of work she assigned to the women, but would hear nothing of the other charges. She argued that the women had borne false witness against her out of hatred and malice called forth by the demands she had made upon them.[26]

Some of Lesly's foreign servants who gave testimony favorable to his wife were put under guard and threatened with torture. The peasant women, however, offered to have themselves put to torture.[27] The servants who remained at liberty fiercely attacked each other, and much blood was spilt on both sides; yet no one was willing to take the blame. Here the Patriarch intervened and convinced His Tsarist Majesty that the foreigners should be deprived of their estates and not be given any thereafter, and that infidel and unbaptized foreigners should not be permitted to treat Orthodox peasants in this way in their homeland and to abuse them in their worship.

The Patriarch lit the fire, and the boyars, who had long wished to lay their greedy hands on the well-run estates of the foreigners, assiduously heaped wood on it. Every day they urged His Tsarist Majesty to carry out the just petition of the Patriarch. Soon Lesly was deprived of his lands and peasants because he was not of the Russian faith, and from this time forth only Russians were permitted to own estates.[28] Not knowing how to support his wife and children without the estate, Lesly let it be known that, if only he were left in possession of the estate and peasants, he and his wife and children would embrace the Russian faith and be rebaptized. The Patriarch and the court responded favorably, and pledged that Lesly's request would be fulfilled. He and his family then entered a monastery and spent six weeks there being instructed in the articles of faith, and especially in the ceremonies, of the Russian church. Then they were immersed in water and rebaptized, and given

[26] While Olearius appears to acquit the Leslys of any wrongdoing, Tsvetaev (*Protestantstvo i protestanty*, pp. 376–77) and Pascal (p. 176) consider the complaints against them justified.

[27] This they did, of course, to emphasize the truth of their charges. Olearius treated this custom in Book III, Chap. Two.

[28] The decree forbidding unbaptized foreigners to hold estates is printed in *Polnoe sobranie zakonov*, Vol. I, No. 103. The religious persuasion of the landholder was clearly the point at issue, for Russians were certainly not deprived of their estates for abuse of their peasants. The order caused consternation, and many foreign officers thought to embrace Orthodoxy, but a majority changed their minds. Many others asked to be released from the service. As Muliukin points out, the measure was not fully enforced, in part to avoid alienating foreigners whose services were especially essential, and in part because the treasury was unable to carry the burden of cash salary payments. For all that, according to one report, after the Lesly family embraced Orthodoxy, 50 other foreigners followed suit. See Kurts, *Sostoianie Rossii*, pp. 97–99, 102, 137; Muliukin, *Ocherki*, pp. 190–94.

new names. The Grand Prince's father-in-law and his wife, who served as godfather and godmother, gave them fine Russian clothes. The colonel then had to be wedded anew to his wife,[29] and Il'ia Miloslavskii arranged a wedding for them in his home. By way of welcome to their new religion, His Tsarist Majesty granted the new Russians 3,000 rubles.

While Lesly and his people were in the monastery, the peasant men and women on his estate, learning that they were to be subjected again to the previous yoke, petitioned to be spared and promised obediently to serve anyone else under whose authority His Tsarist Majesty might place them. Just about then the rebaptized Frenchman Anton de Gron had been promised an estate. He asked about Lesly's properties, and upon learning that the peasants had requested another master, persuaded them to ask His Tsarist Majesty specifically for him. De Gron was granted the estate, and he holds it to the present time. Lesly was persuaded to let the peasants go in peace, since they would anyway have ended by breaking his and his family's necks. Now, therefore, in peacetime, he receives 90 reichsthalers monthly from His Tsarist Majesty, as do the other colonels. His son, too, was granted a colonel's salary, though not as large as his.

As against these instances of inconstancy in religion among men, I wish to tell about a memorable case of remarkable faithfulness in a weak woman. About 32 years ago, the above-mentioned Baron Pierre de Remont came to Moscow and married [Anne Barnesley], the daughter of John Barnesley, who derived from a noble English family and had long lived in Moscow. Only 15 years old then, she was considered the most beautiful of all the foreign women in Moscow. To win the Grand Prince's favor and the magnates' goodwill, the Baron embraced the Russian faith, allowed himself to be rebaptized, and was named Ivan. The Russians, as well as the Baron, would have been very happy if the wife, who was Calvinist in religion, would also have agreed to be rebaptized, and tried to attain this.[30] As she refused, the Patriarch first

---

[29] Inasmuch as the marriage rites of other Christian churches were not recognized by the Orthodox Church, married converts to Orthodoxy had to be remarried.

[30] The Orthodox church not only refused to marry one of its members to a non-Orthodox person but also, as in the case in question, it did not recognize a marriage between two non-Orthodox persons, one of whom subsequently embraced Orthodoxy. The marriage could be legitimized only if the partner was also rebaptized. This requirement was not abolished until the time of Peter the Great. Tsvetaev, *Protestantstvo i protestanty*, p. 511.

tried to win her over with kind words and fine promises. When this had no effect, he began to threaten her severely. At that she prostrated herself and humbly pleaded that her life be taken, rather than her religion; for no matter what they might do to her, she wished to live and die in her religion.

They took away by force and baptized in the Russian faith the children she had by the Baron. The Patriarch thrust away with his foot her father, who also prostrated himself on behalf of his daughter, and ordered her to be baptized by force. He said that since she understood nothing she must be treated as a child and dragged to baptism. During the baptism, she fiercely resisted. After she was taken to the river and had her clothes removed by force, the nuns who were to baptize her bade her, as is their custom, to spit on her religion. Instead, she spit in the face of the nun who asked this of her. When they immersed her in the water, she pulled another nun in and exclaimed, "You may of course immerse the body, but the soul remains unaffected by that." After this forced baptism, she and her husband were sent to the city of Viatka[?], where he was appointed voevoda.

With the elapse of the term, after which voevodas are generally rotated, the Baron was again summoned to Moscow, and he died soon after. His widow then wished to discard her Russian clothing and to go once more to the [Reformed] church with her coreligionists, but she did not succeed. Her two sons were torn from her and given to a Russian nobleman to raise. She and her small daughter were sent to the Beloozerskii Monastery, some leagues from Moscow,[31] and kept there. And there this young woman, a mere 21 years of age, was obliged to spend five years, in misery and without consolation, under the old nuns. She was not only robbed of the company of her sons, her father, and her friends, but she was also never once allowed to write of her life and situation to her relatives, or to receive letters from them. Nevertheless, she still refused to revere or make obeisance to the Russian ikons; and, indeed, she brought the nuns to her way of thinking more than they did her to theirs.

While her misery continued, fortune once contrived to secretly bring her news of her relatives. Once a German roofer was sent from Moscow

[31] The Beloozerskii Monastery was St. Cyrill's, located about 90 miles north of Moscow.

to the monastery to do some repairs, but whenever she wished to speak to him about her people the nuns kept coming in and interfering. In order to find an opportunity to speak to her unobserved by the Russians, the roofer often called his boy to him, and while looking at him with angry expressions and threats, spoke to her as he had been instructed to, and told her where she would find a letter after he left. To the nuns, it appeared that the workman was just scolding his boy for some reason or another, or ordering him to do something. In this way, the good woman received news, and indeed also gave an answer under the guise of asking something of the boy.

Finally, after Patriarch Filaret Nikitich died, owing to the requests and great efforts of her relatives, she was liberated and graciously permitted to live in Moscow.[32] But she could keep only a Russian servant. She was also given leave to go out, though not to the German church, and to visit whomsoever she wished. I met her twice with her brothers-in-law, Messrs. Peter Marselis and [Hermann] Fentzel, who had married her sisters, and heard in astonishment of the patience with which she bore her misery, and how she had managed to find comfort in it. Thus Lady Anne remained constant in her religion to the end. I have heard that she died two years ago. It is remarkable that her grandfather William Barnesley died in England, five years ago, at the age of 126. After becoming a widower, he had married again, though he was already 100 years old.

One hears of no other cases of the Russians forcing someone to adopt their religion. They allow freedom of conscience to everyone, even their subjects and slaves.[33] But if anyone marries someone of their faith, he is no longer allowed freedom of religion. If someone comes to them of his own free will, they gladly accept him and give him support his whole life long. The foreign apostates in Moscow are especially mali-

[32] King Charles I of England had interceded with the Tsar on Anne's behalf, but to no avail. In his reply, Tsar Mikhail insisted that no one was obliged to embrace the Orthodox faith against his will. See Konovalov, "Seven Letters," pp. 36–38, 49–52; a petition on her behalf submitted to the King by Anne's friends and relatives in Russia appears on pp. 62–63.

[33] Olearius puts the matter more strongly than is warranted. Freedom of religion was never proclaimed as an inviolable right. Protestants could not build churches as they pleased, but were obliged to obtain permission in each particular case. As Olearius relates further along, their churches were arbitrarily torn down now and again. Catholics were entirely forbidden to have churches. And even a few decades after Olearius wrote, a Dutch divine named Quirinus Kuhlmann was burned at the stake for heresy. See Schuyler, I, 194. Nevertheless, it is true that in a time of religious fanaticism in the West, Russia showed a comparatively high level of tolerance.

cious to their former coreligionists, who suffer more from them than from the Russians. Examples of this may readily be adduced.

If a Russian goes abroad and there adopts another religion, but reverts to the Orthodox faith upon his return, he must be rebaptized. They undoubtedly borrowed from the Greeks the practice of rebaptizing Christians who convert from other sects to theirs. When the Greeks separated from the Latin church, they began to consider its baptism inadequate, and therefore began to rebaptize those who apostatized from the Western church and wished to become members of theirs. However, they and all those who follow them in this were expelled from the church and anathematized in 1215 by Pope Innocent III, in the fourth decree of the Lateran Council. One may read of this in *Concilia Magna,* XVIII, 165.

The Russians pray in church on certain holidays and festivals; and they do the same each week not only on Sunday but also on Wednesday and Friday (which are their fast days).[34] These holidays are observed much more today than formerly. They used to reason that if they went to church in the morning, they might afterward return to their usual work. Moreover, as Herberstein recorded, they felt that celebrations were for the masters alone, and not for slaves and servants like themselves. Accordingly, even when we were there, one could see them on Sundays, as well as weekdays, plying their trades in their stalls and workshops. Now, however, the Patriarch has ordered that not only on Sundays and holidays but also on Wednesdays and Fridays the stores and workshops are not to be open. On the same days the taverns and saloons are to remain closed, and they must sell nothing, particularly at church time.[35]

The great holidays that they annually celebrate with extraordinary ceremony are 13 in number. Since, as related above, they begin the new year in the fall, on September 1st, their first major holiday comes on September 8th. It is called the Festival of the Holy Virgin's Birth.

[34] Services were apt to be held two or three times a week in the town churches, but only once in the village churches. See Rushchinskii, p. 59.

[35] Decrees banning work and the opening of taverns on Sundays and holidays were published in 1647 and 1653 respectively. See *Akty sobrannye,* Vol. IV, Nos. 19, 63. These orders were manifestations of the reform movement mentioned above. Olearius was mistaken in believing that the bans were in force three days a week.

The second holiday, on September 14th, is the Raising of the Cross; the third, on November 21st, the Presentation of the Holy Virgin to the Temple; the fourth, on December 25th, the Birth of Christ; the fifth, on January 6th, Epiphany, or Day of the Three Saintly Kings; the sixth, on February 2d, Candlemas; the seventh, on March 25th, the Annunciation of the Holy Virgin; the eighth, Palm Sunday, when they have the great procession celebrating Christ's entry into Jerusalem; the ninth, the Great Day, or the Resurrection of Christ; the tenth, the Assumption of Christ; the eleventh, the Descent of the Holy Ghost, or Pentecost; the twelfth, on August 6th, the Transfiguration of the Lord Christ; the thirteenth, on August 15th, the Assumption of the Holy Virgin.

In addition, not a day goes by on which the memory of one or another saint is not celebrated; occasionally, there are even two or three such celebrations on a single day. One may celebrate these days or not, as he pleases, but the clergy are obliged to read, sing, and hold mass [in honor of these saints]. They have a permanent calendar in the old style, in which they very cleverly and rapidly can find both the fixed and the shifting holidays.

On the high holidays and on Sunday, they go to church three times: first, to the sunrise service, the *zautrenia*; then, around noon, to the *obednia*; and in the evening, to the *vechernia*. At these the priest reads several chapters of the Bible, especially some Psalms of David [and selections from] the Gospels, and sometimes a homily from Chrysostom; also the Athanasian creed and some prayers. The priest sings in full voice in a monotone, as in our customary antiphonies. In the course of the reading and singing, he often says, "Gospodi pomilui," and the people repeat this three times, while making the sign of the cross and blessing themselves.

After the reading and singing, the priest goes up to the altar with his deacon (who assists the priest in all holy services) and holds mass, employing the liturgy of the ancient teacher of the church, Basil the Great.[36] He pours red wine and water into a cup, breaks leavened bread into it, blesses it, and reads for a quarter of an hour. Then he spoons the

---

[36] This fourth-century Greek bishop was one of the Church Fathers. Among his important contributions was a monastic rule that came to be widely followed in the Orthodox Christian world, including Russia.

contents of the cup into his mouth, giving none to the other communicants. However, if a sick child is carried into the church for communion, some is given to him.

If the priest has been with his wife on this day, he must not serve mass but must get another to do it in his place. While mass is served, the people stand and bow to their ikons, continually repeating, "God have mercy." As already noted, they ordinarily have no sermons or expositions of Bible passages, but content themselves with unadorned reading of the text and, most important of all, the homilies of the above-mentioned church sage. They explain that at the foundation of the church the Holy Ghost did its work through God's word alone, without further interpretation, and that it can accomplish the same today. Besides, much interpretation calls forth divergent opinions, which only cause perplexity and heresy. Two years ago the archpriest of Murom, named Login, presumed to preach. With some of the priests under his jurisdiction in Murom and other towns, he began to give sermons in the open, to teach the word of God to the people, and to admonish and punish. They were called *kazan'tsi* [*kazan'e* means sermon], and people flocked to hear them. But when the Patriarch was informed, he took harsh measures. He deprived the preachers of their offices, anathematized them in special ceremonies, and exiled them in disgrace to Siberia.[37]

They still have neither preaching nor discussion of religious questions (even though, to use Possevino's words, preaching "is almost the only way divine wisdom has to spread the light of the Gospel"). I am of the opinion that the Russians are hardly likely to be brought onto the right path and to a virtuous life, for no one points out the true path to those who stray. Nor does anyone speak out on behalf of conscience against the many coarse sins so widespread among them.[38] Indeed no

---

[37] Olearius was poorly oriented on movements in the Russian church around mid-century, possibly owing to the deficiencies of his informants. Besides, as Rushchinskii (pp. 2–3) suggests, it was generally difficult for foreign observers to become well acquainted with the inner life of the church. Olearius had little understanding of the pietistic movement launched with the approval of the Tsar and Patriarch. Nor did he realize that Login of Murom and other men were exiled not for preaching, but because they opposed certain of the reforms and the high-handedness of Patriarch Nikon. Login belonged to the circle of activists gathered by Vonifat'ev. See Kapterev, pp. 114–15. His seizure by the authorities is vividly described in the famous autobiography of Archpriest Avvakum. See Zenkovsky, pp. 330–31.

[38] Of course, the Zealots of Piety were concerned and active in regard to these problems. A mine of information on the subject is Pierre Pascal's work. According to Pascal (p. 114), the priest in old Russia fulfilled the function of the preacher at the time of confession, when he counseled the communicant on the conduct of life.

one reproaches them, except for the executioner who lays worthy strokes on their backs for the offenses they commit.

In one of their books, they have detailed descriptions and expositions of some Gospel stories, to which are appended fables, garnished with harmful untruths. They frequently use these to cover up their sins. I will cite just one instance, which Jakob [Ulfeldt] mentions in the description of his journey. In Great Novgorod, he had a conversation on religious matters with his pristav, a gray, old man named Feodor. This Russian proposed that a person need not be distressed by sins, even though they were committed daily, if only he intended in good time to repent. In corroboration of his idea, he cited the example of the repentant sinner Mary Magdalene, an extremely lewd woman who long engaged in harlotry and therefore sinned very often. Once she met on the road a man who asked to spend the night with her. When at first she refused, he continued to importune her, pleading that she fulfill his request "for the sake of God," after which she submitted to him. But as she had done it in God's name, not only was she forgiven all her sins but, in addition, she was inscribed in red letters in the register of saints. This tale is an abominable blasphemy against the holy will of God, and the story of the repentant sinner is befouled and distorted by a coarse lie. . . .[39]

While listening to the chapters of the Bible, the Russians stand before their ikons with bared heads (for no one, not even the Grand Prince, is permitted in church with covered head, except for the priest, who keeps on the *skuf'ia,* or cap, in which he was consecrated), frequently bowing and blessing themselves, in the manner described by Herberstein. They use the first three fingers of the right hand,[40] first touching the forehead, then the breast, then going across from right to left, and each time saying, "God have mercy."

Petr Mikliaev, a recent Russian ambassador to Holstein, gave me an explanation of what intelligent people understand by the sign of the cross. The three fingers symbolize the Holy Trinity; the raising of the

[39] Here Olearius digresses with the tale of a Florentine nobleman who also distorted the story of Mary Magdalene for vicious purposes.

[40] In view of the furor that developed in the church a little later over the number of fingers to be used in making the sign of the cross, it is interesting that, according to foreign reports, part of the population (mainly in the country-side) used two fingers, and part three. Rushchinskii, p. 166.

hand to the forehead, the assumption of Christ, who prepares a place for us in heaven; the touching of the breast points to the heart and the fixing of God's word there; the movement from right to left [indicates] the character of the Last Judgment, in which the pious will be placed to the right and the wicked to the left—the former to be taken up into Paradise, the latter to be cast down into Hell. They execute the sign of the cross at the commencement of all their affairs, whether secular and domestic or spiritual. Without it, they will neither eat nor drink, nor engage in any other activity.

There is no evidence that reverence to ikons was practiced in the Christian church during its first 300 years, up to the time of Emperor Constantine the Great. Although it is probable, as is apparent from Tertullian, that paintings and carvings based upon religious parables and stories were produced, nevertheless the images were not revered as sacred, that is, not prayed to, as with the Russians. The Russians say that they learned it from Damascene, but I believe they adopted it from the Greek church. They do not tolerate carved images, holding that God forbade making and bowing to sculptured—though not painted—images. It is therefore a matter of amazement that they so venerated the carved image of Nicholas the Wonder Worker in Moscow. Perhaps it is because he was, apparently, one of the new rather than one of the ancient saints.[41] Otherwise, they employ exclusively painted pictures, which are rather inartistically rendered in brownish-yellow oil paints on boards usually about one-fourth or one-half an ell in length and somewhat less in breadth.[42]

They revere no ikons except those painted by Russians or Greeks, as if other peoples do not make them beautifully or artistically; or as if something of the artist's religion might be transmitted to the picture![43]

[41] Olearius was wrongly informed, for Nicholas the Wonder Worker became a Russian saint in the eleventh century. See Obolensky, p. 54. On St. Nicholas, see Izwolsky, *Christ in Russia*, pp. 149–53.

[42] Reflecting their cultural conditioning, Western Europeans generally—Possevino was an exception—found Byzantine-influenced Russian painting unattractive. On the other hand, Paul of Aleppo (I, 296–97), who came out of the Eastern tradition, thought Russian art exquisite. "Their images are small," he wrote, "but painted with such exalted skill as to ravish the senses."

[43] More than this, Patriarch Nikon ordered the destruction of ikons done in the Western manner by Muscovite painters, and declared that henceforth persons painting in that style would be punished. See Paul of Aleppo, II, 49. Even a century earlier charges had been made, and with justification, that ikons painted for Moscow churches, such as Blagoveshchensk in the Kremlin, were done under the influence of Western models. See Florovskii, *Puti russkago bogosloviia*, pp. 26–28.

In Moscow they have a special market and shops where they sell such ikons, or as they say, "exchange them for money and silver," since they are loath to admit that people purchase gods.

They also never leave an ikon with anyone not of their religion, for fear that it will not be treated with the proper respect. When, several years ago, the German merchant Karol Möllin bought a stone house from a Muscovite, the Russians scraped the walls clean of all the ikons that had been painted thereon, and carried off the powder with them. They inveigh against us bitterly for making religious pictures, especially of the crucifixion of Christ, on stoves, and for turning our backsides to them. In the villages the peasants did not want us to touch their ikons or to lie on the benches with our feet toward them. Some of those in whose homes we stayed had the priest come with a censer to sanctify the ikons again, as though we had defiled them.

Around the walls of their churches hang large numbers of ikons, the most numerous and important of which represent the Lord Christ, the Holy Virgin Mary, and their principal patron saint, Nicholas. Each has his own saint or ikon before which he prays.[44] If someone commits a coarse offense that warrants his expulsion from the church, his saint [ikon] is also excluded. He may then use this ikon at home, for the excommunicated may no longer enter the church. Those who have the means decorate and ornament their ikons gorgeously, with pearls and precious stones. An ikon is indispensable for prayer and, accordingly, they must be present not only in churches and public processions, but also in everyone's house, apartment, or chamber as well, so that when he is praying he may have it before his eyes. When they wish to pray, they light one or two wax candles and fix them before the ikon. Fires are often caused by their forgetting to extinguish them. For the Russians' sake, the Germans formerly had to keep ikons in their houses; otherwise Russians would not have associated with them, and it would have been impossible to obtain Russian servants. The Patriarch no longer permits ikons in the Germans' rooms, however,[45] for in his opinion, they are unworthy of this honor.

[44] Anyone who prayed to another's ikon was apt to be abused by the owner. However, it was possible to buy a share in another's ikon, which included the right to appeal to it. Rushchinskii, pp. 44–45.

[45] This was connected with the banning of Russian servants from the homes of foreigners. Policy changed from no servants without ikons to no ikons where there are no servants. Decrees forbidding Russian servants in foreigners' homes were issued in 1628 and 1643, and the policy

When a Russian enters another's house or room, he first renders honor to the god, pronouncing his "Gospodi," and only then speaks to the people. He enters the house like a mute, and even though ten or more people may be sitting in the room, pays no attention to anyone. Upon coming in he first turns to the ikon, which is usually placed on the wall in a corner above a table. If he fails to see it, he says, "Is there not a god here?" Once he finds it, he bows and makes the sign of the cross three times. Then he turns to the people, greets them, and takes up his business.

They impute great power to the ikons, as though they could help one in a very special way. The repeatedly cited Danish nobleman, Jakob [Ulfeldt], tells that, in his time, during brewing they held an ikon mounted on a stick in the beer, hoping it would in consequence turn out better. They show timidity and fear before the ikons, as if there were something genuinely divine in them. If they are to have carnal pleasure in its presence, they cover the ikon with a cloth. Sometimes they also frighten people with them. In June 1643, in Moscow, one of their most important ikons began to appear redder than usual in the face. The priests informed the Patriarch and the Grand Prince and made a great fuss, as though this were a great portent. To stave off the threatening disaster they called for repentance and a day of fasting. The Grand Prince, a pious and God-fearing ruler, took all this to heart, called in the Russian painters, and having had them kiss the cross, asked them whether or not the change had occurred naturally. The painters took a good look and said: "This is no miracle. Rather, the paint of the old man's face is coming loose, and therefore the base, which is red, is showing through." With that, the fear subsided.

Sometimes the priests frighten people by devising and painting marks on ikons, to make the people fast and pray and offer the priests contributions and alms, which, out of piety, the simple folk give in great quantity. It is said that something of the sort occurred in Archangel a few years ago. By deception, two priests collected large monetary contributions, but quarreled over the division, fell to blows, and each informed on the other about the fraud. After that the knout made marks appear on them.

---

was reaffirmed in the *Ulozhenie*. Like the decree forbidding unbaptized foreigners to hold estates, however, this one was not rigorously enforced. Nevertheless, foreigners increasingly employed West Europeans or Tatars as servants. See Muliukin, *Ocherki*, Chap. 4.

That the simple, artless folk attribute great power to the ikons is apparent from the following. When, in 1611, the Swedish Colonel Jakob de la Gardie took Great Novgorod, and a fire broke out, a certain Russian held his St. Nicholas ikon before the fire and begged its aid in extinguishing it. When the help did not follow, and instead the fire spread even more widely, he impatiently cast the ikon into the flames and said, "If you will not help us, then help yourself and put it out."[46] To him one might have addressed the words of Lactantius, [*Divinarum Institutionum,*] "Do you not see that it is senseless to expect help from those who cannot help themselves?" At that time, not finding much of value in the houses, the soldiers carried off the ikons. The Russians ran after them forthwith and bought them back at high prices.

To teach their children fear of God, the common people, especially in the countryside and villages, place them before the ikons, and make them bow, cross themselves, and say, "Gospodi," with deep humility and reverence. Nothing is told of what it all means, so from most tender childhood they are accustomed to the idea that the ikons are gods, as the parents call them. In Ladoga, my hostess refused something to eat to her child, which could yet scarcely speak and stand, until in the usual way it had, as she said, shown its respect to God nine times.

However, some of the leading people and those who live in cities near the churches have a somewhat better—and the most intelligent, an entirely different—idea about ikons. In Russian Narva there dwelled a notable and wealthy merchant, who is still alive, named Philip N. An affable, friendly man, he sometimes came to dinner with the ambassadors and gave sound information about one thing or another. Once—it was January 31, 1634—at his request, I and our doctor, Mr. Hartmann Gramann, went to visit him. When we got into a conversation about their religion, and especially ikons, he made a confession of faith from which we could discern that he was a true Christian. Among other things, he said that he attached no significance whatever to the ikons. He took his handkerchief, went up to the ikon, and said: "With this I may wipe off the paint and then may burn the wood. Am I to seek salvation in this?"

He showed me a Bible in the Slavonic language, which he knew very

---

[46] Rushchinskii (p. 79) cites other interesting cases, reported by foreigners, of Russian superstition with reference to ikons.

well, opened it to various places, and translated. He said, "Here is
where I must seek the will of God, and then hold to it."[47] He did not
acknowledge the fasts that most of the Russians observe. "What does
it signify," he said, "if I do not eat meat, when I have costly fish at my
disposal, and get drunk on vodka and mead? The true fast is that which
God made known through the prophet Joel in the first and second
chapters. I fast if I take nothing but bread and water, and zealously
pray." At the same time he lamented that very many of his countrymen
had no such understanding of religious matters, or of the proper fulfillment of Christian duty. When we inquired why he, who was so enlightened about God, did not teach his brothers the better [way], he
answered that he did not have the calling. Besides, rather than believe
him, they would take him for a heretic. If he nevertheless kept ikons in
his home, it was as a reminder of God and the saints. Then he brought
from his chamber a picture of King Gustav [Gustavus Adolphus] of
Sweden, stamped in gilded leather, and said: "We willingly keep in
our rooms a portrait honoring the memory of a brave hero who accomplished many great things. Then why not also have pictures in memory
of the saints, who worked great miracles in the religious sphere?" In
general, when intelligent Russians, in keeping with their religion,
revere and pray to their sacred ikons, they pray not to the material substance, or because they equate them to a representation of God, but out
of love and respect for the saints, who are in heaven. For the honor that
they render to the ikon is received by him whom the ikon portrays. . . .[48]

Recently the archpriest of the Kazan Cathedral in Moscow, Ivan
Neronov, came out against reverence for ikons in the following words:
"It is not right to render to ikons the reverence due to God, for they
are made with the hands, of wood and paint, even though they seek to
represent the image of God and the saints. Would it not be more
appropriate, under the circumstances, to revere and pray to men who
themselves are made in the image of God, and who produced such
ikons? . . ."[49] However, as soon as the Patriarch learned of this, the
good priest was deprived of his clerical hat and was exiled, with harsh

[47] In this, as in other matters, it is apparent that the merchant had been influenced by Protestantism, the faith of his fellow subjects of the Swedish crown. Olearius discerned "a true Christian" in one who had gone far toward acceptance of his own faith.

[48] A passage concerning eighth-century conflicts in the Western church about attitudes toward
religious pictures is omitted.

[49] Various classical references that express this same point of view are cited.

threats, to Kamennyi Monastery on the Volga, so that this teaching might not spread further and the ikons might continue to be accorded the customary reverence.[50]

When their ikons become old and are moth-eaten and falling to pieces, they neither throw them out nor burn them, but instead either set them in flowing water, to float where they will, or bury them deep in the soil of a churchyard or orchard, and endeavor to keep anything unclean away from the place.

As Antonio Possevino correctly writes, the Russians retain the bodies of several putative saints who, they fabulously contend, still accomplish great miracles and can cure the sick. A number of these saints are buried in Moscow. Two years ago, in 1653, they brought there a new saint, named Metropolitan Philip the Wonder Worker, whom they venerate extraordinarily. Deriving from the Kolychevs, an old, noble Moscow family, he lived in Moscow in Ivan Vasil'evich's time, and repeatedly told the tyrant the truth about his peculiar administration and his cruel, unchristian, and even inhuman way of life. The tyrant became indignant, and sent him in disgrace to a distant monastery. However, since he continued to admonish him by letter, and with the point of his pen opened the old wounds again, the tyrant, in a rage, sent one of his servants to the monastery to strangle him with a rope. Kolychev, who was ready to die, surrendered himself to the murderer, only pleading that his life be taken not by strangling but with a knife. This was granted, and the knife was plunged into his body below the heart.[51] The monastery's friars declared him a martyr, took his body to an island called Solovka in the White Sea, beyond Archangel, and buried him there in a chapel.

The present Patriarch, while still Metropolitan of Rostov and Iaro-

[50] Neronov, who was Archpriest Avvakum's spiritual father for a time, did run afoul of the authorities after having enjoyed official support in his campaign for moral reform and religious piety. However, his fall from favor was not caused by criticism of ikons, which Olearius wrongly attributes to him. He was in fact a staunch supporter of veneration of ikons. Rather, like Login of Murom, he fell out with Nikon when the latter gave his support to the religious reforms proposed by Ukrainian clerics who asserted the superiority of the Greek church over the Russian. On Neronov see Kapterev, pp. 107–13, 139–51; Pascal, pp. 35–73; and Ilovaiskii, V, 273–77.

[51] According to a note in Barsov's edition of Olearius (*Chteniia,* 1868, No. 4, p. 338), Metropolitan Philip was smothered with a pillow. Popular legend represented the Metropolitan's death as an act of kenosis, i.e., he offered no resistance, but died in the spirit of Christian self-sacrifice. On kenotic Christianity in Russia, see Fedotov, Chap. 4.

slavl,[52] reported having heard from certain people that many afflicted persons who simply prayed before the still uncorrupted body of this saint were healed. Therefore, he persuaded His Tsarist Majesty to have the corpse brought thence to Moscow. The nobleman Mikhail Levont'evich and a d'iak were assigned to transport it,[53] and took along, among others, Levont'evich's two sons. They set out for the island in two large, open boats. The envoy arrived safely, but the second boat, which carried the d'iak, the envoy's sons, and the others, was lost and never found.

When the saintly Kolychev's corpse had been brought to within a league of Moscow, His Tsarist Majesty and his whole court retinue, as well as the Patriarch and the clergy, went out to meet it. On this occasion, Varlaam, the Rostov-Iaroslavl Metropolitan, a very corpulent man more than seventy years of age, dropped dead not far from the saint. Nevertheless, the saint was brought into the city with great pomp and laid in the Kremlin cathedral or principal church. Here he worked numerous miracles on the sick who came to pray to him, and many who perhaps earlier had been blind, lame, deaf, and dumb, under the Patriarch's careful supervision, were enabled to see, walk, hear, and speak again. Each time such a miracle occurred the great bell was rung, and at first it was heard four or five times a week. Now, however, one does not hear of his working so many miracles; for, as they say, though people became pious upon his arrival, they have once again lapsed into godlessness and no longer approach him with such strong faith. The body is said to lie, still uncorrupted, under a cloth, which, however, no one may raise.

They have another saint, of whom Possevino, Herberstein, and Petrejus all take notice. This saint, Sergei, is located at the Troitskii Monastery, 12 leagues west of Moscow. It is said that he was a great, stout man and initially a brave soldier. Later he renounced the world, became a hermit, and finally went to the Troitskii Monastery[54] to spend the rest of his life there as a monk. Because of his extremely pious

---

[52] The reference is to Nikon, who actually had been Metropolitan of Novgorod. This error, which Olearius subsequently repeats, confuses Nikon with Filaret, who had been Metropolitan of Rostov.

[53] According to Barsov, Olearius incorrectly identifies those who were sent to Solovka for Metropolitan Philip's remains. The persons actually involved were the boyar I. N. Khovanskii and the d'iak Gavrilo Leont'ev. See *Chteniia,* 1868, No. 4, p. 339n.

[54] He in fact founded the monastery.

and God-fearing life, he was elected abbot, and he is said to have helped many people with his prayers and to have performed miracles. He had a disciple named Nikon, who inherited the virtues of his teacher. Sergei died in 1563.[55] Both, after their deaths, were canonized and inscribed as saints. They lie buried near each other at the monastery. It is said that even now they can show the skull of one of them with the brain still undecayed. They relate that the Poles attacked the monastery repeatedly and strove to take it by storm, but when the friars held Sergei's skull and brain toward the foe, they not only were rendered incapable of taking the monastery, but also fell out among themselves and used their swords on one another.[56] Petrejus, too, speaks of the futile siege laid by the Polish colonel Jan Sapieha, but [he attributes] the subsequent rout of his forces to the Swedish army. The monastery took its name from Sergei and is called Troitse-Sergiev, or the Monastery of the Holy Trinity.

As regards the copper pot that Herberstein says is located here, present-day Russians know nothing whatever of it. According to the tale, when certain foods were cooked in it, especially cabbage, it never became empty. No matter how much was taken from it to feed the friars, there was never too much or too little. It is certain, at any rate, that the monastery boasts more than 300 friars and a greater income than any other in the country;[57] for the grand princes and the rich magnates have bequeathed it large sums and continue to do so. Besides, merchants and lords who pass by, if they are able, give rich alms, that their souls may be prayed for and they may be granted protection against all misfortune.

The Grand Prince and his foremost magnates make pilgrimages to this monastery twice a year, on Trinity [Sunday] and on St. Michael's Day [St. Sergius's Day, September 25th]. When they are half a league from the monastery, the Grand Prince dismounts and goes the rest of the way with his suite on foot. He stays to pray several days, during

---

[55] Actually Sergei died in 1393.

[56] The monastery was besieged in 1609, during the Time of Troubles. One of its monks wrote a lively account, full of miraculous events, which appears in *Skazanie Avraamiia Palitsyna*, pp. 132ff.

[57] According to other sources, at the beginning of the seventeenth century the monastery maintained as many as 4,000 persons, including the monks and serving people. Rushchinskii, p. 139. A decade or two earlier, Fletcher wrote that there were 800 friars alone at Troitskii. Bond, pp. 115–16.

which the abbot must furnish, without charge, provisions for the Grand
Prince and his company, and feed for the horses. Since the locality is
extremely pretty and well stocked with game, the Grand Prince usually
goes hunting here for amusement. . . .[58]

[58] Omitted is additional material on other pilgrimages, one to Moscow and one to Novgorod,
both of which have been mentioned earlier.

Religion *(continued)*

ABOVE, IN THE DESCRIPTION of the buildings of Moscow, it was said
that in the Kremlin and in the city there are very many churches,
chapels, and monasteries. Within and without the city walls, they total
more than 2,000, for now every magnate who possesses some property
has a special chapel built for himself. Most of them are made of stone.

The stone churches of Moscow all have round vaults, but the Russians were unable to explain why. I believe that they adopted this design from the ancients, who usually made their temples round (as one
may read in [Joannes] Rosinus, *Antiquatum Romanarum*), imagining
that because these were houses of gods, they should resemble the arc
of heaven. . . .[1]

The Russians have neither chairs nor benches in their churches, for
all must worship standing, kneeling, or prostrate (as they say the late
Grand Prince Mikhail Feodorovich often did). They do not allow
organs or other musical instruments in their churches, arguing that
since they have neither soul nor life, instruments cannot praise God.
When one retorts that people can produce beautiful melodies upon
them, and refers to the Psalms and the example of David, they say,
"These indeed were used in the Old Testament, but not in the New."
In houses and elsewhere outside of the churches, they are glad to have
music, especially during feasts. However, the present Patriarch considered that music was being misused in taverns and pothouses, as well
as in the streets, for all kinds of debauchery and obscene songs. Accordingly, two years ago he ordered the destruction of any tavern musicians'
instruments seen in the streets. Then he banned instrumental music
altogether and ordered the seizure of musical instruments in the

---

[1] There follows a discussion of reasons adduced for the ancient practice.

houses; once, five wagon loads were sent across the Moscow River and burned there.[2] The Germans, however, are permitted to have music in their homes, as is the great magnate Nikita [Romanov], the friend of the Germans, who has a harmonium and many other instruments in his palace. There is little the Patriarch can say to him.

The churches and chapels must without fail have on the summit either a plain or, as on most, a triple cross. They do not consider our churches genuine, since they do not have crosses on them. For they say that the cross signifies the head of the church, which is Christ. Because Christ was crucified on the cross, the cross became the symbol of Christianity, and where that symbol is absent there is no church. As the church is a holy, pure place, nothing impure may enter. They resist letting people of other religions go inside. When we came to the country for the first time and some of us unwittingly went into a church to have a look, we were escorted out again by the arm, and the floor was swept after us with a broom. If a dog or some other unclean thing enters the church, as soon as they become aware of it they immediately wash the defiled place and sanctify it anew with water, fire, and incense. They keep the churchyards equally clean and holy, and it is forbidden to urinate there, on pain of severe punishment.

In their churches hang many bells, sometimes five or six, the largest of which weighs no more than 200 pounds and often a good deal less. With these they summon the people to church; they also ring them when the priest, in celebrating mass, raises the cup. In Moscow, owing to the multitude of churches and chapels, there are several thousand bells. During a service they give forth such varied chimes and tones that a person unaccustomed to it listens in wonder. One person can operate three or four bells. For this purpose they tie the rope not to the bells but to the tongues, and the rope ends one to the hand, the other to the elbow, bringing them into action by turns. In ringing them, they keep to a particular rhythm. They consider the bell indispensable to their worship, and believe that without it the service would not be well received. For this reason, the pristavs were astonished when on Michaelmas, the Swedish ambassadors told them that they wished to celebrate their holiday too. They asked how it was possible [for the

---

[2] The order, dated August 16, 1653, is reproduced in *Akty sobrannye,* Vol. IV, No. 63. See especially p. 97.

Swedes] to celebrate their holiday in Moscow if they had brought no bell with them on their long journey.

Over the church doors, as well as the city gates, they hang or paint ikons so that those who came before them may bow, cross themselves, and say their "Gospodi." They cross themselves and pray not only to the ikons but also to the crosses set on the churches. Consequently, one is always meeting Russians praying in the streets.

The Patriarch, the metropolitans and archbishops, the bishop and the archdeacon, the archpriests, and the priests administer and supervise the ecclesiastical government, the consistory, and the church service. The Patriarch is the supreme head, as the Roman pontiff is to the Catholics. Formerly he was chosen by the Constantinople Patriarch, but later was only confirmed by him. Patriarch Filaret Nikitich was the third, and last, approved by the Constantinople Patriarch;[3] for now both the election and the confirmation is done in Moscow by the Russians themselves. The Patriarch is elected by the metropolitans, archbishops, and bishop from among themselves. For this purpose, they assemble in the Kremlin's greatest church, which they call a *sobor*, and select two, or sometimes four or five, of their number whom they consider the wisest, the most learned, and the most irreproachable in conduct. They report to His Tsarist Majesty, who, after consulting the rest of the clergy, chooses one of them. Sometimes, when the candidates are about equally meritorious and they do not know whom to elect, they cast lots. This occurred, for example, in the case of the preceding Patriarch, who was merely an abbot in a monastery and was drawn into participation in the elections only because of the special respect he enjoyed as a man of unusual intelligence. When the lot fell to him and the others protested, the lots were cast again, and he was selected a second time. When the Grand Prince saw that others still looked askance at him, the lots were cast a third time, and again the choice fell to him. Then His Tsarist Majesty said: "I see that he is destined for it and that God has chosen him. He and no other shall be Patri-

---

[3] Actually no Russian patriarch was ever chosen by the Constantinople Patriarch, for with the establishment of the Russian patriarchate in 1589, the Russian church became autocephalous. The Constantinople Patriarch had a part in the elevation of the first Russian patriarch, but there is no reason to believe that he confirmed the next two, as Olearius contends.

arch."[4] As soon as the Patriarch is elected, he is given a letter of certification, with the signatures and seals of the electors, [affirming] that he is recognized as worthy and that he has been fairly elected with the agreement of all. To this His Tsarist Majesty adds his confirmation or ratification.

After the Grand Prince, the Patriarch enjoys the greatest honor and power in the country. He is judge of the clergy in cases not covered by secular law; he has oversight of religious affairs, good morals, and [the fulfillment of] the Christian way of life. In these affairs, what he thinks right he may order, institute, or abolish at his pleasure, leaving the execution to the Grand Prince. Neither the Grand Prince nor anyone else has the right to advise him, much less to contradict him, in his undertakings, except in such [rare] instances as that of Nikita, who did so on behalf of his foreign clothes.

The preceding Patriarch and, in particular, the present one have changed and abolished very many things that had long prevailed in the country, and have introduced [many] innovations. The present Patriarch, whose name is Nikon, was formerly Metropolitan of Rostov and Iaroslavl. Forty years old, alert and energetic, he lives in the Kremlin in a magnificent palace that he had built for himself. He is amply provided for, according to their custom, lives well, and likes a joke. They tell that when a certain beautiful girl recently came with some friends to be rebaptized and subsequently went to receive his blessing, he said to her, "Lovely girl, I do not know whether to kiss you first or bless you." For they have a custom, after the blessing, of welcoming those newly inducted into their religion with a Christian kiss.

There are four metropolitans: the Novgorod and Velikolukii Metropolitan in Novgorod; the Rostov and Iaroslavl Metropolitan, who resides in Rostov; the Kazan and Sviiazhsk Metropolitan in Kazan; and the Sarskii [Sarai] and Podonskii [Don River area] Metropolitan, who resides in Moscow in the Kremlin. Under them are seven archbishops: the first, the Archbishop of Vologda and Velikoperm, who resides in Vologda; the second, of Riazan and Murom, in Riazan; the third, of Suzdal and Tarussa, in Suzdal; the fourth, of Tver and Kashinsk, in Tver; the fifth of Sibir and Tobolsk, in Tobolsk; the sixth,

[4] The story is about Iosif, who served as Patriarch between 1642 and 1652.

of Astrakhan and Tersk, in Astrakhan; and the seventh, of Pskov and Izborsk, in Pskov.

After these is the Bishop of Kolomna and Kashira, who lives in Kolomna. There are no other bishops in the country. In Moscow, under the Patriarch, there is an archdeacon, who serves as the Patriarch's chancellor and right hand. In the Kremlin Cathedral there is a senior deacon (*protodiakon*). In the towns there are archpriests, priests, and deacons. Then there are the *ponomari*, that is sextons, who open and close the churches and ring the bells. In the monasteries there are archimandrites, monk-stewards (*kelari*), and [nuns], who serve as heads, abbots, and prioresses.

The Patriarch, metropolitans, archbishops, and bishop are not permitted to marry; [if they are already married] when they take these offices, they must abstain from [relations with] their legal wives.[5] All these ecclesiastics, except for the archpriests and deacons, are allowed to wear neither trousers nor rings on their fingers. They may not wear linen next to the body, but only a wool shirt, and must not sleep in a bed. In the monasteries they abstain from meat, and do not have wine, vodka, mead, or strong beer. The Patriarch may not wear a linen shirt either, but may use one of dark silk.

The ordinary daily dress of the Patriarch, metropolitans, archbishops, and bishop, as well as the monks, consists of a long black robe, over which they wear a black cloak. On their heads they wear black hoods, three ells in breadth, in the middle of which is a stiff, round disk, like a large plate. The [headdress] hangs down behind the head. When they walk in the streets, they carry staffs, called *posokhi*, which are bent near the top almost in a right angle.

Owing to the great number of churches, there are around 4,000 priests in Moscow, for some of the larger churches have as many as six, eight, or ten priests. When someone wishes to become a priest, he applies to the Patriarch of the nearest metropolitan or bishop. He is examined, and if he is found worthy, that is if he can read, write, and sing well, he is consecrated and certified.[6] In the investiture ceremony

[5] The men who filled the higher offices of the church were generally recruited from the celibate monks and not from the "white" or secular clergy, who were permitted to marry.

[6] According to Paul of Aleppo (I, 347), the candidate had to have letters of recommendation from the local residents and also was given a short period of training. Pascal (pp. 102–4) gives a detailed account of the steps leading to ordination.

he is dressed in a priestly cloak not much different from a secular one. The hair is shorn from the top of his head, and a little cloth cap, which they call a *skuf'ia*, is put on. It is like our skullcap, and lies against the skin; the surrounding hair hangs down to the shoulders like a woman's. They never take off this hat during the day, except to have their hair cut. It is a sacred article and enjoys great respect. If anyone strikes a priest and comes down on the cap or makes it fall to the ground, he is severely punished and must pay a beschest'e. Nevertheless, priests frequently are beaten, for generally they are more drunken and good-for-nothing than others. Since the sacred cap must be spared, it is first removed; the priest is given a good drubbing and the hat is [then] neatly restored to its place. After such occurrences, nothing is to be wondered at.

In accord with the Greek custom, an archpriest or priest must be married; but should his wife die, he may not marry again and still serve as a priest. They base this [rule] on St. Paul's first letter to Timothy, where he says, "A bishop shall have a wife." They understand this not as a commandment against polygamy but as a prescription that a priest must have a wife and must not marry more than once. Incidentally, both the Russians and the Greeks see this as an important cause of their disagreement with the Roman church, which forbids priests to marry....[7]

Russian priests must be married before they are consecrated. They must wed virgins rather than widows, much less individuals of ill repute or whose relatives are notorious. If the mark of virginity is wanting in the marriage bed and this becomes known, the priest is removed from his office. A priest may not come to the altar and hold mass if he has had carnal relations with his wife the previous night. If a priest's wife dies, he may perform the zautrenia and vechernia but not the obednia, in which the mass and communion are celebrated. He may no longer serve at the altar or conduct baptisms or marriage ceremonies, but may only read and sing.[8] Such priests often are employed in embassies, to assist the envoys in worship. They may not marry a

[7] The difference was based on opposed opinions as to the propriety of accepting the sacraments from a priest with a wife. Olearius discusses this, making reference to various church declarations and commentaries.

[8] As Dr. Samuel Collins put it (p. 5), the priest's calling "is wrapped up in his wife's smock ... which makes them indulge their wives more than ordinary [*sic*] for their office's sake."

second time. It should be added, however, that a young widowed priest who is not prepared to live unmarried has the right to abandon his skullcap and cloak and become a worldly person, engage in trade or some craft or other, and remarry. This frequently occurs. If a priest is old and either cannot perform the zautrenia and vechernia in church any longer or does not want to, he may enter a monastery and become a monk.

Here and there, in and outside of the cities, the Russians have many monasteries, some for monks, others for nuns, most of them operated according to the rule of Basil the Great. People enter them in some cases because of poverty; in other cases because of old age or infirmity, or marital discord; and still others are compelled to enter, for different reasons.[9] Some enter them voluntarily, out of special piety, as indeed some very rich people do. If a wealthy person enters a monastery, he takes with him only a part of his liquid property—the rest goes to his heirs—as was prescribed a few years ago in their new *Sobornoe Ulozhenie*.[10] Previously they took all their property with them into the monastery; so a large part of the land fell under the control of the monasteries. [If that practice had continued] the Tsar might at last have been left without land and peasants.[11] For this reason some of the monasteries have large incomes, while others are destitute.

The monastery's rules must be observed strictly, without lapses. [The monks] nearly always have their rosaries with them, and at certain times of day and night, they zealously do their praying and worshipping. They live an austere life, never eating meat or fresh fish, but feeding only on salt fish, honey, milk, cheese, and garden vegetables, especially raw and pickled cucumbers. They drink kvas, or small beer, sometimes putting diced cucumbers into it and eating it with a spoon.

Outside of the monasteries, however, they permit themselves to be

[9] As a means of terminating the existence of some notable families to which he was hostile, Ivan the Terrible incarcerated their younger members in monasteries. Fletcher, in Bond, pp. 35–36, 117.

[10] See the *Ulozhenie*, Chap. 17, Art. 43.

[11] Though exaggerated, this statement refers to a real problem that led Ivan IV to take steps, in 1550 and 1580, to prevent further accumulation of land by monasteries. See Kluchevsky, *History of Russia*, II, 195–96. His prohibitions were not observed, however, and the *Ulozhenie* (Chap. 10, Art. 42–44) sought once again to halt the transfer of land to the monasteries. Foreign observers estimated that the church owned from one-third to two-thirds of all the land in the country. However, it also contributed substantially to the defense of the country. Patriarch Nikon told Macarius that he had furnished 10,000 soldiers for the war with Poland in the 1650's. Paul of Aleppo, II, 61.

entertained by good friends to such an extent that sometimes it is necessary to carry them drunk from the house to the monastery. Most of them are wretched simpletons; hardly a tenth of them, and indeed of the common people generally (as Clement Adam[s] correctly writes in *Anglorum Navigatio Ad Moscovitas*), can say the "Our Father."[12] Few of them know God's Ten Commandments, for they allow that these are things for the great magnates and the higher clergy, and not for them. On this, see Guagnino Chap. 3, on the religion of the Russians. Henning, on p. 55 of the *Livonian Chronicle*, recalls that when the tyrannical Grand Prince was in Novgorod for the marriage of Duke Magnus of Denmark, he struck several monks on the head with a staff because they were unable to sing the Athanasian creed (in lieu of a wedding song) as rapidly from the book as he did by heart.[13] Monks are frequently seen riding on horesback or in sleighs, like peasants or coachmen. They deal and behave like men of the world, from whom they may be distinguished only by their black habit.[14]

Some Russians, out of special piety, go to the forest, build a chapel along the roadside, and there live an ascetic life as hermits. They live only on the alms they receive from the peasants and passersby. We met such people between Novgorod and Tver.

The Russian church prescribes an extremely severe mode of fasting, which those who wish to be pious and God-fearing observe conscientiously, others less stringently.[15] Everyone I knew, even during the journey, refused meat offered on fast days, although the foremost allowed themselves the finest fish on Wednesdays and Fridays. However, when a major fast begins, as far as one can tell from the outside,

[12] Clement Adams composed a Latin account of Russia based upon Chancellor's report and supplemented with biographical, geographical, and other data. Both Chancellor's and Adams's accounts are printed in Hakluyt, Vol. I. According to other writers, the "Our Father" and the confession of faith were recited by the congregation. Rushchinskii, p. 48. In this respect, as in others, however, practice was apparently not uniform. If this testimony is accepted, then the impression Olearius gives that the congregation said nothing during the service but "Gospodi pomilui" is wrong.

[13] Matters had not changed so much in this respect. Tsar Aleksei Mikhailovich also corrected the clergy, although less violently, in keeping with the different cut of his character. See Paul of Aleppo, II, 246, 247–48.

[14] Though the results may not have been spectacular, the reform movement strove to elevate the quality of monastic life. Many decrees in the 1640's and 1650's were addressed to this problem.

[15] So rigorous were the fasts that Paul of Aleppo, a cleric of a less demanding branch of the Orthodox church, was driven to write in dismay (II, 83–84), "We underwent with them such excess of torment as one might liken to the violence of the rack. . . . There was not a man among us . . . who, after this experience, continued to complain of Lent as [it is] kept with us."

they practice great moderation in eating and avoid everything that comes from meat. Recently they have also begun to abstain from sugar (which they did not formerly consider impermissible), for some years ago a foreign merchant named Bock told the Patriarch that eggwhite was used to purify sugar.

In the course of the year they have more fast days than days on which meat may be eaten. Besides the two fast days each week, they have the great seven-week fast in *Quadragesima*. It begins on Sunday [evening] of *Esto mihi* and runs until Easter.[16] The first week of this fast they call *Maslianitsa* (Butter Week), a period during which they eat neither meat nor fish,[17] but only butter, milk, and eggs; however, they so indulge themselves daily on vodka, mead, and beer that they lose their heads. The consequences are every sort of debauchery and frivolity, and formerly many assaults and murders were committed. Thus their sorry preparation for the fast. Here a reminder of what Basil said (*Homilies*, p. 186) "in praise of the fast" would not have been amiss: "Drunkenness is not the way to the fast, nor temperance the way to licentiousness." In the succeeding weeks they begin to conduct themselves moderately, eating only honey and garden vegetables, and drinking kvas and water; going to baths, sweating, and washing out the sins committed in the previous week; and having the priests bless them. During this period most of those who wish to be more pious do not eat fish either, except on Sunday. A second fast begins on the eighth day after Pentecost and continues until Peter and Paul Day. They call it Peter's fast. A third begins on August 1st and lasts 14 days; a fourth lasts from November 12th to Christmas. In the week between Christmas and New Year's Day, everyone eats meat, and no one does without if he has enough money. They do the same during all the holidays and on Sundays, if these do not coincide with a fast; and they count it a sin not to eat meat on these days. In Guagnino's words, they do not want to violate the apostle's rule, transmitted by Clement, that no one is to fast on Sunday. . . .[18]

---

[16] *Quadragesima* refers to the 40 days of Lent. In 1646 on the eve of Quadragesima, a patriarchal order enjoined sobriety, church attendance, and a reverent attitude upon clergy and laity. Violators were to be reported and punished. See Pascal, p. 133. This is still another manifestation of the reforming activity of the time.

[17] According to Rushchinskii (p. 85), fish could be eaten during this fast.

[18] Clement's canon is omitted.

In the course of a fast, especially the great fast when they eat neither meat nor fish and also for a period of eight days prior to the taking of communion, no one, priest or layman, may copulate with his wife, on pain of heavy fines. [Although this rule may be widely violated] I believe that neither the men nor their wives give one another away, so very little money is taken in.

During the great fast, when the time for confession approaches, some of them purchase birds, which they then set free again. They suppose that by liberating the birds they do a good deed, and that on this account God will free them of their sins.

The Russians consider confession and communion indispensable for conversion and reconciliation with God; and for adults and people who have reached the age of discretion, confession must unfailingly precede communion. Anyone may confess and take communion whenever he wishes, but most do so near Easter. Some go to confession early in Passion Week, but most go on Friday and receive communion on the Saturday before Easter. In the eight days before confession they are supposed to chastise the body with severe fasting, taking nothing but hard bread and kvas, and sour drinks that give them a stomach ache and make them somewhat ill. Confession takes place before the priest inside the church, under the round vault. The person confessing keeps his eyes fixed on the ikon especially designated for the purpose, while telling all the sins he is aware of having committed; and he vows to live a better life. The priest then forgives him his sins and prescribes a penance that accords with their seriousness: a period of fasting; the execution of several hundred or a thousand bows before the ikon of his saint while saying "Gospodi pomilui"; or continence for a specified period of time (in view of their passionate nature, this is a very severe penance, if observed); or denial for a time of the right to enter the church, the sinner being obliged to remain at the door. If the sins are so great that even these forms of penance are inadequate, the sinner must wash in holy water taken from a river that has been sanctified on Epiphany and kept through the year for such purposes in churches, whence the priests sell it for money. With that they consider that they have fulfilled God's commandment given through the prophet Isaiah, are released from their sins, and are pure again.

As Holy Communion may not be taken on days when meat is eaten, the would-be communicant must abstain from meat, even if it is not a fast day. They take communion in two forms, or one may even say three, since they mix together bread, wine, and water. The bread they use must be leavened, and baked by the widow of a priest. This is another reason the Russians cannot adhere to the Roman church: the latter uses unleavened bread, which the Russians say is a Judaic custom, since the Jews were commanded to eat unleavened bread with the paschal lamb in memory of their deliverance from Egypt. As Christians, they themselves have no connection with either Egyptian slavery or deliverance from it. Besides, in establishing Holy Communion, Christ did not eat the Judaic paschal lamb with his disciples, and therefore He must not have had unleavened bread either. When the Jews eat their paschal lamb, they also observe other ceremonies that did not take place during Christ's supper. Christ ate with his disciples not standing but sitting at the table, for otherwise John could not have lain on his breast. Besides, it is not written in the Bible that "Christ ate unleavened bread," but "bread." . . .[19]

Some of the bread the Russians take at communion is consecrated on Maundy Thursday, some on the day they wish to use it. That sanctified on Maundy Thursday is used for the sick and is prepared in the following manner. They take bread that has been baked for the purpose, each piece of which is twice the size of a reichsthaler and has the imprint of a crucifix in the middle. They sing *Agnus Dei* over these, pronounce a blessing, and then, with an iron instrument resembling a spear, pierce and cut the part that shows the crucifix. Then they place these in a wooden dove and hang it over the altar so that mice or other unclean things may not reach them. If someone falls ill in the course of the year and suddenly wishes to take communion, a small piece of one of these wafers is taken from the dove, three drops of red wine are sprinkled on it, and it is put into a cup; then, sometimes, a little water is poured in and he is given it with a spoon (at other times this is not done, depending upon which way is easier for the invalid). If the invalid is incapable of swallowing the bread, he is given wine alone. When communion is publicly administered to healthy people in church, they use a little round wafer, about the size of a half-thaler, shaped and cut like the other. They break off as many pieces as there are communicants and crumble them into red wine and some tepid water (for

---

[19] This point is developed further, and citations are given.

they say that the blood and water that flowed from Christ's wounds was undoubtedly still somewhat warm). Then they bless it, and they claim that with this transubstantiation takes place, that is the bread and the wine are actually transformed into Christ's body and blood. They give it to the communicant with a spoon, saying: "Here is the actual body and blood of Christ, who suffered to gain forgiveness for your sins and the sins of many others. As often as you take it, remember Christ. May God bless you." This method of giving communion, with bread crumbled into wine, was adopted as early as the fourth century by those who were called *intinctores*. In 337, Pope Julius I rejected and anathematized this method, as one may read in the *Concilia Magna*, II, 620.

After receiving communion, Russians who wish to be especially pious lie down and sleep, or force themselves to sleep, the whole day, so that they may not have occasion to sin. On the next Sunday in church, they receive from the priest and eat another small piece of consecrated bread, from which the central part and the crucifix have been cut out for [use in] communion. They call this *kut'ia*, which serves as a gift and a sign of Christian love among them.

They also give a little of the communion to small ailing children. Those who have reached their seventh year receive it in the usual way. For they say that people begin to sin at the age of seven, an idea they undoubtedly borrowed from the ancient church, which considered that children, once baptized, could receive communion. . . .[20]

On a day that a priest has buried a body or kissed a corpse he may not serve communion, for he is considered impure. Neither may he administer it to a new mother in the place where she gave birth to the child; rather, she must first be taken into another room and be well washed. Formerly they sent consecrated bread to those in the countryside who had no priests nearby, and sometimes they even gave it to soldiers and travelers so that if they had made their confession at home they could take it any time they wished thereafter. Ordinarily they kept it until such time as they fell ill, so that in the event they should be unable to raise themselves from bed, they would nevertheless be furnished with provisions for attaining eternal life. . . .[21]

Certain people, for example those who have broken a vow, com-

[20] There follows a discussion of pronouncements and practices of the ancients.
[21] Olearius points out that the ancients are known to have done something of the sort.

mitted a murder and confessed to it, or perpetrated other gross sins, are not given communion before they reach the point of death. They give communion simultaneously with the last rites to a sick person whom medicine will no longer help. After this, the patient may no longer take medicine, but must give himself over entirely to God's care. Nor do they give such a patient anything more to eat unless it becomes apparent that he is regaining strength and it is therefore possible to hope for his recovery. As Possevino observed in *De Rebus Moscoviticis*, p. 5, they often give patients water or vodka into which they have dropped the relics or bones of saints.

Wealthy people who are confined to a sickbed and see that death is approaching sometimes receive communion and then take monastic vows, allowing themselves to be shorn, anointed, and dressed in a monk's habit. Persons who thus attire themselves in seraphic garments (as they call them) may take no more medicine or food for eight days. They say that they are already in the order of holy angels. If, contrary to expectations, such an invalid recovers, he must divorce his wife and enter a monastery, according to his vow.

Russian burials, like all their public actions, take place with very great ceremony. When someone dies, his closest friends assemble, and the women comfort each other with extraordinarily loud wailing and crying. They stand around the corpse and ask, "Why did he die? Did he want food, drink, clothing, or any other necessity? Was his wife not good, young, beautiful, and faithful enough?" And so forth. These laments are repeated at the grave where the body is to be interred. Something of the kind also occurs at the graves at a particular time each year, as told more fully above.

They send for a priest forthwith, offer him beer, mead, and vodka, and ask him to pray for the soul of the departed so that all will go well with it. The corpse is washed clean and dressed in white linen clothing and shoes of fine red leather, and the hands are crossed. It is laid in a coffin (these are sold openly in many parts of the city; they are cut from whole trees and made in various sizes), which is then covered with a cloth or the cloak of the deceased. The coffin is brought into the church, and if the deceased was a notable, in winter time he remains in the church eight days. Here the priest daily sprinkles him with holy water, censes him with myrrh while singing, and celebrates a requiem mass for the departed soul.

The withdrawal of the body occurs in the following manner. Four or six persons carry it out. If the deceased was a monk or nun, then monks or nuns carry the coffin. Before the body walk several veiled women from among the closest friends of the deceased, giving forth extremely sad laments and cries. By turns they cry very loudly, quiet down, and resume bewailing the untimely departure of their friend, wishing he could have lived longer, since he was so pious and dear a person. Meanwhile, some priests go before and after the deceased, carrying ikons and censers, and singing something, of which all that can be made out are the words, "Holy God, Mighty God, Immortal God."

Behind the deceased follow a throng of his closest friends and acquaintances, in no particular order, each carrying a wax candle in his hand. When they reach the grave and the deceased is set down, the coffin is opened and the corpse censed once again. The ikon of the saint he especially revered during his lifetime is held over him; and the priest reads a prayer, frequently reciting the words, "God, think well of this soul." Some passages from the Greek liturgy are also read aloud. Meanwhile, the surviving widow stands near the body and gives vent again to her pitiable laments, repeating once more the questions mentioned above. Then she and the friends go up to the coffin together, kiss it, and sometimes kiss the deceased himself, as a final farewell, and then retire. The priest then comes forward and gives the corpse a passport to [heaven]. In Moscow these are bought from the Patriarch, in other places from metropolitans and archbishops, or in the absence of these, from the priests. The passport is drawn up as follows:

"We N. N., bishop and priest here in N., do hereby acknowledge and witness that [the deceased] actually lived among us as a genuine, righteous Greek Christian. Though he sometimes sinned, he nevertheless repented of his sins, and received absolution and Holy Communion for forgiveness. He revered God and His saints, and fasted and prayed fittingly. With me, N. N., his confessor, he was fully reconciled, and I forgave him all his sins. Therefore, we have issued him this passport to show to St. Peter and the other saints, that he may be admitted without hindrance to the gates of bliss."

The passport is signed by the Patriarch, bishop, or priest, is sealed, and is placed between the deceased's two hands. Simpleminded people consider the passport and letter of recommendation of great importance for gaining admission to the other world. Actually, the priests benefit most of all, since they receive money for these papers. A passport of this kind is mentioned by Guagnino in *De Religione Moscovitorum,* Chap. 2, p. 174. As soon as the passport is given to the corpse, the coffin is closed and interred. They place all corpses with their faces turned toward the sunrise. Once the deceased has been buried, those standing about cross themselves before the ikons and return home. The friends prepare a mourning meal, where they drown their sorrow in drink, and men and women commonly return home intoxicated.

The Russians mourn their dead six weeks. The wealthy, during this period, organize three great feasts, inviting not only the friends, but all the priests who were present at the funeral. They are held the third, ninth, and 20th days, but why they select just these and not other days I have not yet been able to learn from them. No doubt they have borrowed this custom from the Greeks, who, as is evident from Martin Crusius's notes to *Historia ecclesiastica Turco-Graeciae* (p. 213), follow this practice in Constantinople, though they select the 40th rather than the 20th day. The reasons for the feasts, which are of two kinds, may be read in the same place. These three banquets are supposed to have the same significance as the [Roman] *iusta* or *parentalia*: a memorial and an offering for the deceased, [and an admonition] to those left behind to live together in love and friendship. For the purpose, special dishes are prescribed, such as consecrated bread, which the Russians call kut'ia. The Greeks celebrate similar feasts in their churches, and also distribute such little pieces of consecrated bread, which they call "morsels of love," as Crusius, following [Melchior] Gerlach [*Oration von dem jetzigen Zustand der Christlichen Kirchen* etc.], relates. The Russians (the priests as well as others) drink so freely at these fraternal feasts that they then have to crawl home on all fours.

In the cemetery, over the burial place or grave, those who have the means arrange small shelters, usually hung with mats, in which a person may stand. Here, for six weeks, in the morning and afternoon, a priest, chaplain, or monk must read some Psalms of David and several chapters of the New Testament, for the welfare of the soul of the deceased. Though the Russians, like the Greeks, do not believe in purgatory (as Herberstein, Possevino, and Guagnino correctly write), nevertheless they do believe in the existence of two special places that souls reach as soon as they are loosed, where they await the Last Judgment and the resurrection of their bodies. Everyone goes to one place or the other, depending on whether the character of his life was good or evil. The pious reach a cheerful and charming place, where they live in bliss in the company of good angels; the godless a gloomy, frightful valley, where horrible, evil spirits dwell.

They contend that a soul that has left the body and is on its way to the latter place may be brought into the true path to bliss and to life with the good angels by the zealous prayers and intercession of his former confessor, priest, monk, or anyone else. And even though the soul went to the left, to the valley of agony, God may be moved by offerings and prayers to forsake His wrath at his sins; to inscribe him in the book of life; and, in the fullness of time, on the great Day of Judgment, may show mercy. To this end they also give alms.

When a rich person dies, bread and money are daily distributed to the poor for six weeks. One finds among the Russians some who not only contribute large sums to churches and monasteries but also are generous to the poor; yet, on the other hand, they may unconscionably deceive those closest to them in purchases, sales, or other transactions. In the morning when the shopkeepers go from their homes to church, and thence to their stalls, they buy some loaves at the bread market; taking these along, they cut them up and distribute them among the beggars, of whom there are an extraordinary number in Moscow. The poor receive these alms in an abundance surpassing their needs, so they cut the bread into square pieces about an inch in size, dry it in their ovens, and sell these *sukhari*, as they call them, by the bag, to passersby in the markets.

The Muscovites tolerate and have dealings with people of other nations and religions, such as Lutherans, Calvinists, Armenians, Tatars, Persians, and Turks. However, they are very intolerant of Catholics and Jews, and one cannot pain a Russian more than by calling him a Jew [*zhid*], although in business dealings many of the merchants are quite like Jews.

Lutherans and Calvinists have been well received up to the present, not only in different parts of the country but at the court in Moscow as well, both because of the vigorous trade they carry on and because of the offices in which they serve His Tsarist Majesty at home and in the field. There are about 1,000 of them living in Moscow.[22] Each is permitted to worship in his own way in public churches. Both creeds formerly had churches in the Tsargorod section of Moscow. But twenty years ago the Lutherans lost their church because of quarrels and fights among the women, who were embroiled over precedence. When, before the Smolensk siege of that time, [some of] the German officers married servants of the merchants, these women, as wives of captains and lieutenants, no longer were content to sit beneath their former mistresses. For their part, the merchants' wives held that it would be demeaning for them if those who just a little while before had been their maids were to sit above them. Consequently, a great wrangle broke out in the church that finally led to blows. The Patriarch rode by the church just then, observed the tumult, and asked its causes. When he was told that a struggle for superior place was going on in the German church, he said, "I supposed that they came to church with pious thoughts, and to worship, and not for pride [of place] and out of considerations of arrogance." After this, he ordered the church torn down, and it was actually destroyed to its foundation on that very day. However, the Lutherans were permitted to build a new one outside the white wall in the Bol'shoigorod district.[23]

[About this time] the Calvinists had begun to build a fine stone church within the white wall, alongside their wooden chapel, and had completed it almost to the roof. However, since the Patriarch and the

---

[22] This statement has been interpreted variously by different historians, but it seems apparent that Olearius meant 1,000 persons rather than families. For a summary of the conflicting points of view, see Tsvetaev, *Protestantstvo i protestanty*, p. 250.

[23] The reference to the Smolensk campaign suggests that this event occurred in 1632 or 1633. Apart from Olearius's testimony, however, there seems to be no evidence on this event.

Vol. I of *Istoriia Moskvy* mentions no place called Bol'shoigorod. Probably Olearius meant the section outside of Tsargorod that the Russians called Zemlianyi Gorod because it was bordered by an earthen (zemlianyi) wall. In addition to a church in Tsargorod, the Lutherans had one in Zemlianyi Gorod of which Olearius evidently was ignorant. Tsvetaev, *Iz istorii*, p. 41. Perhaps rather than having built a new edifice in this area around 1632–33, the Lutherans all used this church after the destruction of the other.

In spite of the Patriarch's order, the foreigners presently contrived to secure the erection of a new church in the center of the city. One stood in Tsargorod or Belyi Gorod (within the white wall) in 1643, for an order for its destruction was issued that year. Note 24 offers an alternative interpretation.

Grand Prince had not given permission for the structure but had merely looked between their fingers, the Patriarch took it into his head to order it destroyed too, and the chapel near it as well.[24] For a while after this, the Calvinists went to the Lutheran church to hear sermons, until at last they got their own church.

Somewhat later, on the insistence of the Patriarch, the Lutherans were forced to move their church out of Bol'shoigorod too. With His Tsarist Majesty's permission, they took over a lot in an open field outside the wall and built on it a church larger than its predecessor. Recently [in 1652] however, [at the same time] they were forbidden to wear Russian clothes, they once again had to transfer their church to another place. It happened in the following way.

The priests in Moscow had complained for over fifteen years that the Germans living in the city among the Russians bought up and built on the largest and best lots in their parishes, thus causing the priests to lose much of their revenue. However, since the previous Grand Prince was well disposed to the Germans, the priests could get nowhere with him. Now, though, the Patriarch himself complained that the Germans were going about in clothing indistinguishable from the Russians', and, so to speak, were stealing the blessing. The priests seized the occasion to renew their complaints and succeeded in getting enacted a harsh order. It declared that those Germans who wished to be rebaptized in the Russian manner might continue to dwell in the city; but those who refused were obliged in a short space of time to move, with their dwellings, outside the city,[25] beyond the Pokrovskii gate, to Kukui, the place inhabited by the Germans alone forty and

---

[24] Although Olearius couples this event with the Lutheran church's destruction in 1632–33, Tsvetaev (*Protestantstvo i protestanty*, pp. 67–68) places it in 1643, and he is undoubtedly correct. Since there is no documentary evidence for the destruction of the foreign churches in Tsargorod in 1632–33, and an order to that effect is known for 1643 (*Akty istoricheskie*, Vol. III, No. 92, pp. 114–15), one wonders whether Olearius may have confused two separate matters— some unpleasantness growing out of the wrangles of the Protestant women in the early thirties and the actual destruction of the Protestant churches in the city's center a decade later.

The order of 1643 also forbade any further building of homes by foreigners in the city. Thus it anticipated the expulsion of the foreigners from the city in 1652. The 1643 order cites precisely the arguments Olearius attributes two paragraphs later to the priests; indeed, it was issued in answer to their complaints as set forth in a petition to the government.

[25] The order allotting land for dwellings in the new foreign quarter (*novaia nemetskaia sloboda*), is reproduced in *Polnoe sobranie zakonov*, Vol. I, No. 85.

I have found no corroborating evidence of another move imposed on the Lutheran congregation prior to 1652, such as Olearius cites in the preceding paragraph.

more years ago, and where Duke Johann, the brother of King Christian IV of Denmark, was buried.[26]

The place lies on the Iauza River, and received its name Kukui for the following reason. When the wives of the German soldiers who lived there saw something unusual among the Russian passersby, they said to one another, "*Kuck! Kuck hie!*," that is "Look! Look here!"[27] The Russians changed this into the obscene word *chui* [*khui*] (which means the male organ) and shouted as an insult at the Germans whom they chanced to meet [elsewhere], "German, be off to Pricktown!"[?] and so forth (*Nimzin tsizna chui, chui, du Teutscher, packe dich auff* etc.). On this account a petition of grievance was sent to His Tsarist Majesty, complaining, "[The Germans] at present see that for no reason whatsoever they are subjected to abuse by the Russian people. In spite of their loyal service and the goodwill they have manifested to His Tsarist Majesty and his subjects, nonetheless they meet on the streets scoundrelly rabble who assail them and call obscenities. Therefore, they ask His Tsarist Majesty, in keeping with the praiseworthy example of his forebears, to take them under his gracious protection and defend them against such abuse," and so forth.

After this, His Tsarist Majesty issued the following public proclamation, "From this day forth, anyone who shouts [such words] even at the least significant of the Germans will be mercilessly punished by the knout." In fact, some violators of this prohibition were punished and went home with bloody backs. Now the Germans are free of these malicious taunts. Also His Tsarist Majesty has now given this place a new name, "The New Foreign Suburb." Here everyone, according to his condition, office, or profession, has been given a certain place to build on, and the whole suburb is divided into orderly streets. Those who had wooden houses in the city were ordered to take them down and rebuild them in the New Foreign Suburb, where [having escaped

---

[26] As mentioned above, Duke Johann had come to Russia to marry Boris Godunov's daughter, but he died of an illness before the wedding was performed, and was buried in the old Livonian-German foreign quarter. Boris had not insisted on his renunciation of his faith.

[27] Another explanation of the name was offered by the eigtheenth century historian G. F. Müller. According to him, the area where the suburb was built had formerly been so wild that only cuckoos (*kukushki*) could have lived there. See "Dnevnik Generala Patrika Gordona," p. 52n. Both these explanations are contrived. The name undoubtedly stemmed from the location of the suburb, between the Iauza River and a little stream (that later disappeared) called the Kukui or Kokui. See Kurts, *Sochinenie Kil'burgera,* pp. 181–82; *Posol'stvo Kunraada fan Klenka,* p. 524.

from] the fires that frequently break out among the Russians, they now live in far greater safety than in the city. Most of the Germans say that being forbidden to wear Russian clothing and to live in Russian residential areas was as painful to them as it would be, for example, for a crab to be punished by drowning.[28]

When the Germans saw that they had been given something like a town of their own, where they could live in peace, they themselves began to think of tearing down their churches, which were now far from them, and transplanting them to their hearths and homes in the New Foreign Suburb. Now the Lutherans have two German churches, and the Calvinists, a Dutch and an English.[29] Incidentally, at first they suffered a severe shock here, too, as a consequence of the allegation that Colonel Lesly's wife had wilfully thrown Russian ikons into the fire. At that time Russian assailants pulled out the pulpits and altars, and also tore off the roofs. After a certain time they were permitted to restore the roofs, though not the pulpits and altars. The Lutherans enclosed a large cemetery, in which they and the Calvinists bury their dead. For both faiths live together amicably, and there are no conflicts over religion.

The present Lutheran pastor is Mr. Balthasar Fadenrecht,[30] a gifted and clever man. The previous pastor (when we were there) was Mr. Martin Munsterberg of Danzig, also a talented and diligent man, who at first had ample means and was very generous. For that reason, and also in consequence of the ravages of great fires, he lost all his property and was so hounded by his Russian creditors that the grief and woe caused him to fall ill and die before he was 36 years old. His predeces-

---

[28] Nevertheless, the order for the removal of the foreigners to the new suburb initially had caused great dismay—among other reasons, because those who owned houses, which they were obliged to sell quickly, expected to suffer serious losses. Perhaps because of the protests initially expressed, this decree, too, was not completely enforced. Sixteen months after its issuance, the authorities were still pressing some of the foreigners to move out. Even afterward, some 20 families especially trusted by the Tsar were permitted to stay on in the city. See Kurts, *Sostoianie Rossii*, pp. 126–27; Bogoiavlenskii, p. 231.

Tsvetaev finds naïve Olearius's explanation of the foreigners' expulsion, but does not succeed in illuminating the matter more effectively. See *Iz istorii*, pp. 102 ff.

[29] Tsvetaev (*Protestantstvo i protestanty*, p. 86) cogently argues that Olearius must have been misinformed about the English church. Inasmuch as the English merchants were expelled from Moscow to Archangel in 1649, there would have been no group to build or support an English Calvinist church in the first half of the 1650's.

[30] Tsvetaev presents a good deal of information on Fadenrecht and the other pastors Olearius mentions, in *Iz istorii*, Book One, Chap. One. On certain details he corrects Olearius. See, for example, pp. 43–45.

sor, Mr. Georg Ochse, an old man, had been brought to Moscow as a
wine cooper by the Protestant merchant Karol Möllin. The congregation grew, and its members wished to hear sermons from time to
time, but they long had had no ordained minister. Therefore, they
presently selected as pastor this Mr. Georg, who was sufficiently learned
and knew how to handle the prayer book well enough. He filled this
office diligently for several years. When at last he was too old to read
and study, and he began to talk nonsense from the pulpit, the congregation released him from this service and granted him and his wife
maintenance for life. He was still living at the time of our first embassy.

The Reformed [i.e. the Calvinists] also had a learned man as
minister, Magister Heinrich Inchenhoffer of Herzberg, formerly a
Lutheran, who first came to the country with the soldiers and served
as field chaplain in the war at Smolensk. Later, in Moscow, he became
a Calvinist. He wrote a short tract which he published at Bremen
under the title, "The Key to a Proper Understanding of the Closed
Doors." It was refuted by the Superintendent in Borna (in the Meissen
region), Dr. David Auerbach. Inchenhoffer's widow, who still lives
in Moscow, is the daughter of the famous Wittenberg divine, Dr.
Försters. Inchenhoffer never tried to persuade her to defect, which, incidentally, she had no inclination to do. He often said: "Let her remain in the Lutheran faith. She can be saved very well there, inasmuch
as she knows no better." The Reformed also have a learned man now,
Magister Andream Gordium of Scotland.

As has been said, the Russians have nothing against divine worship
by the Lutherans and Calvinists who dwell in the country with them.
Down to the present, however, the Roman Catholics or Papists meet
with little favor among them. Indeed they and their religion have been
a kind of abomination in the Russians' eyes. In 1627, King Louis XIII
of France sent an ambassador named Louis de Hayes to the Grand
Prince [Mikhail Feodorovich] to request that the French nation be
granted freedom of trade in Russia. He also endeavored to secure the
building of a Catholic church, but this was flatly refused.[31]

---

31 France did obtain the trade rights, however. The French ambassador, Louis De Hayes
Courmenin, came to Russia in 1630. The Tsar's answer to the King of France, setting forth
his decision and reasoning, is given in Rambaud, pp. 27–31. On the long, drawn-out efforts to
secure permission for a Catholic church in Moscow, see Tsvetaev, *Iz istorii*, Book Two. The
objective was finally attained in 1696, during the reign of Peter the Great.

When the war at Smolensk was imminent, and there turned out to be some Catholics among the military commanders invited into the country, they were given some presents for having made the journey, and then were escorted across the border again by a good convoy.[32] In the treaties the Russians concluded with us concerning the Persian trade, they included a strict ban on persons of the Latin faith (as they call the Roman Catholics) among our company.[33] Even the name [Catholic] is detested. It is therefore surprising that in 1610 they nevertheless chose Vladislav, the Polish King's son, as Grand Prince. Afterward, however, even prior to the beginning of his real rule, they rejected him and reacted to the Poles and their religion with much greater hatred than before, for the desecrations committed against Russian ikons.[34]

Their forebears received this ancient hatred and seemingly inborn hostility to the Papists from the Greeks, along with their religion, and it was passed on, intensified, to their offspring. Since the Russians are partisans of the Greek Church, they think they must share the hostility that the Greek Church has borne the Latin for many centuries....[35]

The Russians say that they follow the ancient Greeks in all their articles of faith, church laws, and customs, as well as in morals. However, I believe that they learned and adopted nothing from the Greeks so well as drunkenness, for which the latter were famous. "The Greeks," says Cicero, "have a law that reads 'Either drink or be gone.'" In many things, both in fundamental articles of faith and in church

[32] The order empowering Colonel Lesly to recruit troops explicitly instructed him not to hire Catholics. Other recruiters evidently were not so instructed. For instance, Colonel Heinrich Van Dam was advised to recruit Lutherans, like himself, but the order did not specifically ban Catholics. See *Sobranie*, III, 311, 317.

[33] The treaty is printed in *Akty istoricheskie*, Vol. III, No. 181. Muliukin (*Priezd inostrantsev*, pp. 138–43, 218–21) adduces persuasive evidence for the proposition that although the Russian government opposed Catholic proselytization and the establishment of Catholic churches in Russia, it did not as a rule discriminate against Catholics who wished either to enter the Tsar's service or to engage in trade in Russia. Tsvetaev's assertion (*Protestantstvo i protestantly*, pp. 173, 177) that the Holsteiners themselves suggested the ban on Catholics seems inplausible.

[34] Vladislav was chosen by a clique of conservative aristocrats faced with a choice between Polish rule and the wrath of their own insurgent people. As a condition, however, Vladislav was supposed to embrace Orthodoxy. The agreement was never really implemented. For the aristocrats fell out with Sigismund, Vladislav's father, who had unlimited pretensions toward Russia, and the specter of foreign rule aroused a national movement that thwarted Polish designs. See Florinsky, *Russia, A History and An Interpretation*, I, 236ff.

[35] Although there is no doubt a degree of truth in this statement, the Russians' hostility to Catholics was greatly intensified by what they suffered at the hands of the Catholic Poles during the Time of Troubles, as Olearius himself notes above.

An extended discussion of church history that follows is omitted.

customs and ceremonies, they have deviated from the Greeks. Thus the Greeks consider them schismatics, although they refrain from saying so because of the great contributions the Russians send them every year.

In his *Rerum Moscoviticarum commentarii*, Herberstein recalls that, at the request of the Muscovites, the bishop or Patriarch of Constantinople once sent them a learned Greek monk named Maximian to bring into good order the articles, rules, and whatever else pertained to the Greek religion. When the monk set to work, he perceived many crude errors and pointed them out to the Grand Prince. Soon after, however, he was lost sight of, and what became of him is not known. It is supposed that he was secretly slain.[36] The same thing happened to a Greek merchant named Mark, who was disposed of for making similar assertions.[37] The Russians are equally hostile to criticism today, and anyone who proposes anything of the kind fares no better than the abovementioned Archpriest Neronov, who spoke against ikons, or Login of Murom, who began to preach.

Enough has been said of the present condition of Russia and the character of its inhabitants. In describing these, I have given more details than in the account of the journey. Since, however, these things are either new or not generally known, perhaps many will not deem it useless to learn of them. I hope the reader will not take umbrage at this digression.

[36] The monk, generally known as Maxim the Greek, was sent in 1515 by the head of the Mt. Athos Monastery. Part of the work assigned him involved correcting religious books, as well as making new translations. No fault was found with his efforts until he became associated with the opponents of the Grand Prince's divorce, and criticized various ecclesiastical practices, among them landholding by monasteries. After that, he was tried, declared a heretic, imprisoned in a monastery, and denied the sacraments for some time. His repeated requests for permission to return to Mt. Athos were denied. But he was not slain. For a brief account in English, see Cizevskij, pp. 291–300. A major study of the subject is Ikonnokov, *Maksim Grek*.

[37] The note on the Greek merchant is borrowed from Herberstein (I, 83–84). However, as Herberstein represents the matter, Mark was disposed of not for alleged heretical remarks but because he spread reports of Maxim's ill fate.

BOOK IV

CHAPTER ONE

From Moscow to Kazan

Let us return to our journey to Persia. After the passport mentioned above had been issued to our pristav, on June [30th] we departed from Moscow. That whole day we were handsomely feasted by His Princely Excellence's agent Mr. David Ruts. When the last hour of the day arrived (the Russians use Babylonian clocks, which reckon the time from sunrise to sunset), the Tsar sent us the customary horses, on which, accompanied by our old pristavs and many German notables, we rode three versts beyond the city to Simonovskii Monastery. There we met a boat that had gone ahead to allow time for negotiating the meandering course of the Moscow River. We embarked with the warm wishes of our good friends. The Grand Prince had assigned us a pristav named Rodion Matveevich [Gorbatov], who was to escort us to Astrakhan.

We had hardly gotten away from the shore when the young prince's tutor, Boris Ivanovich Morozov, and his trumpeters came up, bringing all sorts of costly drinks. He begged the ambassadors to tarry a while so that he could give them a farewell treat. The ambassadors refused, but since earlier he had provided good sport to some of us on the falcon hunt, we presented him with a silver drinking vessel. Then he rode alongside us in a special little boat for quite some time, having his trumpeters play gaily, and ours answered them. After a while he even transferred to our boat, and drank with our gentlemen until morning. Then, filled with affection and wine, he bade us a tearful farewell.

That night the Russian boatmen—who rowed in alternating shifts of eight men each—were still fresh, and, in addition, they had received a cup of vodka apiece. Consequently, we went with the current so rapidly that soon after sunrise on the next day, July 1st, we reached a nobleman's estate called Dvorianinovo, on the left bank, 80 versts from Moscow. Toward evening we arrived at the village of Marchuk, on our right, 40 versts from Dvorianinovo.

On the 2d, toward noon, near the village and monastery of Bobrenev' [?], we met several large boats loaded with honey, salt, and salt fish. Most had come from Astrakhan and were headed for Moscow. Here there were many large bends and meanders in the river. We disembarked, had our prayer service, and then continued on our way. Toward evening we came to Kolomna, on our right. It is 36 leagues from Moscow by water; in the winter, when one can go directly cross-country, it is reckoned hardly 18. Judging from the exterior, it is well protected by its stone walls and towers. A large wooden bridge spans the Moscow River, which flows past the city walls. The only bishop in the country resides in Kolomna. As there is also a voevoda here, we had to wait while our pristav showed our passport. Meanwhile, an innumerable crowd of people gathered on the bridge to look at us. In order to make way for our boat, which had a rather tall roof, they were obliged to dismantle a part of the bridge, which they did with great speed.

Three versts from Kolomna, the Moscow River falls into the Oka, a wide, deep river that flows from the south. Nearby is the Golutvin-Sergievskii Monastery, said to have been founded by St. Sergei, who is buried at Troitsa. Beyond where these waters join together, the country on both shores of the river is covered with thick vegetation and is well populated, so it was pleasant to look at these cheerful places. We saw more oaks here than at any other place in Russia.[1]

Before sunrise on July 3d, we came to the large village of Dedinovo[2] on the left, which is almost half a league in length and said to have a population of more than 800. Toward noon we came to the village of Omut', on the right, 37 versts from Kolomna. Since it was Sunday, we went ashore here and had our divine worship and a sermon under a pleasant tree, and then went on. Three versts past the village was a long island in the middle of the river, which we passed on the left side.

---

[1] That is why this area was a boat-building center. Zagoskin, pp. 413–14.

[2] In 1667, when the Russian government launched a shipbuilding enterprise intended, in the first instance, to provide security escorts for the waterborne trade with Persia, the vessels were built at Dedinovo. The most important one was the ill-fated *Orel*, which was destroyed at Astrakhan by the Cossack rebel Stenka Razin. On the enterprise and the career of the *Orel*, see *Dopolnenie*, Vol. V, No. 47; Struys; and the letter of David Butler, captain of the *Orel*, which is appended to Volume Three of Struys's book.

We also went by several other villages, of which the most important were Sel'tso and Morozo[vo]. On the 4th, around noon, we arrived at the town of Pereiaslavl, on the right, which also has a voevoda. The town is 107 versts from Kolomna. I calculated the elevation of the pole near there as 54° 42′.

On the 5th we passed Riazan, which was formerly a large city, and indeed the principal one in the whole province of this name. But when, in 1568, the Crimean Tatars invaded, laying waste to everything with fire and sword, this town also was devastated. This province, situated between the Oka and the wall built against the Tatars, was formerly a principality. Besides (as Guagnino and Petrejus correctly point out), it surpassed all the neighboring provinces in grain growing, livestock raising, and abundance of game. Therefore, after its devastation, the Tsar transplanted a large number of people from various places in the country to build up the land again and restore the place to its previous condition. Since they found a more convenient location for the town at [a site] eight leagues from [old] Riazan, they brought the surviving building materials there and constructed an entirely new town. They call it Pereiaslavl-Riazan because the majority, and the most important, of the people who built and settled it were from Pereiaslavl, which lies as far to the north of Moscow as this town does to the south.

I am astonished that Petrejus locates this region to the west of Moscow since, as he admits, it lies between the Oka and the Don, which are not west but east of Moscow, and their courses run eastward as well. The Riazan region lies southeast of Moscow. One of the seven archbishops still resides in Riazan.

On this day we also passed a number of small monasteries and villages, not far from Riazan: Selo, on the left; Kistrus, seven versts farther along on the left; Oblozhitskii Monastery, three versts on; Lipovye Isady, a nobleman's estate two versts farther on the right; Muratovo, two versts beyond; Kalinino, one verst farther; Prestopole, a village belonging to the Riazan archbishop, three versts farther, on the right; and Shilka, two versts farther on the right.

At the first of these, we saw a naked human body floating in the water. It was entirely blackened by the sun and much shriveled. [Our boatmen] supposed that this person had been murdered by the Cossacks or fugitive slaves, who they say frequent the surrounding area.

On the 6th we went past Terekhin Monastery, ten versts along on the left; Tyrinska, ten versts along on the right; Svinchus, eight versts farther on the right; and Kopanovo, two versts beyond on the right. Here we saw another dead body floating on the water. But, as murder is not uncommon here, the Russians paid little attention to it.

On the evening of the 7th, we came to the small Tatar town of Kasimovgorod, which formerly belonged to the Tatar principality of Kasimov.[3] Here, in an old stone building, formerly a castle, lived a young Tatar prince, Res-Kichi, with his mother and his grandfather. The grandfather had submitted to the Grand Prince some years ago, and the town was given him for his support. Here we saw our first Moslem temple. We were told that the Russians proposed to the young lord that if he adopted the Russian faith and was baptized, the Grand Prince would not refuse him his daughter. However, he is said to have answered that he was still too young (he was then only 12 years old), but should give an answer when he attained greater maturity and wisdom.

Our ambassadors sent him their respects and a gift of a pound of tobacco and a bottle of French brandy. He was so pleased with this that he in turn sent his greetings and hearty thanks, and excused himself for being unable to entertain and honor the ambassadors in his home, as he should have liked. [All this] was displeasing to the voevoda, who did not permit foreigners to associate with him. Through his servants, also Tatars, who were able to speak only to the Persian interpreter, he sent us a gift of various victuals, including two sheep, small casks of mead and beer, vodka, some pieces of ice, sour milk, cream, and fresh butter prepared, so they said, by his mother's own hands.

That night, as well as on the following day, we passed on both sides of the river numbers of villages, monasteries, and taverns nestled among the green bushes, the sight of which was very attractive. The chief of these places were: Pochinok Tatarskii, three versts from Kasimovgorod on the right; the village Per'evo, three versts farther on the right; a tavern, eight versts on, on the left; Brod, five versts ahead; the

---

[3] This principality, or tsardom, was created by Grand Prince Vasilii II and was granted in 1453 (not later, as Olearius implies) to one of the first Tatar princes to recognize the suzerainty of Moscow and enter its service. Its seat, formerly called Gorodets-on-Oka, was renamed Kasimov in honor of Kasim, the prince to whom the grant was initially made. See Vernadsky, *The Mongols and Russia*, pp. 330–32.

Moksha River, eight versts farther on the right; a tavern, two versts on; Sateevo, another 13 versts farther on the left; the monastery of Andreianov Pustyn', four versts beyond on the left; Elat'ma, three versts farther on the left. The last of these, a large village of 300 peasants, belonged to the boyar Feodor Ivanovich Sheremetev. After another 20 versts we came to Rusbonor [?], to the right of the river in dry steppe land.

On the 9th, ten versts ahead on the left, we reached the Voskresen'e church. The place is usually called the Voskresen'e Shallow. Then came the big village of Liakhi, five versts ahead on the left (it belongs to the state counselor Prince Boris Mikhailovich Lykov), and the Prechistaia Riazan Monastery, ten versts ahead on the right. Then we reached the town of Murom, inhabited by Russians and Tatars. Here begin the settlements of the Mordvin Tatars, all of whom are subject to the Grand Prince. As there is a market in the city, we sent our interpreters to buy fresh provisions. When we were half a league from the city, we saw some Tatars on the right bank, the Crimean Tatar side of the river. They immediately concealed themselves in the bushes and fired upon us from there, sending one of the bullets over the boat. When we answered with some muskets, however, they remained silent until we passed the town, after which we heard more shots from the same place. We fully expected, as did our Russian boatmen, that they would attack us during the coming night. Therefore we cast anchor near Chukhtskii Island [?], 51 versts from the town, and posted a strong guard. However, we heard nothing more from them.

On the 10th we passed the hamlet of Pavlovo, which belongs to the leading boyar, Prince Ivan Borisovich Cherkasskii. We passed, besides many small villages, two streams—the Vorsma, which comes in from the right, and another, eight versts farther on, which flows from the left. This second one, the Kliazma, runs from Vladimir. Here the terrain on the right begins to rise, making a very high bank that continues at about the same height for almost a hundred leagues along the Volga. From the river below, it looks like a series of contiguous heights. Above, however, it is even, flat country, bare of forest, and good for agriculture. This plain is said to extend more than a hundred versts inland, mostly toward the southeast. The country on the left bank extends to the northwest, and is everywhere low-lying, bushy, wild, and sparsely populated. We found [traces of] snow and ice in some places on this high bank, even when the weather was very hot.

On the 11th, after passing along the right and left of the river such pretty and attractive villages as Izbylets, Troitsa, the Dudin Monastery, and Novinki, toward evening we reached the important town of Nizhnii, or Nizhnii Novgorod. We did not enter the city, but proceeded directly to the ship that had been built for us, which was named the *Friedrich*.⁴ The ship had been constructed of pine planks by the skipper, Michael Cordes, aided by Russian carpenters. It was 120 feet long, and had three masts and a flat bottom. It had a draft of only seven feet and places for 24 oars. It was built mainly for navigation on the Volga, and would enable us to pass over the hidden sandbars and shallows, of which there are many; in case of unfavorable wind, it could be propelled without sails as well.⁵ In the ship's upper part, and below in the hold, there had been built various chambers in which the ambassadors and their suite could be comfortably put up, and there was place as well for a kitchen and for storing provisions. We equipped the ship well with all sorts of powder and missiles, metal- and stone-firing cannons, grenades, and other weapons, in case we were attacked by brigands.

Besides this ship, we had had built and excellently fitted out a sloop, which we thought to use on the Volga, and especially on the Caspian Sea (where the skipper and crew would have to remain aboard ship while we visited the Persian Shah), to journey to uncharted, shallow places, where we should not wish to risk taking the ship. The sloop was also to relieve the ship of some of its load in case of need. To complete the fitting out of the ship, we remained here almost three weeks.

According to Herberstein, Nizhnii Novgorod, which lies below 56° 28′ north latitude, was built by Grand Prince Vasilii and settled by those he exiled from the populous town of Great Novgorod, whence

---

⁴ A collection of documents that relate to the building of the ship are included in Viskovatov, pp. 140ff.

⁵ Of course the ship had to sail on the Caspian Sea as well. At Astrakhan, however, Persians who examined the vessel expressed grave doubts as to its suitability for that purpose and recommended that the masts be shortened. See 1656 ed., p. 378. Subsequent events proved their judgment sound, for the ship went down in a storm not long after setting forth on the Caspian. The wreck is described in Book IV, Chap. 15 of the original.

its name.[6] It is 150 leagues from Moscow by water, and 100 by land. Situated on the right bank of the Oka, on high ground, it is surrounded by a stone wall and towers. There are more people and houses outside the walls than within, distributed over a circular area about half a league in extent. Before the city, the Oka unites with the famous Volga River, called the Rha by the ancient writers. Where the two join, they make a river 4,600 feet wide; a distance I measured twice by crossing the ice, during our journey to Persia and back. I also observed that in this city the magnetic needle is deflected nine full degrees to the west from due north. Nizhnii is inhabited by Russians, Tatars, and Germans. They are all subjects of the Grand Prince, and, when we were there, were governed by the voevoda Vasilii Petrovich [Sheremetev]. We found here the easternmost settlement of Lutherans able to practice their faith in public places of worship.[7] Their congregation then numbered around 100.[8] Many were Scottish officers, some [fully] employed in the Grand Prince's service, others receiving half pay in peacetime and engaged also in beer and vodka brewing and selling— which was allowed them as a special favor. Provisions were extremely cheap in Nizhnii: a young hen or 15 eggs cost one kopek; a sheep 12, 15, or 18 kopeks.

On the 24th, along with our Master of the Horse, Von Mandelslo,[9] the Russian interpreter, Hans Arpenbeck, and the pristav, I was sent to the voevoda to present him with a gift, worth 100 reichsthalers, for the favor and assistance he had rendered our people during the period of more than a year in which they were engaged there in the construction of the ship. It was apparent that the voevoda was very cordial and kind, for he not only entertained us magnificently but also presented us, at our departure, with 20 sides of bacon and other provisions for the

[6] It was Ivan III, rather than Vasilii, who resettled in Nizhnii Novgorod some thousands of people whom he exiled from Novgorod. While this no doubt enlarged the town, it had been founded in 1221. It still has a fortress and two churches that were built in the thirteenth century.

[7] The Protestant community in Nizhnii was created by Ivan IV, who settled there some of those taken prisoner during the Livonian Wars. See Tsvetaev, *Protestantstvo i protestanty*, p. 122. Olearius speaks further of the community in Book VI, Chap. 23, which deals with the return trip from Persia.

[8] Thirty-five years later, when Jan Struys, a member of the crew of the *Orel*, stopped here, the foreign community no longer existed. Struys, I, 290.

[9] Mandelslo, an inveterate traveler, later went on from Persian Ispahan to Jerusalem, and returned home by way of Italy. Subsequently, he made a trip to the East Indies. At his death he left behind an account of this voyage, which Olearius edited and had published. The first edition appeared in 1645. Mandelslo's work is appended to some editions of Olearius's own.

journey. He was indeed an urbane and intelligent man, and his home was kept in excellent condition. When, through our pristav, we had ourselves announced, two persons ushered us into the house through a well-kept passageway, on both sides of which, right up to the staircase, stood servants and slaves. We were received at the porch by two stately old men who escorted us into the voevoda's chamber, which was hung with tapestries and decorated with silver cups and goblets. The voevoda, dressed in gold brocade clothing and surrounded by many other finely dressed men, welcomed us cordially, thanked us with many respectful words for the ambassadors' greetings and the present, and then had us sit down to table. Then he proceeded to drink toasts to the health of His Tsarist Majesty, His Excellence the Prince of Holstein, and the Prince's ambassadors. During the refreshments, which consisted of gingerbread, very strong vodka, and various kinds of mead, he made all sorts of gay and witty remarks, a phenomenon so unusual in Russia that we could not but wonder at him.[10]

He asked if we were afraid of the Cossacks, who engaged in brigandage along the Volga and were not apt to leave us in peace. They were a cruel, inhuman lot, who loved pillage more than their God, and fell upon people as if they [the Cossacks] were beasts. At that he pointed to a lion painted on the table, whose jaws Samson was tearing apart. We replied that if the Cossacks should be lions, we would be Samsons. He expressed the view that the Germans were known throughout Russia for their bravery in His Tsarist Majesty's service; no doubt the Cossacks, too, had heard of it and would refrain from attacking. When we took our leave, he had us escorted out through the house to the gate in the way we had entered.

During these days, the disputes that had arisen among the workers while the ship was being built were settled, and a reckoning of the costs of the construction was demanded. Upon close examination, it turned out that [the recruiter] who had hired the workers persuaded them to promise him a reward of 40 rubles in return for securing higher wages for them. As the blacksmith had perpetrated great abuses and deception in the supplying and working of iron, he was threatened with severe punishment. The voevoda would have carried out anything the

---

[10] Sheremetev, who so charmed Olearius with his urbanity and kindness, later treated some of the leading Zealots of Piety most viciously. See Pascal, pp. 51, 139.

ambassadors wished, even a death sentence. However, the blacksmith fell at the ambassadors' feet and lay there a long time weeping and asking pardon. He was forgiven because of his advanced years—he was more than seventy—and let off without punishment.

We remained in Nizhnii until the end of July, when we became aware that the water level, which until then had been high, was rapidly falling. Therefore we hastened to leave. Ships or large boats that travel to Astrakhan on the Volga wait to start on their way until the river is rising or is at flood level, which occurs in May or June, when the rivers to the north swell and pour their abundant waters into the Volga. Then the boats may pass safely not only over the shallows but also over low-lying islands, which are then deep under water. It happens, incidentally, that boats which have passed the night over such islands become lodged [by morning] because of the water's rapid fall. We encountered rotting boats which had been grounded in this manner at several places on the Volga.

Since this is one of the greatest, longest, and most important rivers in the world, I observed it attentively. With the help of an experienced Dutch mariner, Cornelius Clausen, and some Russian pilots, I was able to map by compass not only its course, coves, angles, and shores, but also its deep channels, shallows, islands, and environs, league by league, and even verst by verst....[11]

The Volga rises (as Herberstein mentions) in the Rzhevsk region, which includes a forest named Volkonskii. In this forest is a lake, whence a stream flows a distance of about two leagues and then across Lake Volgo, which gives the river its name. Before its junction with the Oka at Nizhnii Novgorod, it flows by many important towns: Tver, Kashin, Kholopyi (a hamlet), Uglich, Iaroslavl, Kostroma, Galich, and others. As I did not traverse it, I shall not describe this stretch of the Volga's course but shall begin at the junction of the Oka and the Volga at Nizhnii Novgorod.

Having readied our boat and stocked it with good provisions, and having taken aboard a pilot to point out the proper course, we set out on July 30th, though the wind was against us and was beginning to

[11] Olearius here makes further reference to the map of the Volga that is included in his 1656 edition.

veer. On the ship with us were His Princely Excellence's commissioner in Moscow, Balthazar Moucheron, the voevoda's secretary, the Nizhnii pastor, and our factor, Hans Bernhart,[12] who were accompanying us a few versts of the way to see how the ship sailed. However, we got scarcely two versts from the city, beyond the Gramotin estate, opposite the Pecherskii Monastery, when we ran aground. [To get off] it was necessary to uncoil the anchor [rope] and to drag the ship with great effort for four hours.

The next day, the last of July, after going another verst we were grounded again, but soon got free; then, however, a heavy rain began and a storm from the southeast met us, so we lay at anchor until the following day. Here, on the ship, an oration was made on the danger that we had endured on the Baltic Sea and during the shipwreck at Hochland. We thanked God for His merciful salvation. Our people were advised that in similar circumstances which might be encountered in the course of the long and dangerous journey they should rely firmly on God and not lose courage. At the conclusion of the service, after some joyous music, our good friends who had accompanied us bade us farewell and departed.

On August 1st a guard system was established. The recruited soldiers, as well as the members of the ambassadors' suite, were divided into three companies, which were to take turns on duty. Ambassador Crusius led the first, Brüggemann the second, and the marshal the third. Each of the ambassadors had his captain; for Crusius it was the Master of the Horse, for Brüggemann the Secretary [i.e. Olearius]. To the accompaniment of drumbeats, the captains and the marshal, by turns, escorted the guards to and from their posts. The men posted at the ship's battle stations fore and aft were always numerous.

Later, as the wind continued to blow against us, we tried to advance by oars. However, a musket shot's distance onward we ran aground again. After we got free, we stood at anchor. Some of us went ashore to shoot birds, for very many could be seen in the vicinity. On the high bank, from Nizhnii all the way to Kazan, pleasant bushes and trees are everywhere, as in an unbroken forest.

---

[12] The treaty between Russia and Holstein provided for the creation of Holstein trading company offices along the trade route to Persia, as they might be deemed necessary. It appears that Bernhart acted as the company's representative at Nizhnii Novgorod.

On the 2d, when the wind subsided somewhat, we lifted anchor, hoping to make better progress this day. However, we had hardly gone a quarter of a league when we were grounded once again, at Teliatinskii Island, and soon again, at Sobshchinskii Island. On the latter, a large ship had been grounded during high water [*sic*], and it still stood there, intact. Here we remained nine full hours, until the ship got afloat again.

The sailing had been so unsuccessful at the outset that in four days we had gone hardly more than two leagues (and there remained 550 to the Caspian Sea). Besides, our pilot, who had not traveled on the Volga in eight years, could give us little exact information. Consequently some of us were disheartened.

On the 3d, things went somewhat better. We advanced past several villages and islands, of which the most important were Stolbishchi and Stoba, three versts from Nizhnii; Velikoi Vrag, a village on the right in a valley between two mountains; Zimenki, on a hill to our right; and Teploi Island, 20 versts from Nizhnii. Here we met a large boat coming from Astrakhan, with 200 workers aboard. When the wind is not directly behind them, the Russians do not go under sail. Instead, they carry the anchors, one after another, a quarter of a league ahead in a small boat; then, using the bast [anchor] ropes, a hundred or more men, standing one behind another, pull the boat against the current. However, by this means they cannot go more than two leagues a day. The boats, which are flat on the bottom, can haul 400 to 500 lasts of freight and are loaded chiefly with salt, caviar, and coarse salt fish.

The villages we passed this day lay to the right of the river: Bezvodnaia Ka[d]nitsa, where the elevation of the pole was 56° 21′; Rabotki, Chechenino, Tatinets, and Iurkino. Before the last, ten leagues from Nizhnii, lay two islands, between which the channel attained a depth of 21 feet. As the wind became somewhat more favorable, this day and the next we made use of our sails. We passed many small villages as well as the large ones of Maza and Kremenki on the right. Beyond the latter, we stayed through the night of the 4th.

On the 5th we made good time to the village of Barmino, 90 versts from Nizhnii. Here the peasants came out in three boats and sold us young hens and other provisions at very low prices. Then we passed between two islands, one of which is called Spasa-Belka. Toward evening we saw the little town of Vasil'gorod, and as there was a shoal nearby, we cast anchor and remained before it. Here a courier who had been sent from Moscow overtook us, bringing letters from Germany dated in the month of May. They greatly cheered us.

Vasil'gorod is a little, unwalled town, or hamlet, made up entirely of wooden houses. It lies to the right of the Volga, at the foot of a mountain, at a polar elevation of $55°51'$. It is reckoned 120 versts from Nizhnii. It is said that this town was built by Grand Prince Vasilii, and supplied with soldiers who were charged with repelling raids of the Crimean Tatars. Across the town a rather large river, the Sura, flows from the south. Formerly this river separated the Kazan realm from the Russian.

On the 6th the ship scarcely made it over the aforementioned shoal, almost constantly touching bottom. One could say that the ship capered and danced across the shoal rather than sailed over it. When at noon we passed the town, we ordered our guns fired and the trumpets blown by way of a salute. Thereafter, we repeated this practice at each town that we came to.

From here on, one finds another variety of Tatars, the Cheremiss. Their territory extends far beyond Kazan, on both sides of the Volga. They live mostly in wretched huts, rather than houses, and subsist by raising cattle, collecting honey, and hunting game. They are excellent archers and teach their children to be the same. They are a disloyal, thieving, and superstitious people. Those who live on the right bank of the Volga are called *nagornye,* because they live on and between the heights [*na* means on, in Russian, and *gora* mountain]. Those who live on the left bank are called *lugovye,* from *lugovyi sen,* that is, green pasture and hayfields; for here, owing to the low-lying and damp soil, there are many fine meadows and pastures, from which is gathered a great amount of hay to feed to their flocks.

Guagnino says that this people is partly pagan, partly Mohammedan. As far as I could learn, all those who live around Kazan are pagans, for they are neither circumcised nor baptized. When a child is half a year old, they select a certain day whereon it is to receive its name. On this day, the child is named after whoever first comes to him, or even passes by.

Most of them believe in the existence of an immortal God, who does good on behalf of the earth's people, and to whom one must therefore appeal. But they know neither what He is nor how He wishes to be revered. They do not believe in the resurrection of the dead or in a new life after the present one, contending rather that all is over for a man when he dies, just as it is for a beast. In Kazan, a 45-year-old Cheremiss lived in my host's house. Hearing me speak to my host of religion, including among other things the resurrection of the dead, he began to laugh and clap his hands, and said: "He who once dies is dead for the devil as well. The dead will no more rise again than will my horse and my cow that died some years ago." When I asked him if he knew who created heaven and earth, he answered derisively, "The devil knows." Though they deny the existence of Hell, they believe in demons, whom they call spirit tormentors. They hold that the demons can harass a person during his lifetime and cause him other unpleasantnesses, and they accordingly try to appease them with sacrifices.

In a boggy place in the countryside, 40 leagues south of Kazan, there is said to be a river called the Nemda. They go there on pilgrimages with offerings, and they say, "He who comes here and brings no offering will suffocate or wither away." They suppose that the devil resides there, or more exactly at the Shokshem River, ten versts from the Nemda. It is said that this stream, which is not more than two ells deep, flows between two mountains and never freezes. The Cheremiss are terrified of it and suppose that any of their nation who go to this river die immediately. However, the Russians may come and go there without danger. Sometimes they also make sacrifices to God, slaughtering horses, cows, and sheep for the purpose, stretching the skin out on stakes, and roasting the meat nearby. Then they take a dish full of meat in one hand and a cup of mead or some other drink in the other, and throw the contents against the hide into the fire, exclaiming, "Come, and grant my wish, O God," or "O God, I make this sacrifice to you; accept it favorably and give me cattle," etc., depending on what is wanted. Since they believe in none but the earthly life, all of their requests and prayers are on behalf of worldly things.

They also pray to the sun and the moon, since they observe that the soil and cattle flourish through their action. They especially honor the sun at harvest time. We were told that for a day they revere and sometimes even pray to whatever they may have seen in their dreams, whether a cow, a horse, fire, or water. When my host and I told the Cheremiss that it was not right to revere and pray to cattle and other creatures as to God, he answered: "What then of the Russian gods that hang on the wall? They are nothing but wood and paint." Therefore he had no desire to pray to them. It was much better and wiser to pray to the sun, which has life. They have neither scriptures nor priests nor churches. Their language is also peculiar, as it has little relationship with the usual Turkish or Tatar. Those who live here among the Russians ordinarily use the Russian language.

When one of their substantial people dies, his best horse is slain and eaten at a river by his surviving friends and servants—they carry out all their sacrifices and other ceremonies at rivers. The deceased is buried in the ground, and his clothes are hung on a tree.

They take four, five, and more women in marriage at one time, and without regard to whether two or three of the wives are sisters. The women and girls go about wrapped with coarse, white, linen cloth, and wear veils on their faces. Brides wear an ornament almost like a horn, forward on their heads; it extends upward an ell in length, and at its tip, in a colored tassel, hangs a little bell.

The men wear long, hemp robes over trousers. They shave their heads. But young men who are not yet married wear a long braid from the top of their heads, which they either tie into a knot or allow to hang down like a woman's braid. We ran across many of them not only here but also in Kazan.

When the Cheremiss first saw us on the Volga, on such an uncommon vessel and in such unusual clothing, they were frightened, and some of them ran from the shore. Others remained, but would not respond to our beckoning and come aboard. Toward evening one of them plucked up his courage and came aboard at the Vetluga River, opposite Iungskii Monastery. He brought a large, fresh sturgeon for which he asked 20 altyns, but he gave it for five.

On August 7th we came to the town of Kozmodem'iansk, 40 versts from the preceding town and also on the right bank of the Volga. This town, too, has a namestnik or voevoda. Here grow large numbers of lindens—even whole forests of them—from which the inhabitants peel bast. The bast is distributed throughout the country for use in making sleighs and receptacles or boxes. The trees themselves are cut into cylindrical pieces, hollowed out, and used as tubs, casks, and the like. They also use them to make whole boats, canoes, and coffins, which they sell in markets here and there.

Three versts beyond this town, at Kriusha Island, we anchored, worshipped, and received communion. Here the peasants again brought fresh provisions to sell. When we had gone a league farther and a gale blew up, we again cast anchor and stayed there for the night.

On the 8th a favorable wind arose, so we hoisted sails and easily made it to Turichii Island toward noon. In the afternoon, while under full sail, we struck a sandbar at Maslov Island [with such force] that the masts cracked. We remained here four hours before we were able to get off with the help of three anchors. Here on the right-hand shore we saw many Cheremiss, both mounted and on foot, who had been to their hayfields.

Toward evening we arrived at the town of Cheboksary, 40 versts from [the settlement] encountered the day before. This town, like the preceding two, was built of wood, but in point of location and [the quality of] its houses, it was much the most attractive of them. When, well before our arrival, the inhabitants saw our large ship from afar, they did not know what to make of it. Therefore the voevoda sent a boatload of streltsi to meet us near Mokrits Island, three versts from the town, to investigate and see what sort of people we were. The soldiers circled the boat at some distance and then hurried back to town. While our passport was being presented in the town, three hundred people, young and old, ran down to the shore to look at us. Here, as in neighboring towns on the Volga, though not inland, the voevoda has at his disposal a goodly number of Russian soldiers; so if the conquered Tatars should rebel, an army can be easily collected to subdue them.

On the 9th we came to Kazin Island on the left, 12 versts from the preceding town; then to the village of Sundyr' on the right; and, 20 versts beyond, to the little town of Kokshaia on the left bank, 25 [*sic*] versts from the last town. Near this place, for a distance of several leagues, the Volga is everywhere so shallow that we could barely get over the shoals. For this reason, in the course of this and the succeeding days, we had many difficulties and annoyances in passing, and on the 10th we advanced only a half league. Aboard the ship was heard nothing but "Pull! Row! Back!"

On the 11th, the river's current became somewhat stronger and carried us to the right, against the shore, where we were stuck for several hours. Von Mandelslo and I went ashore and headed for the forest to amuse ourselves by hunting game. However the wind became more favorable, the sails were hoisted, and the ship departed. When we approached the shore and did not see the ship, we ran along the bank for a while, hoping to overtake the vessel. We failed to catch sight of it, but noticed a little boat coming toward us. Initially, we thought it was the Cossacks, but it turned out that the boat had been sent from our ship to meet us. We returned in it to the ship, which stood in a bend of the river, halted by the wind. As the wind became stronger and stronger, we remained here for the night.

On the 12th we attempted with the aid of a small anchor to drag the ship around the bend. But the anchor got entangled in a sunken tree, the rope broke, and the anchor remained at the bottom. They say this sort of thing happens frequently on the Volga because of the trees that are dislodged from the shore in times of flooding and sink to the river's bottom. The Russians say that the anchors in the Volga are so numerous that they are worth a whole principality. Occasionally, one of these anchors would be accidentally pulled up again by another. On the 13th, before noon, we passed on our right two taverns and the village of Viazovka, and then arrived at Sviiazhsk, located to the left on an attractive hill. Here there are a fortress and several stone churches and monasteries, but the town is surrounded by wooden walls and towers.[13] When, because of the shallows that lay before it, we stood at anchor opposite the town, crowds collected on the shore. Since between us and the shore there was a long, sandy mound that interfered with their seeing us clearly, many of them came out in canoes and boats or crossed the narrow part of the river to see us and our ship.

In the 20 versts that remained from there to Kazan, we sailed by many chalky-white sand dunes lying on the right. Toward evening we reached Kazan, where we anchored. Here we encountered the Persian and Cherkassian caravans which had departed from Moscow several days before us. With them was the Persian merchant who had been an ambassador in Moscow. There was also a Cherkassian Tatar prince

---

[13] The fortress of Sviiazhsk was built by Ivan IV in 1551 as a base for his attack on Kazan, then a Tatar town.

from Terki named Musal, who, after his brother's death, received his feudal holding from the Grand Prince.

The city of Kazan lies on the left side of the Volga, seven leagues from the shore, in a flat place on a small hill. Around it flows the Kazanka River, from which the town and the whole district obtained their names. I calculated the elevation of the pole here as 55° 38′. Like all the towns on the Volga, the walls and towers surrounding Kazan, and the houses within, are made of wood. The town's citadel, however, is well protected by thick stone walls, guns, and soldiers. The Grand Prince assigned not only a voevoda to the citadel but also a special namestnik to the city, to govern the inhabitants and administer justice. The city is inhabited by Russians and Tatars, but only Russians live within the citadel, and no Tatar dares to appear there, on pain of death.

The Kazan district, extending leftward, or northward, from the Volga almost to Siberia, and eastward to the Nogai Tatar country, was formerly a Tatar kingdom. As it was well populated, capable of putting 60,000 men into the field, it waged arduous, bloody wars against the Russians and sometimes forced them to pay tribute. In the end, however, the Tatars were subjugated to the Tsar's empire....[14]

After [Ivan the Terrible conquered Kazan], he ordered the reinforcement of the fortress with strong stone walls, towers, round bastions, and thicker rectangular ramparts; the expulsion of the remaining Tatars; and the occupation of the town and the citadel by Russians, who were assigned there from all over. However, the Tatars were permitted to live individually [i.e. not in tribal groups] in the neighborhood and to retain their religion. Thus the tyrant Ivan Vasil'evich subjugated the whole kingdom of Kazan. They say that afterward, when at drinking bouts he wished to show his good humor, he sang a song about the conquest of Kazan and Astrakhan.

The voevoda of Kazan at the time [we were there] was [Ivan Sheremetev] the brother of the Nizhnii Novgorod voevoda. As they had to others, the ambassadors sent to him as a gift a large, fine, ruby ring.

When I learned on August 15th that the ship was to remain anchored all day, I and Von Mandelslo went to the city to see it, sketch it, and buy things that might catch our fancy. We found nothing

[14] An account of the wars of Vasilii III and Ivan IV that led to the conquest of Kazan in 1552 is omitted.

at the market but fruits, which they sold in large quantities, especially melons as large as pumpkins. They also had here old, putrid, salted fish, that gave off a stench so foul that we were unable to go by it without holding our noses. Inasmuch as Ambassador Brüggemann had looked with disfavor on our going into the town, he had the anchor lifted, and the ship went on. When the Kazan people who had been watching the ship from the shore met us on our way back, they informed us that the ambassadors had already gone off. We obtained two wagons and followed along the shore for quite some distance. Finally we transferred to our pristav's boat and were conveyed to the ship, overtaking it toward evening, two leagues from Kazan, where it had stopped for the night.

CHAPTER TWO

From Kazan to Astrakhan

FROM NIZHNII TO KAZAN the Volga flows mostly to the east and southeast, but thereafter generally southward, to Astrakhan and the Caspian Sea. Farther along the Volga [i.e. beyond Kazan] there are many fertile places, but because of the Cossacks and brigands who are met with in these parts, there are very few villages and few inhabitants.

On August 15th we rapidly advanced along the river, which is narrow and swift in these parts. Beyond the village of Kliuchishchi, 26 versts from Kazan, we came to a shallow place, across which, with difficulty, we dragged the ship by the anchor. When we got over, the small anchor again got stuck on the bottom. Throughout the early evening, in spite of varied attempts we were unable to free it, so we remained there through the night. On the next day, the work continued until noon, and the large anchor was also lowered. Then both anchor ropes broke, and [only] by enormous effort were we able to locate and raise the larger of the two. The smaller one was lodged so firmly that it could not be got loose. Therefore we left it and proceeded on our way.

On August 15th [16th] we passed the Ten'kovskii tavern on our right, 30 versts from Kazan. Beyond it was another shoal, and half a league farther on, at the Keshovskii tavern, still another, over which the ship had to be dragged. On the 17th we were grounded on the very large and well-known Ten'kovskii shallows, named after the old tavern we had passed the day before. Several hours were spent hauling the ship over. The river here is quite broad and everywhere equally shallow. Immediately afterward, we saw on the right side a high, undermined bank, a large part of which had collapsed a month before, killing a whole boatload of people who had gone to gather the cherries that grow abundantly there. Our new pilot, who came from Astrakhan, and whom we had engaged at Kazan for the rest of the voyage down the Volga and the return trip, told us that he had encountered the corpses of many of these men and women floating on the water.

In this area, as nowhere else, we saw very many elm trees. They stood very tall and ran gracefully down to the shore. This day we found on the right bank a large amount of ice, with which we were able to freshen our drinks. Toward evening we came to the great Kama River, on the left, 60 versts from Kazan. It rises in the Perm district, flows from the northeast, and falls into the Volga [here]. This river is almost as broad as the Weser in Germany, and its waters are brownish. At its mouth are two cliffs, the taller of which is named Sokol. Opposite it, on a dry place, is the pretty village of Paganshchina, on the left, and three versts farther along is another, Karatai. Then, ten versts from the Kama, came Kireevskaia, where we stopped for the night.

On the 18th we went ahead briskly under full sail, and toward midday encountered another river coming in on the left side, the Chertyg. It rises as a tributary of the Kama some leagues from here and falls into the Volga at this point, 30 versts beyond the Kama. Around noon, we came to the town of Tetiushi, which lies 120 versts from Kazan, on the right. Situated high on a mountain slope, it consists of scattered wooden houses and churches, and is surrounded by a palisade instead of a wall. From this place to the very end of the Volga, not another village is to be seen. In the afternoon, we approached Prolei-Kasha Island, so named because several servants supposedly killed their master here and covered him up with groats.[1]

Beyond the island we met the Terek voevoda, with eight boats. After a three-year administration of the district, he had been called to Moscow [for a change of assignment], according to their practice. He was accompanied by a strong convoy. A boatload of streltsi, which was in the lead, came toward us to have a look at our ship. Since none of us knew what kind of people they were, or whether they could be trusted, we shouted to them not to come too close or they would be fired upon.

---

[1] Prolei-Kasha means "pour out the groats."

The streltsi warned us that approximately three thousand Cossacks were scattered in various places along our way, some on the Volga, others on the Caspian Sea. Moreover, they said that not far from here they had seen on the shore 70 horsemen, undoubtedly scouts, who surely had been sent to attack us; and they went on in a similar vein.

We saluted them with a salvo from a large gun and, continuing on, came to the Utka River, on the left (20 versts from Tetiushi), which flows from the town of Bulgar'. We made 77 versts that day. That night the ambassadors made a test to discover how our people would conduct themselves if it became necessary to give battle. Toward morning a false alarm was sounded. After the first call, the sentinel fired and cried, "Cossacks!" Then the drums were struck, making a great noise, and muskets and cannons were fired. Most of our people took the matter in earnest and went to their assigned stations, prepared to resist. Such false alarms were also staged in Persia, on the return trip.

On August 19th at Staritsa Island, which is 15 versts long, I calculated the elevation of the pole at 54° 31'. Beyond this island the right-hand shore was covered with round stones like lemons or oranges. They were hard and heavy and felt like iron. When they were broken, the insides revealed silver, gold, brown, and yellow star-like forms; they contained sulphur and saltpeter. We took many of these stones with us to use in our stone-firing guns.

Then we came to a green, pleasant place where long ago had stood a Tatar town named Unerovskaia gora [Undory]. There is said to be buried here a noteworthy Tatar who is considered a saint, and to whose grave the Tatars living in the environs still make frequent pilgrimages. This place is 65 versts from Tetiushi. When we got here, we observed two horsemen among the trees on the high bank. We set a sentinel in the crow's nest to keep the high bank under surveillance, but we saw no [further] sign of these people or any others.

Early in the morning of August 20th, several Tetiushi fishermen who had been fishing in these parts came aboard and sold us 55 large, fat bream for 50 kopeks. One of these fishermen was so honest that he would not take an extra five kopeks given him by mistake until he was urged several times to do so. One of their methods of catching fish is as follows. They cast a long rope with a large stone at the end to the bottom, attaching the upper end to some thick logs tied together and floating in the water. To the line they tie hooks baited with very large fish. In this way, they catch big white sturgeon, four, five, or six ells long. These have very white, sweet, and delicious flesh. On our return trip, at another place, we paid a ruble for a fish of this sort brought to Ambassador Crusius's boat. We were able not only to feed everyone aboard ship with this fish, but also to salt away a whole barrel of what was left over.

Russians who must travel from town to town on the Volga on business commonly pull behind them, on a fine line, a hook to which is attached an iron disk, a hand or less in length, covered with a thick layer of tin in the shape of a fish. When pulled through the water, the disk turns this way and that, because of its breadth, giving the appearance of a frolicking fish. In the course of a trip they catch more than they can eat, for the Volga is rich in every sort of fish. Thus, if they have sufficient bread along, with what they find beneath them they have provisions enough for the trip. Since they have so many fast days, they are used to eating fish more than meat and to drinking only water.

Here we abandoned the provisions lighter that we had taken on at Nizhnii and had now emptied. So that it might not be of use to the Cossacks, we set it afire and left it floating behind. Toward noon we came to the three-mile-long Botemskii Island, on the left. It lies opposite a cape called Polivnoi [Vrag]. When a strong head wind began to blow, we anchored behind the cape in the Bot'ma River, on our left—which also appeared to be a branch of the great Kama River —and remained there through the night.

On the 21st we passed two pleasant places on our right where supposedly there once were towns. The more distant of the two, called Simbirskaia gora, is said to have been destroyed by Tamerlane. On the 22d we passed over two shallows, one of which lay before, the other behind, Arbukhim Mountain, which stands to the right of the river. This mountain got its name from a town that was located here.

From the river at this point one can see on the land, between two hills, an enormous rock, ten ells in length but somewhat less in breadth. It is said that on one side of the rock are written the words, "Lift me up and you will have luck." Once, when a Russian boat unable to advance against a head wind had to anchor here, 50 people, thinking to find a great treasure, undermined the rock with great effort and turned it over. However, they found nothing on the underside but the inscription, "What you are looking for is not here."

In this neighborhood, the land on the right is not very high and is without trees, but it has good, fertile soil. All about grows a long, thick grass, but it is not used since the area is uninhabited. Around this locality were apparent signs and traces of the towns and villages that had stood here and were destroyed at the time of Tamerlane's wars.[2]

On the 23d, at the Atroba River, on our left, we again encountered a strong head wind and were obliged to cast anchor. Here the elevation of the pole was 53° 48′. In the afternoon, when the wind subsided, we tried to tack but hardly made half a league in five hours. On the 24th a head wind twice drove us to the shore, and consequently we made little distance that day. During these days, as on the whole journey, the shallows and the wind greatly hindered our progress. When we had a favorable wind, we got lodged on the shallows; and when we came into a deep and commodious channel, the wind came at us head on.

The next four days the wind arose early, at about 9 o'clock, and subsided again at about five in the afternoon, so we either remained in place the best part of the day or had to navigate with great effort and difficulty. As a consequence, our spirits fell again and we were vexed, especially when we considered the long way that still lay ahead and the short period of summer that was left. The people in the suite were worn out and embittered by the constant work. Those who stood guard with the soldiers at night (the guard always comprised 20 people) were obliged during the day to work at the oars or the capstan along with the Russians. And all this time their food consisted of stale bread, dried fish, and water. Besides, they suffered much unpleasantness and oppression from Ambassador Brüggemann, about which it is not worth talking. Thus cares, work, and grief were our daily fare.

On the 25th we came to Solianaia Mountain, on the right, where the Russians had built huts in which they boil salt obtained from nearby mines. They also dry salt that the sun has already largely evaporated. Many lasts of salt are carried from here up the Volga to Moscow.

[2] In the course of a protracted struggle with Tokhtamysh, another Mongol chieftain, in 1391 and 1395 Tamerlane fought military engagements in the middle Volga area. See Vernadsky, *The Mongols and Russia*, pp. 268–77.

Here lies Kostovatyi Island, near where, because of the low banks on either side, the Volga floods on a large scale. A short distance beyond there is a mountain on the right, and below it a river, or more accurately a branch flowing out of the Volga, which, 60 versts beyond Samara, flows into the Volga again. This stream is called the Usa. Because of the thick dark forest that beautifully covers the shore on both sides, this place is pleasing to the eye. But at the same time, it is very dangerous for travelers because of its convenience to brigands. In particular, there are high mountains here, where approaching people may be seen while yet far off and a pillaging attack readied. It is said that Cossacks are usually found around this river. In the past year they seized here a boatload of goods belonging to a wealthy Nizhnii merchant. At this branch, the [Volga's] depth was 60 feet; a little farther on [we came to] Devich'ia Mountain, where a stream of almost the same depth passes through a very narrow place. The mountain lies on the right, is very high, rising steeply from the shore, and is very pleasant to look at. It presents a series of steps, like benches, one above another, of red, yellow, and blue sandstone, and is very much like [a series of] old walls. On the steps grew fir trees [that looked] as if they had been set out in accord with a fixed plan.

On the same day, another courier sent by our agent in Moscow overtook us. He brought us a letter from Nizhnii, advising that among the Russian workers and oarsmen on the ship there were four who were actually Cossacks. It further advised that two or three hundred Cossacks had gathered at some point, and were lying in wait for us. Although we had been very cautious before, we now became even more vigilant.

When toward evening of this day, at twilight, we saw two large fires on the right bank, we supposed that they had been lighted by Cossacks. Therefore we immediately sent some soldiers in the pristav's boat to reconnoiter. When the boat was not far from the shore, the men fired three shots as a signal, which were answered [by the people on] shore with another three, and the information that they were streltsi assigned to convoy the Persian caravan.[3] However, since our soldiers

---

[3] Although it is evident that there was other traffic on the Volga, a good deal of central Russia's trade with Astrakhan was carried on by merchants who twice a year, in the spring and the fall, departed from Nizhnii Novgorod in caravans escorted by streltsi. See Zagoskin, pp. 282, 289–90, and Kostomarov, *Ocherk*, pp. 104–5.

were a little slow in bringing this answer from the shore, Ambassador Brüggemann became suspicious. When a pistol shot from the ship and a shout from Brüggemann brought from our men a reply that we could not make out because of the wind, the ambassador wanted to fire at the Russians with a big gun. But Ambassador Crusius would not agree, holding that it was improper for us to fight except in defense.

On the 26th, during the night, two men in a small boat came very silently down the river, close to our ship. When the sentinel saw them, he made them come aboard. Here they declared that they were fishermen and accustomed to passing close by their fellow Russians' boats, day or night, without thinking about it. However, since we had been informed that the brigands behaved similarly and then cut the anchor ropes; and since, when these people were questioned separately, they evidenced disagreement (one said that 500 Cossacks awaited us on an island near Saratov, which the other denied), we kept them under arrest all night. On the next morning, we sent them ahead with our pristav to the voevoda at Samara, not far off.

On the 27th, on the left near the shore, we saw on a flat place a bare sand hill, which is called the "king's kurgan" [burial mound]. We were told that a Tatar prince named Mamaon was buried in it.[4] He and seven Tatar kings had been planning to ascend the Volga and devastate all Russia, but he died and was buried here. His innumerable host of soldiers brought so much soil for the grave in their helmets and shields that they raised this hill.

A league beyond this mountain, on the same side, that is, the left, begins Sokovskaia Mountain, which extends 15 versts, to Samara. It is high, rocky, and clothed in thick forest. In the middle of the mountain, approximately eight versts from the city, a broad white rock forms a large bare place. Before it, in the middle of the Volga, is a small rocky shoal of which the Russians are wary. When toward noon we approached this place, we met a strong wind and were obliged to anchor and remain until evening. While we were here, two red snakes crept up onto our anchor, which was hanging down just to the water, wound themselves around it, and crawled up onto the ship. When our Russian

---

[4] It is not clear who this prince was. However, Loviagin's supposition that it was Mamai, perhaps best known as the commander of the Tatar forces defeated by Grand Prince Dmitri Donskoi in 1380, is plainly wrong. Mamai died not in the vicinity of the Volga, but at Kaffa, the site of present-day Feodosiia, in the Crimea.

oarsmen saw this they were delighted, and said that the snakes must be left unhindered on the deck, protected, and fed. For these were not poisonous or dangerous, but benign snakes, which brought news that St. Nicholas would furnish a favorable wind and relieve them for a while from rowing and work.

On the 28th we got under way again at a good hour and before sunrise reached Samara, which is reckoned 350 versts from Kazan. The town lies on the left bank, two versts from the shore. It is rectangular in shape and has a few stone churches and monasteries. The town takes its name from the Samara River, which has a branch (they call it "the Samara's son") that falls into the Volga three versts below the city; the main branch flows into the Volga 30 versts farther on.

We should have liked to stop in this town to learn of the additional testimony given by the two arrested men who had been sent ahead with our pristav. But since the wind was extremely favorable, we hoisted sails and continued on. We went a goodly distance this day, more than ever before, and toward evening anchored at Cossack Mountain, 115 versts from Samara. Thus the Russians' prediction of a good wind came true.

Beyond Samara, on the right, the mountains begin again, though they are not as high as before. The first mountain extends 30 versts to the Samara River, opposite which another river, the Askula, also falls [into the Volga]. Here the Volga is three versts wide. Farther along on the right is Pecherskaia Mountain. It is rocky, covered with clumps of trees, and extends down along the river for 40 versts. One hundred versts from Samara, to the west of the river, lies Batrak Island, three versts long; and ten versts from it, another island, Lopatin, five versts long. Here, on the right side, the Syzran River flows in. Beyond it we passed several small islands in the middle of the river before arriving at Cossack Mountain late in the evening, where we stopped. This mountain, which is barren, is 50 versts long. It takes its name from the Don Cossacks, who formerly dwelt here in large numbers and fell upon and plundered passing boats. Since the time that a troop of streltsi sent from Samara attacked them and killed several hundred, they have not appeared here so often. This mountain, like the one beyond it, [here and there] diverged inland and some leagues farther on again approached the shore.

On the 29th at the end of Cossack Mountain we passed Pan'shchina River, on our right, and after making 45 versts in the course of the day, we anchored at Sagerinskii Island, where several fishermen came aboard with a report that 40 Cossacks had been seen nearby on the shore. Here our barrels of beer were exhausted, and our people had to begin drinking water mixed with a little vinegar.

Early on the morning of the 30th we approached the Chagra River, which flows in beyond Sagerinskii Island. Forty versts farther along, we came to Sosnovyi Island, on which, according to one of the fishermen taken aboard above Samara, there were supposed to be several hundred Cossacks waiting for us. We passed the island fully ready for action, but saw no one. Toward noon we came up to Tikhaia Mountain, which makes a large curve on the right; from afar it looks as though this mountain completely cuts off the Volga. Near it the water is shallow everywhere, and one of the principal shoals, which they call Ovechii brod [Sheep Ford] is located here. It is said that the Cossacks cross the Volga here, on horseback and on foot. The many small islands here are convenient for brigands.

We met two fishermen who informed us that eight days earlier the Cossacks had taken a large boat from them and had told them that in a few days a large foreign ship with Germans aboard would be coming. Toward evening we again called aboard two fishermen, an old man and a young one, and asked them about the Cossacks. The old man at first said that he knew nothing about them. However, when the young man turned out to be more communicative and said that there were 40 Cossacks opposite, in the bushes, the old man confirmed this. He said that they had six boats, which they had hidden on the shore in the bushes, but that one should not talk much of all this, since it endangered one's life. He also asked that we take them with us as "prisoners," and put them ashore later, in another place, which we did. We trusted these fishermen as little as the Cossacks, however, and doubled the night watch. In the morning we let them go. We made 60 versts this day.

On the last of August, we again had a very favorable wind, and made 120 versts by evening. First we came to Osinovyi Island, 100 versts from the next town, Saratov. Opposite it we struck a sandy shoal that extends from the shore on the right side. Here the ship touched bottom several times, but we were neither grounded nor slowed down. Twenty versts beyond the shoal was another island, Shismamago[?], and then Koltov, 50 versts from Saratov. Here we determined the depth of the water to be 16, 20, 30, and 40 feet. Between the two islands we met two Russian barges belonging to the Moscow Patriarch, and a large boat, loaded with caviar, belonging to the Grand Prince. Each boat had 400 workmen. As they came toward us they saluted us with their guns, and we answered with a blast from our cannon. Beyond Koltov Island, near the shore, were four more barges, loaded with salt and salt fish, which belonged to a leading Moscow merchant, Grigorii Nikitov [Grigorii Nikitich]. All these vessels were coming from Astrakhan. They reported having met 250 Cossacks not far from Astrakhan. However, they had demanded nothing of them.

Not far from the above-mentioned island, on the right bank, is a very high mountain, 40 versts long. It is called Zmeevaia [Snake] Mountain, because in many places it curves away from and then again toward the shore. A legend has it that the mountain received its name from a snake of supernatural dimensions that lived here a long time. It caused great harm, but at last a brave hero chopped it into three pieces, which thereupon were immediately transformed into stone. It is said that on the mountain one can actually see three large, long rocks lying near one another, exactly as if they had been cut from one piece. From near the end of the mountain right up to Saratov there are many islands lying beside and behind one another. The Russians call these "the forty islands."

Very early on September 1st we passed three large boats with 300 lasts of cargo. They drew 12 feet of water, and pulled behind them several small boats that helped them negotiate the shallows. The largest of the boats belonged to the wealthy Troitskii Monastery, which is situated 12 leagues from Moscow.[5] We exchanged salutes with them, as we had with the other boats. Before noon, about 9 o'clock, we passed the town of Saratov. This town lies four versts from the river in a level meadowland, where a branch of the Volga goes off to the left. Only streltsi live here, under the command of a voevoda and a colonel.

---

[5] Like many other monasteries, Troitskii played an important role in Russian trade. See Kostomarov, *Ocherk*, pp. 137–39.

They are responsible for protecting the country against the Tatars, who hereabouts are called Kalmyks. The Kalmyks live in the area from here to the Caspian Sea and the Iaik River, and not infrequently make raids up the Volga.

Saratov lies under a polar elevation of 52° 12′ and is reckoned 350 versts from Samara. With a favorable wind, this day we passed two islands close together (called Kriusha and Sapunovka), and soon came to Akhmatovskaia Mountain, on the right, the end of which approaches the island of the same name. The latter is reckoned 50 versts from Saratov. This mountain is beautiful to look at thanks to the greenery that covers its summit, the steep grade of its varicolored soil in the center, and the long, green knoll that adjoins its base like an artificial appendage.

Here we met another large boat, which sent several people over to us in a skiff. They told us that this side of Astrakhan they had encountered 70 Cossacks who went quietly ahead and said nothing to them. But four days before that, ten Cossacks had molested them and extorted several hundred rubles. They did not come to their vessel, which was well equipped for repelling brigands, but seized the small boats that had gone ahead with the anchors, without which the vessel could not proceed. They held these boats until the money was turned over to them.

After sunset, as we lay at anchor, we saw ten Cossacks hurrying up the river on the left bank and then crossing over in a little boat to the other shore. Ambassador Brüggemann immediately ordered eight musketeers, some from among the soldiers, some from the suite, to pursue them and bring them to the ship. However, the Cossacks dragged their boat up onto the shore and hid in the woods, so our men accomplished nothing, and returned to the ship after dark. On this account our marshal had a heated argument with Ambassador Brüggemann, whom he gave to understand that it was inconvenient and dangerous to send men out on such missions at night, when we should not be able to support them. Brüggemann answered with sharp words.

On September 2d we passed Akhmatovskii Island, and 20 versts beyond it Zolotoi Island, which is three versts long. Then we came to Zolotaia [Golden] Mountain, which, as they say, was so named because once the Tatars attacked a rich flotilla here, overcame it, and plundered it, after which the brigands divided up the money and gold articles by the hatful. This mountain is 70 versts from Saratov. Just beyond its terminus begins the white Melovaia Mountain, which extends 40 versts along the shore of the river and is as flat on top as though it had been smoothed out by a [leveling] cord. On the river side it descends steeply, and at its foot, near the water, it is handsomely forested. After it comes still another, which we called Column Mountain; it too was very fine to see. Here, on the steep side, are many prominent veins of stone, which remained uneroded after the disappearance of the friable soil [that had once surrounded them]. They were similar to columns, blue, red, and yellow in color, with green bushes scattered among them.

On September 3d we saw on the left side the [E]ruslan River, and opposite it, on the right, the round Urakov Mountain, which is reckoned 150 versts from Saratov. It is said that this mountain got its name from the Tatar sovereign Urak, who, [having] fought against the Cossacks, fell on the field of battle and lies buried here. Further along on the right are the mountain and river called Kamyshinka. This river rises from the Ilovlia, which flows into the great Don River. The latter falls into the Black Sea and forms the boundary between Europe and Asia. They say that the Don Cossacks go to the Volga in their little boats by way of this river. Therefore the place is considered extremely dangerous. Here, on a high bank, we saw many upright wooden crosses. Many years ago a Russian regiment fought here against the Cossacks, who wished to fortify the place and close off free transit on the Volga. In this skirmish a thousand men of both sides are said to have fallen, and the Russians were buried here.

After passing this place, we caught sight ahead of us of the whole Persian and Tatar caravan, consisting of 16 large boats and six small ones. When we noticed that they were waiting for us, having raised their oars and allowed themselves to drift, we hoisted sail and at the same time began rowing vigorously in order to overtake them. When we drew near we had our three trumpets blow gaily, and gave a four-cannon salute. The caravan answered with musket shots from all the boats. Then our musketeers fired too, and there was great frolicking on both sides.

At the head of the caravan, which had been organized at Samara, there were, besides the above-mentioned commercial agent of the Persian Shah and the Tatar prince Musal, a Russian envoy, Aleksei Savinovich Romanchukov,[6] sent by His Tsarist Majesty to the Persian Shah; a Tatar ambassador from the Crimea; the Persian state chancellor's commercial agent; and two other merchants from the Persian province of Gilan. . . .[7]

Toward evening, a swift-moving gale brought a storm and a downpour, in the course of which there were two great claps of thunder. But then calm weather resumed.

On September 4th, a Sunday, our pastor was about to begin the sermon when several Tatars came from the Cherkass Prince Musal. They came to advise the ambassadors that the Prince was indisposed but that as soon as he was better he would personally visit them. The most important of the Tatars, who spoke for all, was a tall, yellow man with entirely black hair and a big, long beard. He was dressed in a black sheepskin coat with the fur outside, and resembled the devil as he is depicted in paintings. The others, who were dressed in black and brown cotton robes, were scarcely more pleasant to behold. After they had been treated to several cups of vodka, they departed, with a gun salute from our streltsi.

Toward noon we came to the Bolykleia River, 90 versts from the Kamyshinka and 90 from the next town, Tsaritsyn. Proceeding another 16 versts, we passed a very high sand hill, Strel'naia, and at its end, 60 versts this side of Tsaritsyn, spent the night. On the 5th we had hardly

---

[6] In a later portion of the book, Olearius wrote of Romanchukov: "This Russian was sent by the Muscovite Grand Prince to the Persian Shah nominally as a minor envoy, but principally to keep our affairs and conduct under observation. He was a man of 30 years, intelligent, and very cunning. He knew several Latin words and, in contrast to the usual attitude of the Russians, had a great love for the liberal arts, especially some of the mathematical sciences and the Latin language. He asked us to help him in the study of the latter; and, in fact, what with diligent attention, constant conversation, and practice, in the five months that we were with him in Persia and, especially, on the return trip, he learned enough to express his ideas, although not too felicitously. Moreover, he also learned geometry and the use of the astrolabe in determining the time and the elevation of the sun. Our watchmaker built him an astrolabe, and whenever we stopped for the night, whether in the city or the countryside, but especially in Astrakhan, Aleksei went into the streets to practice, and told people the heights of houses and other buildings. The Russians, unaccustomed to anything of the kind in their compatriots, marveled extremely at this."

On the return trip from Persia, Romanchukov learned in Nizhnii Novgorod that disgrace awaited him at the court in Moscow, and he took his life.

[7] Visits were exchanged between the Holsteiners and the others, during which Olearius took note of the luxuriously appointed quarters of one of the Persian merchants. The latter complained of the Russians and promised that the Holsteiners would be better treated in Persia. He also advised them confidentially that a Polish envoy had been sent to the Shah, by way of Constantinople, and was then in Astrakhan awaiting permission to proceed home across Russia.

got under way when we struck a shoal at a point where there was barely five and a half feet of water. It was necessary to drag the ship to the side, and at last, with a great shudder, it came loose. Meanwhile the caravan went ahead to Tsaritsyn, where it was to obtain fresh streltsi for the convoy. Toward noon it arrived at the place whence it is hardly a half-day's journey to the great and famous Tanais, or Don, which flows for seven leagues parallel to [and west of] the Volga. A little farther on we came to the mouth of the Akhtubskoe, where the Volga has its first offshoot, a branch going inland from the left shore. This branch at first flows one verst east-northeast away from the river, and then turns southeast and falls into the Caspian Sea. Here the elevation of the pole was 48° 51′.

We were told that five versts farther into the depths of the country, and seven versts from Tsaritsyn, there are still preserved the ruins of a town that the cruel monster Tamerlane built of transported stones, and within which he raised a great pleasure palace. It is called Tsarev Gorod.[8] After this town was destroyed, the Russians brought most of the stones to Astrakhan and used them to build a large part of the city walls, and the churches, monasteries, and other buildings. Even when we were there, several boats loaded with stones were going from there to Astrakhan.

Near this place, a fisherman alongside our ship caught on a hook a beluga almost four ells long, with a girth of one and a half ells. It is much like a sturgeon except that it is whiter and has a large mouth. It was killed just like an ox, with a hammer blow on the head, and sold for one thaler.

On September 6th we met the caravan again, near Tsaritsyn. Those traveling with them had struck their tents on the shore and were awaiting a new convoy. Since the wind was favorable, we passed them by. Tsaritsyn is reckoned 350 versts from Saratov. It is situated on the right bank on a hill, and is small and shaped like a parallelogram, with six wooden fortifications and towers. Its only inhabitants are streltsi, some 400 in number, who are supposed to keep a close watch on the Tatars and Cossacks, and furnish convoys for barges going by. The elevation of the pole here is 48° 23′ [corrected at the end of the book to 49° 42′].

---

8 Evidently the reference is to Sarai, the capital of the Mongol Golden Horde.

From here to Astrakhan, and beyond to the Caspian Sea, the country is desolate, sandy, and unsuitable for cultivating grain. Accordingly, these cities, including Astrakhan, must import their grain, which comes down the Volga, chiefly from Kazan. In spite of this, the grain is brought down the river in such quantity that it is much cheaper here than in Moscow itself. A similar phenomenon is met with often in Holland.

Just below Tsaritsyn, on the right side, lies Sarpinskii Island, 12 versts long. Here the streltsi pasture their cows and other cattle. Not long before our arrival, the Cossacks had observed that the wives and daughters of the streltsi daily crossed over to the island to milk the cows, often without guards; they lay in wait, seized and had their way with them, and then sent them unharmed back to the streltsi homes.

Beyond this island a little stream flows into the Volga from the Don. It is so shallow that only canoes and the lightest boats can navigate on it, as we were told not only by our pilot but also by some of our working hands who earlier had been with the Cossacks and had sailed upon it. The stream is not shown on most maps, except for Isaak Massa's, where it is designated by the name Kamous.[9]

On this day, as on some of the succeeding ones, it was hot all the time, just as on the dog days in our country. The Russians told us that it was always hot here at this time of year.

On September 7th the weather was so cloudy and bad that it was difficult to move forward. After we had dragged along for ten versts, we saw, to the right on a high, red, sandy hill, a gallows, the first we had come across in these parts. The voevoda of the nearest town used it to hang Cossack brigands. They say that no one is ever left hanging longer than eight days, for in that time his comrades manage to make off with him.

At this place Ambassador Brüggemann called together the personnel of the suite and said that he suspected certain of them of a secret plot against him. In case of an emergency he could not rely upon them, and yet he expected and deserved an entirely different attitude from

[9] Isaak Massa, a Dutchman, spent a good many years in Russia beginning in 1609. He produced a valuable, short work on Russian geography, and a series of maps as well. Olearius undoubtedly was referring to one of these that covers the land between the Dnepr and the Volga, published for the first time in 1610. See Adelung, II, 130–33. The map is reproduced in Kordt. Massa also wrote a circumstantial account of Russian affairs, which apparently was first published in the last half of the nineteenth century; see Massa.

them, in view of his difficult position and his daily concern for them. Therefore, he demanded a personal vow of loyalty from the musicians, bodyguards, and table servants. They affirmed that the charges in no wise concerned them and that they [already] reckoned themselves sufficiently obligated to keep faith; nevertheless, they willingly took the vow, and asked only that the ambassador thenceforth should not, as he had done in the past, attack them indiscriminately and without cause, impugning their honor and humiliating them. As far as they were concerned, if only they were decently treated they were ready not only to be true and to serve him with love, but in case of need even to give their lives for him. They were promised that their request would be fulfilled, it is true, but. . . .

On this day we met a large barge. Some of those aboard her came over to our ship in a small boat. They told us that three weeks earlier they had come from Astrakhan. On the way they had been attacked by Cossacks, who took away all their provisions, so they had had nothing to eat for four days. They asked for a little bread to assuage their hunger until they should meet some of their comrades or reach a town. We gave them a bag of dry bread, for which all of them touched their heads to the ground and thanked us profusely.

Forty versts beyond Tsaritsyn, a long, flat mountain stretches away on the right, and opposite it is an island of the same length. Both the mountain and the island are called Nasonovskii. Between the mountain and the island is a narrow, crooked, and deep passage. Several years ago, so they say, the Cossacks here deceived and slew several hundred streltsi who were seeking them out.

Toward evening a fisherman brought to the ship a fish we did not know, which they call a *chiberik*. It is more than two and one-half ells long and has a broad, long nose, like a duck's bill, and black and white spots on both sides, like those of a Polish mottled dog, except that the spots were disposed in an orderly fashion. The belly of this fish is completely white, and the taste sweet and pleasant like that of salmon. The fishermen also supplied us with a kind of sturgeon called *sterliad* [sterlet]; they are less than an ell long, never any larger, and are very delicious. They are abundant everywhere in the Volga and are sold quite cheaply.

On the 8th the caravan again overtook us, at a cape on our right named Popovitskaia [priest's son] Iurka, so called because formerly a

Cossack colonel and ataman, the son of a Russian priest, gathered his detachment here. This place is 70 versts from the preceding town. From here onward for a distance of 40 versts down to Kamennyi Iar Mountain on the right, there are several islands and shallows, upon which both we and the Persians now and again got lodged. Twenty versts farther along on the right was the high-lying Viazovyi Island, four versts long; and beyond it flows a river of the same name. When we had gone another 30 versts, the wind drove us into a cove on the right, whence falls the Volodimirskoe branch. As the wind was very favorable for going on, we did not wish to tarry long here. Accordingly everyone pitched in and, with the aid of two anchors, soon dragged the ship out of this place. Afterward we went under full sail by the settlement of Stupino, from which it was 30 versts to the next town, Chernyi Iar. Twelve versts this side of Chernyi Iar another branch of the Volga, the lower Akhtuby, separates off to the left and joins with the above-mentioned Akhtubskoe branch. We anchored with the caravan beyond this river at Osinovyi [Sennyi?] Island, seven versts from the town, having gone 135 versts, or 27 leagues, this day.

Around this place and almost all the way to Astrakhan, in the shrubbery on both sides of the river, grows a great deal of *Glycyrrhiza,* or licorice, which attains a considerable thickness. Its stem rises to half a man's height, and its seed hangs down in long pods, like black vetch. We found it at Media, too, in all the fields and [in particular abundance] at the Araks River, where the root attained a hand's thickness. It gives as delicate juice as our does.

On the 9th, toward noon, we were driven by a strong wind to the little town of Chernyi Iar, 300 versts from Tsaritsyn, where we anchored. Nine years ago, by order of the Grand Prince, this town was shifted half a league downstream. However, since a high bank before it collapsed and somewhat diverted the river from the town, it was relocated here just two months ago. It lies on the right on a high bank, has eight towers, and is surrounded by a stout, timbered barrier. The town is inhabited exclusively by the streltsi, who are supposed to deal with the many marauding Cossacks and Tatars hereabout. Opposite each corner of the town, at a distance of a quarter-league, is a watch tower built on four tall columns, whence the streltsi can survey the whole area far and wide, particularly since it is flat and unwooded.

The town was built as a consequence of the great amount of slaying and plundering committed by the Cossacks. It is said that 400 Cossacks cunningly waylaid a Russian caravan of 1,500 men, and killed more than half of them. They resorted to the following stratagem. Having observed that the boats did not follow close behind one another, but some—particularly the guards'—went about a musket shot's distance ahead of the rest, the Cossacks hid themselves on a high bank, by which the river flowed most rapidly. They allowed the streltsi to go by and then fell on the others and cut them down. Although the streltsi turned about and hurried back, the swift current hindered their boats so long that [before they arrived] most of the killing and plundering had already occurred, and the Cossacks had gone ashore and made off on their horses.

Here, except on the shore, the right side especially, one sees no more trees, but only dry, baked soil and steppe plants.

On the 10th we had hardly gone by the town when the wind met us head on with such force that in the whole day, no matter how we tried, we could not make more than ten versts. Toward evening some fishermen brought us a very big, fat carp weighing over 30 pounds, and eight large pike the like of which we had not seen before in our entire trip. They would not accept money, arguing that certain Moscow merchants who leased this part of the Volga[10] had sent them there to fish, and that they would have to pay dearly if it was learned that they had sold the least little fish. They were more concerned about vodka, and after receiving half a tankard, delightedly went off with many thanks.

On the 11th, moving continually under sail with a favorable wind, we went 120 versts. Around noon we passed Polovina (Halfway) Mountain, which is so named because it is halfway between Tsaritsyn and Astrakhan, 250 versts from both, to be precise. We spent the night beyond Kiziar Island. On the night of the 11th, when Ambassador Brüggemann was inspecting the guard, a large boat quietly passed our ship in the middle of the river. When no one answered our call to come aboard, 15 muskets were fired, and the cannoneer was ordered to train his gun upon it. Meanwhile, someone from the boat came toward us in a little skiff and reported that they were not foes, but seven Russians carrying a boatload of salt. As they had received a gift of vodka from

---

[10] The exploitation of fisheries on the Volga, in Astrakhan, and elsewhere is treated in Kostomarov, *Ocherk*, pp. 243–51.

the caravan, which lay a short distance from us, they had all lain down and fallen asleep, allowing the boat to drift with the current. When the man was recognized by our pilot, both being from Nizhnii, he was given several cups of vodka and sent back. In the morning, by way of thanks, he brought several sterlets. It was a wonder that no one in the boat was wounded by our unjust volley.

As the wind was very favorable all that night and we did not wish to lose it, toward morning, around 3 o'clock, we got under way again. Soon we came to another branch of the Volga, the Bukhvostov, on our port side, which entered [almost] unnoticed. Then we came to Kopanovskii Island, opposite which, on the right, was a high piece of land called Kopanov Iar. It is 150 versts from Astrakhan. In 20 versts we came to the fourth branch that divides off, the Danilovskoe, on the left, which flows separately to the Caspian Sea. Fifteen versts farther on, almost in the center of the Volga lies a fine, round, little island, Ekaterininskii, which is covered with lovely trees and bushes.

After that we saw from afar a large derelict boat on a sandy mound. Since it looked like a fortification thrown up by the Cossacks, and since several Cossacks were seen in the bushes, our people were commanded to take arms and fire several shots into the bushes. While they were so doing, the musket of our cook's helper, Jakob Hansen, which was doubly loaded, exploded, tearing the thumb off his left hand, which he had against the muzzle, and also inflicting many wounds on his forehead, breast, and hands. Having made 100 versts this day, we anchored beyond Pirushki[?] Island, 80 versts from Astrakhan.

Early in the morning on September 13th, while we were engaged in prayer, and just as we came to Chapter Thirteen of the Fourth Book of Moses, which describes the spying out of the Land of Canaan, and its rich fruits and large grapes, we, too, had occasion to see the first fruits. For two boats from Astrakhan came up and sold us beautiful big grapes, berries almost as large as walnuts, and large and very delicious melons.

The principal place we came to on this day was Mitiushka, on the left, where a branch divides off, part of it flowing into the branch we met the day before, part into the Volga a few versts on. The area is said to be a veritable robbers' nest. When some Cossacks were spotted between two islands ahead of it, the ambassadors ordered that a cannon shot be fired at them. In five versts we came to the last shallows before Astrakhan, Kaban'ia shoal, 70 versts from the city; and in another five, the cape or projection Kabanyi Iar. Then, in five versts, came Ichiburskii Island, 50 versts from Astrakhan, beyond which we remained for the night. Around this place, as well as above it and on the Caspian Sea, we saw large-cropped geese, which the Russians call *babas*. One hundred of them sat together on the shore.

On September 14th we hardly managed to make two versts when, from the southeast, we were met by a most powerful gale, which obliged us to remain here until the next day. The depth beneath us proved to be 80 feet. Here Prince Musal presented the ambassadors with various beverages—beer, mead, and vodka—offering to supply us with more if we liked them.

When early in the morning of the 15th we had good weather and wind, we arose again around 4 o'clock and sailed off smartly to the south, so that in good time we passed Buzan Island, 25 versts along, and the Bolchuk River, or branch, 15 versts from the city. At eight in the morning, from a distance of 12 versts, thanks to the flat and treeless landscape thereabout, we could see the goal of our search—Astrakhan. Just then we went by the Gnilusha branch, which leaves the Volga and rejoins it beyond Astrakhan. This branch flows by many separate mouths into the Caspian Sea.

Toward noon, with favorable wind and weather, we arrived at the far-famed city of Astrakhan. With God's gracious help we had taken the first step, so to speak, from Europe, the first part of the world, into Asia. For all of Astrakhan lies east of the Volga, which separates Europe from Asia.[11] We stopped before the city, in the middle of the river, and fired all our ship's cannons as a salute. This action astonished the inhabitants, more than a thousand of whom stood on the shore.

Since this was [the embassy's] first visit here, before continuing further let us look briefly at this area and its chief city, as well as the condition and characteristics of its inhabitants. . . .[12]

---

[11] The reader will observe that Olearius contradicts himself here, since he stated just a few pages before that the Don is the boundary between Europe and Asia. This contradiction no doubt reflects a lack of agreement in his sources, for there was no consensus on this matter. Ptolemy, whose work Olearius used, was one authority who fixed the Don as the boundary.

[12] In a discussion of the comments of ancient and modern writers on the area and its inhabi-

The Nogai country, the area inhabited by the Nogai Tatars, is the region between the Volga and the Iaik rivers, down to the Caspian Sea. The chief city is Astrakhan, a name some employ for the whole region. It is supposed that the ruler who built and first ruled the city was named Astra-Khan. The city is not—as Herberstein says, and others think—situated several days' journey inland from the Volga; in fact, it is on Dolgii Island, between the river's main stream and one of its tributaries.

By repeated investigations, I calculated the elevation of the pole at Astrakhan as 46° 22′. The climate here is quite warm. In September and October the weather was as fair and warm as in [our] summer, especially when the wind came from the northeast or from the Volga. However, when it blew from the south, that is from the sea, it usually brought with it a chill, and sometimes air that smelled of the sea. When we were there on our return trip, in June, July, and August, the heat was very intense; but since there were constant breezes, it was not too oppressive. Although the winter lasts not more than two months, it is cold enough that—contrary to the opinion of some writers—the Volga entirely freezes over and can support sleighs.

Dolgii Island, as well as the land to its right beyond the river, is sandy and barren. But on the left, eastward all the way to the Iaik, there are said to be good pasture lands. On the side of the river to the west there is a great, flat, dry steppe extending 70 leagues to the Black Sea, and southward 80 leagues to the Caspian Sea. We amply measured it in 11 difficult days of travel. This wasteland furnishes excellent salt, which is found here in various pits, sloughs, and stagnant lakes, of which the most notable are Mochavskoe, Kanikovo, and Gvozdovskoe, situated respectively 10, 15, and 30 versts from Astrakhan. In the lagoons or salt sloughs there are salt veins through which the brine rises. On the surface, the heat of the sun causes the formation of flakes of salt as clear as crystal and as thick as one's finger. It has a pleasant odor of violets. Anyone who wishes may carry it off, paying the Grand Prince a duty of only one kopek for two puds. The Russians do a thriving business with it, transporting it up the shores of the Volga, piling it up

---

tants, Olearius treats different classifications of the Tatar peoples, designating those of this region as Nogais. He also stipulates that he will report only what he himself saw and heard of this people.

in great quantities, and shipping it all over Russia, but not throughout Media, Persia, and Armenia, as Petrejus says in his Muscovy chronicle. . . .[13] As regards the salt sloughs, it is undoubtedly true that the more one takes away the salt flakes, the more they multiply, for there is no want of rich sources of brine.

On the Volga from here to the Caspian Sea, 12 leagues away, there are extraordinarily rich fisheries of all sorts. The fish are extremely cheap, so that one can purchase 12 large carp for one groschen, or 200 sterlets, or small sturgeon (a very delicious fish), for 15 groschen. There also are very many crabs here, but since neither the Russians nor the Tatars eat them, they are simply thrown away. Because of the proximity of the sea and the many reedy and bushy islands that lie below Astrakhan, there are numerous game birds, especially wild geese and large red ducks, which the Tatars know how to catch quickly, using their trained falcons and sparrow hawks. There also are many wild pigs, which the Tatars hunt and sell to the Russians cheaply, since they themselves, in keeping with their law, may not eat them.

As regards garden fruits, they are so marvelous here that we found no better even in Persia. They have apples, quinces, walnuts, large yellow melons,[14] and also watermelons, which the Russians call *arbuzy*, the Turks and Tatars *karpus* (as they are very refreshing), and the Persians *hinduane* (as Hindus first brought them to Persia). They are shaped like [our] melons, or more exactly, pumpkins, and have a green rind and flesh-colored pulp. They are very juicy, sugary sweet, and have black seeds. The Tatars weekly brought ten to twenty loads of these melons to market at Astrakhan and sold them at very low prices.

Formerly they had no grapes at all here. The Persian merchants brought the first vines to Astrakhan, and an old monk planted them in a monastery outside the city. When it became evident that they did very well, in 1613, by order of the Grand Prince, the same monk laid out a proper vineyard, which expanded every year thereafter. It produces wonderful large and sweet grapes, some of which, with other

---

[13] He also disputes Petrejus's fabulous tale about two nearby salt mountains that were said to be colossal and inexhaustible.

The area around Astrakhan was the chief producer of salt in Muscovy, hence the lively traffic of salt-laden barges on the Volga. Because salt fish was a major item in the Russian diet, salt was used in great quantities. Kostomarov, *Ocherk*, pp. 192–93.

[14] The yellow sweet-tasting Russian melon is called *dynia*.

fruits from the same orchard, are sent to the Grand Prince in Moscow, and some of which are sold to the voevodas and boyars in the country. Now some of the Astrakhan burghers have planted vineyards at their homes, and our host told us that his had brought in 100 thalers that year. During the current year, I was reliably informed that so much wine is now produced in Astrakhan that 50 to 60 large barrels will be shipped to Moscow annually.[15] They have a vineyard keeper named Jakob Bothman, who was trained in Gottorp by His Princely Excellence's court gardener.

The monk I mentioned above was 105 years old. An Austrian by birth, he was taken captive in war and brought to Russia while still a boy. He was coverted to the Russian faith, rebaptized, and sent to the monastery. When we were there he had the management of the whole monastery in his hands. He still knew a few words of German and was very kind to those of us who visited him. He also came to visit the ambassadors and brought a gift of fruit from trees that he had planted with his own hands. He was still gay in temper. After he had had two cups of vodka, he began to show his strength by dancing without the help of a stick, although his legs wobbled. He said that the region was healthful and boasted many extremely old people.

As mentioned above, the inhabitants of this Nogai or Astrakhan region formerly were all Tatars. They had a king, who was in amity and alliance with the Kazan and Crimean Tatars, so that an opponent of one of them had to deal with all three. For that reason, two years after his conquest of the kingdom of Kazan, Grand Prince Ivan Vasil'evich was obliged to wage war against the Nogai kingdom, which he also subjugated. The Nogai capital, Astrakhan, was taken by storm on August 1st, 1554. The Tatars were expelled and the Russians occupied the city.[16]

The tyrant subsequently fortified the city with a stout stone wall, and the present Grand Prince ordered its extension and, adjacent to it, the construction of the *streletskii gorod*, in which the streltsi live. Seen from without, on the Volga (which here is 2,260 feet wide), the city

[15] In the 1650's the Tsar's government was taking considerable pains to promote wine production in Astrakhan. As in so many other enterprises, foreign experts were employed to advance the effort and to train Russians to carry it on themselves, without foreign overseers. See *Akty istoricheskie*, Vol. IV, Nos. 63 and 138.

[16] However, the Khanate of Astrakhan as a whole was not subjugated until 1556.

makes a fine appearance, owing to its many towers and church steeples;
but within, [one sees that] it consists chiefly of wooden structures. It is
well looked after by a strong garrison equipped with many (they say
500) metal guns. Among these there are several full-size and half-size
siege guns, which we ourselves saw. It is said that there now are nine
regiments here, each consisting of 500 soldiers. They are commanded
by two voevodas, a d'iak, and several captains, and are ever on the alert
to keep the Tatars in check. In the city, not only the Russians but also
the Persians and the Indians each have their own market. Since the
Bokharans [of Central Asia], the Crimean and Nogai Tatars, and the
Armenians (a Christian people) also carry on a great traffic with all
sorts of goods, the city is said annually to bring His Tsarist Majesty
a large sum, as much as 12,000 rubles, in duties alone.[17]

The native Tatars—partly Nogai and partly Crimean—are not permitted to settle inside the city, but only in designated places outside.
They may close off their settlements with nothing more than a fence.
It should be added that wherever they reside they do not construct
fortified towns or villages, but live in tents. These are round in shape,
commonly with a diameter of ten feet. They are woven of reeds or
rushes, and resemble our chicken coops. They are covered above with
felt, in the center of which is an aperture through which smoke may
escape; attached there is another piece of felt to shut out the wind.
When their fires of dry reeds and dried cow dung have burned out and
the smoke has left, they lower the felt and shut the aperture. The whole
hut is [already] surrounded by felt or reeds so that when the weather
is cold the wife and children may sit around the coals and ashes and be
warmed by the heat, which is preserved for a considerable time.

In the summer they have no definite place of residence but move
whenever they need to find good, fresh pastures for the cattle. Then
they set their dwellings on tall wagons, which they always have near
them, and move on, with the wives, children, and household equipment
loaded onto cows, oxen, horses, and camels. The Russians named them
polovtsy because of their constant migration from one place to another
in quest of pastures.[18] In the winter they divide into several hordes

---

[17] As a link between Russia and Asia, and as a producer of great amounts of salt and fish,
Astrakhan was one of Muscovy's chief trade centers. On Astrakhan's commerce, see Kostomarov,
Ocherk, pp. 107–12.

[18] In Russian the word *pole* means field or pasture.

(similar to the German *Harde*), or companies, go to Astrakhan, and settle closely enough that in case of need they can assist one another. For they are often attacked and plundered by their permanent enemies, the Kalmyks, who are scattered not only from here to Saratov (in this area they are called Bulgarian Tatars), but also beyond the Iaik. The Kalmyks make their raids when the waters have frozen, and it is easy to cross everywhere. So that the Tatars may better defend themselves against their enemies at these times, the Russian arsenal lends them firearms and other military equipment, which they must return at the beginning of the summer. They are not permitted to have any other weapons.

It is true that they pay no tribute to the Grand Prince, but when he wishes to put them into the field against a foe, they must appear. They are glad enough to do so, in the hope of plunder, which they, like the Dagestan Tatars, view as the surest source of prosperity. They can swiftly collect several thousand men, and are very brave in attacking the enemy. They are permitted to have their own princes, headmen, and judges; but in order to diminish the likelihood of rebellion, some of the princes' relatives, by turns, must always be kept as hostages in the Astrakhan fortress.

Both the Nogais and the Crimean Tatars are stout and short, with broad faces and small eyes. Their skin is dark yellow, and the men's faces are as wrinkled as the faces of old women. They have little hair in their beards, and their heads are smooth shaven. Some wear long cloaks of gray cloth; others, especially the Nogais, wear long coats and hats of sheepskin, with the hairy side out. The women, whose faces are not as ugly as the men's, wear white linen cloaks and round, pleated hats, which rise to a point and are not unlike helmets. In front, these hats are hung with Russian kopeks joined in rings. The eldest daughter and any other daughters who, while still in their mother's womb, have been pledged by the parents to God or to a certain *imam*, or holy man, wear a turquoise, ruby, or coral ring in their right nostril, as a mark of their slavery and humility. Boys wear similar rings in their ears. The Persians also have this custom. The children go about naked, with no shirts at all, and all of them have large, protruding stomachs.

The Tatars sustain themselves by raising cattle, fishing, and catching birds. Their horned cattle, like Polish cattle, are large and strong; and their sheep, like the Persian, have big, thick tails of pure fat, which may weigh 20 to 30 pounds. The sheep also have drooping, spaniel-like ears and crooked noses. Their horses are unimpressive looking, but strong and of great endurance. They also have camels, most of which have two humps, but some only one; they call the latter *boggur*, the former *towae*.

Their common food is fish, dried in the sun, which they use in place of bread. They bake cakes of ground rice and wheat in vegetable oil or honey. They eat camel's meat and horse meat, as well as other kinds, and drink water and milk, especially mare's milk, which they prize as a tasty and healthful drink. Thus, when the ambassadors once rode out to see their hordes and camps, we were offered some of this milk poured out of a leather bag.

The Tatars are Moslems of the Turkish rather than the Persian rite.[19] Some of them have adopted the Russian religion and allowed themselves to be baptized. They were very cordial to us, and one of their princes wished to arrange a falcon hunt for the ambassadors' pleasure. However, the voevoda forbade it. . . .[20]

---

[19] That is, the Sunnite rather than the Shiite. These are the two major divisions within the Moslem faith.

[20] The account of the further experiences in Astrakhan treats mainly of exchanges of visits and gifts with other dignitaries, entertainments, and the like. In Astrakhan, Olearius learned that the pristav who escorted the embassy from Moscow had lodged a protest against Brügge-mann, who, in the course of the journey, repeatedly abused him.

Bibliography

Bibliography

Adelung, Friedrich. *Kritisch-literärische Übersicht der Reisenden in Russland bis 1700, deren Berichte bekannt sind.* 2 vols. St. Petersburg, 1846.
Akty istoricheskie. See Arkheograficheskaia Kommissiia.
"Akty o vyezdakh v Rossii inozemtsev, 1600–1640," *Russkaia istoricheskaia biblioteka.* Vol. VIII (St. Petersburg, 1884).
Akty sobrannye v bibliotekakh i arkhivakh rossiiskikh imperii Arkheograficheskoiu Ekspeditsieiu Akademii Nauk. St. Petersburg, 1836. Vol. IV.
Aksakov, S. T. *The Family Chronicle.* New York, 1961.
Allgemeine Deutsche Biographie. Leipzig, 1875–1912. Vol. XXIV.
Amburger, Eric. *Die Familie Marselis.* Giessen, 1957.
————. "Johann Böcker von Delden und seine Nachkommen in Russland," *Personalhistorisk tidsskrift,* 1935, No. 2, pp. 1–8.
Anderson, Matthew S. *Britain's Discovery of Russia, 1553–1815.* New York, 1958.
Arkheograficheskaia Kommissiia. *Akty istoricheskie.* 5 vols. St. Petersburg, 1841–42.
————. *Dopolnenie k aktam istoricheskim.* St. Petersburg, 1846–75. Vols. I, V.
Arsen'ev, A. V. "Pervye russkie studenty za granitsei," *Istoricheskii vestnik,* July 1881.
Bakhrushin, S. V. "Moskovskoe vosstanie 1648 g.," *Nauchnye trudy,* Vol. II. Moscow, 1954. First printed in *Sbornik statei v chest' M. K. Liubavskogo.* Petrograd, 1917.
Baklanova, N. "Ian de Gron, prozhektor v Moskovskom gosudarstve XVII veka," *Uchenye zapiski Instituta Istorii RANION,* 1929, No. IV, pp. 109–22.
Baron, Samuel H. "Plekhanov's Russia: The Impact of the West upon an 'Oriental' Society," *Journal of the History of Ideas,* XIX (June 1958), 388–404.
Basilevich, K. V. "Elementy merkantilizma v ekonomicheskoi politike pravitel'stva Alekseia Mikhailovicha," *Uchenye zapiski Moskovskogo Gosudarstvennogo Universiteta,* vyp. 41, Istoriia, Vol. I (Moscow, 1940).
————. "Kollektivnye chelobit'ia kupechestva i bor'ba za russkii rynok v pervoi polovine XVII veka," *Izvestiia Akademii Nauk SSSR. Otdelenie obshchestvennykh nauk,* 1932, No. 2, pp. 91–123.
————. "Novotorgovyi ustav, 1667 g.," *Izvestiia Akademii Nauk SSSR. Otdelenie obshchestvennykh nauk,* 1932, No. 7.
Bayani, Khanbaba. *Les Relations de l'Iran avec l'Europe occidentale.* Paris, 1937.
Belokurov, S. A. *Adam Olearii o grekolatinskoi shkole Arsenii Greka v Moskve v XVII v.* Moscow, 1888.

334   Bibliography

——. "O Posol'skom Prikaze," *Chteniia* . . . , 1906, No. 3.
Bogoiavlenskii, S. K. "Moskovskaia nemetskaia sloboda," *Izvestiia Akademii Nauk SSSR. Seriia istorii i filosofii*, 1947, No. 3, pp. 220–32.
Bond, E. A., ed. *Russia at the Close of the Sixteenth Century*. London, 1856.
Borodin, A. V. "Inozemtsy-ratnye liudi na sluzhbe v Moskovskom gosudarstve," *Vestnik Imperatorskago Obshchestva Revnitelei Istorii*, No. 2 (Petrograd, 1915), pp. 185–201.
Brückner [Brikner], A. *Die Europäisierung Russlands*. Gotha, 1888.
——. *Kulturhistorische Studien. Die Russen im Ausland, die Ausländer im Russland*. 2 vols. Riga, 1887.
——. *Patrik Gordon i ego dnevnik*. St. Petersburg, 1878.
Bussov, K. *Moskovskaia khronika, 1584–1613*. Moscow, 1961.
Chernov, A. V. *Vooruzhenye sili russkogo gosudarstva v XV–XVII vv*. Moscow, 1934.
Chteniia v imperatorskom obshchestve istorii i drevnostei rossiiskikh pri Moskovskom Universitete. 264 vols. Moscow, 1846–1918.
Cizevskij, Dmitrij. *History of Russian Literature from the Eleventh Century to the End of the Baroque*. The Hague. 1960.
Collins, Samuel. *The Present State of Russia*. London, 1671.
Cross, Samuel H. "Medieval Russian Contacts with the West," *Speculum*, Vol. X, No. 2, pp. 139–44.
——. *The Russian Primary Chronicle*. Cambridge, Mass., 1930.
Dansk biografisk leksikon. Copenhagen, 1933–. Vol. XVII.
"Dnevnik Generala Patrika Gordona," *Chteniia* . . . , 1892, No. 3.
Dopolnenie. See Arkheograficheskaia Kommissiia.
Dvornik, Frances. *The Idea of Apostolicity in Byzantium and the Legend of the Apostle Andrew*. Cambridge, Mass., 1958.
Fedotov, G. P. *The Russian Religious Mind*. New York, 1960.
Fennell, J. L. I. *Ivan the Great of Moscow*. London, 1961.
Fisher, Raymond H. *The Russian Fur Trade, 1500–1700*. Berkeley, Calif., 1943.
Fleming, Paul. *Deutsche Gedichte*. Stuttgart, 1865.
Florinsky, Michael. *Russia, a History and an Interpretation*. New York, 1953. Vol. I.
Florovskii [Florovsky], G. "The Problem of Old Russian Culture," *Slavic Review*, XXI (March 1962), 1–15.
——. *Puti russkago bogosloviia*. Paris, 1937.
Forsten, G. V. *Baltiiskii vopros v XVI i XVII stoletiiakh*. St. Petersburg, 1894. Vol. II.
Giovio, Paolo. *See* Jovii.
Golitsyn, N. V. "Nauchno-obrazovatel'nyia snosheniia Rossii s zapadom v nachale XVII v.," *Chteniia* . . . , 1898, No. 4.
Grekov, B. D. *The Culture of Kiev Rus*. Moscow, 1947.
——. *Kiev Rus*. Moscow, 1959.
Hakluyt, Richard. *Voyages*. New York (Dutton, Everyman ed.), 1962. Vols. I, II.
Hamel, Johannes. *England and Russia*. London, 1854.
Henning, Solomon. *Lieffländische Chronica*. Leipzig, 1594.
Herberstein, Baron S. von. *Notes on Russia*. 2 vols. A Hakluyt Society publication,

edited by R. H. Major. London, 1851. Originally entitled *Rerum Moscoviti-carum commentarii.*

Herbert, Thomas. *Some Yeares Travels into Divers Parts of Asia and Africa.* London, 1638.

Iakubov, K. I. "Rossiia i Shvetsiia v pervoi polovine XVII v.," *Chteniia . . .*, 1898, No. 1.

Ikonnokov, I. V. *Maksim Grek i ego vremia.* Kiev, 1915.

Ilovaiskii, D. I. *Istoriia Rossii. Moscow,* 1876–95. Vol. V.

Istoriia Moskvy. Moscow, 1952–59. Vol. I.

Izwolsky, Helene. *Christ in Russia.* Milwaukee, Wis., 1960.

Johnson, Edgar. *Introduction to the History of the Western Tradition.* Boston, 1959. Vol. II.

Jovii, Paulo [Paul Jovius]. "Posol'stvo ot Vasiliia Ioannovicha, Velikago Kniazia Moskovskago, k Pape Klimentu VII-mu," *Biblioteka inostrannykh pisatelei o Rossii.* St. Petersburg, 1836. Vol. I.

Kapterev, N. *Patriarkh Nikon i ego protivniki v dele ispravleniia tserkovnikh obriadov.* Moscow, 1887.

Kieksee, E. M. *"Die Handelspolitik der Gottorfer Herzöge im 17 Jahrhundert."* Unpubl. doctoral dissertation, University of Kiel, 1952.

Kirchner, Walther. *The Rise of the Baltic Question.* Newark, Del., 1954.

———. "Über den russischen Aussenhandel zu Beginn der Neuzeit," *Vierteljahrschrift für Sozial-und Wirtschaftsgeschichte,* Vol. 42 (1955), No. 1.

———. "The Voyage of Athanasius Nikitin to India, 1466–1472," *American Slavic and East European Review,* V (November 1946), 46–54.

———. "Western Businessmen in Russia: Practices and Problems," *Business History Review,* XXXVIII (Autumn 1964), 315–27.

Kliuchevskii [Kluchevsky], V. O. *History of Russia.* 5 vols. Translated by C. J. Hogarth. New York, 1960.

———. *Istoriia soslovii v Rossii.* 3d ed. Petrograd, 1918.

———. *Skazaniia inostrantsev o Moskovskom gosudarstve.* 2d ed. Petrograd, 1918.

———. "Zapadnoe vliianie i tserkovnyi raskol v Rossii XVII v.," *Ocherki i rechi.* Petrograd, 1918.

Konovalov, Serge. "Anglo-Russian Relations, 1617–1618," *Oxford Slavonic Studies,* Vol. I (1950).

———. "Anglo-Russian Relations, 1620–4," *Oxford Slavonic Studies,* Vol. IV (1953).

———. "Seven Letters of Tsar Mikhail to King Charles I, 1634–8," *Oxford Slavonic Papers,* Vol. IX (1960).

Kordt, V. A. *Materialy po russkoi kartografii.* Kiev, 1899.

Kostomarov, N. *O sostoianii Rossii v tsarstvovanie Mikhaila Feodorovicha i Alekseia Mikhailovicha.* St. Petersburg, 1861.

———. *Ocherk torgovli Moskovskago gosudarstva v XVI i XVII stoletiiakh.* St. Petersburg, 1862.

———. *Russkaia istoriia v zhizneopisaniiakh eia glavneishikh deiatelei.* 4th ed. St. Petersburg, 1895. Vol. II.

Kotoshikhin, G. *O Rossii v tsarstvovanie Alekseia Mikhailovicha.* 2d ed. St. Petersburg, 1859.

Krizhanich, Iurii. *Russkoe gosudarstvo v polovine XVII veka.* 2 vols. P. Bezsonov, ed. Moscow, 1859. A new edition entitled *Politika* was published in Moscow, 1965.

Kurts, B. G. *Sochinenie Kil'burgera o russkoi torgovle v tsarstvovanie Alekseia Mikhailovicha.* Kiev, 1915.

———. *Sostoianie Rossii v 1650–1655 gg. po doneseniiam Rodesa.* Moscow, 1914.

Lakhtin, M. *Meditsina i vrachi v Moskovskom gosudarstve.* Moscow, 1906.

Lappo-Danilevskii, A. S. "Inozemtsy v tsarstvovanie Mikhaila Fedorovicha," *Zhurnal Ministerstva Narodnago Prosveshcheniia,* 1885, No. 9.

———. "Rossiia i Gol'shtiniia. Ocherk po istorii germano-russkikh otnoshenii v XVIII veke," *Istoricheskii arkhiv,* 1919, No. 1, pp. 250–82.

Liubimenko [Lubimenko], I. "Project for the Acquisition of Russia by James I," *English Historical Review,* XXIX (April 1914), 246–56.

———. *Les Relations commerciales et politiques de l'Angleterre avec la Russie avant Pierre le Grand.* Paris, 1933.

———. "The Struggle of the Dutch with the English for the Russian Market in the Seventeenth Century," *Transactions of the Royal Historical Society,* Vol. VII (1924).

———. "Trud inozemtsev v Moskovskom gosudarstve," *Arkhiv istorii truda v Rossii,* 1923.

Loewenson, Leo. "The Moscow Rising of 1648," *Slavonic and East European Review,* XXVI (1948–49), 146–156.

Loviagin, A. M., ed. *Opisanie puteshestviia v Moskoviiu.* St. Petersburg, 1906.

Massa, I. *Kratkoe izvestie o Moskovii v nachale XVII v.* Moscow, 1937.

Matthiae a Michovia. *Descriptio Sarmatiarum.* Cracow, 1521.

Meteren, Emanuel van. *Historia; oder Eigentliche und warhaffte Beschreibung aller furnehmen Kriegshandel.* Hamburg, 1596.

Montaigne, Michel de. *Selected Essays.* New York, 1949.

Morgan, Edward D. and C. H. Coote, eds. *Early Voyages and Travels to Russia and Persia by Anthony Jenkinson and Other Englishmen.* 2 vols. London, 1886.

Moskvitianin. Moscow, 1851. No. 7.

Muliukin, A. S. *Ocherki po istorii iuridicheskago polozheniia inostrannykh kuptsov v Moskovskom gosudarstve.* Odessa, 1912.

———. *Priezd inostrantsev v Moskovskoe gosudarstvo.* St. Petersburg, 1909.

Müller, G. F. *Sammlung Russischer Geschichte.* St. Petersburg, 1732–34. Vol. VII.

Nechaev, V. V. "Inozemskiia slobody v Moskve," *Moskva v ee proshlom i nastoiashchem.* D. N. Anuchin, ed. Moscow, 1910. Part 2, Vol. II.

Nikitin, Afanasii. *Khozhenie za tri moria Afanasiia Nikitina, 1466–1472 gg.* Moscow, 1960. Earlier published in *India in the Fifteenth Century.* R. H. Major, ed. London, 1857.

Obolensky, Dmitri. "Russia's Byzantine Heritage," *Oxford Slavonic Papers,* Vol. I (1950).

Ocherki istorii SSSR. Period feodalizma. Konets XV v.-Nachalo XVII v. Moscow, 1955.

Ocherki istorii SSSR. Period feodalizma, XVII v. Moscow, 1955.

"Otchet niderlandskikh poslov Al'berta Kunratsa Burkha i Iogana Fan Feltdrilia o posol'stve ikh v Rossiiu v 1630 i 1631 gg.," *Sbornik Imperatorskago Russkago Istoricheskago Obshchestva*. St. Petersburg, 1867–1916, Vol. 116.

"Otvet Tsaria Ioanna Vasil'evicha Groznago Ianu Rokite," *Chteniia* . . . , 1898, No. 2.

Pamiatniki diplomaticheskikh snoshenii drevnei Rossii s derzhavami inostrannymi. St. Petersburg, 1854–81. Vol. X.

Pascal, Pierre. *Avvakum et les débuts du raskol.* The Hague, 1963.

Paul of Aleppo. *The Travels of Macarius, Patriarch of Antioch.* 2 vols. Translated from Arabic by F. C. Belfour. London, 1829–36.

Perry, John. *The State of Russia under the Present Tsar.* London, 1716.

Petrejus [Petrei], Peter. *Istoriia o velikom kniazhestve moskovskom.* Moscow, 1867. First published as *Regni Muscovitiici Sciographia* in Stockholm, 1615.

Petrovich, M. B. "Juraj Križanič: A Precursor of Panslavism," *American Slavic and East European Review*, VI (December 1947), 75–92.

Platonov, S. F. "Moskovskie volneniia 1648 goda," *Sochineniia.* 2d ed. St. Petersburg, 1912. Vol. I.

———. *Moskva i zapad v XVI–XVII vv.* Leningrad, 1925.

Plekhanov, G. V. *Sochineniia.* Moscow, 1923–27. Vol. XX.

Polnoe sobranie zakonov rossiiskoi imperii. St. Petersburg, 1830–1916. Vol. I.

Polosin, I. I. "Iz istorii blokady russkogo gosudarstva," in *Materialy po istorii SSSR*. Moscow, 1955. Vol. II (Dokumenty po istorii XV–XVII vv.).

Posol'stvo Kunraada fan-Klenka k Tsariam Alekseiu Mikailovichu i Feodoru Alekseevichu. St. Petersburg, 1900.

Pryzhov, I. *Istoriia kabakov v Rossii.* Moscow, 1868.

Pypin, A. I. "Inozemtsy v Rossii," *Vestnik Evropy*, January 1888.

Rambaud, A. N. *Recueil des instructions données aux ambassadeurs et ministres de France.* Paris, 1890.

Reitenfels, Ia. "Skazaniia o Moskovii," *Chteniia* . . . , 1905, No. 3.

Rikhter, V. *Istoriia meditsiny v Rossii.* Moscow, 1814–20, Vols. I–II.

Rudnitskii, V. T., and S. V. Larin. *Gorod Vladimir, istoriko-ekonomicheskii ocherk.* Vladimir, 1958.

Rushchinskii, L. P. *Religioznyi byt russkikh po svedeniiam inostrannykh pisatelei XVI i XVII vv.* Moscow, 1873.

[Russell, William.] *The Reporte of a Bloudie and Terrible Massacre in the Citty of Mosco.* London, 1607.

Russkii biograficheskii slovar'. St. Petersburg, 1896–1918. Vols. XI ("Ordyn-Nashchokin") and XII ("Olearii, Adam").

Schuyler, Eugene. *Peter the Great.* 2 vols. New York, 1884.

Seredonin, S. M. *Sochinenie Dzhil'sa Fletchera.* St. Petersburg, 1891.

Shcherbachev, Iu. N. *Russkie akty v Kopengagenskago gosudarstvennago arkhiva.* St. Petersburg, 1897. Vol. XVI of *Russkaia istoricheskaia biblioteka.*

Skazanie Avraamiia Palitsyna. Moscow, 1955.

Smirnov, P. P. *Posadskie liudi i ikh klassovaia bor'ba do serediny XVII veka.* 2 vols. Moscow, 1948.

———. "O nachale Ulozheniia zemskago sobora 1648–1649 gg.," *Zhurnal Ministerstva Narodnago Prosveshcheniia*, 1913, No. 9.

Snegirev, N. "Lobnoe mesto v Moskve," *Chteniia* . . . , 1861, No. 1.

Snegirev, V. L. *Pamiatnik arkhitektury, khram Vasiliia Blazhennogo.* Moscow, 1953.
_____. *Pokhozhdenie Berngarda Shvartsa.* Moscow, 1928.
Sobolevskii, A. I. *Obrazovannost' Moskovskoi Rusi XV–XVII vekov.* St. Petersburg, 1892.
_____. *Perevodnaia literatura Moskovskoi Rusi XIV–XVII vekov.* St. Petersburg, 1903.
Sobornoe Ulozhenie Tsaria Alekseia Mikhailovicha. Moscow, 1957. Vol. 6 of *Pamiatniki russkogo prava.*
Sobranie gosudarstvennykh gramot i dogovorov. 4 vols. 1813–28.
Solov'ev, S. M. *Istoriia Rossii s drevneishikh vremen.* 2d ed. Moscow, 1959–65. Vols. V, VII.
Struys, Jan. *Les Voyages de Jean Struys.* Amsterdam, 1718.
Sumner, B. H. *Peter the Great and the Ottoman Empire.* Oxford, 1949.
Sverges traktater med främmande magter. Stockholm, 1909. Vol. V.
Sykes, P. M. *A History of Persia.* London, 1915. Vol. II.
Sytin, P. B. *Istoriia planirovki i zastroiki Moskvy.* Vol. I. Moscow, 1950.
Tel'berg, S. G. *Ocherki politicheskogo suda i politicheskikh prestuplenii v Moskovskom gosudarstve XVII veka.* Moscow, 1912.
Tikhomirov, M. N. *Pskovskoe vosstanie 1650 g.* 2d ed. Moscow, 1935.
_____. *Rossiia v XVI stoletii.* Moscow, 1962.
Tikhomirov, M. N., and P. P. Epifanov, eds. *Sobornoe Ulozhenie 1649 goda.* Moscow, 1961.
Tsvetaev, D. *Iz istorii inostrannykh ispovedanii v Rossii v XVI i XVII vekakh.* Moscow, 1886.
_____. *Pamiatniki k istorii protestantstva v Rossii.* Moscow, 1888.
_____. *Protestantstvo i protestanty v Rossii do epokhi preobrazovanii.* Moscow, 1890.
Ulfeldt, Jakob [Ul'fel'd, Iakov]. *Puteshestvie v Rossiiu datskogo poslannika Iakova Ul'fel'da v XVI veke.* Moscow, 1889.
Ustrialov, N., ed. *Skazaniia sovremennikov o Dimitrii Samozvantse.* St. Petersburg, 1831–34. Vol. I.
Vainshtein, O. L. *Rossiia i tridsatiletniaia voina.* Leningrad, 1947.
Vakar, N. P. "The Name 'White Russia,' " *American Slavic and East European Review,* VIII (October 1949), 201–13.
Vernadsky, George. *The Mongols and Russia.* New Haven, Conn., 1953. Vol. III of *A History of Russia.*
_____. *Origins of Russia.* Oxford, 1959.
_____. *Russia at the Dawn of the Modern Age.* New Haven, Conn., 1959. Vol. IV of *A History of Russia.*
Viskovatov, A. *Kratkii istoricheskii obzor morskikh pokhodov russkikh i morekhodstva ikh voobshche do iskhoda XVII stoletiia.* St. Petersburg, 1864.
Voronin, N. N. *Vladimir, Bogoliubovo, Suzdal.* Moscow, 1958.
Vucinich, A. *Science in Russian Culuture.* Stanford, Calif., 1963.
Willan, T. S. *The Early History of the Russian Company.* Manchester, Eng., 1956.
Wittfogel, K. A. *Oriental Despotism.* New Haven, Conn., 1957.
Wright, Mary. *The Last Stand of Chinese Conservatism.* Stanford, Calif., 1957.

Zagoskin, N. P. *Russkie vodnye puti i sudovoe delo v do-petrovskoi Rossii.* Kazan, 1909.

Zaozerskii, A. I. *Tsarskaia votchina XVII v.* Moscow, 1937. First published as *Tsar Aleksei Mikhailovich v svoem khoziaistve.* Petrograd, 1917.

Zenkovsky, S. A. *Medieval Russia's Epics, Chronicles, and Tales.* New York, 1963.

Zevakin, E. S. "Persidskii vopros v russko-evropeiskikh otnosheniiakh XVII v.," *Istoricheskie zapiski,* 1940, No. 8, pp. 129–62.

Zevakin, E. S., and M. A. Polievktov. *K istorii prikaspiiskogo voprosa.* Tiflis, 1933.

Zviagintsev, E. "Slobody inostrantsev v Moskve XVII veka," *Istoricheskii zhurnal,* 1944, No. 2.

Index